MERRITT PROFESSIONAL PUBLISHING'S
1997 PREPARE TO PASS SERIES

LICENSING SOURCEBOOK

Life and Health

1997 Edition

This book belongs to:

Name Peter [illegible]

Address

MERRITT PROFESSIONAL PUBLISHING

Making business and people more productive

Merritt publishes many insurance and
safety educational materials.
For more information call toll-free:
1-800-638-7597

Editors:
Cindy Davidson, CIC
Richard Morin, CIC
Tracy Lovik, J.D.
Don Schlossman

Production:
Simone Hirzel

Merritt Professional Publishing
1661 Ninth Street/P.O. Box 955
Santa Monica, California 90406-0955

ISBN 0-930868-71-4
B-7593(262)97 1 10M 1

Before You Begin........

This manual has been written to present you, the insurance licensing candidate, with the fundamentals of insurance. As with all Merritt products, the text is updated and reprinted periodically to reflect industry changes and revisions in the insurance licensing requirements as they occur.

Each time the manual is published, we review the topics on the most current examination outlines and attempt to cover all state exam topics in the text. Whenever possible, we encourage state insurance department personnel and industry experts to review the text before it is published. This comprehensive insurance licensing study manual is designed to prepare you to pass your examination, and to provide you with a good educational foundation for the career you have selected.

Manuals like these are being used in almost every state to prepare individuals for the state agent licensing examinations. The product has been available for over 20 years, helping hundreds of thousands of people to pass your exam. Our goal is to prepare people like you to enter the insurance business with a sound understanding of the principles and concepts you will need in dealing with your customers. First, you have to take and pass a state licensing examination. Second, you have to have the knowledge and skills to offer your customers not only what they will pay for, but what fits their needs most accurately.

Your study of this manual is only the first step in your insurance education. There will be many other courses and books to study as you continue growing in the business. The insurance industry is constantly changing from the influence of the clients' needs, and also from the introduction of new regulations and business priorities. The insurance professional who is faithfully and efficiently serving his or her clients' interests must exert a diligent effort to keep abreast of these changes. Continuing education is a necessity to achieve and maintain success in this business.

Congratulations on your choice of an insurance career. We are sure that you will find the majority of your fellow insurance business associates to be a supportive, intelligent, and energetic group of men and women.

The Publishers

Hints for Successful Exam Preparation

In most states, an examination must be taken and passed before an insurance agent's license is issued. This examination is designed to measure your basic knowledge of insurance coverages and practices to ensure that the public is served in a professionally responsible manner. The examination will also test your understanding of state laws and regulations pertaining to the insurance industry.

The Licensing Examination

The questions on your licensing examination will be four-part multiple choice. You may be asked to answer a question, statement, or to complete a statement, or to pick out the exception to the statement. You may expect to see questions of the type illustrated below:

1. Which of the four cities listed below is located in the state of Mississippi?
(A) New York City
(B) Jackson
(C) Miami
(D) Los Angeles

2. All of the following states are located in the southern part of the United States EXCEPT:
(A) New Hampshire
(B) Alabama
(C) Florida
(D) Mississippi

3. An individual who represents an insurance company and sells insurance to members of the general public is:
(A) an insurance professor.
(B) an insurance underwriter.
(C) an insurance agent.
(D) an insurance counselor.

The **Life & Health examination** generally consists of **100-150 questions** which cover insurance topics and state insurance laws and regulations. You will be given from two to four hours, depending on the state, in which to complete your test. This means you will have only a few minutes for each question, so pace yourself accordingly. Check halfway through the exam to make sure you have answered approximately one-half of the questions.

Do not spend too much time on any one question. It is best to skip very difficult questions and return to them after you have completed all of the easier ones. Further questions on the exam may remind you of the answers you are looking for on the difficult ones.

Be sure to read each question carefully. While several of the possible answers may be partially correct, you must select the **best** answer to each question. Watch for words such as "all," "never," and "always." They may help you eliminate some of the choices.

There is no penalty for guessing. If you can narrow the choice of four answers down to three or even two logical possibilities, you have a good chance of picking the right answer by making an educated guess.

The Day of the Exam

Arrive at the exam location on time. Many exam administrators will not allow anyone to enter the testing room once the test has begun. You will also be required to show positive identification (such as a driver's license) to prove who you are, so make sure you have it with you. You will probably want to have a watch so you can budget your time. The use of books and papers, and usually calculators, during the exam is prohibited. It is best if you leave these things at home.

Information and Exam Arrangements

State insurance agent licensing examinations are administered by various testing services. You will need to contact your State Insurance Department for more information and to make arrangements for scheduling your examination.

We Want to Hear From You

We get our best feedback about these manuals from you, the user. Please call us toll-free, write us, or FAX in your comments about how these manuals worked for you. You can reach us by writing or calling:

Sourcebook Editors
Merritt Professional Publishing
1661 Ninth Street
Santa Monica, CA 90404
(800) 638-7597
FAX: (310) 396-4563

How to Get the Most Out of this Book

This study manual has 14 chapters. Chapters 1 and 2 include introductory material, basic insurance terms and concepts, and the fundamentals of insurance law and an agent's responsibilities. The state insurance regulation supplement sold with this Sourcebook will cover the important areas of your state's insurance laws.

Each chapter in the manual is divided into parts so you can easily study the information a little at a time. Review questions are provided at various points in each chapter so that you can check yourself every few pages to be sure you really understand the material you read.

If you have difficulty with any of the review questions, reread the sections covering that material. Be sure to look up any unfamiliar words in the Glossary at the back of the book. Write definitions in the margins to help you remember.

Taking the Practice Exam

When you have completed the text and feel confident about the material, take the sample exam provided in the back of the book. Follow the instructions and time yourself to create an experience similar to the actual licensing exam. We recommend you take the sample exam about one week prior to your planned examination date.

When you finish the test, check your answers against the answer key following the sample exam. Review the text material for any questions you missed by using the page reference located in the answer key.

The Importance of Owning and Using Your Own Book

Why purchase your own book from which to study? These are some of the many important reasons:

- *Create a Personalized Study Source*— By marking up your copy with highlighting and underlining... or any other means... you can target key areas which are particularly difficult for **you**. In your final study sessions before taking the exam the identification of these problem areas will be an invaluable study aid.
- *Use as a Workbook*— The Review Questions interspersed throughout the text are designed so that you can write in the appropriate responses. Writing out the correct answer is a reinforcement exercise which will help you remember important material.
- *Handy Reference Source*— These manuals function as a useful reference guide long after you pass your exam. Successful agents use the manuals often in their day-to-day business for answers to technical and legal questions regarding the practice of insurance in their state.

CONTENTS

1

INTRODUCTION TO INSURANCE

INSURANCE PRINCIPLES & CONCEPTS

Every day, all of us face various risks; such as the risk of unemployment, disability, sickness, premature death, damage, or loss of our property. These risks evolve from uncertainty which result in personal financial loss. **Risk** is the possibility that a loss might occur and is one of the reasons that people purchase insurance.

Insurance is a social device for spreading the chance of financial loss among a large number of people. By purchasing insurance, a person shares risk with a group of others, reducing the individual potential for disastrous financial consequences.

Insurance originated in the 13th century with shipowners who wanted to insure their ships and cargo against loss at sea. These shipowners met at coffee houses to transact business with groups of wealthy individuals willing to insure property against potential loss. The leading coffee house eventually became Lloyd's of London in the 17th century. Fire insurance was first offered in the 16th century. In the United States, the first fire insurance company was started in 1752 by Benjamin Franklin, and was known as the Philadelphia Contributionship for the Insurance of Houses from Loss by Fire.

The insurance company or **insurer** receives relatively small amounts of money, referred to as **premium**, from each of the large number of people buying insurance. A large uncertain loss is exchanged for a specific small amount of premium.

The agreement between the insurer and the **insured**, the person who is covered by the insurance, is established in a legal document referred to as a contract of insurance or a **policy**. The insurer promises to pay the insured according to the terms of the policy if a loss occurs. **Loss** is defined as reduction in the value of an asset. To be paid for a loss, the insured must notify the insurer by making a **claim**. The claim is a "demand" for payment of the insurance benefit to the person named in the policy.

The costs and benefits of insurance to society are obvious. Due to the sharing, or pooling, of a large number of similar risks, insurance coverage is available to most individuals for a reasonably affordable premium. When losses occur, insurance helps individuals to maintain their customary standard of living, which helps the whole economy. In the absence of insurance, a major disaster (such as fire or earthquake) could cause the entire economy in local communities to stagnate. If medical bills wiped out family savings and people did not have the funds to rebuild damaged homes, the uninsured losses could lead to a drop in construction activity and a decline in all areas of consumer spending. Insurance is the device that allows individuals and society in general to recover from unexpected losses.

TYPES OF RISK

There are two types of risks, only one of which can be covered by insurance.

Speculative risk (such as gambling) creates a risk situation and offers the opportunity for gain as well as the possibility of loss. Insurance is not designed to protect against speculative risks. It is this type of risk that insurance and its underwriting practices are designed to eliminate. Examples are found in new business ventures, stock market investments, and race track bets. There is a chance that the new business will not succeed, that the stock will not go up, or that the horse will not win, place or show. However, there is a chance that in each of these instances the speculator will make a profit.

Pure risk is the possibility of loss only and is the type of risk that insurers accept; for example, the possibility of financial loss due to an accident, sickness, or premature death. The purpose of insurance is to make the person whole again, to restore the insured to his or her original financial position. Insurance is not designed to provide a person with the opportunity of making a gain or profit.

RISK MANAGEMENT & INSURANCE

The risk management process involves identifying the **loss exposures** of the client and then making recommendations on how to avoid those exposures. Risks must first be identified in terms of items which are subject to loss with regard to specific perils and hazards and the resulting financial loss.

A **peril** is the cause of a potential loss. Accident, fire, explosion and flood are common perils which may be covered by insurance.

A **hazard** is a condition which increases the seriousness of a potential loss or increases the likelihood that a loss will occur due to a peril. Slippery floors, unsanitary conditions, and improperly stored gasoline are hazards that might increase the severity or frequency of losses caused by perils. Actually, there are four types of hazards which may contribute to losses:

- **Physical hazards** arise from material, structural, or operational features of a risk situation (slippery floors or unsanitary conditions would be physical hazards)
- **Moral hazards** arise from people's habits and values (filing a false claim is an example of moral hazard)
- **Morale hazards** arise out of human carelessness or irresponsibility (failing to take safety precautions is an example of morale hazard)
- **Legal hazards** arise from court actions which increase the likelihood or size of a loss (legal hazards are illustrated by the growing tendency of people to file lawsuits and of courts to award enormous sums for alleged damages, or to require insurance payments which were not intended)

Once the risks and hazards are identified, they must be evaluated and analyzed, and then steps to reduce the loss exposures must be examined and implemented. Finally, the results must be analyzed and techniques modified if appropriate.

Methods of Managing Risk

The first step in dealing with risks is to identify and analyze **loss exposures**, and then to evaluate alternatives for dealing with them.

There are four ways to manage risk. A risk may be *retained, avoided, reduced, or transferred.* A risk is **retained** when a person decides to assume financial responsibility for certain events. The deductible amount on a health insurance policy may be seen as a way the insured retains some portion of the risk. In addition his or her premium is reduced because of this assumption of risk. To **avoid** a risk a person might ride a bus or take a taxi instead of owning an automobile and risking the loss of the car due to an accident or theft. A risk is **reduced** when a person practices living a healthier lifestyle, thereby reducing the chance of major illness.

A risk may be **transferred** in two ways. If someone's negligence causes an injury, the person injured could sue the negligent party, transferring the burden of the risk to the negligent party.

The second method for transferring risk is accomplished through the use of insurance. The risk of loss is transferred to the insurance company. However, unlike the first instance of risk transfer, the entire burden is not merely transferred to one party, it is shared between a number of insureds who share the same chance and uncertainty of an event occurring. The characteristics for determining which group of individuals share a common risk are such things as age, sex, and occupation.

Once a risk management program has been decided upon and implemented, the results must be monitored, and the loss control measures reevaluated, and changed. New exposures may arise while old exposures change or disappear. New methods of dealing with loss exposures may become appropriate. It is the risk manager's, and sometime the producer's function, to stay in constant contact and remain familiar with the client's needs.

Insurance companies predict the potential losses of a large group by studying the past experiences of the group using the mathematical principles of probability and statistics. Looking at groups of individuals, rather than individuals, to make predictions is called the **pooling concept** and is an accurate way of predicting potential losses.

Law of Large Numbers

The law of large numbers allows an insurance company to predict the expected losses of a group. The basic principle of this law is that the larger the number of separate risks of a like nature combined into one group the more predictable the number of future losses of that group within a given time period. For the law of large numbers to operate, it is essential that a large number of exposure units be combined. **Exposure unit** means the item of property or the person insured. The exposure unit in life and health insurance is the economic value of the individual person's life. In property and casualty insurance it is the number of cars, homes, etc. Insurance companies can only predict the number of losses expected for a group, not for each individual.

If a large enough number of exposure units are combined, the degree of error in predicting future losses decreases as the number of individual exposure units in a group increases. Thus, the larger the group, the more closely the predicted experience will approach the actual loss experience. Insurance companies deal only with averages, in the sense of establishing actuarial predictions of loss experience. By providing for the average risk, the extremes in loss experience cancel each other out.

Actuaries are mathematicians who study and compile statistical data regarding exposure units and risks. This data is the basis for mortality and morbidity tables used to predict probable losses due to death (mortality) or sickness (morbidity) of large groups of people.

Insurance companies collect premiums to cover expenses, profits, and the cost of expected losses. The expected losses are based upon the past experience of the average risk. The fact that some people never experience an automobile accident or that some live well beyond their life expectancy is immaterial, for other people are involved in accidents or die prematurely. Those insureds who suffer loss are compensated, while many other insureds do not experience sizable losses.

Insurable Interest

Individuals may not be able to purchase any kind of insurance they desire. To be insurable a risk must involve the possibility of loss only and not gain, and the applicant must have a legitimate "interest" in the preservation of the life or property insured. This requirement is called **insurable interest**.

A person is presumed to have an insurable interest in his or her own life. An individual is also considered to have an insurable interest in the life of a close blood relative or a spouse. In these cases insurable interest is based on the love that individual would have for the family member and a real interest in protecting the life of that family member.

Insurable interest can also be based on a financial loss that will take place if an insured individual dies. Examples are two partners in a business, each of whom brings substantial expertise to that business. If one partner dies, the business could fail, resulting in a loss to the other partner.

For life insurance, insurable interest must exist at the time of the application for insurance, but it need not exist at the time of the insured's death. For property and casualty insurance, insurable interest must exist at the time of loss.

In the early history of insurance people did profit by obtaining insurance on persons they had no insurable interest in. An example of this would be a person obtaining insurance on a stranger. If the stranger dies, the policyholder obtains the benefit of the policy with no appreciable emotional or financial loss. It was this type of potential gain that caused some to mistakenly associate insurance with gambling.

Insurable Risks

An insurance company must conduct its operations efficiently to be successful. The first requirement for success is to be able to predict future losses accurately. Also, the company must deal only with **insurable risks**. Not all risks are insurable, and thus it is important to outline those risks to which insurance concepts can be properly applied.

Large Numbers of Homogeneous Units. The expected loss experience of a group of exposure units cannot be predicted with any certainty unless there are a large number of exposure units in that group. Risks are not considered insurable unless the insurance company has a large enough number of similar (homogeneous) risks and knows enough about their previous loss experience to be able to reliably predict possible future losses.

Loss Must Be Ascertainable. Since the purpose of insurance is to reduce or eliminate the uncertainty of economic loss, it is essential that the insured's economic loss be ascertainable. In other words, the insurer must be able to place a monetary value on the loss. In life insurance, monetary value is placed on the insured's human life value or ability to earn an income. It is especially difficult to determine economic loss under health insurance. For this reason economic loss is measured by lost wages, or by actual medical expenses incurred. The potential loss must be measurable so that both parties can agree on the precise amount payable in the event the loss occurs. If the insured is incapable of determining the amount of his or her loss, the law affords no remedy.

Loss Must Be Uncertain. Since the purpose of insurance is to reduce or eliminate uncertainty, it is obviously not in the public interest to permit the writing of insurance for intentional acts, such as a man jumping off a skyscraper two days after purchasing an insurance policy. Uncertainty arises out of not knowing what is going to happen or being unable to predict what is going to happen to the individual exposure unit. If insurance is provided for other than uncertain losses, the element of chance is not a factor. Nor is there any element of uncertainty in losses occasioned by natural wear and tear or deterioration, depreciation, or defects in property covered under insurance. Losses are expected in these situations, therefore such losses would not be uncertain.

Economic Hardship. The nature of the loss must be such that an economic hardship would occur should the loss occur. There would be little point in obtaining insurance to cover occurrences so minor that a loss would not produce economic hardship. For example, if a person loses two days pay because of an injury, a loss occurs, but it is not significant enough to be covered by insurance.

The nature of the loss must be of such magnitude that it is worthwhile to incur the premium cost to cover potential loss. It must be economically feasible to insure. Thus, a comparison of the potential loss with the cost of premium is a major consideration to the insurance buyer.

Exclusion of Catastrophic Perils. While the ability to predict future losses with a reasonable degree of accuracy is critical to the insuring function, certain types of perils do not lend themselves to prediction. Such perils, when they cause losses, do not establish a pattern of predictability that can be relied upon for future predictions of anticipated loss. Accordingly, these perils are usually excluded from coverage. Examples of excluded catastrophic perils are war, nuclear risk, and floods.

Indemnity

The concept of indemnity restores the insured, in whole or in part, to the condition he or she enjoyed prior to the loss. Restoration may take the form of payment for the loss, or repair or replacement of the damaged or destroyed property.

In life and health insurance, the concept of indemnity has a slightly different meaning in that a person's economic value or human life value is the individual's present and future earning power. For example, a family is indemnified for the financial loss of the breadwinner by being provided with life insurance proceeds with which to replace present and future income and thus enable the family to maintain its lifestyle.

COVERAGE CONCEPTS

Limit of Liability

While the term "limit of liability" is not used in the life and health insurance field as commonly as it is in the property and casualty field, it means the maximum amount the insurer will pay for a specified insured contingency.

Life insurance policies usually use the term **face amount** to refer to the maximum liability of the insurer for a death claim. However, the face amount may not always be the maximum amount payable. In the case of a double indemnity provision, the limit of liability for an accidental death may be expressed as "twice the face amount" shown on the face of the policy.

Health and disability policies are more likely to specify a **maximum benefit** amount or period instead of a limit of liability. Basic medical insurance often has a maximum benefit amount (such as $10,000), and major medical insurance usually has a lifetime maximum benefit (such as $1 million). Disability income policies often limit benefits to a specified maximum benefit period (expressed in weeks or months). Within the maximum benefit limits found in health and disability policies there may be various **sublimits** — such as daily dollar limits on covered room and board charges, scheduled maximum amounts for various surgical procedures, and weekly dollar limits for disability income benefits.

Deductibles

Deductibles are a common feature of medical insurance coverages (the term has no application in life insurance). A deductible is simply the initial amount of a covered loss (or losses) that the insured must absorb before the insurer begins to pay for additional loss amounts. For example, if a basic medical expense policy only pays losses above a $250 deductible and an insured incurs $1,000 of covered medical expenses, the insured would have to pay the first $250 and the insurer would then pay the additional $750 of expenses.

Although the term is not used in disability income policies, disability insurance usually has a "time deductible." It is called the "elimination period" or a "waiting period," but the concept is similar to a deductible. The elimination period is simply a number of days that an insured must be disabled before disability income benefits become payable. For example, if a policy specifies an elimination period of seven days and an insured is disabled for 30 days, the policy would only pay benefits for the 23 days following the elimination period.

The purpose of a deductible is to minimize small nuisance claims and to keep premiums down. It might cost an insurer much more just to process the paperwork on $10 and $25 claims than the amount of the claims. Naturally, these costs would have to be reflected in insurance rates if such small claims were covered. Deductibles help eliminate this problem and keep rates down. Insurers usually offer a standard deductible, but give applicants the option of purchasing higher deductibles which result in even lower premiums.

Coinsurance

Coinsurance is another concept commonly found in medical insurance policies. It means that within a specified coverage range, the insured and insurer will share the allowable expenses. It is usually expressed in percentages (such as 20%-80%). For example, if a policy has a $500 deductible and a 20%/80% coinsurance provision for the next $10,000 of expenses, a $5,500 medical bill would be settled in the following manner: the insured would pay the first $500 (the deductible amount) and $1,000 of the additional expenses (the insured's 20% share); the insurer would pay the remaining $4,000 (the insurer's 80% share).

A coinsurance provision is also designed to keep insurance premiums down, but it does so primarily by discouraging unnecessary or excessive treatments. An insured who is faced with paying 20% of the bill is more likely to question the doctor about whether proposed treatments are necessary, and whether there might be less costly alternatives.

REVIEW QUESTIONS

1. Insurance protects against uncertainties or ________.
2. The term used to describe the individual who is covered by the insurance is ________.
3. The application of the law of large numbers enables actuaries to (select only one):
   a. predict the future losses of specific individuals.
   b. estimate the future losses of a class or group of people.
4. The estimation of future losses is more accurate when information is from (select only one):
   a. a small select group.
   b. a large group.
5. Name the conditions of insurable risk that must exist for the concept of insurance to apply:
   a. ________
   b. ________
   c. ________
   d. ________
   e. ________

Answers to Review Questions are located at the back of the book.

TYPES OF INSURANCE & INSURERS

TYPES OF INSURANCE

Insurers market a variety of insurance products. The most common products offered are property, casualty, life, and health insurance, and annuities.

Property insurance includes a wide variety of insurance contracts for personal and business situations. Property insurance policies cover the risk of damage or loss to property. Property includes building, equipment, stock or contents. Property insurance also includes many related and contingent property losses, such as business interruption.

Casualty insurance includes insurance policies covering losses resulting from a number of occurrences. Casualty insurance contracts include automobile policies, general liability policies, workers compensation coverage, crime insurance and suretyship coverages, boiler and machinery coverages, and many others.

Almost every insured has a need for both property and casualty insurance coverage, whether personal or business (commercial). Some of the property and casualty coverages are sold together in special policies called "packages."

Life insurance is designed to protect against the risk of premature death — dying too soon. Premature death exposes a family or a business to certain financial risks such as burial expenses, paying off debts, loss of family income and business profits.

An **annuity** is designed to protect against the risk of living too long; that is, outliving one's financial resources and income during retirement. By definition, an annuity is a guaranteed income for the life of an annuitant.

Health insurance, also referred to as accident and sickness or disability insurance, protects the insured against financial loss caused by accidents and sicknesses. It may reimburse the insured for actual medical expenses incurred due to an accident or illness (hospitalization insurance) or it may provide protection for loss of income experienced by the insured during periods of disability due to accident or sickness (disability income insurance). Health insurance can be written on both an individual and group basis and includes medical expense, hospital indemnity, major medical, hospital, surgical, disability, cancer, accident, dental expenses, eyeglasses, prescription medication and other health-related expenses.

Disability income insurance provides protection against the financial effects of illness or injury. It provides protection for **loss of income** due to illness and injury (disability), and can be written on both an individual and group basis.

TYPES OF INSURERS

Insurance is provided to the public by three major sources: private commercial insurers (profit-making), private noncommercial insurers (nonprofit service organizations), the United States Government (special nonprofit). Other types of private insurers include reciprocals, fraternals, Lloyd's, reinsurers and self-insurers.

Private life and health insurers are in the business to make a reasonable profit, and are, therefore, called **commercial insurers**. Stock and mutual insurers are private insurers. Private **noncommercial** service organizations, like Blue Cross and Blue Shield, operate on a nonprofit basis. A nonprofit status exists when profits are returned to subscribers in the form of reduced premium or expanded benefits (similar to mutual insurers).

Commercial Insurers

Stock Insurers. A stock insurance company, like other stock companies, consists of stockholders who own shares in the company. The individual stockholders provide capital for the insurer. In return, they share in any profits and any losses. Management control rests with the board of directors, selected by the stockholders. The board of directors elects the officers who conduct the daily operations of the business. Capital stock companies control two-thirds of the premiums in the property and liability field and nearly one-half of the premiums in life insurance. If the board of directors declares a dividend, it will be paid to the stockholders. Often a stock company is referred to as a **non-participating** company because policyholders do not participate in dividends.

Mutual Insurers. In a mutual company, there are no stockholders. Formation funds must be contributed by someone or some group. Because of the difficulties involved today in obtaining the funds to organize a mutual company, many mutual companies start as stock companies and then mutualize.

In a mutual company, ownership rests with the policyholders. They vote for a board of directors which in turn elects or appoints the officers to operate the company. Funds not paid out after paying claims and not used in paying for other costs of operation are returned to the policyowners in the form of policy dividends. As such, mutual companies are sometimes referred to as **participating** companies because the policyowners participate in dividends. Although in theory, policyowners should share in losses as well as profits, these losses are actually only felt in the discontinuation of dividends. Mutual companies write nearly one-third of the property and liability business in the country and one-half of the life insurance business.

Nonprofit (Service) Organizations

Service insurers are unique to the health insurance field, and technically they are not insurers. They are organizations providing prepaid plans for hospital, medical, and surgical expenses. They do not provide cash benefits (except under certain limited conditions) to the plan subscriber, but instead pay the provider of medical services used by the plan subscriber to the extent covered in the contract. Best known of the service insurers are the various Blue Cross and Blue Shield plans. Blue Cross plans cover hospital expenses and Blue Shield plans cover medical and surgical expenses.

The "Blues" are a **cooperative** group of separate insuring organizations loosely coordinated by a national association, the Blue Cross and Blue Shield Association, that sets standards and seeks to enforce those standards by authorization or denial of use of the Blue Cross or Blue Shield designation. Originally, Blue Cross and Blue Shield had separate associations. As a result of the merger of the national associations on July 1, 1982, some local Blue Cross and Blue Shield associations have merged into one association for Blue Cross and Blue Shield. Blue Cross and Blue Shield associations are, with very few exceptions, incorporated under special legislation in most states.

Other Types of Private Insurers

Reciprocal Insurers. Reciprocal insurers are unincorporated groups of people providing insurance for one another through individual indemnity agreements. Each individual who is a member of the reciprocal is known as a "subscriber". Each subscriber is allocated a separate account wherein his or her premiums paid and interest earned are kept track of. If any subscriber should suffer a loss provided for by the reciprocal insurance then each subscriber account would be assessed an equal amount to pay the claim. Administration, underwriting, sales promotion, and claims handling for the reciprocal insurance is handled by an "attorney-in-fact". The attorney-in-fact is often controlled and overseen by an advisory committee of subscribers.

Fraternal Insurers. Fraternal benefit societies are primarily life insurance carriers that exist as social organizations and usually engage in charitable and benevolent activities. Fraternals are distinguished by the fact that their membership is usually drawn from those who are also members of a lodge or fraternal organization. They operate under a special section of the state insurance code and receive some income tax advantages. One distinctive characteristic of fraternal life insurance is the open contract, which allows fraternals to assess their certificateholders in times of financial difficulty.

Lloyd's. Lloyd's of London is not an insurance company, but may be compared to a stock exchange. Just as an exchange provides facilities for its members but does not buy or sell securities itself, Lloyd's provides a meeting place and clerical services to its members who actually transact the business of insurance.

Members are grouped into syndicates but they remain individually liable and responsible for the contracts of insurance they enter into. Their individual fortunes and resources are pledged as the capital behind their assumption of risk. A syndicate is represented in a Lloyd's Organization by an underwriter. Lloyd's of London assures full and adequate performance by its members through a governing committee and rules of eligibility. Such things as character, experience, business integrity, and amount of capital are factors considered for any new member.

Assessment Insurers. An assessment company retains the right to charge policyholders additional premiums if those paid in are insufficient to meet claims. Some go one step further and charge nothing until a loss occurs and then charge each member his or her pro rata share. Such a policy is referred to as an "open-end" contract.

Reinsurance

Reinsurance is a form of insurance between insurers. It occurs when an insurer (the reinsurer) agrees to accept all or a portion of a risk covered by another insurer (the ceding company). In many cases, the original insured has no knowledge of the transaction. In the event of loss, the insured has no claim against the reinsurer. The ceding company is responsible for the coverage it has written, but it will have a legitimate claim against the reinsurer for any portion of its own loss that is reinsured.

Companies often use reinsurance to reduce the risk of a catastrophic loss. Insurance against loss by earthquakes, floods, and aviation accidents might not be available if a single carrier had to assume all of the risk. Large life insurance cases are also often reinsured. For example, a $1 million life insurance policy on an insured may be shared through reinsurance with one or more insurers. Reinsurance makes it possible for a carrier to issue a policy and then share the risk with another insurer or a group of insurers. Another reason for reinsurance is that it helps carriers avoid capacity problems. Insurers must keep unearned premium reserves and certain levels of surplus in relation to premiums written. A shortage of capacity occurs when the ratio of premiums to surplus and reserves gets out of balance. By reinsuring a risk, many insurers are able to avoid or minimize capacity shortages.

Specific, or **facultative**, reinsurance is negotiated on an individual risk basis. The reinsurer retains the "faculty" to accept or reject each risk offered by a ceding company, so there must be an offer and acceptance on each reinsurance contract. Some carriers form agreements under which they engage in **treaty** reinsurance, which involves an automatic sharing of risks assumed by the ceding company. Whether reinsurance is facultative or on a treaty basis, it may be written on an **excess of loss** basis, which means the reinsurer will pay only the portion of loss which exceeds a threshold retained by the ceding company, or on a **quota share** basis, which means that the insurers will share loss on a pro rata or fixed percentage basis.

Excess and Surplus Lines

Occasionally, it may be difficult to place a risk in the normal marketplace. If the risk is very large or unusual in nature, typical carriers may be unwilling to assume it. For some special risks, the only market may be with specialty carriers. Excess and surplus lines is the name given to insurance for which there is no market through the original agent or broker, or which is not available through authorized carriers in the state where the risk arises or is located. Such business must be placed through a licensed excess or surplus lines broker, who will attempt to place it with an unauthorized carrier.

The United States Government as Insurer

The federal government provides life and health insurance through various sources. The federal government has offered a variety of military life insurance plans including United States Government Life Insurance (to veterans of World War I), National Service Life Insurance (in 1940) and Servicemen's Group Life Insurance. Additional occupations are eligible for federal government insurance provided through the Railroad Retirement Act, the Civil Service Retirement Act, and the Federal Employees' Compensation Act.

Because private insurance policies exclude catastrophic risks, the federal government has stepped in to provide War Risk Insurance, Nuclear Energy Liability Insurance, National Flood Insurance, Federal Crime Insurance, Federal Crop Insurance, and insurance on mortgage loans. At the state level, governments are involved in providing unemployment insurance, workers compensation programs and second-injury funds, and state-run medical expense insurance plans.

Federal, state and local governments provide **social insurance** to a segment of the population who would otherwise be without disability income, retirement income, or medical care.

Social Security provides survivor benefits in the event of death of a covered worker. These benefits include a lump sum burial amount of $255 plus monthly income benefits to eligible survivors. Social Security also provides disability benefits in the event of the total disability of a covered worker. In addition, the program also provides retirement benefits to covered workers at age 65 or earlier if elected by the individual. The Medicare program is also part of Social Security and accordingly provides medical expense benefits for covered workers beginning at age 65. All of these programs will be discussed in more detail in later chapters.

Medicaid is primarily a state governmental program which provides health care benefits for the financially needy. Medicaid is financed by the states with some federal subsidies.

Social insurance is distinguishable from private insurance in four significant areas:

- Participation is mandatory and automatic for all eligible citizens.
- Benefits are not provided under a contract or policy, but are prescribed by law. Individuals do not elect changes to the benefit plan. Any changes to the benefit structure and provisions are made by changes to the law.
- Social insurance seeks to be adequate, to meet the needs of the public, rather than equitable. As income is redistributed through the governmental system, insureds who put less into the system (the poor, the elderly, and those with many dependents) get greater benefits.
- The government, as an insurance provider, has a clear, and strong monopoly.

Self-Insurers

Self-insurance is a means of **retaining risk**. For a risk to be truly self-insured, two important characteristics will be present: (1) a large number of homogeneous exposure units, so that the law of large numbers can be used to predict expected losses, and (2) sufficient liquid assets to pay claims and other costs of retaining risk. The advantages of self-insurance are that money can be saved if losses are less than those predicted, expenses may be reduced by the elimination of such things as administrative costs and commissions, and the self-insurer has use of the money that would normally be held by the insurance company. The main disadvantages of self-insurance are that actual losses may be more than predicted, and expenses could be higher than expected if additional personnel have to be hired to administer the program.

Insurer's Domicile (Domestic, Foreign and Alien Insurers)

An insurer is defined not only by its corporate status, but also by its locality, or "domicile of incorporation." If an insurer is conducting business in the state where it is incorporated, that insurer is considered to be a **domestic insurer** in that state. If an insurer conducts business in a state where it is not incorporated, the insurer is considered to be a **foreign insurer** in that state. If an insurer is incorporated in a country other than the United States, it is considered to be an **alien insurer** if it is doing business in any jurisdiction within the United States.

Therefore, an insurer incorporated in California, and conducting business in California, is a domestic insurer in California. An insurer incorporated in New York and conducting business in California, is a foreign insurer in California. An insurer incorporated in Canada and conducting business in California, would be an alien insurer.

Authorized vs. Unauthorized (Admitted vs. Nonadmitted)

Before an insurance company can conduct business it must, by law, receive the authority to do so. Insurance statutes require a company to secure a license from the department of insurance to sell insurance in a particular state. Once the insurer receives the license, it is considered "admitted" into the state as a legal insurer, and is "authorized" to transact the business of insurance. Those insurers not licensed to transact insurance within the state are referred to as unauthorized or nonadmitted. This licensing power (sometimes companies are referred to as licensed and nonlicensed) is used to regulate company activities. Licenses may be issued to domestic companies, foreign companies, or alien companies. Stricter requirements are often imposed on alien and foreign companies because of their inaccessibility. Out-of-state mail order companies may sell insurance to residents of a state without obtaining a license in the state.

REVIEW QUESTIONS

6. What type of policy is designed to protect against the risk of living too long? ______________________

____

7. What are the two types of reinsurance?

   (1) ______________________
   (2) ______________________

8. What three terms are used to describe insurers based on where they are incorporated and doing business?

   (1) ______________________
   (2) ______________________
   (3) ______________________

9. Self insurance is an example of which method of handling risk?______________________

10. Which of the following are used to denote insurance companies? (check one or more)
    a. Broker
    b. Exchange
    c. Corporation
    d. Insured
    e. Insurer

11. Which of the following is a type of insurance company owned by its shareholders?
    a. Mutual
    b. Stock
    c. Lloyd's

12. Name at least five different types of insurers.

    (1) ______________________
    (2) ______________________
    (3) ______________________
    (4) ______________________
    (5) ______________________

> ☞ ***Answers to Review Questions are located at the back of the book.***

TYPES OF DISTRIBUTION SYSTEMS

Insurance companies market their products generally in one of two ways: by using agents to sell their products or selling directly by mass marketing. The vast majority of policies are sold through agents.

Agency System

Companies that use agents to sell their products vary by whether the agents are employees or independent sales representatives.

Independent Insurance Agents sell the insurance products of several companies and work for themselves or other agents. They sell their clients the policy that fits their needs best among the many insurers they represent, and are paid a commission for each sale. The independent agent owns the expirations of the policies he or she sells, meaning that that individual may place that business with another insurer upon renewal if in the best interest of the client.

Exclusive or captive agents represent only one company. These agents are sometimes referred to as career agents working from career agencies. Most often, these captive or career agents are compensated by commissions. A career agent's compensation will normally consist of first year commissions and renewal commissions in subsequent years. Usually, the first year commissions may represent 50% or more of the first year life insurance premium. Thereafter the renewal commissions will usually be 10% or less each year.

However, frequently these agents may also be paid a training allowance which serves as a salary for a limited period of time during which the new agent is being trained. Generally, this allowance may be paid for several months or possibly a year or two. Most companies will require that the career agent validate this training allowance by producing a certain amount of new business each month.

If an agent hires, trains and supervises other career agents within a specific geographical area, he or she is referred to as a **general agent or managing general agent** (MGA). The MGA is compensated by commissions earned on business sold by him or herself as well as an overriding commission (overrides) on the business produced by the other agents managed by the general agent.

An MGA may also receive additional compensation for administrative and service functions performed for policyholders. This compensation is paid in accordance with a separate contractual agreement with the insurer. This supplemental agreement may be referred to as an expense allowance as it is designed to help cover some of the agency's overhead expenses.

Direct writing companies usually pay salaries to employees whose job function is to sell the company's insurance products. Technically, these salaried employees do not function as agents. Commissions are usually not paid and the insurer owns all of the business produced.

Mass Marketing

Mass marketing has grown in general use over the past several years. The most common types of mass marketing systems are direct-response, franchise, noninsurance sponsors, and vending machine sales.

Direct-Response. Direct-response marketing is conducted through the mail, by advertisement in newspapers and magazines, and on television and radio. Policies sold using this method have limited benefits and low premiums, such as disability only.

Franchise Marketing. The franchise marketing system provides coverage to employees of small firms, or to members of associations. Unlike group policies where benefits are standard for classes of individuals, persons insured under the franchise method receive individual policies that vary according to the individuals' needs.

Franchise plans are attractive to employers who do not, according to the laws of their state, meet the qualifications for a "true group." It allows the employers to offer individual insurance to their employees at a lower premium than for insurance purchased on an individual basis. Premiums may be deducted from the individual's paycheck.

Noninsurance Sponsors. Noninsurance sponsors are being used more and more. The most common are banks, and companies that issue credit cards. This marketing system reaches a select group of individuals who have a history of periodic payments. Usually the sponsor is responsible for the billing of premium, and it is added to the billing statement, or deducted from checking accounts.

Vending Machine Sales. Vending machine sales have traditionally been of travel accident policies sold from coin operated machines at airports. A large amount of coverage is available at low premiums. The coverage is good only for the duration of a single trip.

REVIEW QUESTIONS

13. The two types of insurance distribution systems are:
    (1) ______________________
    (2) ______________________

14. Which of the following people represents several insurance companies but owns the policy expirations?
    a. Independent agent
    b. Exclusive agent
    c. Direct writing agent

15. A sales campaign conducted through the mail is called a ________________ solicitation.

> ☞ ***Answers to Review Questions are located at the back of the book.***

PRODUCERS

Categories of Producers

The largest single group of insurance workers, and perhaps the most vital to insurance companies, consists of producers — the men and women who sell insurance policies to the public. Producers can be generally categorized as agents, brokers, and solicitors.

Producers are not only categorized by their function in the industry, but also by the line of insurance they sell.

Life and Health Agents. Generally, life and health insurance agents represent the insurer to the buyer with respect to the sale of life and health insurance products. The agents are appointed by the insurer and usually the agent's authority to represent the insurer is specified in the agency agreement between them, which is a working agreement between the agent and the insurer. Life and health insurance agents generally do not have the authority to issue or modify insurance contracts. Customarily, life and health insurance agents are authorized to solicit, receive, and forward applications for the contracts written by their companies. The agent may receive the first premium due with the application, but usually not subsequent premiums, except in industrial life insurance. The insurance company approves and issues the contract after receiving the application and premium from the applicant through the agent. The agent **cannot bind** coverage. This means that an agent cannot commit to providing insurance coverage on behalf of the insurance company.

Property and Casualty Agents. Agents appointed by property and liability insurance companies generally are granted more authority. These agents **may bind** or commit their companies by oral or written agreement. They sometimes inspect risks for the insurance company and collect premiums due. They may be authorized to issue many types of insurance contracts from their own offices.

Brokers. In contrast to the agent-client relationship in which the agent represents the insurer to the purchaser, a broker represents the buyer to the insurer. A broker may do business with several different insurers. Brokers are independent sales representatives who select insurance coverages from these various companies for their clients.

Brokers must be licensed just like agents and generally their routine activities and functions are similar to that of agents. Brokers solicit applications for insurance, may collect the initial premium and deliver policies. Brokers do not have the authority to bind coverages.

Solicitors. A solicitor is a salesperson who works for an agent or a broker. This working relationship is most common in the property and casualty insurance field. Most often the solicitor will be licensed as a solicitor. Depending on the state, the solicitor may obtain an agent or broker's license. Solicitors normally have a working agreement with an agent or broker. In accordance with this agreement, the solicitor's primary functions are to solicit insurance, collect initial premiums and deliver policies. Solicitors cannot bind coverage.

Insurance Consultants. A very small group of insurance professionals call themselves insurance consultants. Consultants are not paid by commission for the sales of insurance policies. Instead, they work strictly for the benefit of insureds and are paid a fee by the insureds they represent.

Agency Law Principles

An understanding of the law of agency is important as an insurance company, like other companies, must act through agents.

Agency is a relationship in which one person is authorized to represent and act for another person or for a corporation. Although a corporation is a legal "person," it cannot act for itself, so it must act through agents. An agent is a person authorized to act on behalf of another person, who is called the principal. In the field of insurance, the principal is the insurance company and the sales representative or producer is the agent. When one is empowered to act as an agent for a principal, he or she is legally assumed to be the principal in matters covered by the grant of agency. Contracts made by the agent are the contracts of the principal. Payment to the agent, within the scope of his or her authority, is payment to the principal. The knowledge of the agent is assumed to be the knowledge of the principal.

Presumption of Agency. If a company supplies an individual with forms and other materials (signs and evidences of authority) that make it appear that he or she is an agent of the company, a court will likely hold that a presumption of agency exists. The company is then bound by the acts of this individual whether or not he or she has been given this authority.

Power and Authority of Agents. The authority of an agent is of three types: express, implied or apparent.

Express authority is an explicit, definite agreement. It is the authority the principal gives the agent as set forth in his or her contract. It is very important for an agent to know the limitations of the contract and to operate within its limits. To do otherwise could place him or her in a position of personal liability. His or her actions and knowledge are binding on the insurance company, so he or she must be alert to the consequences of his or her actions and words.

Implied authority is not expressly granted under an agency contract, but it is actual authority which the agent has to transact the principal's business in accordance with general business practices. For example, if an agent's contract does not give him or her the express authority of collecting and submitting premium, but the agent does so on a regular basis, and the company accepts the premium, then the agent is said to have implied authority. That is, it is a general business practice to collect premium, and by accepting the premium from the agent, the company has implied that the agent has the authority to conduct this practice.

"Lingering implied authority" means that the agent carries "signs or evidences of authority." By having these evidences of authority an agent who is no longer under contract to an insurer could mislead applicants or insureds. When the agency relationship between agent and company has been terminated, the company will try, or should try, to get back all the materials it supplied to the former agent, including sales materials.

On the other hand, the public cannot assume that an individual is an agent merely because he or she says so. The agent must carry the credentials (for example the agent's license and appointment) and company documents (such as applications and rate books) that represent him or her as being an agent for an insurance company.

Apparent authority is the authority the agent seems to have because of certain actions undertaken on his or her part. This action may mislead applicants or insureds, causing them to believe the agent has authority which he or she does not, in fact, have. The principal adds to this impression by acting in a manner that reinforces the impression of authority. For instance, an agent's contract usually does not grant him the authority to reinstate a lapsed policy by accepting past due premiums. If, in the past, the company has allowed the agent to accept late premiums for that purpose, a court would probably hold that the policyowner had the right to assume that the agent's acceptance of premium was within the scope of his or her authority.

Collection, Financing and Remittal of Premium

All premiums received by an agent are funds received and held in trust. The agent must account for and pay the correct amount to the insured, insurer, or other agent entitled to the money.

Any agent who takes funds held in trust for his or her own use is guilty of theft and will be punished as provided by law.

An agent may establish an account separate from a personal account to deposit the trust funds. All trust funds may be deposited into the single separate account, however, the agent's records must clearly distinguish the funds held for each individual.

Agent's Responsibility to Insured/Applicant

An agent has a fiduciary responsibility to the insured, the insurer, the applicant for insurance, current clients, etc. The agent has a fiduciary duty to just about any person or organization which he or she comes into contact with as part of the day-to-day business of transacting insurance. By definition, a **fiduciary** is a person in a position of financial trust. Thus, attorneys, accountants, trust officers and insurance agents are all considered fiduciaries.

As a fiduciary, the agent has an obligation to act in the best interest of the insured. The agent must be knowledgeable about the features and provisions of various insurance policies as well as knowing the use of these insurance contracts. The agent must be able to explain the important features of these policies to the insured. The agent must recognize the importance of dealing with the general public's financial needs and problems and offering solutions to these problems through the purchase of insurance products.

As a fiduciary, the agent must know and comply with the state's insurance laws. Many of these laws are for consumer protection. It is the agent's duty to comply with these laws and thus protect the interests of the insured at all times.

As a fiduciary, the agent must collect and account for any premiums collected as part of the insurance transaction. It is the agent's duty to make certain that these premiums are submitted to the insurer promptly. Failure to submit premiums to the insurer or to put these funds to one's own personal use, is certainly a violation of the agent's fiduciary duties as well as possibly embezzlement period. The insured's premiums must be kept separate from the agent's personal funds. Failure to do this can result in **commingling** — mixing personal funds with the insured or insurer's funds.

Waiver and Estoppel

The legal doctrines of waiver and estoppel are directly related to the responsibilities of insurance agents. An insurer may, by waiver, lose the right of making certain defenses that it might otherwise have available. **Waiver** is defined as the intentional and voluntary giving up of a known right. An insurance company may waive its right to cancel a policy for nonpayment by accepting late payments.

Waiver and estoppel often occur together, but they are separate and distinct doctrines. **Estoppel** means that a party may be precluded by his or her acts of conduct from asserting a right that would act to the detriment of the other party, when the other party has relied upon the conduct of the first party and has acted upon it. An insurer may waive a right, and then after the policyowner has relied upon the waiver and acted upon it, the insurer will be estopped from asserting the right.

The agent must be alert in his or her words, actions, and advice to avoid mistakenly waiving the rights of the insurance company. As a representative of the company the agent's knowledge and actions may be deemed to be knowledge and actions of the company.

Agent's Responsibilities to Company

The agent's contract or agency agreement with the insurer will specify the agent's duties and responsibilities to the principal. As previously mentioned, the agent has a fiduciary duty to the insurer. In all insurance transactions, the agent's responsibility is to act in accordance with the agency contract and thus for the benefit of the insurer. If the agent is in violation of the agency agreement, then he or she may be held personally liable to the insurer for breach of contract.

An agent has a duty to act with a degree of care that a reasonable person would exercise under similar circumstances. This prudent person rule is to protect the insurer and the insured from unreasonable insurance transactions on the part of the agent.

In accordance with the agent's fiduciary obligation to the insurer and his or her agency agreement, the agent has a responsibility of accounting for all property including money which comes into his or her possession. The agent must not embezzle or commingle these funds.

As part of the agent's working relationship with the insurer, it is important that pertinent information be disclosed to the insurer, particularly with regard to underwriting and risk selection. If the agent knows of anything adverse concerning the risk to be insured, it is his or her responsibility to provide this information to the insurer. To withhold important underwriting information could adversely affect the insurer's risk selection process. In accordance with agency law, information given to the agent is the same as providing the information to the insurer.

It is the agent's responsibility to obtain necessary information from the insurance applicant and to accurately complete the application for insurance. A signed and witnessed copy of the application becomes part of the legal contract of insurance between the insured and the insurer and thus it is critical that the application be accurate.

Finally, the agent has a responsibility to deliver the insurance policy to the insured and collect any premium which may be due at the time of delivery. The agent must be prepared to provide the insured with an explanation of some of the policy's principal benefits and provisions. If the policy is issued with any changes or amendments, the agent will also be required to explain these changes and obtain the insured's signature acknowledging receipt of these amendments.

Company's Responsibility to the Agent

The company likewise has a responsibility to the agent. It is required to permit the agent to act in accordance with the terms of the agent's employment contract, and the company must recognize all of the provisions of that contract.

In addition, the company must pay the agent the compensation agreed upon in the contract, must reimburse the agent for proper expenditures made on behalf of the principal, and must indemnify the agent for any losses or damages suffered without fault on the part of the agent but occurring on account of the agency relationship.

Potential Liabilities of Agent/Errors and Omissions (E&O) Exposure

Errors and omissions insurance is needed by professionals who give advice to their clients. It covers negligence, error, or omission by the insurer, or agent who is the insurer's representative. E&O policies protect agents from financial losses they may suffer if insureds sue to recover for their financial loss due to an agent giving them incorrect advice (error) or not informing them of an important issue (omission). Since an agent's office is very busy, he or she must take special care to follow strict procedures (and train all employees to do the same) in regard to taking applications, explaining coverages, collecting premiums, submitting changes to policies upon an insured's request, and preparing claim forms. Any error or omission could result in losing a client and could lead to a lawsuit. All E&O policies have certain basic characteristics in common:

- The policy covers only losses due to negligence, error, or omission. For example, the agent who fails to tell a client that his or her purchase of a new policy means that waiting periods have to be met again, can be sued for this omission if the event previously covered occurs and the insured finds that he or she is not currently covered.

- The policy usually has a high deductible, such as $500 or $1,000. The high deductible provides an added incentive for an agent to reduce his or her errors.
- The coverage may be written with both a limit per claim, and a limit for all claims during the policy period.
- Except for obvious exclusions, like an agent committing unfair trade practices, the policy has few other exclusions.

REVIEW QUESTIONS

16. Which of the following can bind an insurance company by oral or written agreement?
    a. Property/Casualty agent
    b. Life agent
    c. Broker
    d. Solicitor
17. Name the three types of agent authority.
    (1) ______________________________
    (2) ______________________________
    (3) ______________________________
18. Life and health insurance agents (have/do not have) ____________ the authority to bind an insurance company to a contract agreement.

> ☞ ***Answers to Review Questions are located at the back of the book.***

NOTES

2

INSURANCE REGULATION

REGULATION OF THE INSURANCE BUSINESS

Insurance is a highly regulated industry. It is regulated to protect the public interest and to make sure insurance is available on an equitable basis. Regulation of the insurance industry is undertaken from several perspectives and is divided among a number of authorities. The three major channels of regulation of the insurance industry are:

- Federal regulation
- State regulation
- Self regulation

Most of the regulation takes place at the state level, but there are some important regulations at the federal level. The body of laws at the state level is called the **Insurance Code.** State regulation consists of statutes, and rules and regulations. **Statutes** are the body of law developed by the Legislative branch of government. They outline, in general terms, the duties of the Commissioner and the activities of the Insurance Department. **Rules and regulations** are developed by the Insurance Department to expand upon statutory requirements and carry out legislative intent.

FEDERAL REGULATION

Federal regulation of insurance is primarily used as a means to oversee those areas not covered by state regulation of the industry. The most important sources of federal regulation are outlined below and include both legislative and judicial aspects.

Paul versus Virginia. In the case of *Paul v. Virginia*, an agent working for insurers in New York began to transact insurance in Virginia, where the New York insurers had failed to comply with state law. The case was brought before the Supreme Court in order to determine if the individual states had the right to regulate the business of insurance. The Court's decision established, as law, that the transaction of insurance across state lines was not interstate commerce and therefore should be regulated by local law. This decision held in case after case for 75 years.

South-Eastern Underwriters Decision. In 1944 the South-Eastern Underwriters Association was indicted for violating the Sherman Antitrust Act. The Association defended its action by stating the fact that federal regulation did not apply to the business of insurance. For the first time in 75 years the issue of transacting insurance across state lines was looked at another way. The issue, this time, related to the effect of an Act of Congress on insurance transactions conducted across state lines.

The Supreme Court overturned the previous decision by saying that insurance transacted across state lines was, in fact, interstate commerce. This decision had the capability of turning the insurance industry upside-down, because for the past 75 years the states had been regulating the industry locally.

McCarran-Ferguson Act. In order to waylay any impending confusion, Congress enacted the McCarran-Ferguson Act in 1945. This act stated that the federal government had the right to regulate the business of insurance, but only to the extent that such business is not regulated by state law. The main intent of the law was to exempt the insurance industry from most of the provisions of the federal anti-trust laws.

Other Regulating Agencies. Some insurance products are regulated by both the federal and state government. For example, the Securities and Exchange Commission (SEC) and the state Insurance Departments regulate variable contracts. Variable annuities and variable life insurance are insurance company products but these products present a degree of investment risk to the buyer and accordingly, they have also been identified as securities in accordance with SEC regulations.

PRIVACY, DISCLOSURE & FAIR REPORTING

With the increase in recordkeeping and computer information systems, the question of individual privacy became an issue in three areas; access to private and personal information, disclosure of private and personal information, and the fair reporting of private and personal information.

Government studies determined that the insurance industry is one of the largest collectors and users of personal information. It was, therefore, one of the industries studied. The two laws having the greatest impact on the insurance industry are the Fair Credit Reporting Act, and the Privacy Act of 1974. The NAIC Model Privacy Act has had an important impact by helping individual states to enact regulations governing privacy. These Acts do not protect insurers but operate to serve the public interest by protecting individuals.

In regulating insurers, many states have enacted privacy laws under the Unfair Trade Practices Law.

Fair Credit Reporting Act

When an application is submitted to a life or health insurance company, a consumer reporting agency is hired to obtain personal information about the applicant to be used in the underwriting evaluation. To protect the consumer's right to privacy in this situation, the federal Fair Credit Reporting Act was passed in 1970. The Act sets up procedures for consumer reporting agencies to follow in their dealings with businesses to ensure that records are confidential, accurate, relevant and properly used.

Consumer Reports. Consumer reports include written, oral and other forms of communication which a consumer reporting agency has regarding a consumer's credit, character, reputation, or habits, which is used or collected to determine whether or not a consumer is eligible for credit, insurance, employment or other purposes authorized under the Act. Consumer reports may only be issued to persons who have a legitimate business need for the information. Governmental agencies may also be provided with a consumer's name, present and former addresses, and present and past places of employment.

Investigative Consumer Reports. An investigative consumer report includes information on a consumer's character, general reputation, personal habits, and mode of living that is obtained through investigation, i.e., interviews with associates and friends and neighbors of the consumer. Such reports may not be made unless the consumer is clearly and accurately told about the report in writing within three days of the date on which the report was first requested. The consumer must also be notified that he or she is allowed to request additional information. If that person requests such information in writing, the person who caused the investigative report to be made must make a complete and accurate disclosure of the report to the consumer about whom it is written. The disclosure must be made within five days of receipt of the report, or when the report was first requested, whichever date is later. If there is an investigative consumer report prepared subsequent to the first one, any adverse information must be verified, or must have been received during the three months preceding the subsequent report.

Pretext Interviews. A pretext interview is an interview whereby a person, in an attempt to obtain information about another person, pretends to be someone he or she is not, misrepresents the true purpose of the interview, or refuses to properly identify him or herself.

Generally, pretext interviews are prohibited. However, such an interview may be conducted when there is evidence of criminal activity, fraud or misrepresentation.

Consumer Reporting Agencies. Consumer reporting agencies collect information on individuals, prepare reports, and make the reports available to persons or organizations having a legitimate reason to receive such information. These agencies may operate for profit; for example, a credit union. Or, agencies may be nonprofit, such as the Medical Information Bureau (MIB).

Prohibited Information. Consumer reporting agencies are specifically prevented from putting information in their reports about bankruptcies over 14 years old; suits and judgments over seven years old or in which the statute of limitations has expired, whichever period is longer; paid tax liens or accounts placed for collection or charged to profit which are over seven years old; arrests, indictments, or conviction of crime reports; and any other adverse information which took place seven years prior to the report.

These restrictions are not applicable when the consumer credit report is used in connection with a credit transaction of $50,000 or more, a life insurance policy of $50,000 or more, or when it concerns employment of an individual earning $20,000 or more.

Consumers' Rights. Consumers who feel that information in their files is inaccurate or incomplete may inform the consumer reporting agency of any information in dispute. The consumer reporting agency is then required to reinvestigate and record the current status of the disputed material (unless the agency has reasonable grounds to believe the dispute is frivolous or irrelevant) in a reasonable period of time. If the information is no longer accurate or verifiable, it must be deleted promptly. If the dispute is not resolved after reinvestigation, the consumer may file a brief statement (not more than 100 words) concerning the problem. If this statement is filed, the consumer reporting agency must note it in future consumer reports which contain that information (unless it is determined to be frivolous or irrelevant). If credit or insurance is denied, or charges are increased, based wholly or partially on information contained in a consumer report, the user of the information must notify the consumer of this fact and report the name and address of the consumer reporting agency which made the report. If credit or insurance is denied, or charges are increased, wholly or partially due to information obtained from a person or organization **other** than a consumer reporting agency, the user of the information must disclose the nature of that information to the consumer if it has been requested within 60 days of the disclosure. It is the responsibility of the user of the information to inform the consumer of his or her right to request this information when the adverse action is communicated to him or her.

Penalties. Failure to comply with the provisions of the Act makes the guilty party liable to the consumer for the sum of actual damages sustained as a result of the noncompliance; punitive damages deemed proper by a court; and the costs of an action which enforces liability, plus reasonable attorney's fees. When the noncompliance is due to negligence, the guilty party must pay the consumer the sum of the consumer's actual damages, the costs of any successful action to enforce liability, plus reasonable attorney's fees.

The maximum penalty for obtaining consumer information reports under false pretenses is $5,000, or imprisonment for one year, or both. The same penalty is imposed on officers or employees of consumer reporting agencies who have knowingly and willfully provided consumer information to a person not authorized to receive it.

Privacy Act of 1974

In the 1970s the *Privacy Protection Study Commission* was established. The job of the Commission was to study (1) the collectors of personal information, (2) the users of personal information, and (3) the manner in which personal information is circulated. The study found insurers to be one of the major collectors and users of personal information. Because of the abundance of personal information, and the numbers of agencies collecting and using personal information, it became vital that some controls be established to protect the public from inaccurate, or misused information.

The Commission's findings were summarized in a report entitled *Personal Privacy in an Information Society.* A large portion of the report dealt with the insurance industry. The report outlined three goals:

- To minimize intrusiveness
- To be fair and impartial in collecting, analyzing, and presenting information and reports
- To make it known to the public that they can expect personal information to be handled in confidence

Disclosure Authorization. Applicants for insurance must be given advance notice of the insurer's practices regarding collection and use of personal information. Notice must be given promptly and in writing. Notice should be given in the following cases and in the following manner:

- If a third party is interviewed, the applicant must be given notice when the collection of information has begun
- If only the applicant is interviewed, the applicant must be given notice when the policy is delivered
- If a policy is being renewed, the insured must be given notice by the renewal date
- If a policy is being reinstated, the applicant-insured must be given notice at the time the request is made
- If an insured is requesting a change in benefits, the insured must receive notice at the time the request is made

The notice must give the applicant or insured the following kinds of information:

- The people with access to personal information
- The kind of information to be collected
- The kind of information the insurer can receive without the applicant's prior approval
- The sources of information
- The persons to whom information may be disclosed without the applicant's prior authorization

Disclosure authorization forms are now required by law to be prescribed and approved by the Commissioner. The disclosure form must be written in accordance with the plain language laws of the state, and dated. Disclosure forms state the types of persons authorized to disclose private and personal information (e.g., neighbors, employers, and previous or other insurers); the kind of information which may be disclosed (e.g., personal habits, work habits, health habits such as smoking and drinking). The form must also state the reason information is collected, and how it will be used. For instance, the *reason* personal information is gathered is because the applicant requested a life insurance policy; the information will be used by the underwriting department for the *purpose* of determining the applicant's risk category.

The applicant's signature on the disclosure form authorizes the insurer to collect and disseminate information in the manner described in the notice. The authorization is only good for a certain period of time. For example, if authorization is given to an insurer to collect information with regard to a claim settlement, the authorization is good for 30 months. At the end of this period another authorization must be obtained. The applicant or insured may request, and receive, a copy of the authorization form.

Personal information may be disclosed to persons other than the requesting parties under certain conditions. Among those to whom an insurer may disclose information are agents, other insurers, insurance organizations (such as the MIB) and Insurance Departments. This type of third-party disclosure may require authorization, but in some instances authorization is not required, just as long as the applicant or insured has received proper notification of the insurer's information practices. In some cases information is passed on to those conducting scientific research, audits, or marketing approaches.

Penalties. The Commissioner of Insurance has the authority to investigate any insurer, or any agency used by the insurer to collect information, to determine if the company is in compliance with the Insurance Act. If the Commissioner believes that a violation of the Act has taken place he or she can conduct a hearing to determine the facts. If a violation is found, the Commissioner can issue a cease and desist order, but if the violator continues to violate the Act, the Commissioner can institute a fine of up to $10,000 for each violation. If the violation is one that happens with such frequency that it appears to be a general business practice, the fine for each violation can be up to $50,000.

The NAIC Model Privacy Act also provides for the enforcement of individual rights. The individual has the right to information concerning himself or herself, and the right to correct inaccurate information, the right to know the reasons for being turned down for insurance, or any other adverse underwriting decision. These rights are those found under the Fair Credit Reporting Act.

A fine of $10,000, or up to one year in jail is the penalty for any person who obtains information that he or she has no legitimate reason to receive.

STATE INSURANCE REGULATION

Commissioner's Scope and Duties

The Insurance Code of each state authorizes the establishment of an Insurance Department to administer and carry out the insurance laws. In each state, a public official will head the Department — the title of the official will be the **Commissioner, Superintendent,** or **Director** of insurance. The titles differ state-to-state. A majority of the states use the title "Commissioner." In all cases, the public official in charge of the Insurance Department has broad powers to supervise and regulate the insurance affairs within the state.

The insurance laws of the state usually confer upon the Commissioner all of the following powers and duties:

- To conduct investigations and examinations
- To make reasonable rules and regulations
- To hire employees and examiners, and delegate any power, duty, or function to such persons
- To examine the accounts, records, documents, and transactions of any insurer, agent or broker
- To subpoena witnesses and administer oaths in order to further any examination, investigation, or hearing on insurance matters
- To issue orders and notices on decisions made or matters pending
- To issue insurance licenses and Certificates of Authority
- To impose penalties for violations of the Insurance Code, including but not limited to fines, suspensions or revocations of licenses and Certificates of Authority, and requesting that the Attorney General prosecute a violator
- To approve insurance policy forms sold within the state
- To approve rates and rate increases for regulated lines of insurance

SELF-REGULATION

The last channel of regulation of the business is self-regulation, that is those restraints from within the industry either by individual company conscience or by group pressure of insurance associations. This was the first type of regulation of the business and is still the predominant type in Great Britain.

There are several inter-company organizations or associations that impose "codes" on their members. These include the National Association of Life Underwriters (agents) through its state and local associations, the International Association of Health Underwriters (agents), and the American Society of Chartered Life Underwriters (agents). In recent years, these industry associations have had a major impact on prelicensing and continuing education laws. For example, often the state Association of Life Underwriters will be the organization which is the major force in obtaining passage of these laws through the state legislature. Continuing education laws are designed to protect the consumer by mandating certain continuing educational requirements if an agent is to maintain his or her license. These educational requirements usually focus on product knowledge, insurance regulations and ethics. The majority of states have continuing education requirements.

The NAIC

The **National Association of Insurance Commissioners (NAIC)**, an association of state insurance commissioners, although without legal authority as a group, also imposes a strong influence in the area of the industry's self-regulation. The NAIC is the organization that has done the most to standardize law between the states. Although the wording, and sometimes the provisions themselves differ from state to state, for the most part the differences are only slight as each state attempts to follow, in essence, the wording of the "model laws" established by the NAIC.

The model laws include the *Individual Accident and Sickness Policy Provisions Law, Standard Nonforfeiture and Valuation Laws, Fair Trade Practices Act, Unauthorized Insurers Service of Process Act, Insurance Holding Company System Regulatory Act, Variable Contract Law,* "group life definition and standard provisions bill," and "credit life and credit health insurance regulation bill."

REVIEW QUESTIONS

1. What is the case of *Paul v. Virginia*? ____________

____

____

____

2. What was the South-Eastern Underwriters Decision? ____________

____

____

____

3. What was the purpose of the McCarran-Ferguson Act? ____________

____

____

____

4. What are the three channels of regulation of the insurance business?

(1) ________________________

(2) ________________________

(3) ________________________

5. A(n) ____________ report is any written or oral communication about an individual which is used by a consumer reporting agency to determine if the individual is eligible for credit, insurance, or employment.

6. Unauthorized persons who misrepresent themselves for the purpose of gaining personal and confidential information are (collecting "prohibited information"/conducting pretext interviews)____________

____

7. The maximum penalty for collecting personal information under false pretenses is $ ____________.

8. What is the purpose of the Privacy Act of 1974?

____

____

9. In most cases, if an insurer is requesting information, notice of this request must be given to the applicant who agrees to this activity by signing a ____________ form.

10. The fine for continued violation of the Privacy Act is $____________, but can be up to $ ____________ if the violation appears to be a general business practice.

☞ ***Answers to Review Questions are located at the back of the book.***

AREAS REGULATED — COMPANIES

The State Insurance Code prescribes the procedures that must be followed in order for an insurance company to be formed. It specifies the manner in which the company must be organized, the requirements for incorporation, such as, the amounts for minimum capital and surplus requirements for a domestic stock insurer; and the minimum surplus requirements and securities deposit for a domestic mutual insurer. While the bulk of the Code pertains only to domestic insurers, some of the laws regulate foreign and alien insurers' eligibility to transact insurance business as well as establishing requirements for maintaining assets and liabilities.

Protection against insurer insolvency is one of the principal concerns of the insurance industry. Insurance insolvency regulations govern such areas as the organization and ownership of a new company, capital and surplus requirements, reserves, accounting, investments, annual statements, and the rehabilitation and liquidation of impaired insurers. In addition to these areas of regulation, Insurance Departments in many states have adopted regulations for the establishment of guaranty associations in the event that an insurer does, in spite of regulations and precautions, become insolvent.

Before individuals can form an insurance company they must receive prior approval from the Insurance Department to organize. They must meet the requirements for incorporation, certificates of intention and bylaws in the same manner as other corporations. They are required to draw up a charter which states the proposed name of the insurer, the location, the lines of insurance to be sold, and method of operation. The Insurance Department will also conduct an investigation to ensure that the organizers are of good moral character.

The majority of individual life and health insurance is written by stock and mutual companies. A mutual company must have a minimum number of applications for insurance, the advanced premium payment for each application, and a surplus. A stock company must have a specified amount of capital, which is invested, and a surplus amount. In many states domestic insurers must deposit securities which insurance regulations specify as relatively stable and safe, such as government bonds.

Insurer Solvency

The Insurance Department has the right to compute the reserve liabilities of a company; to value its assets; to approve or disapprove its investments, dividends, and expenses; and the power to require it to deposit securities to cover its liabilities in the state.

Because insurance companies collect premiums before losses are paid, there is a great need to guard against insolvencies. The Department will attempt to rehabilitate a company in a hazardous condition, or if this fails, handle the liquidation.

Various state statutes impose capital and surplus requirements, the preparation of annual financial statements, and require periodic examinations of insurers by the Insurance Department. These laws establish initial financial requirements and help in the early detection of financial problems.

Each insurer's capacity to write new business is limited by the levels of capital and surplus it currently maintains. Most states discourage or prohibit the writing of net premiums in excess of some multiple of an insurer's existing surplus. Without such controls, a carrier might assume excessive amounts of risk, experience losses beyond the capacity to pay claims, and become insolvent.

Despite checks on policywriting capacity, there are a number of other factors which could undermine or improve the financial status of an insurer. Insurance always carries an element of uncertainty, and above average underwriting profits or losses might cause a company's financial status to shift. Investment income or loss is another factor that can have a profound impact on an insurer's status. Agents and insureds therefore have an interest in having coverage placed with carriers who have a sound financial condition.

Annual Statement

Each insurance company must report its financial condition in an annual statement. The annual statement generally reports the following information:

- Summary of company assets (listed by type)
- Summary of company liabilities
- Summary of company surplus, and other funds
- Summary of company operations
- Analysis of operations (listed by line of business)
- Analysis of reserve increases
- Statements regarding changes in financial condition

Valuation of Assets

The Mandatory Security Valuation Reserve (MSVR) was created in 1951 to prevent radical changes in policyholder surplus from fluctuations in the value of securities and other investments. The MSVR absorbs the smaller changes in the values of security investments up to a maximum amount. When the maximum is reached, the surplus is increased or decreased, depending upon whether there was a gain or a loss in the value of the security. Other regulatory bodies and state statutes regarding assets are intended to assure that insurers invest only in high quality assets to prevent insolvencies.

Investments

All states have regulations governing insurance company investments. Life insurance companies may invest funds in concerns that are fairly stable in value. These safe investments include municipal bonds, corporate bonds, real estate mortgages, and even policy loans.

Regulations require that all investments and loans be approved by the company's board of directors, and that no board members have a personal interest in the investment being made. Committee meetings where discussion of investment or loans has been undertaken must have minutes recorded. Such minutes will be open to inspection by the Commissioner.

Foreign companies seeking a license to transact business in a state must meet investment requirements similar to those required of a domestic insurer.

Taxation of Life Insurance Companies

Life insurance companies are taxed on both their investment income and underwriting profits. For stock insurance companies, investment income is taxed in the year it is earned, while 50% of underwriting profit is taxed during the year earned, and the other 50% is taxed when paid out to stockholders. The one-half of the underwriting income that is taxed becomes shareholders' surplus, and the half that has not been taxed becomes policyholders' surplus. Both types of surplus are collectively known as the **earned surplus** of an insurance company.

Mutual insurers pay out their underwriting income as dividends to policyholders, so this tax regulation does not generally apply.

Company Ratings

Agents have a responsibility to place coverage with financially sound carriers. There are several organizations that rate the financial strength of insurance carriers, based on an analysis of a company's claims experience, investment performance, management, and other factors. These organizations include A.M. Best Company, Standard & Poor's Insurance Rating Services, Moody's Investors Service, Duff & Phelps Credit Rating Company, and Weiss Ratings. These ratings are one of the most widely used indicators of financial health (or the lack of it) in the insurance industry.

The approach taken by A.M. Best illustrates one approach to evaluating companies. Best uses nine alphabetical ratings for insurers to which it gives an assigned rating, and uses other designations to evaluate financial health, which are explained below:

- A++, A+ (superior — strongest position)
- A, A- (excellent)
- B++, B+ (very good)
- B, B- (good)
- C++, C+ (fair)
- C, C- (marginal)
- D (below minimum standards)
- E (under state supervision)
- F (in liquidation)

Various **modifiers** (one of eight lower case letters) are added to assigned ratings, which are shown in upper case, to qualify the status of a rating. For example, "g" is used to indicate a *group* rating involving a pool of affiliated companies. The letter "e" indicates a *parent company* rating, when the financial strength of the parent is used to evaluate a newly affiliated company. Caution is signaled by a "w" which means *watch list* — meaning that some decline has occurred, but not enough to cause a drop in the assigned rating. An overall rating might look like this — B+w (very good, but watch).

About 30% of the companies reported on by Best do not qualify for an assigned rating. These are categorized and reported as "not assigned," but Best assigns one or more of 11 suffix codes to indicate the reason why the company was not assigned a letter rating. For example, NA-3, insufficient operating experience, indicates that the company has not accumulated five consecutive years of representative operating experience.

In making its evaluations, Best considers such things as underwriting, reserves, investments, and management practices. It also considers whether a company could absorb an unusual loss or other financial shock.

Examination of Insurers

The state Insurance Department must examine the **financial affairs**, transactions, and general business records of domestic insurers in accordance with specific state insurance laws. Generally, these laws will state that the Commissioner of Insurance may examine the insurer's records as often as necessary but at least once every three to five years.

The non-financial regulatory activities of an insurance department fall under the broad heading of **market conduct**. Proper market conduct means conducting insurance business fairly and responsibly.

A market conduct examination is when state insurance department investigators examine the business practices and operations of an insurer and its agents in order to determine their authority to conduct insurance business in the state. During a market conduct examination, state examiners investigate the records and practices of an insurance company and determine whether the company is in fact in compliance with state laws regulating the sales and marketing, underwriting, and issuance of insurance products. Some states conduct market conduct exams in conjunction with their regular financial examinations of insurers; others conduct independent market conduct exams.

As part of these examinations, the insurer's records of commissions paid to agents will be reviewed to determine if commissions were paid in accordance with state statutes. Most states require that commissions may only be paid or shared with licensed agents or producers. Generally, agents may share commissions with other agents provided they are both appointed with the same insurer and licensed in the same lines of insurance.

Rehabilitation and Liquidation

Despite regulatory controls, some insurers become insolvent, or find themselves in financial difficulty. In this event the Department has the authority to assume control over company funds and management. If an insurer becomes impaired (in financial difficulty) the Department will attempt to put the insurer back on a sound financial standing. If an insurer becomes insolvent (unable to meet financial obligations) the Department will attempt to make the insurer solvent again. Rehabilitation efforts are undertaken if the Department believes that an impaired insurer has a chance of restoring solvency. Liquidation proceedings are instituted when the insurer is insolvent and cannot be restored to solvency.

The 1977 NAIC Model Insurers Supervision, Rehabilitation, and Liquidation Act is divided into four sections designed to facilitate actions of insolvency. *General Provisions* establishes the Act's absolute authority for the rehabilitation or liquidation of insolvent insurers. *Supervision Proceedings* offers alternative plans for use prior to the need for the Department's full intervention. *Formal Proceedings* outlines methods for transferring authority from the insurer to the Department. *Interstate Relations* provides for the transfer of an insurer's assets and records to the state of domicile.

Rehabilitation proceedings can occur for the following reasons:

- The company's continued operation would not serve the best interests of policyowners, creditors, or the general public.
- The company's officers and directors have violated the law by committing certain acts or omissions.
- The company's officers, directors, or owners have attempted to transfer a significant amount of assets, or have attempted a merger without the Department's approval.

Guaranty Associations

State Guaranty Associations are organized to protect claimants, policyholders, annuitants and creditors of financially impaired or insolvent insurers by providing funds for the payment of claims and other related policy benefits. The Association is composed of insurers authorized to transact insurance business within the state. Association membership exceptions include fraternal organizations and non-profit companies. Member insurers are assessed certain sums of money to cover the Association's operating expenses. If an insurer insolvency should occur, each member insurer will be assessed additional fees to cover the insolvency.

Guaranty associations are often compared to the Federal Deposit Insurance Corporation (FDIC), which protects bank depositors from bank failures. Like the FDIC, coverage by the guaranty association is subject to limitations, usually something like $300,000 for death benefits, $100,000 for life insurance cash surrender/withdrawal values, $100,000 for health benefits, and an overall cap for individuals.

Some of the characteristics of the Association include the following:

- It establishes accounts to collect funds for the administration and assessment of the association
- It is supervised by the Commissioner, and a board of directors (usually nine members)
- The duties of the board and the Commissioner are specified by law
- An insurer's authorization to transact business in the state is contingent upon membership in the association
- Member insurers are assessed on the percentage of premiums each insurer has individually earned in the state

The NAIC has helped to establish a National Organization of Life and Health Insurance Guaranty Associations (NOLHGA) which helps facilitate cooperation and communication among the state guaranty associations.

Marketing and Advertising Life and Health Insurance

States often regulate the marketing and advertising of life and health insurance policies to assure truthful and full disclosure of pertinent information when selling these policies. As a rule, the insurer is held responsible for the content of advertisments of its policies. Advertisements cannot be misleading or obscure, or use deceptive illustrations, and must clearly outline all policy coverages as well as exclusions or limitations on coverage (such as preexisting condition limitations).

Most states require insurers to keep a permanent **advertising file** of all advertisements used in the state until the next regular examination of the insurer by the Insurance Department, or for a specified minimum number of years, such as two or three.

Also, many states require the delivery of a Buyers Guide and Policy Summary or Outline of Coverage at the time of policy delivery. The Buyers Guide is a document providing basic information about the insurance policies, and the Policy Summary (life insurance) or Outline of Coverage (health insurance) is a written statement describing the elements of the policy being sold. Generally, it must include the agent's name and address, the name and office address of the insurer, and the generic name of the policy and each rider.

REVIEW QUESTIONS

11. Insurance companies must report their financial condition in a(n) ____________________

    ____

12. Who assumes control over company funds and management if an insurance company becomes insolvent?____________________

    ____

    ____

13. ____________ efforts are instituted when an insurer is insolvent but might be able to restore solvency.

14. The mechanism used to pay covered claims and prevent financial losses to claimants and policyholders when an insurer becomes insolvent is a

    ____

    ____

15. What company produces evaluations of insurer financial status often used by Insurance Departments? ____________________

16. Each insurer's capacity to write new business is limited by the levels of ____________________ it currently maintains.

☞ ***Answers to Review Questions are located at the back of the book.***

AREAS REGULATED — AGENTS

Agents and brokers, and other producers are also governed by the Insurance Code with respect to licensing and unfair trade practices.

License Required

Under the statutes of most states, no person is permitted to be, or act as, an insurance agent, broker, or solicitor unless currently licensed as such. In many states, adjusters, consultants, and service representatives must also be licensed.

No agent, broker, or solicitor shall take application for, process or place for others, any kinds of insurance for which he or she is not then licensed. Nor shall an agent place any insurance with any insurer to which the agent does not then hold both a license and appointment as agent.

Licensing regulations include the following in most states:

- Those eligible to become agents (for example, those with good moral character, or who are 18 years or older)
- Those ineligible to become agents (such as, those found guilty of dishonesty, or those convicted of a felony)
- The form of the application for license (the form must solicit such information as insurance experience, personal history, and the purpose of the license)
- Those who must take and pass a qualifying examination (for example, agents, brokers, and solicitors)
- Those who are exempt from the examination (such as those who renew a license on time, or ticket-selling agents of airlines)
- Types of licenses (agent, broker, temporary)
- Educational requirements (pre-licensing education needed prior to taking the exam or continuing education)
- Maintaining a license (expiration and renewal of license, or suspension, or revocation of license)

Qualifications — Agents, Brokers, Solicitors

To be eligible for a license as agent, broker or solicitor, an individual typically must meet the following requirements:

- Be at least **18** years of age
- Depending on the state, may or may not be a citizen of the United States, or have applied with the U.S. Department of Immigration for permanent residence and have declared the intent to apply for citizenship
- Have been a bona fide resident of the state in which application is being made for whatever amount of time the state requires
- Be trustworthy, have a good reputation, and not have been convicted of a felony or a crime involving moral turpitude
- If applying for a brokers license, have filed any bond which may be required and be able to demonstrate to the satisfaction of the Insurance Department that the necessary competency exists due to experience or special education to fulfill a broker's responsibilities
- Compliance with any required prelicensing education laws and pass the required licensing examination in order to demonstrate competency in the kinds of insurance to be transacted under the license
- Intend to actively engage in the insurance business with members of the public, and not use the license principally for transacting a disproportionate amount of **controlled business**

License for Controlled Business Prohibited

The head of the Insurance Department will not grant, renew, continue, or permit to exist any license that probably will be used, has been, or is being used principally for writing **controlled business**. "Controlled business" means insurance on the agent's, broker's, or solicitor's own property or interests, or those of his family, his employer, or any partnership, association, or corporation in which he or a family member has an interest as an officer, director, stockholder, partner or employee.

A certain amount of controlled business is permitted. But a licensee is not permitted to earn commission or compensation from controlled business in excess of a stated amount (35% to 50% of total compensation, depending upon the state) during a stated time period (usually a calendar-year). If a greater proportion does come from controlled business, the practice is in violation of law and the license may be revoked or suspended.

Resident Agent

A resident agent or broker is one of the following:

- If an individual, is domiciled and residing in the state issuing the license
- If a firm, is one with all members domiciled and residing in the state issuing the license
- If a corporation, is incorporated under the laws of the state issuing the license, or maintains its only

places of business in that state and all shares of the corporation are owned by residents of the state

Nonresident Agent

A nonresident agent is one who resides in a state different from the state in which he or she is applying for a license. A state may issue a license to any agent who does not reside in that state when the nonresident agent represents an insurer authorized to do business in the licensing state.

Some states have **reciprocal** agreements and will only issue a nonresident agent license if the state in which the agent resides issues nonresident licenses to agents in their state.

Other states require that the nonresident agent split his or her commission with a resident of the licensing state.

Countersignature

A countersignature is the signature of a resident agent on a policy sold by a nonresident agent. The basic purpose of the countersignature in life and health insurance is to ensure that resident agents take part in the commissions earned from business written in their state.

If the commission is above a certain amount the nonresident agent is legally obligated to share some portion of his or her commission with the cosigning resident agent. If the commission owed to the resident agent is less than a certain amount, for example $5, the resident agent can waive the right to such commission split.

Exceptions to License Requirements

Salaried employees of insurers who devote full—time to clerical or administrative duties and who do not solicit insurance or earn commission are not required to be licensed in most states, even though they may have incidental functions with regard to insurance transactions (such as collecting premiums).

OBTAINING A LICENSE

Application for License

Application for an insurance license is made to the head of the Insurance Department on whatever forms have been designated and furnished for that purpose. Such licenses shall be issued upon proper filing of the application, satisfaction of all statutory requirements, and payment of the appropriate fee. Applications usually require personal information showing the identity, personal history, business record, and insurance experience of the applicant, along with a statement about the purpose for which the license will be used. Applications frequently include questions to elicit the following information:

- Whether or not the applicant was ever previously licensed to transact any kind of insurance in any state
- Whether or not any license was ever refused, suspended or revoked
- Whether or not the applicant is indebted to any insurer or general agent
- Whether or not the applicant has ever had an agency contract cancelled

If a firm or corporation applies for an agent or broker license, similar information is required with regard to the firm or corporation. In addition, the names of all members, officers, and directors of the firm or corporation must be listed, and each person who is to exercise agent or broker powers must be identified and shall furnish the same personal information required of an individual applicant.

An application for an agent license must show the kinds of insurance to be transacted and the name of the authorized insurer which the applicant represents. An application for a solicitor license must be accompanied by a written appointment of the applicant as solicitor by a licensed agent or broker.

Examination

Unless exempt, each applicant for an insurance license must personally take and pass an examination, which will reasonably test the applicant's knowledge of both insurance and related legal responsibilities. The examination must cover all the kinds of insurance for which the applicant has applied. If the applicant is a firm or corporation, each individual who will be named in the license as having authority to act for the applicant must take the examination.

Exemptions from Examination

Examinations may not be required for the following:

- Those applying for and meeting the requirements for temporary licenses
- Nonresident agent applicants who reside in a reciprocal state
- Transportation ticket agents of common carriers applying for a limited license to sell only travel accident insurance and baggage insurance
- Title insurance agents
- Applicants for a license covering the same kinds of insurance for which he or she was previously licensed in the same state within the previous 12 months

The last stipulation does not apply if the previous license was a temporary license, or if the previous license was suspended, revoked, or not renewed.

Issuance of License

Licenses shall be issued to persons who are properly qualified and, when applicable, have passed the exam. A license will usually state the name of licensee, issue date and expiration, kind(s) of insurance covered, and any conditions which may apply.

Combination Agent and Broker License

A licensed agent may be licensed as a broker and be a broker to insurers for which he or she is not licensed as an agent. A licensed broker may be licensed as and be an agent to insurers authorizing the individual as agent. The sole relationship in transactions between a broker and an insurer for which the broker is licensed as an agent shall be that of insurer and agent.

Licensing of Firm or Corporation

A firm or corporation may usually be licensed as an agent or broker, but may only be so licensed if one of its principal functions is the transaction of insurance or if it receives any commission or compensation dependent upon the placement of insurance. At least one person in each office or place of business shall represent the same insurer(s) that the firm or corporation represents and shall be individually licensed.

Solicitors

A solicitor may not be appointed by or licensed to more than one agent or broker. Generally, the solicitor's license will cover all the kinds of insurance for which the appointing agent or broker is licensed. A solicitor does not have authority to bind risks or countersign policies. All transactions of a solicitor shall be in the name of the agent or broker, and the agent or broker shall be responsible for acts of omissions of the solicitor within the scope of his appointment. The solicitor's license shall remain in the custody of the agent or broker by whom appointed. Upon termination of the appointment, the agent or broker shall give written notice thereof to the Insurance Department and return the license for cancellation.

Temporary Agent Licenses

In most states, temporary agent licenses may be issued to qualified individuals who pay the appropriate fee and meet the age, residency, and trustworthiness requirements for licensees. A temporary licensee is not required to take an examination. Temporary licenses are commonly issued in the following cases:

- To the surviving spouse or next of kin of a deceased licensed agent
- To the administrator or executor, or one of their employees, of the estate of a deceased licensed agent
- To the spouse, next of kin, employee, or legal guardian of a licensed agent disabled by injury or physical or mental illness
- To an employee of a firm, or officer or employee of a corporation, licensed as agent, upon the death or disability of the person designated in the license to exercise agent powers
- To the designee of a licensed agent who is entering active duty in the U.S. armed forces

A temporary license may cover the same kinds of insurance for which the agent being replaced was licensed. Temporary licenses are generally issued for 90-day periods. Under certain situations, they may be renewed for additional 90-day periods. For example, an estate administrator of a deceased agent may require more than 90 days to complete the business of the agent and accordingly, the temporary license may be renewed for a subsequent 90-day period.

MAINTAINING A LICENSE

Change of Address

Every licensee must promptly give to the head of the Insurance Department written notice of any change of business address.

Office and Records

Every agent or broker (except nonresident licensees) must have and maintain in the state issuing the license a place of business accessible to the public. The designated place of business must be where the licensee principally conducts transactions under the license. The licenses of the licensee and solicitors appointed by the licensee shall be conspicuously displayed in a part of the place of business which is customarily open to the public. The agent or broker must keep at the place of business the usual and customary records pertaining to insurance transactions.

Continuation/Expiration/Renewal of License

All licenses continue in force until their expiration dates, unless revoked, suspended or terminated at an earlier date. Each state establishes procedures for continuation or renewal of licenses. Renewal fees are normally charged. An increasing number of states have established continuing education requirements for licensees. Generally, these laws require the agent to earn a specific number of continuing education credits through approved self study or classroom programs within a specified period of time prior to the license renewal. If the agent fails to comply with the continuing education requirements, the license will not be renewed.

Appointment of Agents

Each insurer appointing an agent is typically required to file the appointment with the Insurance Department in writing and pay the specified appointment fee. The filing must specify the kinds of insurance to be transacted by the agent, and one appointment fee shall cover all the kinds of insurance to be transacted for the one insurer.

Subject to continuation of the appointment and payment of the periodic continuation fee, each appointment shall remain in effect until the agent's license is revoked or terminated. Appointments not continued by the periodic filing and payment of fees shall expire at midnight on the last day of the period during which the prior appointment was effective. Late charges may be added to the fee if a filing of an appointment is late. It should be noted that the agent's license is with the state and the agent's appointment is with an insurer. Loss of an appointment does not necessarily mean that an agent has lost his or her license. It simply means that the agent may no longer represent that particular company although he or she is still licensed within the state.

Termination of Appointment

Subject to an agent's contract rights, if any, an insurer may terminate any of its appointed agents at any time. The insurer must give prompt written notice of the termination and the date to the Insurance Department (and to the agent when reasonably possible), and must file a statement of facts related to the termination and reasons for it.

Disciplinary Actions

In most jurisdictions, an agent's or broker's license may be revoked, suspended for up to 12 months, or renewal may be refused if any of the following causes are found to exist:

- Any cause for which the original license or any renewal would have been refused
- Willful violation of or noncompliance with any insurance statute, lawful rule or regulation
- Misrepresentation or fraud in obtaining or attempting to obtain an insurance license
- Misappropriation or conversion to personal use, or illegal withholding, of monies belonging to policyholders, insurers, beneficiaries or others and received during the conduct of insurance business
- Suspension or revocation of an insurance license in any jurisdiction
- Conviction by final judgment of a felony involving moral turpitude
- Conduct of insurance affairs showing the licensee to be incompetent or a source of injury and loss to, or repeated complaints by, the public or any insurer

The license of a firm or corporation may be suspended, revoked or refused for cause if such cause applies to any individual designated in the license. The revocation or suspension of an agent or broker license will automatically revoke or suspend the licenses of all solicitors appointed by that agent or broker.

In addition to suspension, revocation and nonrenewal of license, an agent may be fined or imprisoned for violation of state insurance laws. Depending on the violation, fines can range from $100 to several thousand dollars. If an agent is in violation of civil law, the Commissioner can refer the matter to the State Attorney General for criminal prosecution and possible imprisonment.

REVIEW QUESTIONS

17. No one may act as an insurance agent unless currently ____________ as such.
18. Which of the following help an agent's eligibility for licensing:
    a. being a citizen of the United States
    b. intending to primarily transact controlled business
    c. passing the required examination
    d. being a resident of the state in which application is made
19. Define **countersignature**.

    ____

    ____

    ____
20. The following generally are not required to take licensing examinations **except**:
    a. transportation ticket agents selling only travel accident and baggage insurance
    b. resident agents
    c. nonresident agents in a reciprocal state
    d. temporary agents
21. A solicitor (has/does not have) the authority to bind risks and countersign policies. __________
22. Licensees must notify the Insurance Department within six months of any change of business address. (True/False) __________
23. Willful violation of or noncompliance with any insurance statute, rule, or regulation may result in

    ____

Answers to Review Questions are located at the back of the book.

THE LEGAL FRAMEWORK

Insurance Contract Law Principles

Insurance policies are legal contracts and are subject to the general law of contracts. This is a distinct body of law which is separate from criminal law (crimes against society) and tort law (legal liability issues usually involving damages for negligence). Contract law dictates the formation and enforcement of legal contract rights.

A contract is a binding agreement between two or more persons that is enforceable in a court of law. Under the law, the following elements are necessary for the formation of a valid contract:

- Agreement (offer and acceptance)
- Consideration
- Competent parties
- Legal purpose

Agreement (Offer and Acceptance). There can be no contract without the agreement or mutual assent of the parties. A common intention on all terms of the contract is essential to an agreement and no essential terms of the contract may be left unsettled. Further, the intention of the parties to a contract must be communicated to one another.

The parties to an insurance contract are the insurance company and the applicant, who may become the insured or may name another person to be insured. Unless otherwise indicated, it is assumed that the applicant is the prospective insured.

Offer. An offer is a proposal that creates a contract if accepted by another party according to its terms. A contract arises only if the acceptance indicates clear assent to the exact terms and conditions of the offer. Generally, any words or actions by the person receiving the offer which imply agreement will be interpreted as acceptance of the offer.

The offer may come from the insurer (company) or the applicant. In either case the offer must be definite and clear in its terms. If an applicant gives the insurer a completed application and pays the first premium, the application is an offer. If the policy is issued as applied for, the insurer accepts the offer.

There is no offer if the applicant sends the application to the insurance company without payment of the premium. Such an application is merely an invitation to the company to make an offer. The insurance company makes an offer by issuing the policy. The applicant accepts it by paying the first premium.

Acceptance. An acceptance must be unconditional and unqualified. A qualified or conditional acceptance rejects the offer and may constitute a counter offer. If an insurance company, after receiving an application and premium payment, issues a policy with more restrictive coverage than that applied for, the company has made a counter offer.

For example, a counter offer occurs if an applicant applies for a standard health insurance policy, pays the premium, and receives a policy containing an exclusionary endorsement for specified physical conditions. The applicant must decide whether or not to accept the policy as modified. If he or she accepts the policy, then there is a contract. If he or she rejects the modified policy, there is no contract, and the applicant is entitled to a return of his or her premium.

Consideration. Each party to the contract must give valuable consideration. In the insurance contract, the value given by the insurer consists of the promises contained in the policy contract. The consideration given by the insured consists of the statements made in the application and the payment of the initial premium.

The consideration may consist of any of the following:

- A monetary payment
- An act
- A forbearance from action
- The creation, modification or destruction of a legal right
- A return promise

In other words, each of the parties to the contract gives up something of value or forbears from exercising a right.

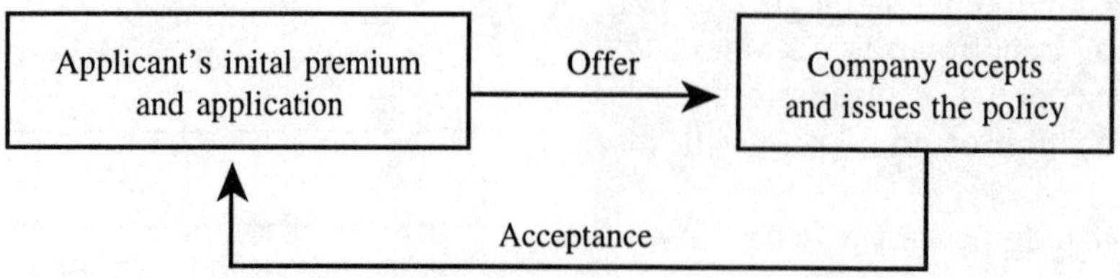

It is important to know that part of the applicant's consideration consists of the statements in the application. A great deal of importance is placed on the representations in the application, since the insurance company's entire decision of whether to contract is based on its evaluation of the information in the application.

The application should be complete and accurate. The agent must take the time to ask each and every question and to record the answers fully and legibly. The agent must be careful to avoid haphazard or cursory completion of application forms on behalf of applicants since incomplete or inaccurate application information hurts both the insurance company and the applicant. Further, the agent must not assist the applicant in deliberately deceiving the company regarding material facts in the application. Later discovery of false information in the application may be cause for denying coverage.

Failure to complete all required information on the application in a thorough, honest, and detailed manner could subject the agent to the embarrassment of having to explain to his or her client why the insurance policy is invalid. This failure could also lead to disciplinary action by his or her insurance company and by the state.

Competent Parties. For a contract to be binding, both parties must have the legal capacity to make a contract.

To have the legal capacity to make insurance contracts, an insurance company must have authority under its charter to issue contracts and be authorized by the state to issue contracts. The company's representative must also be licensed by the state. The legal effect of a contract made by an unlicensed insurer depends on state law.

The insured or applicant must be of legal age and be mentally competent to make an insurance contract. Applications of minors must usually be signed by an adult parent or guardian to comply with the legal age requirement for making contracts.

Legal Purpose Public Policy. To be valid, a contract must be for a legal purpose and not contrary to public policy. Wagering or gambling contracts are contrary to public policy. An insurance contract, however, is not against public policy where an insurable interest exists.

Insurance Contract Features

The insurance contract has certain characteristics not found in the typical noninsurance contract.

Utmost Good Faith. The insurance contract requires utmost good faith between the parties. This means that each party is entitled to rely upon the representations of the other and each party should have a reasonable expectation that the other is acting in good faith without attempts to conceal or deceive.

Aleatory. An insurance contract is said to be "aleatory," or dependent upon chance or uncertain outcome, because one party may receive much more in value than he or she gives in value under the contract. For example, an insured who has a loss may receive a greater payment from an insurer for the loss than he or she has paid in premiums. On the other hand, an insured may pay his or her premiums and have no loss, so the insurer pays nothing.

Adhesion. In insurance, the insurer writes the contract and the insured "adheres" to it. Any ambiguity in the wording of the contract is resolved in favor of the insured, because the insurance company draws up the original contract and the insured has little or no control over its content.

Unilateral. Contracts may be bilateral or unilateral. An exchange of a promise for a promise is bilateral, whereas an exchange of an act for a promise is unilateral. Generally, insurance contracts are unilateral. This means that after the insured has completed the act of paying the premium, only the insurer promises to do anything further. The insurer has promised performance and is legally responsible. The insured has made no legally enforceable promises and cannot be held for breach of contract. For example, the insured may stop paying premium because he is not legally responsible to continue paying premium.

Executory. An insurance contract is an **executory contract** in that the promises described in the insurance contract are to be *executed in the future, and only after certain events (losses) occur.*

Conditional. Insurance contracts are also **conditional** contracts because when the loss occurs certain conditions must be met to make the contract legally enforceable. For example, a policyholder might have to satisfy the test of having an insurable interest, and satisfy the condition of submitting proof of loss.

A condition is a contract provision which limits the rights contained in the contract. A **condition precedent** means that an act must be performed, or an event must take place before the right is met. For example, an insured must become injured to collect the medical benefit; or the insured must die before a spouse can collect the death benefit. A **condition subsequent** exists when an act or event is of such nature as to cancel a right. For example, if the contract contains a provision that denies payment of the death benefit in the case of suicide, within a two-year period of the policy effective date, the insured who commits suicide within one year cancels the existing right of payment of the death benefit.

Personal Contract. Generally, insurance policies are personal contracts between the insured and insurer. Except for life insurance and some marine coverages involving transportation and cargo, insurance is not transferable to another person without the consent of the insurer. Fire insurance, for example, does not follow the property. If an owner sells an insured building and no arrangements are made for transferring coverage to the new owner, no insurance exists — the previous owner no longer has insurable interest, and the new owner has no personal coverage.

Warranties and Representations

A **warranty** is something that becomes part of the contract itself and is a statement which is considered to be **guaranteed** to be true. Under a strict interpretation, any breach of warranty provides grunds for voiding the contract.

A **representation** is a statement **believed** to be true to the best of one's knowledge. An insurer seeking to void coverage on the basis of a misrepresentation usually has to prove that the misrepresentation is material to the risk.

Under most state laws, an applicant's statements or responses to questions on an application for insurance (in the absence of fraud) are considered to be representations, and not warranties.

An example would be a question on the application asking for your sex or date of birth. You represent yourself to the insurance company as being male or female, and a certain age. The accuracy of these items is very important to the insurance company issuing the policy. If they are incorrect, they may be considered misrepresentations, and the policy may be voided as a result.

There is a difference between representation of a fact and an expression of opinion. A good example is a question on many applications: "Are you now to the best of your knowledge and belief in good health?" If the applicant answers "yes" while knowing in fact that he or she is not, there is a misrepresentation of actual fact. If, on the other hand, he or she has had no medical opinion and suffers from no symptoms recognizable to a layman, his or her answer is an opinion and thus not a misrepresentation.

Impersonation

Impersonation means assuming the name and identity of another person for the purpose of committing a fraud. The offense is also known as false pretenses. In the case of life insurance, an uninsurable individual applying for insurance may ask another person to substitute for him to take the physical examination.

Misrepresentation and Concealment

A **misrepresentation** is a written or oral statement which is false. Generally, in order for a misrepresentation to be grounds for voiding an insurance policy, it has to be material to the risk.

Concealment is the failure to disclose known facts. Generally, an insurer may be able to void the insurance if it can prove that the insured *intentionally* concealed a material fact.

Material information or a **material fact** is something which is crucial to acceptance of the risk. For example, if the correct information about something would have caused the insurance company to deny a risk or issued a policy on a different basis, the information is material.

Fraud

Fraud is an intentional act designed to deceive and induce another party to part with something of value.

Fraud may involve misrepresentation and/or concealment, but not all acts of fraud. If someone intentionally lies in order to obtain coverage or to collect on a false claim, that would be a matter of fraud. If someone misrepresents something on an application (perhaps a medical treatment the person is embarassed to talk about) without any intent to obtain something of value, no fraud has occurred.

Parol (Oral) Evidence Rule

The parol evidence rule limits the impact of waiver and estoppel on contract terms by disallowing oral evidence based on statements made *before* the contract was created. It is assumed that any oral agreements made before contract formation were incorporated into the written contract. Once formed, earlier oral evidence will not be admitted in court to change or contradict the contract. An oral statement may waive contract provisions only when the statement occurs after the contract exists.

REVIEW QUESTIONS

24. In an insurance contract, there must be an "offer." Who makes this offer?________________

____

____

25. What is the "consideration" in an insurance contract in the case of the applicant and in the case of the insurer?________________

____

26. What is necessary for a person to have the legal capacity to enter into an insurance contract?______

____

____

> ☞ ***Answers to Review Questions are located at the back of the book.***

FORMATION OF A LIFE & HEALTH INSURANCE CONTRACT

The formation of a life or health insurance contract differs from the formation of other insurance contracts in that the life or health agent usually does not have the authority to bind the insurer.

The life or health insurance agent has no authority to put a policy into effect. The agent can only solicit offers from prospective insureds, securing their applications and initial premium payments. The application and premium must be sent to the insurance company underwriter, who determines whether or not the company wishes to accept the risk.

The restricted underwriting authority of the life insurance agent is related to the nature of life insurance contracts. Life insurance policies are generally non-cancellable, long-term contracts. A life insurance policy is contestable for a one or two-year period. Property and casualty insurance, however, involves a short-term contract often for one year or less and the insurance company usually reserves the right to cancel the policy if the risk appears to be undesirable. In addition, life and health insurance underwriting decisions frequently rest on medical questions. The life or health insurer employs medical experts and has at its disposal various investigative reports that shed light on the desirability of a risk. The insurance company is in a much better position than the agent to evaluate the applicant's insurability.

INSURANCE CONTRACTS & THE COURTS

Contract Construction

When the courts have a case involving contracts it looks at the "rules of construction" to interpret the contract. The rules of construction help to identify and establish the intent of the parties to the contract. There are five major areas which the courts review in order to interpret the contract, establish the intent of the parties, and hand down a ruling.

Plain Language and Word Definitions. If the language of the contract is clear the courts do not have to interpret the meaning of the contract. The courts give the words in the contract their "ordinary meaning." In cases where ordinary words have been used in a technical capacity, then the technical meaning of the word is accepted.

The Entire Contract. The courts look at the entire contract to determine the intent of the parties. It does not consider material added to the basic contract, nor does it take only parts of the contract to make a determination. Once the intent of the contract has been established, individual clauses which might tend to contradict the general intent of the contract will not take precedence over the intent of the entire contract.

Interpretation in Favor of Valid Contract. Because the courts assume that when people make a contract they intend for it to be valid, the courts will, if possible, render an interpretation of the contract which makes it valid rather than invalid. Even if a party to the contract did not have the intention of making a valid contract, the courts will if possible, interpret the contract as being valid, and the dishonest party then becomes involved with charges dealing with fraud.

Unclear Contract of Adhesion Interpreted Against the Insurer. If a contract contains wording which is unclear the courts will interpret the language used against the writer of the contract, unless the wording used is required by law to be stated in a specific manner. Insurance contracts are contracts of adhesion, which mean the insured had no part in determining the wording of the contract, therefore the courts will interpret the contract in favor of the policyholder, insured, or beneficiary.

Written Contracts. If a contract contains unclear or inconsistent material between printed, typed, or handwritten material in the contract, the typed, or handwritten material will determine intent. Where there is a discrepancy between typed material and handwritten material, the handwritten material will determine the intent. This procedure is used because printed material is standard and for general use, but typed or handwritten material is added to the existing printed material and is a better indication of the parties' intent.

More and more states are developing regulations dealing with these areas of contract construction. Regulations now govern areas of contract construction, which include the following:

- Commonly accepted definitions of words
- The use of "plain language" in the contract
- The kind of type or print used in contracts

PARTS OF THE INSURANCE CONTRACT

While it is not a legal requirement that all contracts be in writing, insurance contracts always are, because of their complex nature. The number of pages which make up an insurance contract varies because of the types of insurance and the individual risks being insured, but all life/health insurance contracts contain four basic parts:

- Policy face (Title page)
- Insuring clause
- Conditions
- Exclusions

Policy Face (Title Page). The policy face is usually the first page of the insurance policy. It includes the policy number, name of the insured, policy issue date, the amount of premium and dates the premium is due, and the limits of the policy. The policy face also includes the signatures of the secretary and president of the issuing insurance company. In addition, there are generally clauses required by law to give the insured information on his or her right to cancel, and a warning to the insured to read the policy carefully.

Insuring Clause. The insuring clause generally also appears on the policy face. It is a statement by the insurance company which sets out the essential element of insurance — the promise to pay for losses covered by the policy, in exchange for the insured's premium and compliance with policy terms.

Conditions. This section spells out in detail the rights and duties of both parties. Conditions are provisions which apply to the insured and insurer. For example, the conditions include the reinstatement provision, suicide clause, payment of claim provision, and similar standard policy provisions.

Exclusions. In this section, the company states what it will not do. The exclusions are a basic part of the contract and a complete knowledge of them is essential to a thorough understanding of the agreement. Certain risks must be excluded from insurance contracts because they are not insurable. Such risks would include, war and act of war, self inflicted injuries, certain exclusions for hazardous occupations or avocations, such as sky diving, scuba diving, auto racing, etc. In reality, it is likely that coverage for persons who engage in hazardous activities would be available for an additional premium.

REVIEW QUESTIONS

Match the following descriptions with the concepts listed below by selecting the correct letter for each concept and writing it next to the description.

_____ 27. A promise to pay for losses in exchange for the insured's premium.

_____ 28. The company states what it will not do.

_____ 29. Includes information such as the name of the policyowner, name of the insured, and premium required.

_____ 30. Details the duties and rights of both parties.

A. Policy Face
B. Insuring Clause
C. Conditions
D. Exclusions

☞ ***Answers to Review Questions are located at the back of the book.***

UNFAIR TRADE PRACTICES

The Unfair Trade Practices Act is divided into two parts — Unfair Marketing Practices and Unfair Claims Practices. In each state, statutes define and prohibit certain trade and claims practices which are unfair, misleading and deceptive.

Misrepresentations

It is a violation of Unfair Marketing Practices for any person to make, issue, or circulate any illustration, sales material, or to make any statement which is false, misleading or deceptive. A misrepresentation is simply a lie. Misrepresentations include (but are not limited to:

- Misrepresenting the benefits, advantages or terms of any policy
- Misrepresenting policy dividends by implying or stating that they are guaranteed
- Misrepresenting the financial condition of an insurer by means of an inaccurate or incomplete financial comparison

Misrepresenting an insurance policy by using any name or title which is untrue or misleading or by indicating that an insurance policy represents shares of stock

False or Deceptive Advertising

It is unlawful for any person to formulate or use an advertisement or make a statement which is untrue, deceptive or misleading regarding any insurer or person associated with an insurer.

Twisting

Twisting is illegally inducing a person to drop existing insurance in order to purchase similar coverage with another agent or company. For example, an agent may misrepresent another insurer by falsely making statements about the financial condition of the company or by giving an incomplete comparison of policies. This misrepresentation (illegal inducement) is used to persuade a person to drop existing coverage and purchase insurance with a different agent.

False Financial Statements

It is a violation of Unfair Marketing Practices for any person to deliberately make a false financial statement regarding the solvency of an insurer with the intent to deceive others.

Defamation

It is unlawful for any person or company to make any oral or written statements or to circulate any literature which is false, maliciously critical, or derogatory to the financial condition of any insurer, or which is calculated to injure anyone engaged in the insurance business.

Discrimination

It is unlawful to permit discrimination between individuals of the same class or insurance risk in terms of rates, premiums, fees and policy benefits, due to their place of residence, race, creed or national origin.

Rebating

In most states, rebating is a violation of the Unfair Trade Practices Act. Rebating is any inducement in the sale of insurance which is not specified in the insurance contract. The offer of sharing commissions with the insurance applicant is an inducement in the sale of insurance which is not part of the insurance policy and thus, rebating. Rebates include not only cash but also personal services and items of value.

Illegal Premiums and Charges

It is unlawful for any person or insurer to collect premiums or make charges which are not specified in the insurance contract.

Boycott, Coercion or Intimidation

It is a violation of the Act for any person or organization to commit or be involved in any act of boycott, coercion or intimidation which is intended to create a monopoly or restrict fair trade in the transaction of insurance. For example, it is unlawful for a bank to force a person to purchase insurance from a particular company or agent as a condition for receiving a loan from the bank. The bank may require that adequate insurance be purchased or be in force to back such a loan but the bank cannot force or intimidate a person into purchasing coverage from a specific insurer as a condition for the granting of a loan.

Unfair Claims Practices

Claims settlement practices are regulated, in the public interest, for two main reasons: (1) it is for the purpose of settling claims that insurance companies have collected policyowners' money, and (2) when insureds are denied claims, or claim payments are delayed or altered, the consequences go beyond the policy benefits, and can drastically affect other areas of the insured's financial situation. The Unfair Claims Practices provisions of the Unfair Trade Practices Act are designed to protect the insureds and claimants from any claims settlement practices which are unfair, deceptive or misleading. The following are considered unfair claims practices:

- Misrepresenting pertinent facts or insurance policy provisions relating to coverage at issue
- Failure to acknowledge and act reasonably promptly upon communications with respect to claims arising under insurance policies
- Failing to adopt and implement reasonable standards for the prompt investigation of claims arising under insurance policies
- Refusing to pay claims without conducting a reasonable investigation based upon all available information
- Failing to affirm or deny coverage of claims within a reasonable time after proof of loss statements have been completed
- Not attempting in good faith to effectuate prompt, fair, and equitable settlements of claims in which liability has become reasonably clear
- Compelling insureds to institute litigation to recover amounts due under an insurance policy by offering substantially less than the amounts ultimately recovered in actions brought by such insureds
- Attempting to settle a claim for less than the amount to which a reasonable person would have believed he or she was entitled by reference to written or principal advertising material accompanying or made part of an application
- Attempting to settle claims on the basis of an application which was altered without notice, knowledge or consent of the insured
- Making claims payments to insureds or beneficiaries not accompanied by statements setting forth the coverage under which the payments are being made
- Making known to insureds or claimants a policy of appealing from arbitration awards in favor of insureds or claimants for the purpose of compelling them to accept settlements or compromises less than the amount awarded in arbitration
- Delaying the investigation or payment of claim by requiring an insured, claimant, or the physician of either, to submit a preliminary claim report and then requiring the subsequent submission of formal proof of loss forms, both of which submissions contain substantially the same information
- Failing to promptly settle claims where liability has become reasonably clear under one portion of the insurance policy coverage in order to influence settlement under other portions of the insurance policy coverage
- Failing to promptly provide a reasonable explanation of the basis relied on in the insurance policy in relation to the facts or applicable law for denial of a claim or for the offer of a compromise settlement

Some states have added another provision which makes it an unfair claim practice to *offer a settlement or payment in **any manner** prohibited by law.*

Penalties

Following an investigation and a hearing, if the Insurance Department finds that any person or insurer is engaged in any unfair trade or unfair claims practice, the Commissioner may issue a **cease and desist order** prohibiting the individual or company from continuing the practice. Failure to comply with the cease and desist order can result in a substantial fine (usually $10,000). In addition, fines and loss of license may also be imposed for any company or person guilty of violating the Unfair Trade Practices Act.

The Insurance Department may also issue a **consent order**, which is a disciplinary action in which the party at fault (the insurance company or agent) agrees to discontinue a particular practice (usually an unfair trade or claims practice) through a written agreement with the Insurance Department. Usually the individual denies the allegations but consents to the action taken by the Insurance Department. Consent orders (also known as consent decrees) may or may not involve a fine.

REVIEW QUESTIONS

Match the following descriptions with the concepts listed below by selecting the correct letter for each concept and writing it next to the description.

____ 31. Making a statement that is derogatory to the financial condition of an insurer, and which is intended to cause injury

____ 32. Making incomplete comparisons of policies, for the purpose of inducing a policyholder to change or replace an existing policy

____ 33. Using any name or title of any insurance policy that does not reflect the true nature of the policy

A. Misrepresentation
B. Twisting
C. Defamation

Answers to Review Questions are located at the back of the book.

NOTES

3

LIFE INSURANCE BASICS

SELLING LIFE INSURANCE

Costs Associated with Death

When an individual dies, he or she typically leaves behind the unfinished business of a lifetime. This is particularly true of individuals who die earlier than normal life expectancy would predict. Costs associated with death include:

- Doctor and hospital bills from a final illness or accident
- Funeral expenses
- Estate taxes
- Paying off debts (credit cards, loans)

In addition, to those individuals leaving behind a family or other dependents financially dependent on them for support, the following financial needs will immediately become apparent:

- Mortgage payments
- Immediate income needs — to pay for groceries, utilities, car payments, and other day-to-day living expenses
- Longer term needs — money to pay for children's educations, retirement income for a spouse

The insurance agent is the person most qualified to help potential insureds select the contract of insurance that will best meet their needs.

This needs analysis can be accomplished by identifying the specific financial objectives of the individual by means of a fact finding interview. This interview would cover the following financial needs:

- Cash needs to cover the expenses of dying (funeral, taxes, last illness, etc.)
- Cash needs for payment of debts (charge cards, loans, bank notes, etc.)
- Home mortgage payments
- Family income needs during the dependency period and in later years
- Educational funds for children's college education
- Retirement income needs
- Health insurance needs such as hospitalization insurance and disability income coverage

After the needs analysis is complete, the agent should then make recommendations as to the amount and type of insurance needed by the individual. These recommendations should consider the following:

- Should the coverage be permanent or term insurance; or a combination of the two?
- How much premium can the individual afford to pay?
- Should the premium be level, increasing or decreasing?
- Is the individual insurable?

MEETING CONSUMER NEEDS

Under-Insurance is Common

Studies show that only 43% of American adults own individual life insurance, and the average American adult has just $45,000 of life insurance. Relying on the group life insurance provided at work can build a false sense of security, since coverage is usually insufficient for family needs and coverage generally ceases when employment terminates. Experts agree that few people protect their own "full value" with life insurance, leaving their families at risk.

Human Life Value Approach

The human life value concept was developed in the 1920s by Dr. S.S. Huebner. His concept was based on the fact that when a working person dies his or her ability to produce income or support a family is lost. By comparison, a piece of machinery can help its owner to generate income or help in the support and maintenance of the business until it breaks down. While theoretically true, Dr. Huebner realized that value cannot be placed on a human life the way it is on a piece of machinery. So the value was placed, not on the life itself, as the name of the concept may imply, but on the earning potential of the insured, calculated and projected over a period of years (capitalized).

In formulating the items to determine need, Dr. Huebner looked at four general areas:

- The individual's net annual salary
- The individual's annual expenses
- The number of years the individual has left to work (the present to retirement age)
- The value of the individual's dollar as it depreciates over time (capitalized rate)

The human life value concept was a way of determining what a family would lose in income by the death of the principal wage earner. By this method, if the insured died, the family could be reimbursed for that loss.

Needs Approach

Looking at the needs of an individual and his or her dependents is considered the best method for determining the amount and kind of insurance a prospect should buy. Basically, the needs method looks at such things as:

- Needs for last illness and burial expenses
- Maintenance income for the family for a period of time after the death of the principal wage earner
- Education for dependent children
- Continuing income for the surviving spouse, etc.

After determining needs, the agent must present a plan of insurance that will meet these needs. However, this is not always so simple. The agent must also find out how much the prospect can afford to pay in premium, and make further adjustments based on the prospect's financial position keeping in mind the various term policies and riders.

Estate Planning

Life insurance can also create an immediate estate for the insured, and provide funds that will help preserve the greatest amount of value in the estate. The field of estate planning is very complicated. It requires expertise in the areas of wills, taxes, law and life insurance. Some of the items to be considered when planning an estate are:

- The needs of the beneficiaries
- The type and amount of property that is in the estate
- How to best administer the estate to fulfill the wishes of the insured
- The amount of insurance needed to cover expenses and costs
- How to dispose of any business interest
- Who will settle and administer the estate

There are two methods of distributing the estate; *inter vivos transfers,* or *testamentary transfers.*

Inter vivos transfers are made while the estate owner is still alive. Transfers can be made as:

- Gifts
- Trusts
- Policy ownership under rights of survivorship

Testamentary transfers are made by will after the death of the estate owner. If the estate owner dies without leaving a will, which is called dying **intestate**, the property will be transferred as an intestate distribution under the laws of the state.

Other Sources of Funds

In determining the amount and kind of insurance an applicant needs, the agent must consider other sources of income or benefits the applicant currently has, or for which he or she may be eligible under other insurance plans, government programs (such as Social Security), and retirement plans (pensions, IRAs, Keoghs, etc.).

These other assets will help in determining the amount, and kind, of insurance necessary to meet the applicant's current and future needs. For example, Social Security benefits may not pay the retirement benefit a dependent spouse needs prior to age 65. It is important to remember that there is a period of time, often called the **blackout period**, after a surviving spouse no longer receives survivor's benefits (after her youngest child is no longer eligible) and before she is eligible for retirement benefits. Some other sources of funds to be considered are:

- Medicare
- Medicaid
- Group retirement plans
- Savings
- Investments
- Other income (e.g., income from property rental)
- Annuities
- Other insurance

COMPARING COSTS OF INSURANCE POLICIES

As with many other products, consumers have a wide range of options when considering which life insurance policy to buy. To help insureds make cost-effective selections, there are two basic methods: the traditional net cost method, and the interest-adjusted cost method. There are advantages and disadvantages to both. The discussions below are general since the actual calculations require an advanced knowledge of mathematics.

Traditional Net Cost Method

The formula used adds premiums expected to be paid over 10 years (or the maximum number if the term is less than 10 years), then subtracts the cash value expected to be accumulated and dividends to be paid by the end of the 10-year period. This number is averaged (divided by 10 in this case) for a final number referred to as the "average annual surrendered net cost." All of the premium, dividend, and cash value numbers can be obtained through the insurance company, and calculations should be done per $1,000 of insurance. By making this calculation with several policies, an insured can determine the policy with the lowest number, and theoretically, the lowest cost.

There are three main problems with this calculation of cost. One, it assumes that the policyowner will have the policy for exactly 10 years. The averages would be different for a 20-year period. Two, dividends are only assumptions. If dividends are higher or lower than predicted, cost averages are affected. Last, this comparison does not take into account when premiums and benefits are paid — the time value of money.

Interest-Adjusted Cost Method

This method is similar to the traditional net cost method, with the exception that it accounts for an interest rate. After the selection of a time period for analysis (such as 10 years) and the selection of an interest rate (such as 5%), the calculation is as follows: Add annual dividends at interest to the cash value at the end of the period. Divide this amount by an interest factor which converts it to a level annual amount. This result is subtracted from the annual premium.

Even with this method, comparison of policy costs is still inexact. Coverages provided may differ in policies and dividend amounts are assumptions only. No policy is cost-effective for an insured if it does not meet that individual's needs.

REVIEW QUESTIONS

1. Define inter vivos transfer. ____________

   ____
2. Define testamentary transfer. ____________

   ____
3. Name four sources of funds an insured may have, other than life insurance.

   (1) ____________

   (2) ____________

   (3) ____________

   (4) ____________

☞ ***Answers to Review Questions are located at the back of the book.***

USES OF LIFE INSURANCE

PERSONAL USES OF LIFE INSURANCE

Life insurance is the only financial services product which guarantees a specific sum of money will be available at exactly the time that it is needed. Bank savings accounts, mutual funds, stocks, bonds and other investments cannot make such a guarantee. The death of the insured creates an instant estate for the benefit of the individual's family. From a personal perspective, life insurance may be used to provide:

- Peace of mind and financial security for a family
- Cash for funeral costs and related expenses
- Cash to pay off a home mortgage
- A college education for surviving children
- Income for a family and surviving spouse
- Cash for emergencies or to supplement retirement
- A means of maintaining a family's lifestyle
- Funds to preserve an estate and avoid a forced liquidation of capital to pay estate taxes and debts
- Bequests to non-family members or to charitable or civic organizations
- Advance payment of proceeds prior to death through accelerated benefits or viatical settlements

If an insured has a terminal illness, a life insurance policy may be his or her last substantial source of money. The life insurance benefits may be made available for medical expenses and living expenses prior to death through accelerated benefit provisions or viatical settlement agreements. **Accelerated benefits** are living benefits paid by the insurance company which reduce the remaining death benefit. The government does not consider accelerated death payments to be taxable income, and the policyowner gets between 50-95% of the policy's full benefit.

Under a **viatical settlement**, the policyholder sells all rights to the life insurance policy to a viatical settlement company, which advances a percentage (usually 60% to 80%) of the eventual death benefit. The viatical settlement company then receives the death benefit when the insured ultimately dies. Beginning in 1997, proceeds from viatical settlements and accelerated benefits are not taxable as income. While accelerated death benefits may require a life expectancy of one year or less, viatical settlements may be available for a person who has up to five years to live.

BUSINESS USES OF LIFE INSURANCE

There are generally three types of business organizations: the sole proprietorship, the partnership and the corporation. Regardless of business type, a business has the same need as an individual — protection against premature death and the delivery of cash exactly when it is needed.

This cash need relates to the disposition of a business interest upon the death of the sole proprietor, a partner or a corporate stockholder. Disposition of the deceased's business asset usually means the sale of the business, retention of the business within the family or liquidating the business. The difference between a sale and liquidation is that a sale will usually result in the family receiving a fair market value for the business interest. Liquidation is a forced sale which may only bring one-tenth of the true business value.

In some situations, liquidation of the business is necessary or mandated by law. However, liquidation is the least desirable method of disposing of the deceased's business interest. The sale or retention of the business requires:

- Proper planning and implementation of business agreements
- A willing and competent successor—buyer
- Cash with which to implement the plan

Sole Proprietorship. A sole proprietorship is an unincorporated form of business whereby an individual, utilizing his or her own special talents and abilities, owns and manages a business. Even though a sole proprietorship may have several employees, it is the sole proprietor who is generally directly responsible for the success of the business.

The sole proprietor has **unlimited liability** with regard to the business operation. Creditors can claim both the sole proprietor's business assets as well as personal assets. When the sole proprietor dies, the business also dies. This business asset becomes part of the deceased's estate and is commingled with other personal assets subject to taxation, the payment of debts and claims of creditors.

Generally, the business is the principal asset in the sole proprietor's estate. It is also normally the only source of income for the family. Upon the death of the sole proprietor, family income ceases and, unless adequate planning has occurred, the business may have to be liquidated for a fraction of its value in order to pay estate settlement costs.

Life insurance can be used to solve the problems created by the death of the sole proprietor. Life insurance may fund a **business continuation agreement** (also known as a buy-sell agreement) by providing necessary cash with which to keep the business doors open until possibly the business can be sold at its fair market value for the benefit of the family. Life insurance can also be used to provide funds for a competent employee or other qualified person to purchase the business from the surviving family members.

The Funded Business Continuation Plan
Between a Sole Proprietor and a Key Employee

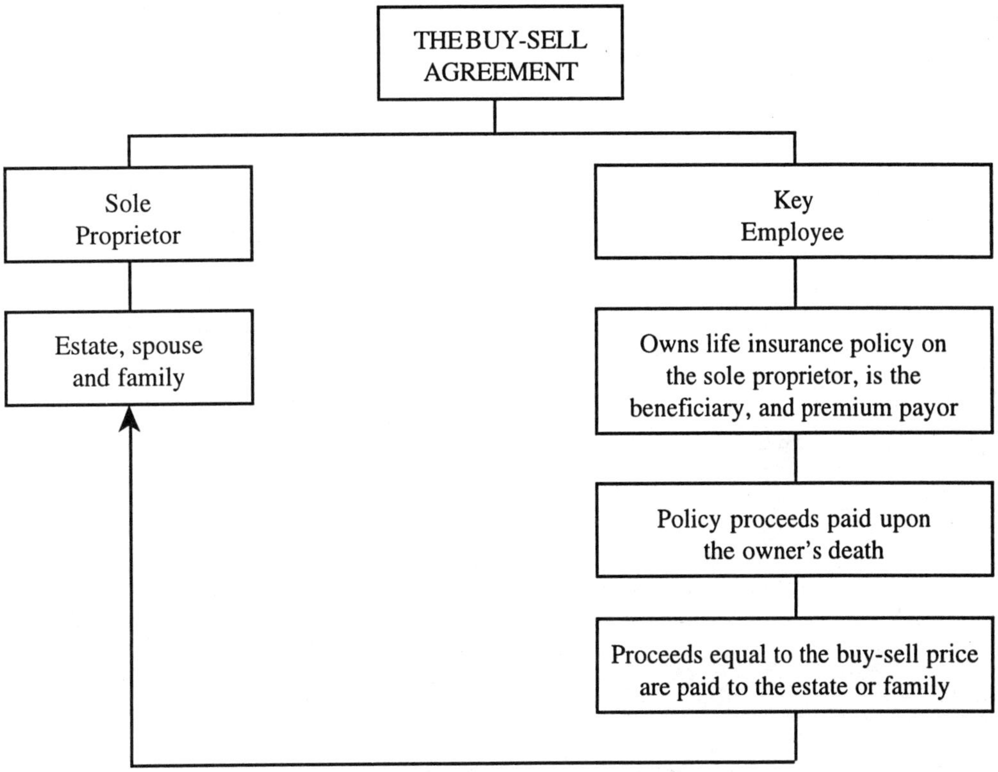

Chart 3-1

If the business is to survive the death of the sole proprietor and the family is to be able to maintain its standard of living, adequate planning and the implementation of certain business agreements (such as a business continuation agreement) is necessary. Finally, these plans and agreements must be funded with adequate amounts of life insurance to guarantee that the sole proprietor's financial plans will be realized.

Partnership. A partnership is a legal, non-incorporated business relationship involving two or more individuals who each contribute their unique skills, talents and capital for the purpose of owning and operating a business enterprise. As a partnership, each partner has unlimited liability with regard to partnership functions. As such, business creditors may claim personal assets for payment of debts.

Generally, by law, when a partner dies, the surviving partner(s) must dissolve the business. The survivor becomes a liquidating trustee and in essence liquidates the business, his or her own job, as well as eliminating the family's principal source of income. Disposition of the deceased's business asset is required in order to settle the deceased's estate.

To a large degree, the problems created by the death of a partner can be resolved by means of a properly drawn **buy-sell agreement**. If there are only two or three partners, a **cross purchase** plan may be advisable in which each partner is bound by the terms of the plan and agrees to purchase a share of the deceased partner's interest. If there are more than two or three partners, the **entity type** plan is usually recommended whereby the partnership agrees to purchase the interest of a deceased partner.

Funded Cross Purchase Partnership Plan

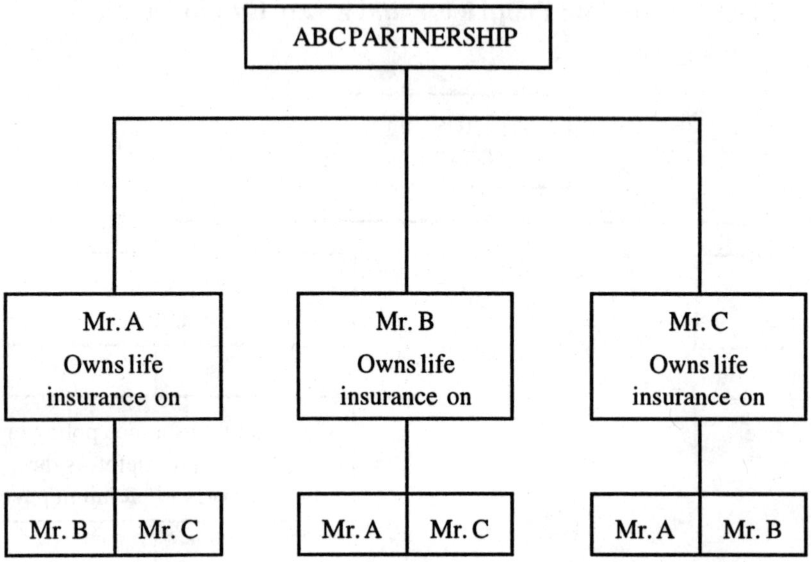

Chart 3-2

Funded Entity Partnership Plan

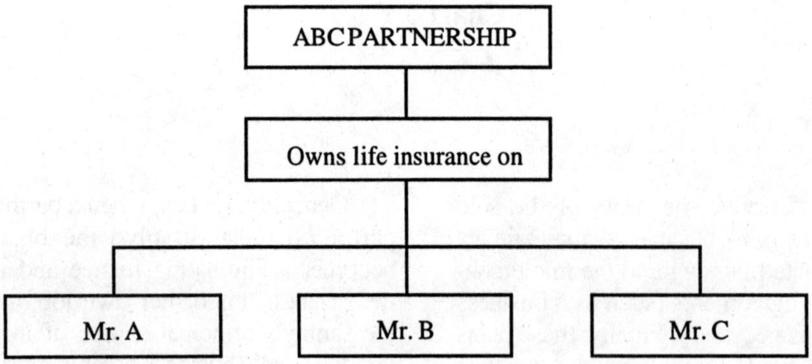

Chart 3-3

The key element for partnership planning is the funding of the agreements. Life insurance is the ideal choice which will guarantee that the required amount of money will be delivered exactly when it is needed. A cross purchase plan covering two partners would require that each partner own, pay the premium and be the beneficiary of a life insurance policy on the life of the other partner.

If the partnership consisted of six partners, then each partner would be the owner of five policies for a total of 30 life insurance policies. This is the reason why an entity agreement is usually recommended if there are more than two or three partners. Under an entity agreement involving six partners, the partnership would own six policies.

The principal advantages of the funded buy-sell agreement include:

- A fair market value is established, funded with life insurance, for the benefit of the surviving family
- Buyers of the partnership interest are predetermined and legally bound by the agreement
- The partnership and employee's jobs are secure
- The necessary funding to implement the plan is readily available

Corporations. A corporation is an "artificial person." It is a legal entity which is owned by its stockholders. One of the characteristics which distinguishes a corporation from the other business forms is that its life is **unlimited**. When a working stockholder dies, the corporation continues. Another distinguishing characteristic is that stockholders have limited liability. A stockholder's risk is limited to his or her investment in the corporation. Personal assets are generally save from the claim's of creditors.

Generally, a corporation is a larger business concern than the sole proprietorship or the partnership.

Corporations may be classified as closely held or publicly held. A close corporation is typically one which is owned by a few stockholders, often members of the same family. A publicly owned corporation may be owned by several thousand stockholders, such as General Motors. This discussion of corporate insurance needs will be limited to the close corporation.

The death of a stockholder in a closely held corporation means the loss of services of this key person and quite possibly loss of business income. However, the most immediate effect will be the loss of income to the deceased's family. The choices available to the family are to sell the deceased's stock; attempt to live off of any dividends which the corporation may pay; or assume a working position within the corporation.

Probably, the most desirable alternative is to sell the deceased's stock. Attempting to live on dividend income only will probably not enable the surviving family members to maintain their standard of living for very long. Assuming the surviving spouse has inherited the deceased stockholder's shares, he or she may not be knowledgeable or competent enough to assume the position of the deceased within the corporation. In addition, the surviving stockholders may not want a new, inexperience stockholder working in the corporation. Thus, the purchase of the deceased's stock becomes a viable alternative, provided there has been adequate planning and there is cash available for the stock purchase.

Business planning to resolve the problems created by the death of a stockholder involves the implementation of a stock purchase or stock redemption plan. A **stock purchase plan** is similar to a cross purchase partnership plan whereby a price is determined and each stockholder agrees to purchase a proportionate share of the deceased shareholder's stock. The purchase price is naturally funded with life insurance and each shareholder is the owner, premium payor and beneficiary of a life policy on the lives of the other stockholders. This arrangement is feasible when there are only a few shareholders.

In situations with several shareholders, the stock redemption plan is better. Under a **stock redemption plan**, the corporation is the owner, beneficiary and premium payor of the life insurance policies and the corporation agrees to purchase the deceased's stock.

The advantages of the life insurance funded corporate buy-sell plan include:

- The establishment of a fair price for the stock
- A binding agreement which identifies the buyers
- Corporate assets and jobs are secure
- Life insurance guarantees delivery of the purchase price

Section 303 stock redemption is a special type of stock redemption which permits a corporation to **partially** redeem a shareholder's stock for purposes of providing cash to cover estate settlement costs. Tax laws generally require that stock redemptions be total to avoid taxing the proceeds payable to the family as a dividend. The Internal Revenue Service will permit a partial redemption by the corporation to pay funeral expenses, taxes and related estate settlement costs.

Key person life insurance protects the corporation from the financial loss sustained when a key employee (the owner, for example) dies. In addition, to the corporate owner, a key person could be a sales manager, a vice president, etc. When a key person dies, the corporation could experience a loss of

Funded Corporate Buy-Sell Plan

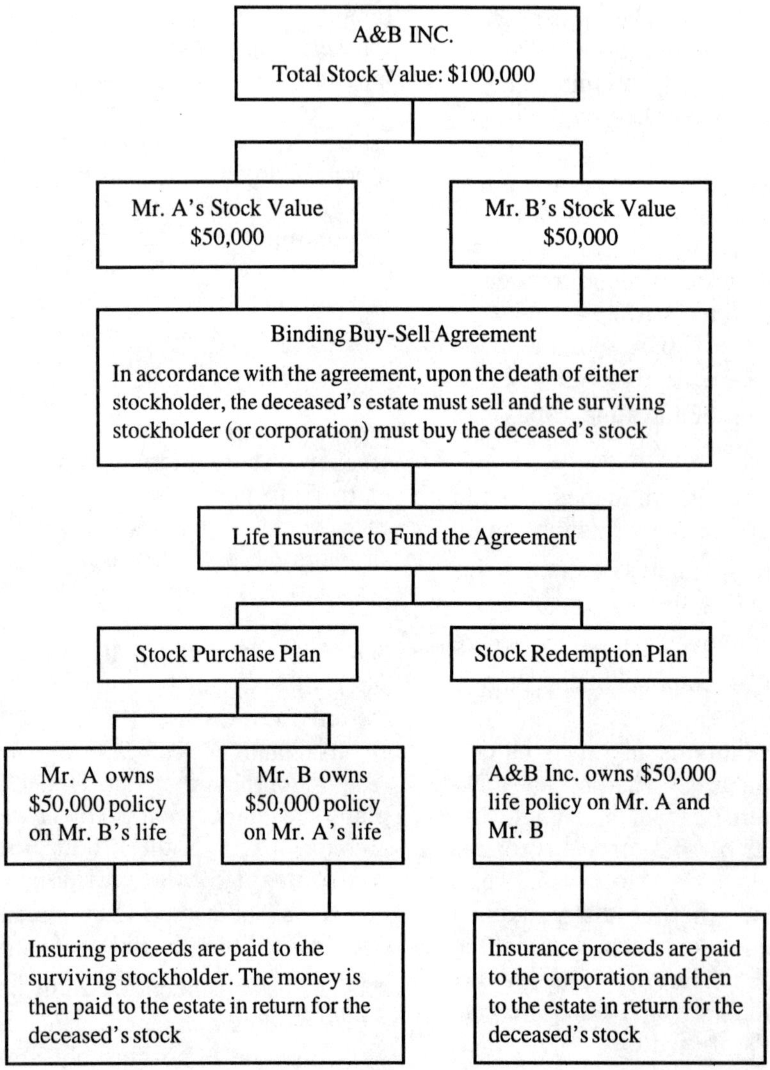

Chart 3-4

income, impaired credit standing, loss of jobs and customers. To offset this financial impact, the corporation may purchase a life insurance policy on the life of the key person. Some contracts include a **change of insured** provision that allows the employer to change the person insured when there is a change in personnel, without the need to cancel the existing policy and issue a new one.

The corporation would be the owner, premium payor and beneficiary of the policy. The face amount of the policy would generally relate to the amount of lost corporate income plus the costs of hiring and training a replacement for the deceased key person.

Deferred compensation is an executive benefit which enables a highly paid corporate employee to defer current receipt of income such as an executive bonus and have it paid as compensation at a later date (retirement, death or disability) when presumably the employee will be in a lower tax bracket. Generally, the employee will enter into an agreement with the employer which specifies the amount of money to be paid, when it will be paid and the conditions under which the deferred compensation may not be paid.

The agreement will specify that the amount deferred will be paid as a retirement benefit or in the event of the premature death or disability of the employee. It will further indicate that the individual will forfeit the right to this sum of money if he or she leaves the employer except for retirement, death or disability.

The advantage of this agreement for the employee is avoidance of current taxation since receipt of the money is deferred. This is allowed by IRS Section 457. However, there are some disadvantages. Usually, deferred compensation is a nonqualified plan and as such, it may be funded or unfunded. An unfunded deferred compensation plan is nothing more than an unsecured promise to pay a future benefit. As a funded plan, the assets funding the plan are considered corporate assets and thus subject to the claims of corporate creditors or to other uses by the employer.

The principal advantage for the employer is that the services of the employee are usually secured for life since the employee will forfeit the right to the deferred compensation except for retirement, death or disability. In addition, deferred compensation can be viewed as a desirable executive benefit and thus enable the employer to attract and retain key personnel.

Funding for the deferred compensation may be life insurance contracts, disability income policies, annuities, mutual funds, etc.

Split Dollar plans are not actually types of life insurance policies but rather methods of purchasing life insurance. Under a split dollar arrangement, a plan of permanent life insurance is jointly purchased by the employee and the employer. Permanent life insurance is used because it provides guaranteed cash values.

The employer's share of the premium is an amount equal to the annual increase in the policy's cash value. Accordingly, in the early years of the plan, the employee's cost will be higher than in the later years when the policy will contain higher amounts of cash value and the employer's share of the premium will be greater.

The death benefit is also shared between the employee and the employer in proportion to the amount of the premium each is paying. Usually, the employer is the policyowner and thus has control of the policy including its cash value.

Split dollar plans are an attractive benefit whereby a key employee is able to purchase life insurance at an attractive cost because of the joint premium payments.

CHARITABLE USES OF LIFE INSURANCE

Another use of life insurance is for charitable purposes. In accordance with tax laws, a policyowner may purchase a life insurance contract on his or her life, pay the premiums and designate a charitable organization as the beneficiary; such as a church, school, hospital or similar organization. Generally, the premium paid by the insured-donor is tax deductible.

REVIEW QUESTIONS

4. Insurance purchased to cover a top executive or other important employee is called ____________

    ____
5. If a business partner dies a(n) ____________

    ____________ is a legal document which will allow the remaining partners to purchase the deceased partner's interest in the business.
6. To fund an employee pension plan, or to finance a child's future education, an individual might buy a "cross-purchase plan." (True/False)____________

☞ ***Answers to Review Questions are located at the back of the book.***

CLASSES OF LIFE INSURANCE

Life insurance markets can be divided into four basic classes; individual life insurance, group life insurance, credit life insurance, and industrial life insurance.

INDIVIDUAL LIFE POLICIES

Life insurance has been transacted in the United States since the mid-1700s, but it wasn't until the 1840s that the industry made a significant impact on the American business scene. Since that time individual insurance has grown steadily, due primarily to the agency distribution system.

Today, individual insurance represents the greatest percentage of in-force business in the United States. It may be characterized as life insurance issued for face amounts of at least $1,000. The face amount is paid when the insured dies. Premiums are paid directly to the insurance company. If the agent has the authority he or she may collect the premium. Basically, however, it is designed for direct premium payment to the insurance company. The term **ordinary insurance** is sometimes used to describe individual insurance. There are three broad types of individual or ordinary life insurance — whole life, term life, and endowment policies. These types of insurance and others will be discussed in more detail in a subsequent chapter of this book.

Frequently, ordinary policies may be further described as **participating (par)** or **nonparticipating (non-par)**. Par policies are issued by mutual life insurance companies. Non-par policies are issued by stock life insurance companies. A participating policy is one in which the policyholders share in dividends (if a dividend is declared). A nonparticipating insurer does not pay dividends to policyholders.

GROUP LIFE POLICIES

Social and economic changes due to industrialization of our society, the growth of large cities and the growth of the union movement in the United States, have contributed to the development of group insurance. The influence and political strength of unionized workers have compelled employers to offer group insurance as an employee benefit. Group insurance is usually written as one-year term insurance.

Legal Requirements

In keeping with the NAIC Model Group Life Insurance Bill, the legal requirements of group insurance are uniform throughout the majority of states and include the following six basic characteristics:

- All states define a "true" group as having at least 10 people covered under one master contract. Some states make allowance for even smaller groups.
- Coverage is generally available without individual medical examinations.
- The policy is issued to the employer, trust, union, or other association. Certificates of insurance are issued to the individual insured.
- The insurance cannot be obtained to benefit the employer, trust, union, or other association. It must be for the benefit of the covered employee or member, and their dependents.
- Premiums are based on the experience of the group as a whole. Premium may be paid entirely by the policyowner, or it may be paid jointly by the policyowner and the insured. If premium is paid entirely by the policyowner (employer or association) it is a **noncontributory** plan, and all eligible employees or members must be covered. If premium is paid by both policyowner and insured the plan is a **contributory** plan, and at least 75% of all eligible employees or members must be covered. Eligible employees refer to the eligible class of employees, such as, full time employees, salaried workers (as opposed to hourly workers), non-union workers, etc. It is permissible to exclude certain groups of employees from the eligible class as long as these exclusions are based on some occupational criteria. The employer or association is always required to pay some portion of the premium. Insureds are, by law, not permitted to contribute more than a specified amount.
- Individuals covered under the plan are classified in such a way (usually by salary, position, or time on the job) that they do not choose the benefit levels.

Standard Provisions

Group insurance policies have special provisions unique to group insurance. Some of these provisions are the same as those found in policies of individual insurance. Most states have enacted, or adopted the standard provisions found in the NAIC Model Bill for Group Life Insurance. Group policies must contain provisions relating to the following:

- Grace period (usually 31 days)
- Incontestability (usually one or two years after the policy becomes effective; usually two years from the insured's effective date of coverage)
- Entire contract (the application must be attached to and made part of the contract)
- Representations (statements regarding the individual's health are representations not warranties)

- Evidence of insurability (individual insurability must be proven if the employee or member joins the plan after the enrollment period)
- Misstatement of age (*premium is adjusted* to the correct age; under individual insurance *benefits are adjusted*)
- Facility of payment (allows payment of policy proceeds to a close relative or friend if no beneficiary is named, or living)
- Conversion (the right to convert to an individual policy when the insured's coverage is terminated because of termination of employment, or the elimination of a class of insureds)
- Termination of master policy (the right to convert to an individual policy because the master policy has been terminated)
- Individual certificates (issued as evidence of coverage under a master policy)

In addition to the rights of conversion listed, an insured who dies after coverage has terminated, but before the end of the 31-day conversion period, will receive the group policy benefit.

Certificates

In group insurance, the policy is evidence of a contract between the insurer and the employer or association (the policyowner). The policy is purchased for the benefit of the individuals who are covered under the policy, but is issued to the insured (the employer or sponsor). Because of this situation it is obvious that the individual insureds would not receive a copy of the policy, since there is no agreement between the insureds and the insurer. But because the insureds have an interest in the policy they must receive some evidence that they are covered by the master policy; the certificate of insurance is that evidence. They must know something about the plan under which they are covered, and the certificate provides enough information so that they are aware of the benefits available to them, and their rights and obligations.

The face page of the certificate has information on the coverage effective date, dependent coverage, and life insurance benefit amounts. The certificate covers such information as benefit amounts, benefit descriptions, age limits, notice of claim, proof of loss, and the insured's right to convert to individual coverage in the event of policy termination, or employment termination.

Policy Forms

There are five main types of group life insurance being marketed to eligible groups: group term life, group permanent life, group creditor life, group paid-up life, and group survivor income benefit insurance. Group insurance is also written to include the dependents of the group members.

One disadvantage of group life insurance is that it is usually only temporary coverage, and an individual member of the group may lose that coverage when he or she leaves the group.

To lessen this disadvantage group term policies must include provisions to provide for conversion to individual coverage. They may also include continuation of insurance provisions, and waiver of premium provisions. Some employers continue group term insurance at reduced amounts for retired workers.

Dependent Coverage

Life or health insurance benefits may be extended to members of a primary insured's family. Dependents may be any of the following:

- The insured's spouse
- The insured's children
- The insured's dependent parents
- Any person for whom dependency can be proven

The insured's children can be stepchildren, foster children or adopted children. Dependent children must be under a specified age, usually age 19, or to age 21 if attending school full time. The law further requires that any other person dependent on the insured is eligible for coverage. Such dependency is proven by the relationship to the insured, residency in the home, or the person being listed on the insured's income tax return as a dependent. A child may be a dependent beyond the ages of 19 or 21 if that child is permanently mentally or physically disabled prior to the specified age. Dependent coverage is not provided under credit life insurance.

Group Conversion Option

By law in most states, any employee covered by a group life insurance plan must be allowed to convert to an individual permanent life policy upon termination of employment. Evidence of insurability cannot be required. The conversion period is usually 30 or 31 days, and coverage is automatically in force during that period. Coverage is often limited to $5,000 or $10,000 or the amount of coverage under the group policy, whichever is less.

FEGLI and SGLI

FEGLI, Federal Employees' Group Life Insurance, provides group life insurance automatically for federal employees unless they choose not to be included in the plan. Life insurance in the amount of one year's salary is customarily provided. Another one year's salary may be added but is contributory (the employee must pay that portion of the premium).

SGLI, Servicemen's Group Life Insurance, is automatically provided for members of the armed forces. The life insurance is provided on a group term life basis as soon as a member enters active duty. The maximum limit is now $200,000, with automatic full-time coverage applicable to qualified reservists, as well. Premiums are deducted from the servicemember's paycheck.

Both FEGLI and SGLI policies are underwritten by private insurers in very large group life insurance contracts.

CREDIT & INDUSTRIAL LIFE POLICIES

Credit life insurance is written specifically to protect the balances of unpaid loans. Credit insurance is written on the lives of debtors, and the policy benefits are payable to the creditor. Industrial life insurance is a special type of policy issued for small face amounts and characterized by frequent premium payments, such as weekly or monthly. Industrial insurance was once popular among factory workers, but is no longer a practical solution for most workers insurance needs. These special policies will be discussed in more detail in a later chapter of this manual.

REVIEW QUESTIONS

7. Name three people who could be named as dependents for life and health insurance benefits:
   (1) ______________________
   (2) ______________________
   (3) ______________________
8. Name the three broad types of individual life insurance:
   (1) ______________________
   (2) ______________________
   (3) ______________________
9. Group insurance is usually written as ____________
   ____
   ____

☞ ***Answers to Review Questions are located at the back of the book.***

SOCIAL SECURITY

Since the time of the Industrial Revolution most individuals and families have not been self-sufficient economic entities. We no longer grow our own food, and many people live long distances from their families. Particularly since the Great Depression, society has wrestled with the problem of numbers of individuals being unable to care for themselves due to unemployment, disability or death of the family wage-earner. The Social Security System was a political response to this issue.

Covered Workers

The Social Security System was enacted in 1935 to provide retirement benefits for covered workers. It became effective January 1, 1937. By 1939, Social Security also provided survivors benefits to the families of covered workers. Almost all jobs are covered by Social Security and nine of every ten workers are currently paying into the system. What we refer to as Social Security is more properly called Old Age Survivors and Disability Insurance (OASDI).

Types of Benefits

Today, Social Security pays four types of benefits:

- Retirement benefits to workers and their dependents
- Survivors benefits to a worker's family
- Disability benefits to workers
- Medicare benefits

Retirement and survivor benefits help satisfy the covered worker's need for income and death benefits (life insurance). Disability and Medicare benefits provide needed health insurance protection for the disabled and the aged. Thus, these benefits could be classified as federal life and health insurance benefits.

Eligibility for Social Security

Generally, most workers must be covered under Social Security. This includes common law employers and employees, most self employed persons, Armed Forces personnel, and employees of non-profit organizations.

The main excluded worker groups are railroad workers and federal employees hired before 1984. Federal employees hired after 1984 are covered. Railroad workers contribute to their own railroad retirement system.

In addition, employees of state and local governments are not covered unless the government entity has entered into an agreement with the Social Security Administration or does not have a retirement program. Generally, most government workers are covered.

Finally, there are certain types of family employment situations in which a family member may not be covered under Social Security. These include: employment of a minor child (under age 18) by his or her parent; employment of a parent as a domestic in the home of the parent's child; and employment of a parent to do work not in the course of a son's or daughter's business.

Insured Status

A covered worker becomes qualified for Social Security benefits by attaining either **fully or currently insured** status. A person reaches insured status by accumulating a specific number of **quarters of coverage**.

A quarter of coverage is equal to a minimum amount of wages paid (and taxed by Social Security) in a calendar quarter. The minimum amount of wages usually changes every year. For example, for years prior to 1978, a covered worker received one quarter of coverage for each calendar quarter in which wages paid were $50 or more. In 1996, this wage base was $640 so that a worker received a quarter of coverage for each quarter in which at least $640 of wages were taxed by Social Security. In 1997, the amount is $670. This taxed wage base usually increases each year to account for cost of living increases.

Generally, a worker is fully insured if he or she has acquired 40 quarters of coverage (10 years of covered work).

Fully insured = 40 calendar quarters

A worker is currently insured if he or she has acquired a minimum of six quarters of coverage during the full 13-quarter period ending with the calendar quarter in which the worker: died, became totally disabled or eligible for retirement benefits.

Currently insured = 6 calendar quarters in a 13 quarter period.

A special insured status is required if a worker is eligible for disability benefits under Social Security. This status requires that the worker be fully insured and to have earned at least 20 quarters of coverage in the 40 calendar quarter period ending with the calendar quarter in which the disability begins. This requirement is modified slightly if a covered worker is disabled prior to age 31.

All covered workers (and spouses), age 65 and over are entitled to Medicare benefits under Social Security. Usually this will mean that the worker is fully insured and has attained age 65.

The individual's insured status determines eligibility for Social Security benefits. A fully insured person and eligible dependents are entitled to all Social Security benefits. A worker who is only currently insured has limited benefits available. If a worker is only currently insured at death, Social Security benefits would only be payable to a dependent child in addition to the lump sum death benefit of $255.

Chart 3-5 illustrates the relationship between insured status and Social Security benefits.

Retirement Benefits. Benefits begin when a fully insured worker retires, after age 62. However, benefits are reduced to 80% when they are paid at age 62 and reduced by lesser amounts when paid at ages 63 and 64. To receive full benefits the worker must work until age 65. (In the year 2000 retirement age for full benefits will increase to age 67.) Benefits are not only paid to the worker, but also to the following members of the worker's family:

- Wife or husband 62 or over
- Wife under 62 if she is caring for the worker's minor or disabled child(ren)
- Unmarried children under 18
- Unmarried children under 19, if full-time students
- Unmarried children 18 or over who were severely disabled before age 22 and continue to be disabled

The benefit amounts payable vary with every worker. Amounts are contingent on the worker's average earnings under Social Security, the worker's age at retirement, and additional earnings after retirement. The amount of income a worker will receive under Social Security after adjusting for the above factors is referred to as the **Primary Insurance Amount (PIA)**. The benefit is also adjusted over time to reflect increases in the cost of living, as measured by the Consumer Price Index. All Social Security benefits are equal to the PIA or some fraction thereof depending on the benefit being provided.

Survivors Benefits. A lump-sum burial benefit of $255 is paid at the time of a currently or fully insured worker's death, usually to the surviving spouse or minor child. Monthly survivors benefits are also payable to eligible dependents in an amount equal to the worker's PIA (see the chart below for the insured status required). These monthly benefits are payable to:

- Widow or widower 60 or over, provided the worker was fully insured
- Widow or widower, or surviving divorced mother or father if caring for the worker's children under age 16 or disabled child(ren)
- Unmarried children under 18
- Unmarried children under 19, if full-time students in elementary or secondary school
- Unmarried children 18 or over who were severely disabled before age 22 and continue to be disabled
- Others such as dependent parents in certain circumstances

Disability Benefits. A covered worker may be eligible for disability income benefits if the required insured status is achieved, the worker is under age 65, and can satisfy the Social Security definition of total disability.

Social Security defines total disability as the inability to engage in any substantial gainful activity due to physical or mental disability and such disability must last for at least 12 months or is expected to end in death. Substantial work activity means significant mental and/or physical duties for which a person is compensated.

This definition does not refer to the individual's occupation prior to disability or to the level of predisability compensation. A surgeon earning $200,000 annually may be disabled to the degree that he or she could no longer perform surgery. However, if this person could perform other meaningful work duties

Social Security Benefit	Insured Status Requirement
Retirement	Fully Insured
Survivor's Benefits	Fully Insured
Lump Sum Death Benefit	Currently Insured
Children and Dependent Parent Survivor Benefits	Currently Insured
Disability Income Benefits	Fully insured plus 20 quarters in the 40 quarters preceding the disability
Medicare	Fully insured and attained age 65

Chart 3-5

(bank employee, school teacher, salesperson, etc.), he or she would probably not be eligible for disability benefits since they could not meet the Social Security definition of total disability.

The amount of the disability benefit is equal to the worker's PIA which in essence is the same as the individual's monthly retirement benefit. Disability benefits are only payable for total disabilities. Disability benefits begin with the sixth month of disability. No benefit is paid for a partial disability.

Medicare. Covered workers and others, such as railroad employees covered under the railroad retirement system are eligible for Medicare upon attainment of age 65. Medicare consists of two parts; **Part A** (Hospital Insurance) and **Part B** (Medical Insurance).

Part A benefits are provided automatically when the worker attains age 65. These benefits have been "prepaid" during the individual's working years through the Social Security taxes. Part A benefits generally cover hospital expenses incurred while the person is hospitalized as an inpatient.

Part B provides coverage for certain medical expenses incurred outside of the hospital such as physicians charges, lab tests, etc. Part B is optional and a premium is charged for coverage. Generally, the individual needs both Part A and Part B of Medicare to have adequate coverage.

Both Part A and Part B are subject to deductibles and copayments which are increased each year. Medicare is discussed in more detail in the Health Insurance section of this text.

Social Security Taxes

Taxes (contributions to the Social Security system) are automatically deducted from each covered worker's paycheck. Earnings subject to taxation include wages, salaries, tips, and commission (earned income only). The employer contributes a matching amount. Tax rates and the maximum amount of taxable income vary by year. The employer "withholds" the employee's taxes from his or her gross income, and remits these taxes, along with its own taxes, to the Internal Revenue Service. Individuals who are self-employed pay taxes according to a special rate schedule.

Self-employed workers basically pay the employee's and the employer's share of the required Social Security taxes.

It should be noted that since 1992, the Social Security tax paid is broken down into the OASDI portion and Medicare percentage. Both the maximum wage base (the amount taxed by Social Security) and the tax rate generally change annually.

The 1996 maximum Social Security taxes are shown in the chart below. Since 1994, there has been no maximum wage base for Medicare taxes.

It must be remembered that the employees tax rate and amounts are duplicated by the same rates and amounts contributed by the employer. Thus, the maximum OASDI tax is in reality equal to the maximum wage base, $65,400 x 6.2% x 2 which equals $8,109.60.

Excess Earnings Cap

Workers under the age of 70 who continue to work after age 65 may have their benefits reduced depending on the amount of money they earn. For 1996, the excess earnings cap on post-retirement earned income is $1,125 per month or $13,500 per year. A retired worker collecting Social Security benefits may earn up to $11,520 per year without penalty.

For a worker between ages 65 and 70, excess earnings will result in one-third of the excess amount being deducted from the retirement benefit. In other words, there is a loss of $1 of Social Security benefits for every $3 of excess earnings. A worker over age 70 may earn any amount of income and still receive full Social Security retirement benefits.

Taxation of Social Security Benefits

A portion (up to 85%) of the Social Security benefit is includable in the worker's adjusted gross income for tax purposes. Various formulas apply depending on the level of adjusted gross income, whether the taxpayer is married or single, and if married whether filing separate or joint returns.

Maximum Social Security Taxes — 1997

Employee Amounts		Employee and Employer Totals	
OASDI	**Maximum Wage Base**	**Maximum Tax**	**Total OASDI Tax**
6.20%	$65,400	$4,054.80	$8,109.60
Medicare	**Maximum Wage Base**	**Maximum Tax**	**Total Medicare Tax**
1.45%	NONE	1.45% x wage base	2.9% x wage base

Chart 3-6

Retirement and Survivor Benefits as a Factor of the PIA

Social Security Benefit	Benefit Amount Equal To:
Normal retirement at age 65	100% of the PIA
Early retirement at age 62	80% of the PIA
Spouse's retirement benefit	50% of the PIA
Child's benefit (retired or disabled worker)	50% of the PIA
Child's benefit (deceased worker)	75% of the PIA
Survivor's monthly benefit caring for a minor child	75% of the PIA
Survivor's monthly benefit at age 65	100% of the PIA
Survivor's monthly benefit at age 60	100% of the PIA reduced

All benefits are subject to the maximum family benefits as determined by current Social Security rules and cost of living indexes.

Chart 3-7

Current Financial Status of Social Security

The financial soundness of the Social Security System has been the source of controversy for some time. There has been a realistic concern that individuals working today will not be able to count on this system to provide them with retirement income. The reason for this problem is that when Congress first enacted Social Security, almost 20 workers were paying into the system for every one retired individual drawing out of it. Today, the ratio is only three-to-one, and decreasing. When the large post-WWII baby boom generation begins to retire, there may be only two workers paying in for each retired worker needing that income. In order to offset this trend, Social Security tax increases and benefit decreases were seen in the 1980s. Additional changes, such as increasing the normal retirement age from 65, possibly to age 67 or even 70, will become necessary during the coming decade.

All benefits are subject to the maximum family benefits as determined by current Social Security rules and cost of living indexes.

REVIEW QUESTIONS

10. What are the four classes of benefits provided under Social Security?
    (1) ________
    (2) ________
    (3) ________
    (4) ________
11. Retirement benefit amounts are contingent upon what three factors?
    (1) ________
    (2) ________
    (3) ________
12. Self-employed workers are exempt from paying Social Security taxes. (True/False) ________

☞ ***Answers to Review Questions are located at the back of the book.***

TAX CONSIDERATIONS

This section is designed to give the new insurance agent a basic understanding of the taxation of life insurance premiums and proceeds. What follows is by no means a complete description. Further study of tax consequences will make the insurance professional much more responsive to the needs of his or her clients. Life insurance proceeds represent a great deal of money, often the bulk of an insured's estate, so tax considerations become very important.

Proceeds

Life insurance proceeds may be subject to federal income taxes and federal estate taxes. One of the big advantages of life insurance is that **lump sum proceeds** are not taxable as income. This is true whether the policy is an individually owned contract or a business owned policy. Thus, a beneficiary pays no federal income tax on life insurance proceeds and neither does a corporation.

If the life insurance proceeds are taken other than in a lump sum by the beneficiary, part of the proceeds received will be tax free and part will be taxable. The basic concept is that the principal (the face amount) is returned tax free. However, the installment received is part principal and part interest. Therefore, the interest portion of the installment is taxable. All interest is taxable as income.

Federal estate tax is a tax on the transfer of property upon the death of an individual, and may range from 0% to 55% of the adjusted gross estate. Life insurance proceeds are subject to inclusion in the deceased's estate for federal estate tax purposes if:

- The estate was the named beneficiary; or
- The deceased was the policyowner; or
- The deceased transferred the policy to another person within three years of death

Thus, a corporate owned life insurance policy on the company's president with the corporation as the beneficiary, would not be included in the deceased president's estate since the corporation was the owner and beneficiary.

Whether the life insurance proceeds will actually be taxed in accordance with federal estate tax laws will be dependent on the deceased's estate situation. There are deductions and exemptions which may be applied to adjust a person's estate for tax purposes. For example, there is a **unified tax credit** of $192,800 (which roughly equals a $600,000 exemption), which is a dollar-for-dollar reduction in gift and estate taxes due. Other estate planning techniques such as the use of trusts and gifts can also reduce the size of a person's taxable estate. There is an annual gift tax exclusion of $10,000 per donee. This basically allows a donor to give away property, tax free, up to a value of $10,000 per person, thus reducing the value of the remaining estate. The main point is that regardless of the tax consequences, the life insurance proceeds are included in the estate.

Accelerated Benefits and Viatical Settlements

Beginning in 1997, income received from accelerated benefits or viatical settlements for the chronically or terminally ill are not taxable as income. Previously, accelerated benefits were not considered taxable but proceeds from viatical settlements were taxed.

Transfer for Value Rules

Life insurance proceeds may not be exempt from income taxes if the benefit payment results from a transfer for value. If the benefits are transferred under a beneficiary designation to a person in exchange for valuable consideration (whether it be money, an exchange of policies, or a promise to perform services), the proceeds would be taxable as income. This section of the tax laws is designed to prevent a tax exemption for benefits which are purchased from another party, since the intent of the transaction would be to exchange something of value for tax-free income.

Taxation under the transfer of value rules *does not apply* to an assignment of benefits as collateral security, because a lender has every right to secure the interest in the unpaid balance of a loan. Nor does it apply to transfers between a policyholder and an insured, transfers to a partner of an insured, transfers to a corporation in which the insured is an officer or stockholder, or transfers of interest made as a gift (where no exchange of value occurs).

Cash Surrender Value

If a policyowner surrenders the policy for its cash value, some of the cash value received may be subject to ordinary income tax if it exceeds the sum of the premiums paid for the policy (this is known as the Cost Recovery Rule). For example, Mary cash surrenders her whole life policy and receives $5,000. Total premiums paid into the policy were $4,700. Mary owes federal income tax on $300.

1035 Exchanges

In accordance with section 1035(a) of the Internal Revenue Code, certain exchanges of insurance policies (and annuities) may occur as nontaxable exchanges. Generally, if a policyowner exchanges a life policy for another life policy with the same insured and beneficiary and a gain is realized, it will not be taxed under section 1035(a). This same concept applies to exchanges involving annuities and other life insurance products.

Premiums

Premiums paid for life insurance are generally not tax deductible. For individuals, they are considered a personal expense and therefore not deductible. When businesses buy life insurance to perpetuate the continuation of the business, the premiums are considered to be a capital investment, and for this reason, not deductible. However, when a business buys group term insurance for its employees, premiums are generally considered a necessary business expense and are deductible. Employer contributions for permanent life insurance are treated as taxable income of the employee.

Dividends

Dividends are considered to be a return of excess premium paid by the policyowner. They are not included as income for tax purposes. However, interest earned on dividends and accumulated by the insurer or paid to the policyowner is taxable in the year received.

Endowments and Annuities

Part of an endowment or annuity payment is taxable, and part is not. The non-taxable portion is the expected return of the principal paid in. The taxable portion is the actual amount of payment minus that expected return of the principal paid in. Since these amounts would be difficult to calculate, the IRS makes up tax tables for this purpose.

By definition, **cost base** is money which has already been taxed. **Tax base** is money which is yet to be taxed. A person investing $1,000 in an annuity is investing $1,000 cost base. Any interest earned is tax base, but the taxes are deferred during the accumulation period.

The taxation of annuity contracts is based upon an **exclusion ratio**. The exclusion ratio is the relationship of the total investment in the contract (cost base) to the total expected return under the contract (calculated based on average life expectancy tables). This ratio (expressed in a percentage) shows how much of each annuity payment is taxable, and how much is excluded from taxation.

Once an annuitant recovers his or her cost base during the annuity period, the total payments received will be taxed at ordinary income tax rates.

If an endowment is paid as a death claim in a lump sum, the benefit is not subject to income tax.

If an annuitant dies and the balance of a guaranted amount is paid to a beneficiary, the payment is not taxable as income until the investment in the contract has been received tax free (the amount received by the beneficiary is added to the tax free amounts received by the annuitant, and only any amount which exceeds the total amounts paid in will be taxable).

If an annuitant dies and payments continue to a surviving annuitant under a joint and survivor annuity, the same percentage that was excludable before the first annuitant's death will continue to be excluded from taxes.

In most cases where a corporation owns a deferred annuity contract as an investment, it is not treated as an annuity contract for tax purposes — all income and gains received or accrued during a tax year are taxed as ordinary income. This does not apply to annuities

TAXATION OF LIFE INSURANCE

Income Tax Consequences

Proceeds: *	
Lump Sum	No income tax
Installments	Interest portion taxable as income
Cash Surrender Value	Cost Recovery Rule (portion in excess of premium payments taxed as income)
Premium Payments	Individual - not deductible; Group paid by employer - cost for the first $50,000 of life insurance is deductible for employer, and the cost for coverage in excess of $50,000 is taxable as income to the employee

* Proceeds may be subject to Estate Taxes depending upon who owns the policy and who is the beneficiary

Chart 3-8

which are owned by a corporation for the purposes of funding pension plans, profit sharing plans, and other plans which are treated differently under the tax laws.

Estate and Gift Tax

Since 1916 the federal government has levied a tax against the estate of an individual who recently died. Currently, the maximum amount of that tax is 50%. One exception to this is the marital deduction. An entire estate may be left to a surviving spouse with no tax consequence.

One way to reduce an estate to reduce the amount of tax to be paid upon death is to provide gifts to individuals or charitable organizations during a lifetime. Gifts of amounts up to $10,000 per year, per donee may be given with no tax consequence to the donor.

Modified Endowment Contracts

There are special tax requirements for modified endowment contracts, including retirement income or semi-endowments. In a retirement income endowment, the amount payable upon survival (of the endowment period) is greater than the face amount, and the amount payable at death is the greater of the face amount or cash value. The semi-endowment pays upon survival one half the sum payable if the insured dies during the endowment period. Because the investment return may be greater than the amount invested, the tax considerations can be complicated.

In November 1988, Congress passed the Technical and Miscellaneous Revenue Act (TAMRA) which makes any withdrawal, loan, or collateralizing of the cash in these policies taxable. In fact, depending on the policyowner's age, the amount may be taxable and subject to a 10% penalty. In order to avoid the taxation and subsequent penalties, the policyowner must limit his or her investment according to the **seven pay test** established by the government, which limits the amount that may be paid into the policy during the first seven policy years. This information should be provided to policyowners by the insurance company.

Group Life Insurance

A variety of special tax rules apply to life insurance products which are provided as benefits to employees. Generally, the cost of the first $50,000 of **group term life insurance** coverage provided to an employee by an employer is not taxable to the employee. The cost of life insurance coverage in excess of $50,000 is taxable as income to the employee.

To the extent that an employee is taxed on the cost for incidental life insurance protection, the employee only pays a tax on the cost for pure protection. For cash value insurance, the taxable cost would be the one year term rate for the amount of protection at risk (face value minus accumulated cash value), regardless of the premium actually being paid by the plan. For term insurance protection, the entire actual cost for protection would be taxable to the employee, because that is the cost for pure protection.

REVIEW QUESTIONS

Match the following numbered definitions with the lettered terms below:

____ 13. Generally not tax deductible for individuals.

____ 14. Considered a return of excess premium and not subject to income tax.

____ 15. The amount that exceeds premiums paid in is subject to ordinary income tax.

____ 16. Subject to estate taxes.

A. Dividends
B. Lump sum benefits
C. Premiums
D. Cash surrender value

☞ ***Answers to Review Questions are located at the back of the book.***

NOTES

4

UNDERWRITING, ISSUING, & DELIVERING THE LIFE INSURANCE POLICY

THE PROCESS OF ISSUING A LIFE INSURANCE POLICY

IMPORTANT RESPONSIBILITIES

Sales Presentations

Agents are subject to a number of laws and regulations which shape their behavior during sales presentations. For example, agents are prohibited from misrepresenting policy terms. In addition, agents are often required to disclose facts about information practices and the products they are proposing for sale. In many jurisdictions, agents must provide prospective insureds with a policy summary and a buyers guide at the time of application. A **policy summary** is a document that summarizes the coverages, benefits, limitations, exclusions, and terms of the policy proposed for sale. A **buyers guide** is a consumer publication that describes the type of coverage being offered, and provides general information to help the applicant compare different policies and reach a decision about whether the proposed coverage is appropriate.

Policy Issuance

Once the prospect has agreed to purchase the life insurance contract, three important functions must take place:

- The underwriting process will begin
- The application will be approved and the policy issued (or declined)
- The agent will deliver the policy to the policyowner.

Each of these activities is important — not only to provide the best possible service to the policyowners — but to comply with state laws regulating the writing of life insurance policies.

It is important to clearly understand all of the individuals who might be involved and the parts they play in the life insurance process. These might include the applicant, the insured, the policyowner, and the beneficiary. Although these are four separate roles, they may all be played by one person, or by two, three, four, or more persons. Let us define them individually.

Applicant — the individual who fills out the application and applies for the insurance.

Policyowner (usually also the applicant) — the individual who pays the premium, accepts the policy when it is delivered by the agent, has the special owner's rights, such as designating beneficiaries.

Insured — the individual whose life is covered by the policy.

Beneficiary — the individual or individuals who the policyowner has named to receive the benefits of the policy.

Most of the time, the applicant, policyowner and the insured are the same person. For example, a husband may apply for insurance on his own life, naturally is the insured as well and most often will also be the policyowner.

The term **third-party ownership** refers to a situation where the policy is owned by someone other than the insured. For example, in a business situation, a corporation may apply for insurance on the life of a key employee. In this case, the corporation is the applicant and the policyowner, and the key employee is the insured. The corporation would also be the beneficiary.

THE UNDERWRITING PROCESS

By definition, underwriting is the process of selection, classification and rating of risks. Simply put, underwriting is a risk selection process. The selection process consists of evaluating information and resources to determine how an individual will be classified (standard or substandard). Once this part of the underwriting procedure is complete, the policy will be rated in terms of the premium which the applicant will pay. The policy will then be issued and subsequently delivered by the agent.

Loss Ratios and Related Concepts

Loss and expense ratios are basic guidelines as to the quality of company underwriting. A **loss ratio** is determined by dividing losses by total premiums received. Loss ratios are often calculated by account, by line of insurance, by "book of business" (all accounts placed by each agent or agency), and for all business written by an insurer. Loss ratio information may be used to make decisions about whether to renew accounts, whether to continue agency contracts, and whether to tighten underwriting standards on a given line of insurance. An **expense ratio** is determined by dividing an insurer's operating expenses (including commissions paid) by total premiums. When the combined loss and expense ratio is 100%, the insurer breaks even. If the combined ratio exceeds 100%, an underwriting loss has occurred. If the combined ratio is less than 100%, an underwriting profit, or gain, has been realized.

For example, let's assume that the ABC Insurance Company realizes $3 million in underwriting losses for all term insurance policies. This same block of business also generates $10 million in premium. The loss ratio would be calculated as follows:

Loss Ratio = Losses/Premiums
Loss Ratio = $3 million/$10 million = 30%

Further, let's assume that the ABC Insurance Company has operating expenses totaling $2 million for this same block of term insurance. The expense ratio would be:

Expense Ratio = Operating Expenses/Premiums
Expense Ratio = $2 million/$10 million = 20%

The combined loss and expense ratio equals 50%. Thus, the ABC Insurance Company has an underwriting gain or profit on this block of term insurance.

Selection Criteria

An underwriter's job is to use all the information gathered from many sources to determine whether or not to accept a particular applicant. Individuals applying for individually owned life and health insurance receive more underwriting scrutiny than members of a group. The following concepts apply primarily to individual underwriting. Group underwriting considerations are discussed later in this chapter. The underwriter must exercise judgment based on his or her years of experience to read beyond the facts and get a true picture of the applicant's lifestyle. Are there any factors (occupation, hobbies, lifestyle) which make this individual likely to die before his or her natural life expectancy? An underwriter cannot, and is not, expected to foresee all circumstances. However, the underwriter's purpose is to protect the insurance company insofar as he or she can against **adverse selection** — very poor risks, and those parties with fraudulent intent.

Adverse selection exists when the group of risks insured is more likely than the average group to experience loss. For instance, in a randomly-selected group of 1,000 25-year-old individuals, only two might be expected to die in a given year. However, human nature is such that many healthy 25-year-olds do not see the need to buy life insurance and prefer to spend their money elsewhere. It is only those 25-year-olds who are ill or perhaps employed in dangerous occupations who are likely to buy insurance. An underwriter must take care not to accept too many of these poorer-than-average risks or the insurance company will lose money.

Besides the problem of adverse selection, the underwriter must guard against moral and morale hazards. A **moral hazard** is the tendency of an applicant to misrepresent him or herself to the insurance company with reference to health status, occupation or other pertinent information. In other words, a moral hazard deals with an individual's tendency to lie or be dishonest.

A **morale hazard** is the applicant's indifferent attitude toward risk. For example, an applicant with a history of speeding tickets and drunk driving, would display an indifferent or apathetic attitude toward his or her own health and well being and thus present a morale hazard to the underwriter.

Sources of Underwriting Information

The underwriter has various sources of information to provide the necessary information for the risk selection process. These sources include:

- The application
- Medical exams and history
- Inspection reports
- The Medical Information Bureau (MIB)
- The agent

The Application. The form of the application may differ from one company to another. However, most applications provide the following information:

- Part I — General Information
- Part II — Medical Information
- The Agent's Statement or Report

- Proper signatures of all parties to the contract

A sample application appears in the Sample Policy Section at the end of this manual.

Part I of the application asks for general or personal data regarding the insured. This would include such information as: name and address, date of birth, business address and occupation, Social Security number, marital status, and other insurance owned. In addition, if the applicant and the insured are not the same person, then the applicant's name and address would be included in Part I.

Part II of the application is generally designed to provide information regarding the insured's past medical history, current physical condition and personal morals. If the amount of insurance applied for qualifies as "non-medical", then the agent and the insured will complete Part II of the information. If the amount of insurance applied for is relatively high, then Part II is not completed by the agent and the proposed insured. In such cases, the proposed insured is required to take a medical examination and Part II of the application is completed as part of the physical exam.

Increasingly, underwriters are relying on paramedical exams and blood tests for information in order to accurately evaluate a health risk. Blood testing is almost universally used to determine cholesterol levels, elevated liver enzymes, and the presence of HIV infection. In many jurisdictions, HIV testing requires informed consent of the applicant, confidentiality of results, and proper notification procedures.

Part II of the application provides information regarding the past medical history of the insured by asking questions related to the types of illnesses and accidents experienced by the insured; periods of hospitalization and any surgery and reasons for visits to any physician.

In addition, Part II requires information regarding the current health of the insured by asking for current medical treatment for any sickness or condition and types of medication taken. The name and address of the insured's physician is also required.

Usually Part II of the application will also include questions regarding alcohol and any drug use by the insured. Avocations and high risk hobbies are also usually reported on Part II. Generally, any plans for a prolonged trip or stay in a foreign country are also reported in Part II. Naturally, questions regarding alcohol and drug use are designed to help determine the moral attitude of the insured.

Another source of medical information available to the underwriter is an **Attending Physician's Statement (APS)**. After a review of the medical information contained on the application or the medical exam, the underwriter may request an APS from the proposed insured's doctor. Usually, the APS is designed to obtain more specific information about a particular medical problem.

Simplified issue life insurance requires no medical exam and only asks very basic health-related questions on the application. Usually this type of insurance is only available in low face amounts, to reduce the risk of adverse selection against the company.

The Agent's Statement is part of the application and requires that the agent provide certain information regarding the proposed insured. Generally, this includes information regarding the agent's relationship to the insured, data about the proposed insured's financial status, habits, general character and any other information which may be pertinent to the risk being assumed by the insurer.

The application will also record information regarding the policyowner/insured's choices with regard to the mode of premium (monthly, annually, etc), the use of dividends and the designation of a beneficiary.

Finally, the signatures of the insured (and the policyowner if different from the insured) are required in the appropriate places on the application. Usually, the agent also signs the application as a witness to the applicant's signatures.

Inspection Reports. To supplement the information on the application, the underwriter orders an inspection report on the applicant from an independent investigating firm or credit agency, which covers financial and moral information. This information is used to determine the insurability of the applicant. If the amount of insurance applied for is average, the inspector will write a general report in regard to the applicant's finances, health, character, work, hobbies, and other habits. The inspector will make a more detailed report when larger amounts of insurance are requested. This information is based on interviews with the applicant's associates at home (neighbors, friends), at work, and elsewhere.

Medical Information Bureau. Another source of information which may aid the underwriter in determining whether or not to underwrite a risk is the Medical Information Bureau (MIB), based in Westwood, Massachusetts. This is a nonprofit trade association which maintains medical information on applicants for life and health insurance. The MIB has 650 member companies that write 80% of the health insurance and 99% of the life insurance policies in the U.S.

MIB information is reported in code form to member companies in order to preserve the confidentiality of the contents. The report does not indicate any action taken by other insurers, nor the amount of life insurance requested. In addition, an insurer may not refuse to accept a risk based solely on the information contained in an MIB report. There must be other substantiating factors which lead an insurer to decide to deny coverage. Beginning in 1995, the MIB must provide explanations to applicants who are denied coverage, allowing consumers to challenge possibly inaccurate information about their medical history.

The Agent As Field Underwriter

A key element in the underwriting process is the role of the insurance agent. It can be argued that the agent is the most important part of the risk selection process. The agent is in a position to see and talk to the proposed insured, to ask the questions contained on the application and to accurately and completely record the answers to those questions.

Thus, one of the most important functions of the agent is the completion of the application. Much of the information reported on the application becomes the basis upon which to accept or reject the proposed insured. In addition, a signed and witnessed copy of the application becomes part of the policy, the legal contract between the insured and the insurer.

As a field underwriter, the agent can help expedite the underwriting process by the prompt submission of the application, by scheduling the applicant for a physical exam (if necessary) and by assisting the home office underwriter with other requirements such as obtaining an APS.

The most important element of this process for the agent is the accuracy, thoroughness and honesty displayed when completing the application. Answers to questions must be recorded accurately, and completely by the agent. In addition, honest reporting is required. The agent may not omit pertinent information or report it inaccurately in order to get the policy issued. The ethical conduct of the agent with regard to the underwriting process must be above reproach.

Finally, if the proposed insured is rated or declined for the insurance, it is the agent's role as a field underwriter to explain the reasons for the underwriting action. Seldom is an individual declined for life insurance but it does happen that they may be classified as substandard and thus a rated or substandard policy may be issued in lieu of the one applied for. When this occurs, the agent must be prepared to not only explain the reasons for the substandard rating but also to explain the rated policy which the company has issued. In addition, there are usually some underwriting forms (amendments or revisions) which must be signed by the applicant when the policy is delivered and it is the agent's responsibility to return these signed forms to the home office.

GROUP UNDERWRITING CONSIDERATIONS

Each individual application for insurance is underwritten on an individual basis including the necessary application, medical information, inspection reports, etc. When the underwriting process is complete, an individual policy is issued to the applicant.

Group life insurance is usually written on a group basis as opposed to an individual basis. Each group participant completes a very short application form which usually consists of the individual's name, address, Social Security number, dependent information and beneficiary designation. There are no medical questions. Thus, no medical underwriting takes place. (However, evidence of insurability must be furnished by an employee who wants to join a contributory group after the period of eligibility has ended.)

It is therefore possible for individuals in poor health to receive group insurance benefits because there is no medical underwriting. All eligible participants obtain coverage. But underwriting, the risk selection process, does occur.

The group underwriter is concerned with the following underwriting factors:

- Adverse selection
- The size of the group
- The nature of the group (industry, specific work functions)
- The financial stability of the group
- The number and frequency of new entrants to the group

Adverse selection is the tendency for poor risks to seek and be covered for insurance more often than average risks. Thus in a group situation, the underwriter must consider such things as the type of work done, the ages of the participants, and the probability of this particular group being an adverse risk to the company. For example, a group of coal miners presents a much different risk than a group of bank employees.

The larger the group to be insured, the more predictable will be the expected losses from the group. Thus, it is more difficult for the underwriter to anticipate expected losses from relatively small groups (10, 20 or 25 participants).

Once a group is written, the underwriter wants the business to stay on the books and thus is concerned about the financial stability of the company. If the company has a history of financial problems, i.e., bankruptcy, layoffs due to no work, seasonal employment, then possibly the group may be declined for these financial reasons.

The group underwriter is concerned with the number of new group entrants. The insurer does not necessarily want a group in which there is no turnover. If the loss experience is to be favorable, employees must leave the group due to retirement or terminations and new (younger) employees must take their place. This turnover of employees helps bring some stability in terms of loss experience and possible adverse selection.

Adverse Underwriting Decisions

A risk will be rejected when the insurer believes the applicant cannot be profitable at a reasonable premium or with reasonable coverage modifications. If a risk is rejected based on information in an investigative report, the applicant must be notified and given the name and address of the reporting company. In health insurance, when renewal is denied, the insured must be given a written explanation for nonrenewal or be notified that the explanation is available upon written request.

Issues Relating to AIDS

The disease Acquired Immune Deficiency Syndrome (AIDS) is beginning to have a large impact on the insurance industry. The cost of AIDS to society in the 1990s will be in the tens of billions. The costs associated with AIDS are those of premature death and medical costs including long hospital stays and very expensive drug treatments. These costs affect medical, disability, and life insurance coverages.

Blood tests for the AIDS virus prior to policy issuance are a common underwriting requirement. Typically, the proposed insured must sign a **consent form** before the blood test is performed. AIDS testing is almost always required whenever a large amount of insurance is applied for. Each insurance company sets thresholds for the ages and amounts of insurance for when medical underwriting (including blood tests for the AIDS virus) will be required.

Test results are confidential and certain procedures must be followed to inform the applicant of any positive results. A signed **release form** is required whenever test results will be disclosed to any party who is not otherwise entitled to the information.

REVIEW QUESTIONS

1. The underwriter's main purpose is to protect the insurance company from ____________________ ____________________, poor risks and persons who intend to defraud the insurance company.
2. An insurer may not refuse to accept a risk based solely on the information in an MIB report. (True/False)____________________
3. A blood test for the AIDS virus may be conducted prior to insurance policy issuance provided the proposed insured____________________ ____________________ ____________________

☞ ***Answers to Review Questions are located at the back of the book.***

CLASSIFICATION OF RISKS

As was previously stated, underwriting is the process of selection, classification and rating of risks. Risk classification refers to the determination of whether a risk is standard or substandard based on the underwriting or risk evaluation process. Basically, a standard risk is simply an average risk.

Standard risks are those who bear the same health, habit, and occupational characteristics as the persons on whose lives the mortality table used was compiled. Most insurers offer special but higher rates to persons who are not acceptable at standard rates because of health, habits or occupation. This is sometimes called "extra risk" insurance. Some companies have coined euphemistic names for it in order to avoid the rather insulting implication that persons offered this type of coverage are **substandard**. About 90% of individuals covered are standard risks. Less than 2% of individuals applying are turned down for coverage completely.

There are several methods of determining the extra rate for the substandard class of risk:

- **Rated-Up Age:** This plan assumes that the insured is older than his or her actual age, which is a way of saying that he or she will not live as long as a "standard" risk. Thus an impaired risk of age 35 may be issued a policy as applied for but with the rate of age 40. While having the merit of simplicity of handling, this method is no longer widely used.
- **Flat Additional Premium:** A constant (that is, not varying with age) additional premium is added to the "standard" rate.
- **Tabular Rating:** Applicants are classified on the basis of the extent to which mortality of risks with their impairment or degree of impairment exceeds that of the "standard" risk. Percentage tables are developed and used to calculate the amount of extra premium to be charged for any class of impaired risks. Extra percentage tables are usually designated as "Table A," "Table B," etc. Each usually reflects about a 25% increase above 100%,

or "standard." Insurers vary in the number of tables on which they will accept risks. One may not accept anything lower (or "higher," depending on viewpoint) than, say, Table C (175%). Another may write through Table F (250%). Companies can be found that will write up to 1,000% — or perhaps even higher. More and more high risk cases are becoming acceptable (and, also, many conditions once considered "high risk" are now, on the basis of more experience, being accepted as "standard"). Today it is a rare case when coverage cannot be found anywhere for almost any risk.

- **Graded Death Benefits:** The insured pays the standard premium for, say, $20,000 of insurance but receives a policy with a face amount of perhaps $15,000. After some time has elapsed the company may increase the amount of insurance periodically and when the company considers the substandard condition to no longer exist, the full $20,000 of coverage would be granted.

Preferred Risks. If a substandard risk presents an above average risk of loss, a preferred risk presents a below average risk of loss. In an effort to encourage the public to practice better health, the insurance industry has developed preferred risk policies with lower (or preferred) premium rates. Those applicants who may be eligible for preferred risk classification are those who:

- Work in low risk occupations and do not participate in high risk hobbies (scuba diving, sky diving, etc.)
- Have a very favorable medical history
- Presently are in good physical condition without any serious medical problems
- Do not smoke
- Meet certain weight limitations

DETERMINATION OF PREMIUMS (RATING CONSIDERATIONS)

The final step in the underwriting process is the rating of the risk or the determination of the premium. There are three factors used in determining life insurance rates:

- Mortality
- Interest
- Expenses

Mortality

If an underwriter could predict exactly how long each insured would live, he could charge a premium for each risk that was precisely correct for covering the policy face amount, and expenses, while taking into account the interest to be earned on the premium paid. Of course an underwriter cannot do this on an individual policy, but he can predict the probability of numbers of deaths for a large group of people by using a standard mortality table, such as the 1980 Commissioners' Standard Ordinary Mortality Table. The table is based on statistics kept by insurance companies over the years on mortality by age, sex, and other characteristics.

The deaths per 1,000 (mortality rate) is taken from the mortality table and converted into a dollar and cents rate. For instance, if the mortality rate for a particular age group is 3.00, it means, on the average, three out of every 1,000 can be expected to die at that age.

An insurance company would need to collect $3 from each of 1,000 policyowners in order to have sufficient premium to pay out $1,000 in benefits for those who die in that age group.

To illustrate: 1,000 x $3 = $3,000
3 deaths x $1,000 = $3,000

Interest

Because premiums are paid in advance of claims, insurance companies have money to invest to earn interest. This interest helps to lower the premium rate.

As explained, the basic cost of life insurance is the cost of mortality, however, in constructing a rate, interest enters in. It is assumed that all premiums are paid at the beginning of the year and all claims paid at the end. Therefore, it becomes necessary to determine how much should be charged at the beginning of the year, assuming a given rate of interest, to have enough money at the end of the year to pay all claims.

Expenses

Using the cost of mortality and discounting for interest, there is enough money to pay claims, but we have no money to pay operation expenses. The premium without expense loading is a "net" premium. (Do not confuse "net" as it is used here with the same term sometimes used to indicate a participating premium minus dividends paid.)

An expense loading is added to the net premium in order to: (1) cover all expenses and contingencies, (2) have funds for expenses when needed, and (3) spread cost equitably among insureds.

Loading consists of four main items:

- **Acquisition Costs** — All costs in connection with putting the policy on the books are charged as incurred in the insurance accounting. In most cases, these costs will be so proportionately high in comparison to ensuing years that they must be amortized over a period of years. One of the highest acquisition costs is the agent's first year commission. (This is the reason a policy that lapses in the first two or three years creates a loss for the insurer. It has not yet recovered acquisition costs.)

- **General Overhead Loading** — Clerical salaries, furniture, fixtures, rent, management salaries, etc., must be considered when determining expenses. The allocation of these costs is unaffected by the size of the premium, probably little affected by the face amount, but is most likely affected by the number of policies.
- **Loading for Contingency Funds** — Once a level premium policy has been issued, the premium can never be increased. However, unforeseen contingencies could make the rate inadequate. Assessment companies reserve the right to charge additional premiums in such a case. Legal reserve companies establish contingency reserves to draw on in such cases.
- **Immediate Payment of Death Claims** — In rate-making, it is assumed that all claims are paid at the end of the year. This is not literally true, of course. Relying on the law of large numbers, it is safe to assume that death claims will be spread throughout the year. Therefore, theoretically, all claims will be paid six months before the end of the year. Allowance must be made for this loss in the expense loading.

The **gross annual premium**, the amount the policyowner actually pays for the policy, equals the mortality risk discounted for interest, plus expenses. By definition, the **net premium** is the mortality risk discounted for interest, without any expense adjustment.

By formula:

Gross Premium = Mortality - Interest + Expenses

Net Premium = Mortality - Interest

The mortality risk factor increases with age. This is the reason that some life insurance policy premiums increase periodically. For example, the premium for a one-year renewable and convertible term insurance policy increases each year because each year the insured is one year older and thus the mortality risk is greater. This can result in very expensive premiums as the insured becomes older.

The **level premium** concept was devised to solve this problem of increasing premiums. Mathematically, the level premiums paid by the policyowner are equal to the increasing sum of the premiums caused by the increased risk of mortality. Accordingly, in the early years of the policy, the level premiums paid are actually more than the amount necessary to cover the cost of mortality. Conversely, in the later years of the policy, the premiums paid are less that the amount necessary to cover the increased cost of mortality. This "shortage" in the later years of the policy is accounted for by the overcharges (plus interest earned) in the early policy years.

Premium Mode. Once the single premium amount has been determined, the company will break this amount into smaller amounts (annual, semi-annual, quarterly, or monthly) which will be more convenient for the insured to pay. This frequency of payment is called the premium mode. This is important because the insurance company invests the premium amounts it receives and uses the income as part of the eventual settlement. The more payments the insured wishes to break his premium into, the higher the total premium. This is because of the interest lost by not receiving money for coverage in advance and because of increased administrative expenses.

RESERVES

Reserves are accounting measurements of an insurer's liabilities to its policyholders. Theoretically, the reserve is the amount together with interest to be earned and premiums to be paid that will exactly equal all of the company's contractual obligations.

A life insurance reserve is a fixed liability of the insurer. This liability represents the insurer's promise to pay the face amount of the policy at some future time. By law, a portion of every premium must be set aside as a reserve against the future claim from the policy as well as other contractual obligations such as cash surrender and nonforfeiture values. Accordingly, the policy reserve is equal to the premiums paid plus the interest earned on those premiums and other policy obligations.

Insurance companies demonstrate their solvency to the state Insurance Departments by showing their assets as well as adequate funds to cover their reserve obligations. In addition to its assets, the insurer must show that it will continue to receive future premiums plus interest in order to cover its reserve obligation.

By law, the Insurance Commissioner requires that a specific reserve be maintained if a company is to be solvent. The reserve must be calculated using a mortality table and an interest specified by the Commissioner. Most states require that premiums be calculated using the 1980 Commissioner's Standard Ordinary table. In addition, the estimated investment return or interest rate paid on the premiums will also be determined by the Insurance Commissioner. Usually, a very conservative interest rate is specified.

REVIEW QUESTIONS

4. What are the three factors used in determining life insurance rates?
   (1) ____________________
   (2) ____________________
   (3) ____________________
5. A premium without an expense loading is called a(n) ____________ premium.
6. Under the level premium system, premiums are (higher/lower) ________ than needed in the early years of the policy.
7. The frequency of premium payment is called the ____________ .
8. Define reserves. ____________________
   ____
   ____

Answers to Review Questions are located at the back of the book.

DELIVERING & SERVICING THE POLICY

RECEIPTS

Once the underwriting process is complete and the applicant has been approved, the life insurance policy will be issued by the insurance company. The coverage is not effective until the policy is delivered and the initial premium has been paid. However, usually the applicant will pay the initial premium with the application. When this occurs, the agent will provide the applicant with a receipt for the initial premium and the effective date of coverage will depend on the type of receipt issued.

Conditional Receipt

A **conditional receipt** can be given to the applicant if the premium is paid at the time of the application. This receipt makes the coverage effective on the date of the application, if the applicant is found to be insurable under the company's general underwriting rules in effect at the time of application. However, some conditional receipts make coverage effective on the date of application, or the date of the medical examination, whichever is later.

For example, an applicant has paid the initial premium, completed and signed the application. The agent provides the applicant with a conditional receipt which basically states that the applicant is covered as of the date of the application (or receipt) provided he or she is insurable as a standard risk. Thus, if the applicant were to die before the policy was issued, the beneficiary would receive the face amount of the policy.

On the other hand, if the applicant was found to be a substandard risk, then the conditional receipt is null and void and no coverage would be effective until the substandard policy was delivered and additional premium paid. If the policy is not issued as applied for (a substandard rating, for example), then no coverage would be in force until the applicant accepts the substandard policy and pays the additional premium required by the rating.

Binding Receipt

A few companies use an "unconditional" or **binding receipt** that makes the company liable for the risk from the date of application. This coverage lasts for a specified time or until the insurer issues the policy. The specified time limit is usually 30 to 60 days.

With a binding receipt, regardless of the applicant's insurability, he or she is covered for a specific period of time following completion of the application and the payment of the initial premium. Use of this type of receipt is rare.

Temporary Insurance Agreement

This type of receipt or agreement provides the applicant with immediate life insurance coverage while the underwriting process is taking place whether or not the individual is insurable.

For example, an applicant submits the initial premium and application and is provided with a temporary insurance agreement which states that coverage is effective immediately and will continue during the underwriting process. If the applicant should die during this period, the coverage is in force regardless of the individual's insurability or risk classification as a result of the underwriting process.

Temporary Term

Strictly speaking, temporary term is not actually a type of receipt but it does provide insurance protection for a specified period of time until a policy is issued. Some applicants want immediate life insurance protection but for some reason or another, want to defer the actual issuance of the policy until a later date such as three or six months from the date of the application.

In these situations, the insurer covers the applicant with term insurance, sometimes referred to as preliminary or interim term insurance as it covers the applicant during the interim before the primary policy is issued. Usually, this situation occurs when the applicant does not wish to begin making premium payments on the primary policy until several months later. Thus the individual has term insurance protection (at a low cost) until he or she is ready to being pay the premiums on the primary policy.

AGENT'S COLLECTION OF PREMIUM

The agent is encouraged to collect the initial premium with the application. Evidence shows that this procedure is most effective in having the insured accept the policy when it is issued. If the insured does not pay the initial premium at the time of application, chances increase that he or she will not accept the issued policy. Also, a point that you, as agent, can make to the applicant is that if the applicant waits to pay the premium, he or she may become uninsurable, or may die before the policy takes effect. Remember, the policy is effective only after the initial premium has been paid.

When the initial premium is not paid with the application, no contract is in force. The applicant is not making an offer to the insurer. He or she is merely inviting the insurer to make an offer by issuing the policy. Since there is no insurance in force under these circumstances, when the agent delivers the policy and collects the initial premium, there may be additional underwriting requirements which must be satisfied. Most commonly, the insurance company may require that the insured sign a health statement verifying that no change in health has occurred since the date of the application.

SUBMITTING THE APPLICATION & INITIAL PREMIUM

It is important for the agent to submit the application, initial premium, and any questionnaires or other forms to the home office underwriter promptly. The agent should review all forms for completeness and be sure that they are properly signed. Not only does this make for good relationships with the home office underwriter, but it is extremely important to the applicant. Unnecessary delays in delivering the policy can cause the applicant undue anxiety and result in a loss of confidence in the agent. Since agents are handling money belonging to their clients, it is extremely important that an accurate record of such transactions be kept. It is also wise for the agent to keep copies of applications and other information. This avoids unnecessary delay or other problems if the originals are lost.

Issuing the Policy. A life insurance policy may be **issued as applied for**, **modified**, or even **amended** if the applicant does meet the underwriting standards of the insurance company. While uncommon, an insurer may issue a waiver with the policy which states that death by a particular event will not be covered. This might be done if the insured had a particularly hazardous occupation or hobby. More commonly, an insurer might issue a more limited form of policy or at lower limits than that which was applied for.

Personal Delivery. Since delivery is necessary to complete the sale of a life insurance policy, the best way to assure delivery is to do it in person. If a conditional receipt has not been previously issued, the insurer may require the agent to obtain a statement of good health at the time of policy delivery. In addition to knowing the policy has been delivered, this method also gives the agent an opportunity to:

- Thoroughly explain all coverage provisions, exclusions, and riders to the applicant/policyowner. Although most policies contain a provision barring an agent from changing the policy contract in any way, the company may be liable for errors made by the agent if the agent incorrectly represents the policy being sold. It is important for the agent to sit down with the insured at the time of policy delivery and explain all policy provisions, particularly the exclusions, and any riders that may restrict the coverage given in the policy.
- Review the purpose of the policy and how it fits into the policyowner's total life insurance plan
- Reinforce the relationship and good will established with the client
- Allow the agent to explain the possible need for additional coverage
- Ask the insured for referrals under favorable circumstances

Mailing the Policy. Legally, the policy is considered "delivered" when it is mailed or turned over to the policyowner or someone acting on his or her behalf. Some companies do mail policies directly to policyowners. However, many prefer to have the agent make a personal delivery.

In some cases, a **constructive delivery** is deemed to occur when the insurer mails a policy to its agent for actual delivery to the policyowner, because the insurer has issued the policy and released it for delivery. However, a legal delivery has not yet occurred if the insurer requires personal delivery for verification of good health at the time of delivery, or if the policy is being provided to the applicant merely to review and inspect at that time, and not necessarily to buy.

REPLACEMENT

Replacement, simply, is the purchase of one life insurance policy to replace another. Because of the cash values that can build up in a policy, and the favorable loan interest rates in older policies, replacement can be disadvantageous to consumers. However, there are good reasons to replace a policy, particularly if it does not meet the current needs of the consumer.

Commissions paid to agents for selling a new policy are particularly lucrative. For this reason, unscrupulous agents have persuaded consumers to give up old policies for new ones, even if it was not in the best interests of the policyholder.

When replacement of life insurance is involved, the agent must comply with all pertinent federal and state regulations. Each state has rules and regulations regarding replacement of life insurance products which are designed to protect the interests of the insuring public. Frequently, it is not in the best interests of the insured to replace existing life insurance with a new policy. The reasons for this are many:

- New insurance requires the applicant to prove insurability
- Premiums may be higher for a new policy
- New policy provisions will have to be complied with such as a new incontestable period

- The existing policy's provisions may be more liberal than a new policy's provisions
- Generally, a new policy will not have any current cash values

The National Association of Insurance Commissioners (NAIC) has adopted a Model Life Insurance Replacement Regulation. The majority of states have replacement regulations based on this model.

Duties of Agents and Brokers

Technically, replacement means any transaction in which new life insurance or a new annuity is to be purchased, and it is known, or should reasonably be known to the agent or broker, or to the insurer if there is no agent, that as part of the transaction, existing life insurance or annuity will be:

- Lapsed, forfeited, surrendered, or terminated
- *Converted* to reduced paid-up insurance *continued* as extended term insurance, or *reduced* in value by the use of nonforfeiture benefits or other policy values
- Amended to produce a reduction in the benefits or in the term for which coverage would otherwise remain in force, or for which benefits would be paid
- Reissued with reduction in cash value

Generally, the duties of the agent or broker include: obtaining, along with the application, a signed statement from the applicant as to whether or not insurance is to be replaced; and submitting the statement to the insurer.

If replacement is involved, the agent or broker is required to:

- List all existing life insurance policies to be replaced
- Give the applicant a completed **Comparison Statement,** signed by the agent or broker, and a **Notice to Applicants Regarding Replacement of Life Insurance** (a copy of the forms should be left with the applicant)
- Give the insurer a copy of any proposals made, and a copy of the Comparison Statement with the name of insurer that is to be replaced

The agent must take special care when replacing an existing policy with a new policy to make sure that the insured is not misled into purchasing a policy which is to the insured's disadvantage. The agent also needs to be aware of his or her own errors and omissions liability, particularly in the area of replacement.

Duties of the Insurer

The duties of the replacing insurer include:

- Making sure that all replacement actions are in compliance with state regulations
- Notifying each insurer whose insurance is being replaced and upon request, furnishing a copy of any proposal and Comparison Statement
- Maintaining copies of proposals, receipts and Comparison Statements

Each individual state has established time limits for the performance of duties. You should check your state's regulations to learn specific time limits, such as:

- The time within which an agent must supply the applicant with a Comparison Statement
- The time and manner within which the agent must notify the insurer of replacement activities
- The time within which the insurer must notify the insurer being replaced that such action is in operation
- The time within which the insurer being replaced must respond to the replacing insurer and the applicant

Also, individual state law specifically outlines the method in which records are to be maintained and the length of time the records are to be made available. A common wording for laws on record keeping is: *These records shall be maintained for at least (three years) or until the next examination of the company by the Insurance Department.*

POLICY RETENTION

Although much of the business of the agent is involved in attracting potential clients, retaining the account and servicing it through the years is very important as well.

The agent becomes involved with the client after original application and delivery at times of change. The client's needs change at such times as marriage, the birth of a child, and death. The agent acts as the representative of the company in changing beneficiaries, when desired, adding amounts of insurance, and facilitating payment of claims. The effectiveness of the agent at these times will lead to retention of the account for the lifetime of the client, and often over generations.

SUMMARY OF THE AGENT'S RESPONSIBILITIES

The insurance agent is a key person in the process of marketing, underwriting and delivery of insurance policies. As a marketing representative of the insurer, it is the agent's responsibility to represent and market the insurer's products in an ethical and professional manner. This requires knowledge of various insurance products, being aware of a prospect's insurance needs and problems and the ability to solve these needs with the proper insurance products.

The agent also has a responsibility to be aware of insurance laws which pertain to marketing of insurance products; such as state required standards for advertising and sales literature. Generally all advertising, sales presentations and illustrations must be truthful, may not misrepresent or omit material information.

As part of the underwriting process, the agent is the primary source of underwriting information. It is the agent's duty to accurately and thoroughly complete all applications for insurance, and collect initial premiums and promptly submit them to the company. In addition, the agent is responsible for providing the insurance applicant with privacy notices and information such as the Notice of Insurance Information Practices, and finally to provide the insurance applicant with necessary receipts for the initial premium collected.

Another objective of the agent as a field underwriter is to help protect the insurer from adverse risks. If an applicant is substandard, the agent is responsible for delivering the substandard policy and explaining its limitations and/or extra premium to the applicant.

REVIEW QUESTIONS

9. Which of the following statements is/are **true** about submitting the application, premium, and other forms to the insurance company?
   a. The application and any questionnaires must be signed by the applicant
   b. The agent must keep accurate records of all transactions involving the applicant's money
   c. Since coverage is effective immediately, it is not necessary to send the forms to the home office underwriter more often than weekly
10. Which of the following statements describe the best use of an agent's time when personally delivering the policy?
    a. Agent Jones delivers a policy and makes a special point of finding out how the insured's son performed in the gymnastics competition
    b. Agent King delivers a policy and reiterates the same sales pitch she used to make the initial sale
    c. Agent Ritley delivers a policy and restates the advantages of the policy and how it can be amended to meet future insurance needs
11. Which of the following statements is/are **true** regarding delivery of the policy?
    a. If delivered in person, it gives the agent a chance to reinforce a good relationship
    b. Mailing the policy directly to the policyowner constitutes legal delivery
    c. Delivery of the policy is necessary to complete the life insurance sale
    d. Delivery of the policy is not necessary if a permanent conditional receipt has been issued
12. Which of the following statements is/are **true**?
    a. Replacement is illegal
    b. Replacement is the purchase of one life insurance policy to replace another
    c. Replacement laws are designed to protect the interests of life insurance purchasers
    d. Replacement laws concern themselves with the use of false and misleading statements used in the sale of insurance
13. If replacement is involved, the agent must:
    (1) ________________________________
    ____
    (2) ________________________________
    ____
    (3) ________________________________
    ____
14. Since the agent is an agent of the insurer, the insurer must make sure that ________________
    ____
    ____

☞ ***Answers to Review Questions are located at the back of the book.***

5

LIFE INSURANCE POLICIES

There are four basic types of life insurance: ordinary (individual), group, industrial, and credit life. It is important for the agent to know and understand each of these types of life insurance. However, most often, the agent will be recommending some form of ordinary life insurance to an individual or in a business situation. In this chapter, we will examine individual policies in detail and review industrial and credit life insurance policies briefly.

There are several types of ordinary life insurance. These various policies can be used separately or in combination with each other to solve an individual's life insurance needs.

TERM INSURANCE

Term policies provide temporary insurance protection for a specific term of years only. The term may be for one year, five years, 10 years, 20 years, to a specific age, or anything in between, although the intervals mentioned are the most common forms. The policy will only pay benefits if the policyholder should die *during* the term. If the insured lives beyond the period of coverage, the policy will expire with nothing due the insured.

Term insurance may be issued as renewable, renewable and convertible (R&C) or nonrenewable. Nonrenewable term is temporary protection for a specified period of time and when the term period ends, the coverage ends.

A **renewable** term policy is one which may be renewed at the end of the specified period of time for another term period *without evidence of insurability* (however, the renewal policy premium will be based on the insured's attained age). Thus, a one year renewable term policy expires after one year but is renewable for additional one year periods. A five year renewable term policy can be renewed for subsequent five year periods. Renewability may be limited to a certain number of renewals or to a specified age.

A term policy which is **convertible** allows the policyowner to convert or exchange the temporary protection for permanent protection without evidence of insurability. Usually, this conversion feature is used to convert term insurance to some form of whole life insurance. If the conversion privilege is exercised it will be at attained age; meaning the premium paid for the new policy will be the insured's age at the time of conversion.

Most often term insurance policies are issued as renewable and convertible (R&C).

Types of Term Policies

The types of term policies are defined by the way the face amount of the policy changes throughout the life of the policy. The **face amount**, or **face value**, of the policy is the amount of money listed on the face page (first page) of the policy. This is the amount that will be paid in the event of the insured's death. There are three types of term policies. **Level term** provides a level death benefit and level premium during the policy term. For example, if an individual purchases a 10-year R&C term policy with a face amount of $100,000, both the premium and the face amount will remain constant for the entire 10-year period.

Assuming the level term policy is issued as renewable and convertible, every time the policy renews for a subsequent term period, the policy's premium will increase due to the increased age of the insured.

For example, an insured has purchased $50,000 of one-year renewable and convertible term insurance. Each year the policy is simply renewed at the same face amount by the payment of the new, higher premium. A new application is not required nor is a new policy issued. The only thing which changes is the age of the insured and subsequently the policy's premium.

LEVEL DEATH BENEFIT
FOR THE LIFE OF THE POLICY

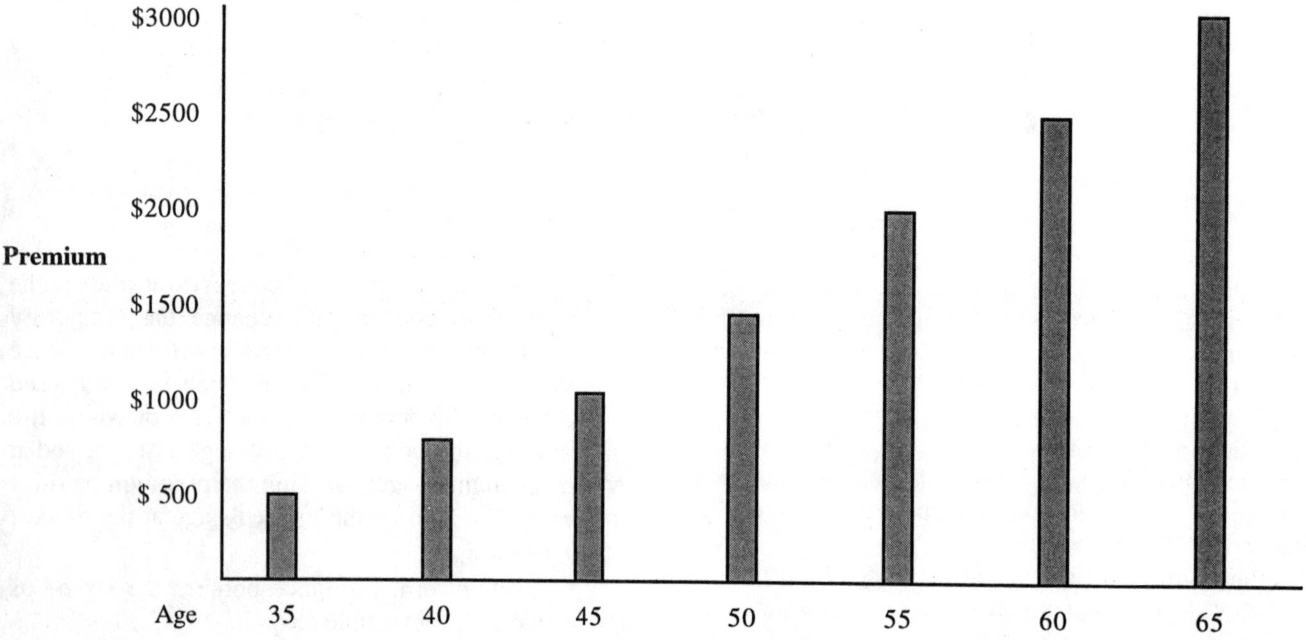

Chart 5-1
$100,000 5 Year R&C Term

Decreasing term is also temporary protection for a specified period of time. The face amount decreases throughout the life of the policy down to zero at the date of policy expiration. The annual premium remains level during the term of the policy. This type of insurance is appropriate for individuals having a declining need for coverage over time; for example, the amount needed to cover the outstanding balance on a home mortgage.

Decreasing term is usually written as convertible but generally is not renewable at the end of the term period. The convertible feature allows the policyowner to convert to permanent insurance usually at any point during the decreasing term of the policy for the available amount of insurance at that point in time. As is true with any conversion feature, this option is exercised at the insured's attained age at the time of conversion.

LEVEL PREMIUM AMOUNT
FOR THE LIFE OF THE POLICY

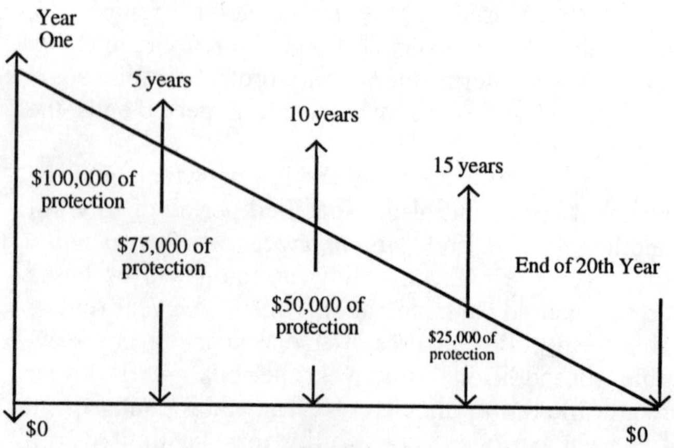

CHART 5-2
$100,000 20 YEAR DECREASING TERM INSURANCE

Increasing term is another type of term insurance which is not used as often as level or decreasing term. Increasing term is basically the opposite of decreasing term. The death benefit increases over the life of the policy, and the premium remains level.

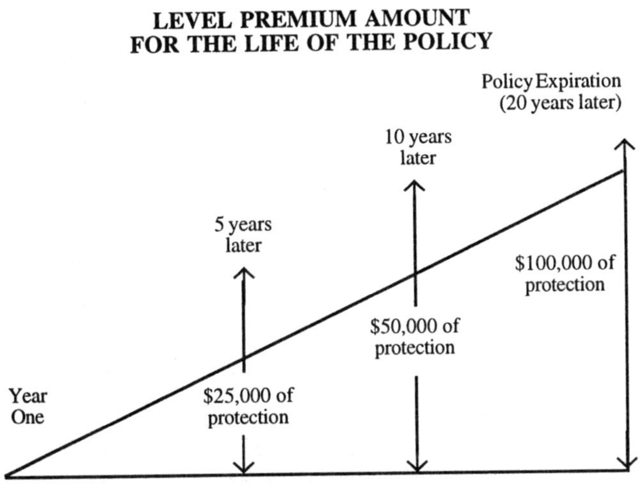

CHART 5-3
$100,000 20 YEAR INCREASING TERM INSURANCE

Advantages and Uses of Term Insurance

Some of the advantages and uses of term insurance are as follows:

- Initially, the cost of term insurance is low and accordingly, it is often used by individuals or businesses who may have a large need for insurance but limited financial resources to pay for it.
- As temporary protection, it is often used to help cover temporary needs. For example, decreasing term is frequently used to cover the decreasing financial obligation associated with a home mortgage.
- Term insurance can be flexible. Frequently it is used to provide additional protection for an insured. For example, a husband has a relatively small whole life policy and becomes a father of twins. His responsibilities have suddenly changed and there is a need for possibly large amounts of additional life insurance. Term insurance could provide the solution to this problem. Often, the additional insurance is added to the existing policy by means of a rider.

Disadvantages of Term Insurance

Some of the disadvantages associated with term insurance are:

- Over a long period of time, renewable term insurance becomes very expensive. Although initially the level term premium is low, it increases with each renewal based on the increased age of the insured and the increased risk of mortality for the insurance company. Thus, a relatively low premium at age 35 becomes an expensive and sometimes prohibitive premium at age 55 or 60.
- Even though the premium for decreasing term remains level for the life of the contract, this level premium pays for less and less insurance. In the later years of a decreasing term policy, the actual cost of the remaining insurance tends to be expensive.
- One of the disadvantages of term insurance is its very nature — it is temporary protection for a limited period of time. If the policy is not renewable or due to the increasing cost of the policy, the insured can be left without insurance at a time (older ages) when he or she needs the protection the most. Some experts put it this way: term policies are actuarially designed to expire before you do.
- Term insurance is pure death protection only. It offers no living benefits such as guaranteed cash values.
- Even if the term policy is renewable, it generally is not renewable beyond a certain age such as age 65 or 70. Again, there is the danger of losing or not being able to afford the protection at these ages.

WHOLE LIFE INSURANCE

Although the first policy of life insurance on record was issued in 1563, all policies issued for the next 200 years were either short term or endowment. The few "whole life" policies issued were for undetermined face amounts. The formula for a policy issued for the whole of life on a level premium basis eluded mathematicians until 1762. In that year, the Society for the Equitable Assurance of Lives & Survivorships (today commonly referred to as "Old Equitable" and one of Britain's leading life insurance companies) came out with a whole-life, level-premium, fixed-amount policy. This is the form known today as "whole life" or "permanent life."

As the name implies, this policy form offers insurance coverage for the whole of life (or up to age 100, which is the ultimate age on the mortality table now in common use; if the insured lives to 100, the cash value equals the face amount and is paid to him or her in a lump sum). Chart 5-4 is a diagram of a $100,000 whole life policy to help you conceptualize whole life insurance.

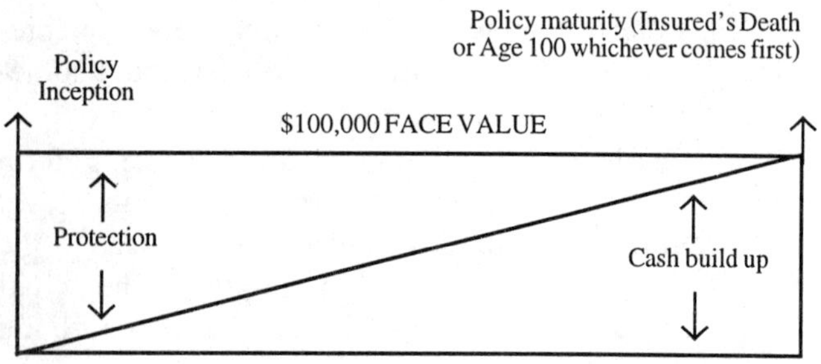

CHART 5-4
WHOLE LIFE INSURANCE

As you can see, the first day the policy is in force, the insured has $100,000 of protection. If the insured should die one week, one month, one year, 10 years, or 50 years later his beneficiaries would be paid $100,000 at the time of his death. The face amount of the policy remains the same throughout the life of the policy (and the insured).

Since the face amount of the policy is payable upon the death of the insured, the element of risk to the insurance company is much different than it is for, say, an automobile policy. When an insurance company issues an auto policy it hopes that the insured will be a safe driver and will never have an accident. When an insurance company issues a whole life policy, it knows it will someday be called upon to pay a claim because every human being dies. For the insurer, the only unknown is whether the claim will be made in one year, or in 50.

Characteristics of All Whole Life Policies

Level Premiums. Premiums for whole life policies are level and guaranteed for the life of the contract. There will not be an increase in the premium. The premium paid by the policyowner at age 25 will be the same premium paid at age 75.

Level Face Amount. Not only does the premium remain level for the life of the policy, but also the face amount of the policy. Generally, the policy's basic face amount will not change for the life of the policy.

Guaranteed Cash Value. Unlike term insurance which is pure death protection only, whole life provides a guaranteed "living benefit", the policy's cash value. Usually, in the first couple of years of the policy, the cash value is equal to zero but over the life of the policy, there is a steady increase in the amount of the cash until at age 100, the cash value is exactly equal to the policy's face amount.

The policyowner is entitled to this living benefit at any time. If the policyowner decides to cease paying premiums, he or she may "cash the policy in" for the available cash value.

The cash value can also be "loaned" to the policyowner. The term, "loan" is used but this loan does not have to be repaid unless the policyowner elects to repay it. Often, the cash value of the policy may be needed by the policyowner for emergencies, to help pay the cost of a child's college education or for any purpose whereby the policyowner simply needs cash.

If the policyowner takes a cash value loan (for the available amount of cash at that point in time) and elects not to repay it, the amount borrowed will reduce the face amount of the policy. This unpaid loan amount will be identified as an indebtedness against the policy and accordingly the policy's face amount will be reduced by the amount of indebtedness.

For example, an insured dies with a $10,000 whole life policy which has an outstanding loan of $1,000, the beneficiary would receive $9,000.

As a policy loan, it is also subject to interest. A modest amount of interest is charged on the unpaid loan balance. If this interest is not paid by the policyowner, it too will become an indebtedness against the policy and will subsequently reduce the face amount of the policy.

Types of Whole Life

Continuous premium whole life is the most common type of whole life insurance sold. These policies stretch the premium payments over the whole life of the insured (to age 100). This type of policy is often referred to as "straight life" insurance.

Single premium whole life is simply a whole life policy with one premium payment. The entire cost of the policy is paid up at the time of purchase. For example, instead of paying $600 per year for a $50,000 whole life contract, a 35-year old policyowner elects to pay one premium which pays the policy for life. This single premium is not equal to $600 times the 65 years (to age 100) or $39,000. The single premium will be discounted by the insurer since the entire payment for the life of the policy is subject to interest. Accordingly, this discounted single premium may only be $22,000 depending on the interest and the discount.

Except for the premium payment, the single premium whole life policy has all of the characteristics of continuous payment whole life.

Limited payment whole life policies allow the policyowner to pay for the entire policy in a shorter period of time. The premium for any whole life policy can be broken down into any desired number of installments.

Common forms of limited payment whole life are 20-payment life (meaning payments spread out over

20 years); 30-payment; and life paid-up at age 65. For example, 20-pay life means premium payments for 20 years but lifetime (to age 100) protection. Life paid up at 65 means premium payments to age 65 but the policy provides lifetime protection. A 20-pay life policy matures at age 100 or upon the death of the insured, whichever occurs first. The principal difference with limited pay policies is simply the length of the premium paying period.

Chart 5-5 illustrates the 20-pay life concept.

20-Pay Life

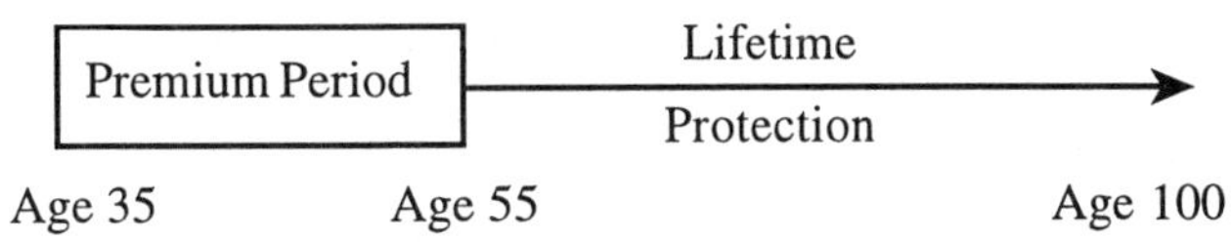

Chart 5-5

A secondary difference between limited pay and continuous pay whole life is the size of the premium and the policy's cash value. Limited pay premiums will be higher than continuous pay whole life policies because the limited pay premium will be paid to the insurer for a shorter period of time. Therefore, the actual premium paid each month or each year will be higher than the premium paid by a policyowner who theoretically will pay premiums to age 100.

Because more premium is being paid, the policy's cash value will be higher than continuous payment whole life. This higher cash value will generally be apparent during the premium paying period of the limited pay life policy. In the later years of the policy and at age 100, the cash value of a limited pay policy will be equal to the cash value of a continuous pay whole life contract.

Indeterminate premium whole life policies are nonparticipating contracts which were developed to compete with participating policies. These policies employ a *dual premium* concept — a maximum premium and discounts which may reduce the premium. The discounts will vary with insurance company investment performance, but the actual premium charged will never be more than the maximum premium specified in the contract.

To bring this discussion of the various types of ordinary policies into some perspective, the following examples illustrate the differences in these ordinary policy types.

These premium examples illustrate the fact that an individual, age 35, who purchases a one-year R&C level term contract pays only $1.20 per $1,000 of insurance. This same person would be paying $28.87 per $1,000 at age 65 due to the annual increase in the premium. This demonstrates that initially the cost of term is low but over the life of the policy, the cost becomes expensive. This is especially true when compared to a level premium whole life contract. A whole life policy purchased at age 35 generates a $16.05 level premium for life. The term premium becomes higher than the whole life sometime after age 55.

Note of course, that the limited pay contracts produce a higher level premium because of the limited premium paying period. Also note that a life paid up at age 65, purchased at age 55, actually becomes a 10-pay life with a relatively high premium.

Chart 5-7 demonstrates the differences in cash values among some of the whole life contracts. The primary reason for the differences is due to the amount of premium paid for these policies. The higher the premium, the higher the initial cash value. However, at age 100, all cash values are equal.

Examples of Annual Premiums Per $1,000 of Insurance

Age	1-Year R&C Term	Whole Life	Life Paid Up at Age 65	20-Pay Life
35	$ 1.20	$16.05	$22.11	$27.00
45	3.90	23.01	37.12	37.12
55	12.92	33.66	66.98	57.18
65	28.87	46.09	—	79.90

Chart 5-6

Cash Value per $1,000 of Insurance — Issue Age 35

Policy Year	Whole Life	Life Paid Up At 65	20—Pay Life
1	$ 0	$ 0	$ 2
2	0	4	10
3	1	11	19
4	5	21	33
5	14	38	57
10	90	160	204
20	322	429	509
At Age 65	502	688	707
At Age 100	1,000	1,000	1,000

Chart 5-7

Current Assumption Whole Life

This type of whole life offers flexible premium payments which are tied into current interest rate fluctuations. The insurance company reserves the right to increase or decrease the premium within a certain range depending on interest rate fluctuations. During a period of relatively high interest rates, premiums could be reduced. During periods of low interest rates, premiums could be increased within certain limits. Usually, any premium adjustment is made on an annual basis.

Economatic

This is a whole life-type policy with a term rider which uses dividends to purchase additional paid-up insurance. Let's assume that an individual wants $100,000 of whole life but can't quite afford it. Instead, he purchases $70,000 of whole life with $30,000 of term insurance. Thus, he has $100,000 of death protection at a lower cost.

As policy dividends are declared, they are used to purchase additional paid-up insurance. As the paid-up insurance is added, an equal amount of term insurance is removed from the policy thus maintaining the full face amount of $100,000 at no additional cost. In reality, the cost of the insurance may decrease as the term amounts are eliminated if a level term rider was used. If a decreasing term rider were used, the reduction of the term insurance would become "automatic" but a level premium would be paid for the decreasing term.

When the paid-up additions equal $30,000, the insured now owns $100,000 of whole life but only pays an economical premium for $70,000.

Advantages and Uses of Whole Life

The principal advantage of whole life is that it is permanent insurance and accordingly can be used to satisfy permanent needs such as the cost of death, dying and final burial expenses.

The level premium allows the policyowner to always know exactly what the cost of insurance will be and basically offers a form of forced savings.

Whole life builds a living benefit through its guaranteed cash value which enables the policyowner to use some of this cash for emergencies, as a supplemental source of retirement income and other living needs.

Disadvantages of Whole Life Insurance

Some of the disadvantages of whole life insurance are:

- The premium paying period may last longer than the insured's income-producing years.
- It does not provide as much protection per dollar as term insurance.

REVIEW QUESTIONS

1. ______________ policies provide temporary insurance protection for a specific term of years only.
2. ______________ means an insured has the right to change his or her term policy to a whole life or endowment type of policy.
3. A ______________________________ whole life policy is purchased with one lump sum payment.

☞ ***Answers to Review Questions are located at the back of the book.***

ENDOWMENTS

The third principal type of ordinary life insurance is the **endowment**. Endowments can generally be perceived as a forced savings plan with a death benefit feature. An endowment policy has all of the same elements as a whole life policy. The primary difference is that it matures earlier (at a specified age or date) so the cash value must build up more rapidly and the premium is higher per $1,000 of coverage.

If a person were to open a savings account in a local bank with the intention of accumulating $10,000 in a 20-year period of time but died one month later, his or her survivor would only receive what had been deposited (plus interest) in the savings account as of the date of death.

Conversely, if the same person had purchased a $10,000 20-year endowment policy and died one month later, the beneficiary would receive $10,000 (the amount the insured wanted to accumulate over 20 years). Thus, an endowment might be defined as a forced savings plan with a death benefit.

Specifically, an endowment provides for the payment of the policy's face amount if the insured dies during the endowment period or it pays the face amount to the insured, if the insured survives to the end of the endowment period. The endowment period is the length of time that the policyowner pays the premium. When the premium period is ended, the endowment matures on the maturity date and pays the face amount to the insured (policyowner). Endowments are purchased for various periods of time, i.e., 10 or 20 years, or to age 65. Chart 5-8 illustrates a 20-year endowment.

20-year endowment

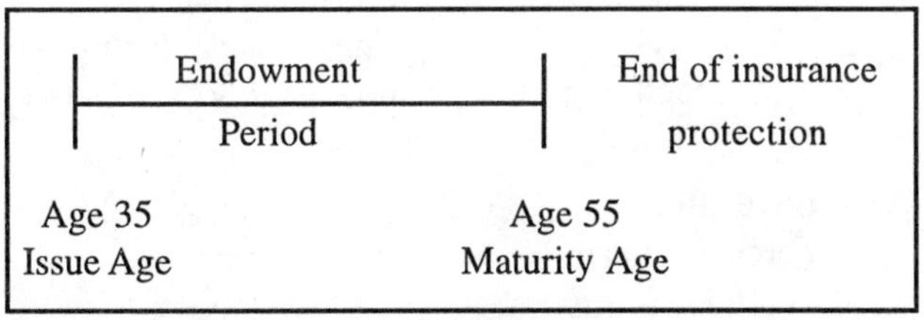

Chart 5-8

It should be noted that when the policy matures, there is no longer any insurance protection. The policy matures for the face amount as a living benefit. The overall concept of an endowment is very similar to that of whole life, except that the cash value accumulates more rapidly and the premiums are higher. It could be said, that whole life matures at death or at age 100 whichever occurs first. It could be said that whole life is an endowment at age 100.

Types of Endowments

A **retirement endowment** is one of the most commonly sold endowment contracts. Typically, this type of policy is issued to mature at age 65 when the insured plans to retire. Like whole life insurance, the face value is payable as a death benefit if the insured dies before the maturity date. However, at maturity, the full face amount becomes payable as a living benefit, usually in the form of monthly installment income.

Another version of the endowment concept is the **pure endowment**. This policy offers no life insurance protection. The pure endowment provides for the payment of the policy's face amount only if the insured lives to the maturity date. If the insured dies prior to the endowment date, all benefits are forfeited. Because this is essentially a high risk savings plan (all savings are lost upon early death), it is rarely sold.

Endowment life insurance is a combination of a pure endowment plus term insurance for a specified period of time. The pure endowment provides living benefit at the end of the endowment period. The term insurance pays a death benefit to the insured's beneficiary if he or she dies prior to the end of the endowment period.

Juvenile endowment policies are designed to mature at a specific age, such as age 18 so that the maturity value is available to help fund a college education.

The charts that follow provide a comparison of the endowment to the other forms of ordinary life insurance with respect to the premiums paid and the cash values.

Since a 20-year endowment matures as a death claim or as a living benefit after 20 years, all of the necessary premium must be paid in a relatively short period of time thus the cost of the endowment is considerably higher than the cost for the other policy forms.

The greater the premium paid, the higher will be the cash value in the early years of the contract. The 20-year endowment ends after 20 years. Thus, it matures for the policy's cash value within 20 years.

Advantages and Uses of Endowments

The primary advantage of an endowment is its forced savings with a life insurance benefit. The insured is able to systematically save a sum of money with the death protection element during the endowment period.

Examples of Annual Premiums per $1,000 of Insurance

Age	1-Year R&C Term	Whole Life	20-Pay Life	20-Year Endowment
35	$ 1.20	$16.05	$27.00	$42.04
45	3.90	23.01	37.12	55.16
55	12.92	33.66	57.18	78.11

Chart 5-9

Cash Value per $1,000 of Insurance — Issue Age 35

Policy Year	Whole Life	20-Pay Life	20-Year Endowment
1	$ 0	$ 2	$ 10
2	0	10	42
3	1	19	86
4	5	33	130
5	14	57	199
10	90	204	466
20	322	509	1,000
Age 65	502	707	
Age 100	1,000	1,000	

Chart 5-10

The endowment is primarily a vehicle which provides a living benefit.

Disadvantages of Endowments

Endowments are not primarily life insurance. They do provide a death benefit for a limited period of time only. Endowments should not be purchased if the person's primary need is life insurance protection.

Because an endowment matures in a relatively short period of time as a living benefit (10 or 20 years for example), the premiums are extremely high in comparison to other forms of life insurance. Thus, endowment insurance is very expensive.

REVIEW QUESTIONS

Match the following numbered definitions with the lettered terms below:

____ 4. Covers for the whole of life, or up to age 100

____ 5. A policy having a face amount which decreases throughout the life of the policy

____ 6. Type of whole life policy paid for in a given period of time

____ 7. Type of policy that provides life insurance protection plus a specific sum of money at the end of the protection period

____ 8. Allows the insured to convert his or her term policy into a whole life or endowment policy without providing new evidence of insurability

____ 9. Type of life insurance policy not many can afford because it requires one lump sum payment

____ 10. Characteristic of whole life policies that, regardless of the premium payment method chosen, premiums never increase

____ 11. Only pays if the insured dies during the specific policy period; usually 5 years, 10 years, etc.

A. Convertible
B. Decreasing term
C. Level premiums
D. Limited payment whole life
E. Term insurance
F. Single premium whole life
G. Whole life insurance
H. Endowment insurance

Answers to Review Questions are located at the back of the book.

SPECIALIZED POLICY FORMS

There are a number of life insurance policies that have been designed to fit specialized situations. Some of the more frequently used forms will be discussed here. These forms are merely combinations or modifications of the three basic ordinary policy forms: whole life, term, and endowment. Many of these special policy names vary by company, and many companies have produced variations of these basic combinations.

Family Income Policies

One of the most popular, and perhaps most useful, of the combination life insurance contracts is the family income policy. Combining *whole life* insurance with *decreasing term* coverage, this policy provides temporary protection and permanent coverage. The term portion of the coverage provides monthly income benefits for the family and the permanent (whole life) part of the policy provides a lump sum payment.

Some family income policies split the lump sum payment into two payments. In this case one-half the policy's face amount would be paid to the beneficiary after the insured's death to assist in paying for the funeral expenses and the costs of last illness. This would then be followed by the specified income (installment) payments for a period of years. At the end of the payment period, there would be another lump sum payment equal to one-half the face amount of the policy.

Thus, a family income policy provides a family income period plus a lump sum benefit. Accordingly, the policy has two time elements. The family income portion of the policy corresponds to the decreasing term time period. The base part of the policy is usually whole life and thus some degree of protection is provided for the whole of life (to age 100).

If the term part of the policy is represented by 20-year decreasing term, then the family income period is for 20 years. This 20-year period begins with the effective date of the policy as does the 20-year decreasing term portion. The actual monthly family income benefit is triggered by the death of the insured.

If the insured outlives the term of years specified in the family income coverage, the decreasing term insurance ceases, and the insured continues the basic policy to maturity, which is either death or the attainment of age 100 (in the case of whole life insurance).

The family income policy fulfills the need for higher amounts of coverage during the initial child rearing years. When the children become self-supporting the need for protection and coverage is reduced.

Chart 5-11 illustrates the family income concept.

If the insured died at age 50, the family income benefit would be payable for five years. If the insured died at age 57, then only the whole life portion would be paid as a death benefit.

Family Maintenance Policies

The family maintenance policy consists of a combination of permanent whole life insurance plus level term insurance. It too consists of a temporary income period plus lifetime protection. The level term part of the policy provides a monthly income (triggered by the death of the insured) and the whole life portion provides the lifetime protection.

The monthly income benefit is usually based on multiples of $10 or $20 per $1,000 of whole life insurance. Thus, a $20 family maintenance policy with a $10,000 base of whole life would provide $200 of monthly income upon the death of the insured for a specified period of time such as 10, 15 or 20 years.

The primary difference between the family income policy and the family maintenance policy is the length of the income period. The income period begins on the date of the insured's death provided that the insured dies during the period of the level term protection.

Chart 5-12 demonstrates the family maintenance concept.

Since death occurs within the 20-year level term portion of the policy, monthly income benefits are payable for a full 20 years.

The Family Policy (Family Protection Policy)

The insurance industry has developed a package life insurance contract to protect all members of a family under one policy, usually termed a "family policy" or "family plan". Its purpose is to provide minimal amounts of coverage on each member of the family. Usually, most of the premium dollar purchases *whole life* insurance for the head of the household, while *term* insurance in smaller face amounts is written on the other members of the family. The coverage for children begins automatically, usually when they are a few days old, and continues up to a stated age, often 18.

Generally, family plans are sold or purchased with reference to units of insurance. A unit might equal $2,500 (or some other amount) of coverage. Thus, when a family plan is purchased, it would be stated for example that the husband/father has four units of coverage and the wife/mother, two units of coverage and each child, one unit of coverage. This translates into $10,000 of whole life on the husband, $5,000 of

20-Year Family Income Plan
$20 per $1,000 Face Amount
Issue Age 35

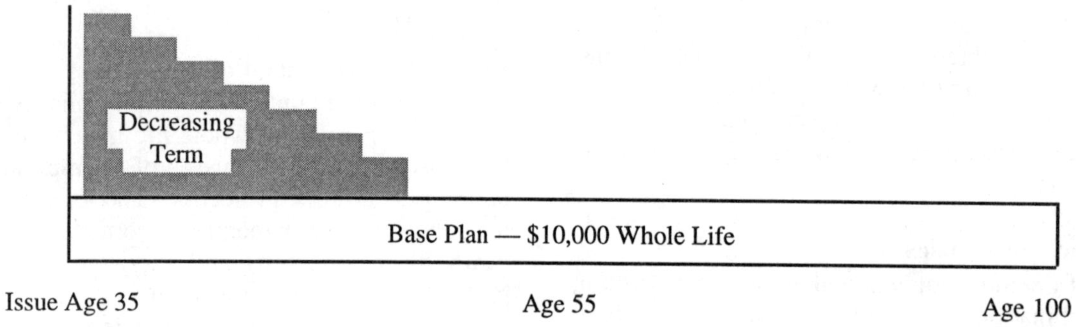

Chart 5-11

20-Year Family Maintenance Plan
$20 per $1,000 Face Amount
Issue Age 35

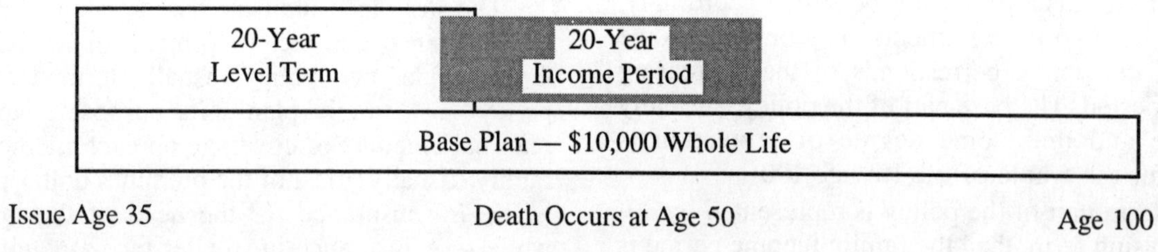

Chart 5-12

level term on the wife and $2,500 of level term on each child currently alive (and under age 18) or yet to be born of this marriage.

Occasionally the term insurance may be written as decreasing term instead of level term. Typically, if decreasing term is used, the amount of insurance will decrease to zero when a child reaches age 18. The decreasing term placed on one of the spouses will normally decrease to zero by the time the person reaches age 65. Whether decreasing or level term is used, the term coverage is written as convertible term.

Retirement Income

The retirement income policy accumulates a sum of money for retirement while providing a death benefit. Upon retirement, the policy pays an income such as $10 per $1,000 of life insurance for the insured's lifetime or a specified period. These policies are expensive, and cash value accumulation is high to pay for the monthly income. Once the cash value in the policy becomes greater than the face amount, that cash amount becomes the death benefit.

Joint Life Policies

These are whole life contracts written with two or more persons as named insureds. Most commonly, the policy is issued on two lives with the insured amount payable on the death of the first insured only. However, policies may be found that pay on both deaths and even (usually for business insurance purposes) pay on the first death and then increase the amount of coverage on the remaining insured or insureds so that the total coverage remains the same.

A variation of the joint life policy is the **last survivor policy**. It pays the insured amount, not to the beneficiaries of the first insured to die but to those of the last.

Usually, a joint life policy will provide a conversion or exchange privilege for the surviving insured whereby that person may continue the coverage on his or her life following the death of the other insured.

Juvenile Policies

Juvenile life insurance is any form written on the lives of minors. One type of policy is commonly called the "jumping juvenile policy" because it automatically increases in face amount at a given age, usually 21, but the premium remains level. The usual "jump" is from $1,000 to $5,000.

A **payor benefit** provision may be added to a juvenile policy for an extra premium which provides that the premiums on the child's policy will be waived if the applicant (usually a parent) dies or becomes disabled before the child attains a stated age (usually 21).

Minimum Deposit

This is a high cash and loan value *whole life* form, usually offering a loan immediately upon payment of the first premium (instead of at the end of the first year). Such policies were devised in the late 1950s to take advantage of the fact that at the time, Internal Revenue allowed the interest paid on a policy loan to be deducted in full for income tax purposes. Thus a prospect could buy such a policy and immediately borrow back the loan value so that, in effect, his or her initial premium outlay was very small. Since that time, however, Internal Revenue has placed restrictions on the interest deduction when the loan is to finance insurance so that the popularity of the form has diminished.

Modified Life

Modified life is typically a whole life product which is purchased at a very low premium for a short period of time (three to five years) followed by a higher premium for the life of the policy. The policy may be a combination of *term* for the "modified" period automatically converting to a *whole life* premium so that premiums are lower than average during the modified period and slightly higher than average (to make up for the early deficit) thereafter. Generally, this type of policy is sold to an individual who desires whole life but for the next few years is unable to pay the typical premium for whole life. The individual is thus afforded the opportunity to purchase whole life with a modified premium for the initial three to five years of the policy. Chart 5-13 depicts this concept.

Graded Premium

Graded premium whole life is similar to modified whole life in that initially the premium is very low. Unlike modified life which has one increase to a higher, level premium for the life of the contract, graded premium policies provide for an increase in premium each year for the first 5 to 10 years of the policy. At the end of this "step rated" premium period, the premium remains level for the life of the policy.

Graded premium policies, like modified life contracts, are designed to allow the policyowner to purchase a version of whole life without the initial cost of whole life. These contracts are aimed at the young individual just beginning a job or career and whose income will increase in future years.

It should be noted that graded premium (and modified life) policies build cash value but the amount of the cash value is usually less because of the smaller outlay of premium. Typically, a graded premium policy will have very little, if any, cash value during the graded premium period. Chart 5-14 illustrates the graded premium policy.

$10,000 Modified Life Plan
Issue Age: 35

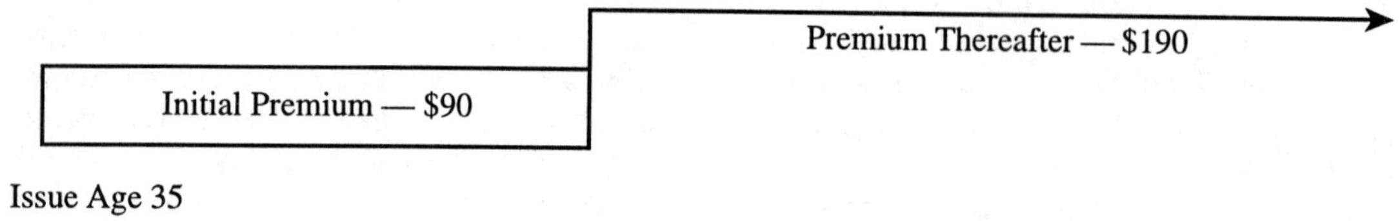

Chart 5-13

$10,000 5-Year Graded Premium Policy
Initial Premium:

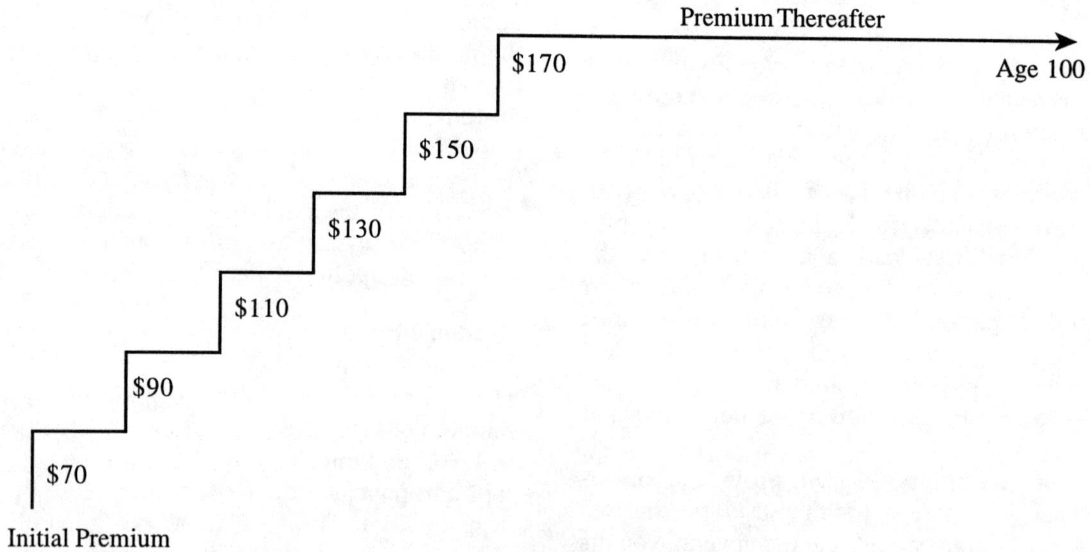

Chart 5-14

Split-Life Policy

The split-life policy is a combination of a whole life or a term life insurance contract and an annuity contract. The savings feature is a retirement annuity to age 65, and the life insurance feature is usually yearly renewable term insurance. The sale of the split-life policy has not been approved in all states, because it seems to discriminate in favor of those individuals who purchase annuities. Those who do not purchase an annuity along with their life insurance do not receive the same low cost benefits as those who do purchase the annuity. The insurance contract may be renewed as long as the annuity premium continues to be paid. The most common amount of coverage found is up to $10,000 of term insurance for each $10 of annuity premium paid.

Mortgage Redemption

The mortgage redemption policy or rider is simply decreasing term insurance. The benefit amount of the term element is intended to be sufficient to pay off the unpaid remainder of the mortgage loan, if the insured dies before paying it off himself or herself.

Multiple Protection

Multiple protection policies are combinations of whole life and term whereby the amount of protection is higher in the early years of the policy and less in the later years. For example, the current death benefit may be described as equal to two times the benefit at age 65 (double protection). If the age 65 (and thereafter) benefit is $5,000, then the insured has $10,000 of protection up to age 65. In essence, the additional death benefit prior to age 65 is term insurance.

Index-Linked Policies

Due to high inflationary periods, many companies offer policies with face amounts increasing by the amount of inflation. The policy amounts are generally linked to the Consumer Price Index. There are two ways of providing this additional coverage. Either the premium is increased every year to cover the increased insurance amount, or the life insurance company makes assumptions about what it expects the increases to be at policy inception and the insured pays the same (but higher than average) premium over the life of the policy.

Deposit Term Insurance

Deposit term insurance is a level term insurance policy that has a much higher premium for the first year than for subsequent years. The initial premium is significantly higher than the average premium needed to cover the cost of mortality during the term period. The excess front end premium (the deposit) is then set aside to earn interest, and these dollars (deposit plus interest) will be applied to reduce the premium payments required in the following years. The premium levels are set so that the entire deposit will be exhausted when the final annual premium is paid. In effect, this arrangement provides a method of paying a portion of the premium in advance.

For example, the annual premium for a 10-year level term policy for a particular insured may be $500 (total outlay of $5,000). The same type of policy may be purchased as a deposit term contract for an initial premium of $2,500 followed by annual premiums of $200 (total outlay of $4,300). The initial deposit and interest are used to make up the difference in premium. Mathematically, the insurance company actually receives an equal amount of premium for these two policies when the time factor and interest earnings are taken into account.

REVIEW QUESTIONS

12. What types of life insurance makes up the:
    a. Family Income Policy? ____________________
    ____
    b. Family Maintenance Policy? ____________________
    ____
    c. Family Policy? ____________________
    ____

☞ ***Answers to Review Questions are located at the back of the book.***

FLEXIBLE POLICIES

While traditional policies have served the needs of the public for many decades, more recently several new types of life insurance products have been developed and marketed to meet the needs of the public. These new products include adjustable life, universal life and variable life insurance. Each of these contemporary products has its own unique features and characteristics. However, one factor that each of these policies has in common is its flexibility. These newer life insurance products generally offer the policyowner flexibility in terms of premiums, face amounts and investment objectives.

Adjustable Life Insurance

Adjustable life is a policy which offers the policyowner the options to adjust the policy's face amount, premium and length of protection without ever having to complete a new application or have another policy issued. Adjustable life introduces the flexibility to convert to any form of insurance (such as from term to whole life) without adding, dropping, or exchanging policies. Adjustable life is based on a money purchase concept.

The basic premise becomes not so much which type of policy does a person buy but rather how much premium is to be spent. For example, if an applicant, age 25, states that he or she can afford to pay a $500 annual premium, it then becomes a matter of using this premium commitment to meet the individual's needs and to identify the type of insurance to be purchased.

To further illustrate, let's assume the 25 year old applicant is married with three children and a large home mortgage and has no other life insurance. This person naturally needs a large amount of insurance. Based on the $500 premium, it might be recommended that all or most of that premium be used to purchase several hundred thousands of term insurance.

In later years, this same individual may adjust the premium, the face amount or the period of the death protection to meet current needs. For example, the insured is now 50 years old and possibly is planning for retirement. The same $500 premium could now be used for some form of permanent insurance protection with guaranteed cash values. The temporary protection is changed to permanent coverage and the death benefit (face amount) would be reduced due to the insured's age and premium commitment.

If the insured makes an adjustment in the policy which results in a higher death benefit, then proof of insurability may be required for the additional coverage.

Universal Life

Universal life was the insurance industry's answer to the extremely high interest rates we experienced in the decade of the 70s. Traditional whole life contracts have earned 3½-5% interest. In an effort to be more competitive, many insurers developed universal life products with relatively high interest rates (8, 10, 12%). These higher interest rates provide universal life with its distinctive characteristic — flexibility.

Flexibility is realized by the following factors:

- The policyowner may increase or decrease the death benefit subject to any insurability requirements
- Premium amounts may be changed as long as enough premium is paid to maintain the policy

Most universal life policies are sold based on the accumulation values and tax-deferred retirement income, rather than on the proposed death benefit. However, policyholders often misunderstand that returns can and do fluctuate, based on investment performance and interest rates. The universal life policy was designed for people who need flexible coverage over the course of their lifetime.

Universal life is basically a whole life policy divided into its two components — death protection and cash value. In essence the death protection takes the form of one-year renewable term insurance and the cash value account realizes current interest rates.

For example, let's assume that the insured's universal life premium is $1,000 annually for $100,000 of coverage. When the premium is paid, an amount necessary to provide one-year renewable term coverage is used to cover the death protection element of the policy. The balance is "deposited" into the cash account where it will earn competitive current interest rates.

Although possibly over simplified, Chart 5-15 illustrates the universal life concept. Annually, the cost of the death protection will increase. The cash account is credited with current interest rates which are guaranteed on an annual basis relative to current market conditions. Many insurers will deduct a sales or administrative charge from the cash value account before crediting interest. Other companies may have a "back end load" whereby a charge is made for any policy withdrawals.

There are actually two interest rates associated with the universal life policy — the current year guaranteed rate and the contract rate. The current guaranteed rate refers to the annual rate which is reflective of current market conditions. Thus, the current rate can change every year. The contract rate is the minimum guaranteed interest rate which the policy guarantees will be paid. For example, the policy's guaranteed rate may be 5%. This amount would be credited to the cash account if the current year's rate fell below 5%.

$100,000 Universal Life Policy
Male, Age 35
Annual Premium: $1,000

PREMIUM				
Death Protection (1-Yr. Renewable Term)		**Cash Account** +	**Interest** =	**Total ***
Age 35	$200	$800	10%	$ 880
36	210	790	10%	869
37	225	775	12%	868
38	245	755	11%	838
39	270	730	11%	810
			TOTAL:	$4,265

* Figures do not take into account the effect of sales charge deductions or compounding of interest.

Chart 5-15

Chart 5-15 also demonstrates the characteristic of flexibility. Assuming interest rates remain relatively high, the cash account can very easily take care of the annual premium for the cost of the death protection so that the policyowner could actually not pay the premium and the required cost for the death protection could be transferred from the cash account.

There are two options regarding the death benefit payable under a universal life policy. **Option 1** (or option A) provides a level death benefit equal to the policy's face amount. As the policy's cash value increases, the mortality risk decreases. Thus, the cost of the death protection actually decreases over the life of the policy and accordingly more of the premium can be placed in the cash account. This is exactly the same concept which applies to whole life (see chart 5-4).

However, due to the higher current interest rates credited to the account, if the cash value increases to an amount equal to or in excess of the policy's face amount, then the death benefit will automatically be increased. Under current tax laws, if the universal life policy is to maintain its status as life insurance and thus provide a tax free death benefit, there must be a degree of mortality risk until the insured's age 95. This is the reason for the automatic increase in the death benefit if the cash value equals or exceeds the policy's face amount. This buffer or corridor between the death benefit and the cash value must be maintained.

Option 2 (or option B) provides for an increasing death benefit equal to the policy's face amount plus the cash account. If we refer back to chart 5-15, at age 39, the insured's death benefit under option 2 would equal $100,000 plus $4,265 of cash value. Unlike option 1, the mortality risk remains at a level amount equal to the policy's face value. Thus, the policyowner will incur a higher expense for the cost of the death protection over the life of the policy and less of the premium will be deposited in the cash account.

Universal life provides for cash value loans in the same manner that whole life or any permanent plan of insurance does. If a loan is taken, it is subject to interest and if unpaid, both the interest and the loan amount will reduce the face amount of the policy.

Many universal life policies will also permit a partial withdrawal or surrender from the cash account. This is not treated as a loan. A partial surrender is not subject to any interest and will reduce the total cash value in the account. If this withdrawal is later repaid, it will be treated as a premium subject to any sales load that the policy may have.

Variable Life Insurance

Variable life insurance products have been marketed in Europe for several decades. They are a relatively recent development in the United States. They are often referred to as **equity products** because they use equity investments and securities as backing for policies. The amount paid as a death benefit varies according to the success of the investment chosen. There is usually a guaranteed minimum death benefit which may increase over the life of the policy. Cash values are not guaranteed and often are determined daily.

Primarily, variable life insurance is a whole life policy designed to protect the policyowner and the beneficiaries from the erosion of their life insurance dollars due to inflation. Thus, it could be said that variable life is designed to be a hedge against inflation.

Historically, during periods of inflation, the stock market usually has kept pace with inflationary trends by increasing in value. In recognition of this fact, the insurers have established **separate accounts** which consist primarily of a portfolio of common stock and other securities-based investments.

In contrast, the insurer's general account consists primarily of safe, conservative investments such as high grade bonds, real estate, certificates of deposit, etc. The premium from traditional life insurance contracts is placed in the company's general account and the entire contract is fully guaranteed by the insurer.

Premiums paid for variable life insurance contracts are placed in the insurer's separate account consisting primarily of common stock and thus there is considerable investment risk to the policyowner and few guarantees. Due to this element of investment risk, the federal government has declared that variable contracts are securities and are thus regulated by the Securities and Exchange Commission (SEC), the National Association of Securities Dealers (NASD) and other federal bodies.

The variable life product is regulated by the Securities Act of 1933, the Securities and Exchange Act of 1934, and the Investment Company Act of 1940. Following is a brief review of these acts as they apply to variable life insurance:

- The Act of 1933 requires a prospectus be delivered at or before the point of sale of a variable life product
- The Act of 1934 requires registration of the company and the company's sales representatives with the federal authorities
- The Act of 1940 provides for the registration of separate accounts as an investment company

Other requirements of the federal laws include a mandatory 45 day free-look provision from the date of policy application. Also, variable life policyowners have voting rights. Under the Act of 1940, the policyowner is allowed one vote for each $100 of cash value. The policyowner must be permitted to convert to traditional whole life insurance within 24 months of policy issuance.

Variable life insurance is also regulated by the state Insurance Department as an insurance product. This dually regulated product requires the following compliance:

- Agents selling variable life products must be registered with the NASD by passing the appropriate licensing exam (usually Series 6 or Series 7).
- The separate account backing the variable policies must be registered with the federal government in accordance with federal laws.
- Agents must also be licensed on a state level to sell life insurance.
- In some states, agents are required to have a separate state variable contracts license.
- All variable contracts must be filed and approved by the state Insurance Department

The 12% Rule. At the time of solicitation, variable life illustrations may not be based on projected interest rates greater than 12%. This prevents both the agent and the policyholder from assuming excessive and unrealistic rates of return. A variety of policy performance illustrations at different rates would be the preferred method for clearly explaining variable life products. Agents should also stress that rates are not guaranteed and historical performance may not be duplicated in the future. Over-reliance on the maximum permissible illustrated rates may mislead the buyer into thinking the rates are guaranteed.

Types of Variable Life. There are basically two types of variable life insurance: scheduled premium variable life and flexible premium variable life.

Scheduled premium variable life requires a periodic level premium be paid to keep the policy in force. Because a specific premium will be paid, this type of variable life provides a guaranteed minimum death benefit equal to the initial face amount of the policy. Excess death benefit may be paid depending on the performance of the policy's separate account. If the portfolio of common stock in the separate account does well, then the variable life policy will perform well. However, the policyowner is guaranteed a minimum death benefit regardless of the performance of the separate account.

The cash value of the scheduled premium variable life policy is not guaranteed. The values are solely dependent upon the performance of the separate account. Due to this factor, any cash value loan is usually limited to 75% of the policy's available cash value.

In most other respects, the scheduled premium variable life contract is very similar to traditional whole life. Chart 5-16 illustrates the scheduled premium variable life policy.

Flexible premium variable life is basically variable universal life. It provides the flexibility of universal life and the hedge against inflation of variable life. Although, flexible premium variable life may provide a minimum guaranteed death benefit, most often there is no guarantee of death benefit or cash values. The performance of the policy is solely based on the performance of the separate account.

There is usually no guaranteed death benefit because of the flexible premium concept. It is very difficult to provide a guaranteed death benefit when the amount of premium to be paid is unknown. Thus, the principal difference between scheduled and flexible premium variable life is the method of paying the premium. Chart 5-17 illustrates a comparison of traditional life insurance forms and variable life insurance.

Scheduled Premium Variable Life Policy

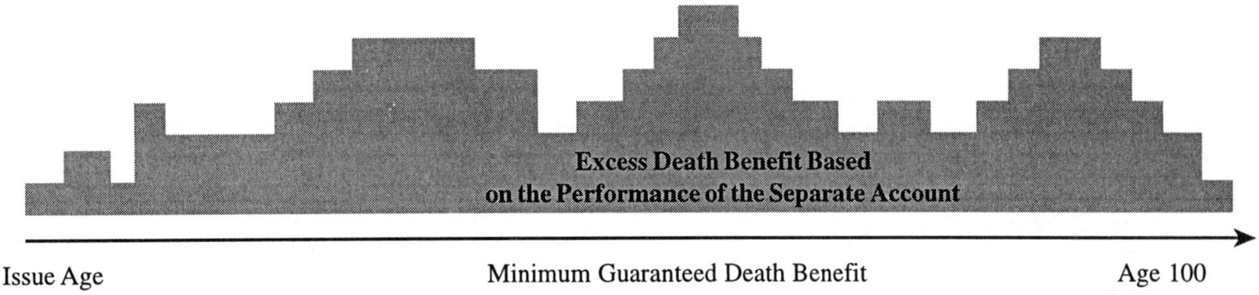

Chart 5-16

Comparison of Traditional Life Insurance Forms and Variable Life Insurance

	Scheduled Premium VL	Whole Life	Flexible Premium VL	Universal Life
Death Benefit	Guaranteed minimum death benefit	Guaranteed death benefit	Not guaranteed	Guaranteed and flexible
Premium	Fixed	Fixed	Flexible	Flexible
Cash Value	Not guaranteed	Guaranteed	Not guaranteed	Guaranteed
Risk	The insured	The insurer	The insured	The insurer
Performance	Based on Separate Account	Based on General Account	Based on Separate Account	Based on General Account
How Regulated	State and Federal	State	State and Federal	State
Taxed as	Insurance and Securities	Insurance	Insurance and Securities	Insurance

Chart 5-17

Variable Universal Life

Variable universal life insurance is a combination of variable life insurance and universal life insurance. The benefits of such a plan are that it combines what are considered the outstanding features of both products.

The policy is variable in that the benefits vary according to the investments backing the contract, and many companies allow the insured to choose the type of investments he or she favors. The insurer will often permit the insured to switch from one investment to another at the insured's option. An insured will make his or her selection based on the investment he or she believes will provide the greatest interest return. The investments the insured selects are not limited to the insurer's portfolio. Eligible investments may include any of the following: stocks, bonds, mutual funds, precious metals, diamonds, real estate in various forms, stamps, coins, or art objects.

This policy is universal in that the following features make it versatile enough to be used over the insured's lifetime:

- Flexible premium
- Adjustable benefit
- Term or endowment insurance
- Tax-deferred savings

The flexible premium feature allows the insured to choose the amount of his or her premium payment. The life insurance benefit will be that which the premium paid will purchase.

The adjustable feature allows the insured to change the benefit, that is, the amount of life insurance in force. The premium payment will then become the amount needed to provide such benefit. The premium payment amount, or the benefit amount, or both the premium and the benefit amounts are dependent upon the performance of the stock portfolio backing the contract.

The term feature provides the insured with adequate life insurance protection at a low cost. The endowment feature provides retirement income, or funds for the children's education. It also provides the insured with money to get started in business. Only the funds which exceed the total amount of premium paid is taxable as income, and only at the time that the funds are actually withdrawn.

REVIEW QUESTIONS

Match the following definitions .with the lettered terms below.

____ 13. Whole life plus level term policy combination

____ 14. Combines life insurance with equity investment (stock)

____ 15. Whole life coverage for the breadwinner and term insurance for other family members

____ 16. Offers a loan value upon payment of the first premium

____ 17. Whole life for two or more insureds

____ 18. Policy combination including whole life and decreasing term

____ 19. Usually a term policy automatically converting to whole life so that premiums are lower during the initial period of coverage

____ 20. Written on the lives of minors

____ 21. Whole life and term life to 65 combination policy

____ 22. Type of policy in which the premium and face amount can be increased or decreased at any time

____ 23. Variable rate of interest credited to cash value based on current market rates

A. Family Income
B. Family Maintenance
C. Family Policy
D. Multiple Protection
E. Joint Life Policies
F. Juvenile Policies
G. Minimum Deposit
H. Modified Life
I. Adjustable Life
J. Variable Life
K. Universal Life

☞ ***Answers to Review Questions are located at the back of the book.***

INDUSTRIAL LIFE & CREDIT INSURANCE

INDUSTRIAL LIFE INSURANCE

The industrial policy is written for a small face amount, usually $1,000 or less, and the premiums are payable as frequently as weekly, and occasionally, monthly. It derived its name from the fact that it was originally sold in England to the "industrial class" of factory workers. This form of insurance was originally sold in America to workers in industry.

The insured would determine how much he could pay each week and the face amount would be determined by the amount of premium the insured could pay. A company representative would call on the insured each week, usually at home, to collect the premium, which usually ranged from five cents to one dollar. The policy benefit was used primarily to pay for last **illness** and **burial expenses.**

This method of distribution is very expensive for two reasons. First, the mortality rates are higher for industrial policyowners because these insureds tend to have higher than average health risks and poorer than average living standards. Second, having the agent collect the premium each week at the customer's home increases the cost of this type of policy.

With the rising incomes of workers, increasing consumer awareness, and the growth of group life insurance, the need for industrial life has decreased considerably over the last several decades. Today, industrial life represents about 1% of life insurance in force. Federal Social Security benefits have also filled a need which was once met by industrial life insurance.

The basic characteristics of industrial life insurance are:

- Premium payments are made frequently.
- Benefits are usually less than $1,000.
- Premiums are collected, by the agent, at the insured's home or workplace.
- Sales are made in premium units rather than in insurance units. The rate book lists the amount of insurance that can be bought with a specified weekly or monthly premium. (This has been changing for larger amounts of insurance.)
- All family members are covered from birth to age 65 or 70.
- Usually a medical examination is not required.

Most of the provisions required in ordinary life policies are also required in industrial life policies. There are some differences in the content of the provisions, but the basic intent is the same. The required industrial provisions are: grace period, entire contract, incontestability, misstatement of age, nonforfeiture, reinstatement, 10-day free look, settlement, owners' rights, and values and options.

Home Service Life Insurance

Today we find a variation in the industrial life concept known as home service life insurance. Policies are usually modest in size, ranging from $10,000 to $15,000 in face value, and are typically sold on a monthly debit plan (automatic bank draft) or payments by mail.

CREDIT LIFE INSURANCE

Billions of dollars of consumer credit are being used in this country today. Most of us make time payments on automobiles, bank loans, and similar obligations.

The unexpected death of an individual who has time payment obligations can create serious problems for his or her family. Credit life insurance provides that, in the event of the death of an insured debtor, the outstanding balance is usually paid off in full.

Credit life insurance can be written on a group basis or in individual credit life policies. It is usually written as a decreasing term type of coverage so the amount of insurance reduces as the amount of the obligation reduces. Level term insurance may also be written which would remain level for the term of the loan. The benefits are payable to the policyowner (the creditor) and are used to reduce or extinguish the unpaid indebtedness.

Usually, the individual debtor pays the total premium. The premium is added to the finance contract amount so that, in effect, the insurance premium is being financed along with the item being purchased. The insurance company receives full premium up front.

If a debtor prepays or refinances the loan, he or she is entitled to cancellation of the credit insurance and a refund of the unearned premium.

SPECIFIC PROVISIONS

Many of the policy provisions gain their uniformity from the NAIC model laws. The standard provisions for group insurance, previously discussed, are similar to the required and optional provisions for individual life found in Chapter 6. Industrial and credit life insurance provisions have some unique features that should be discussed.

Industrial Life Policy Provisions

Most of the provisions found in individual life insurance policies are also found in industrial life insurance. However, consideration should be given to these provisions and their unique application to industrial policies. Because the face amount of the policy is so small, and the cost of this type of insurance is expensive, certain provisions do not have the same impact on industrial-insureds as on individual insureds:

- 31-day grace period (28 days for weekly premium policies)
- The application is not required to be part of the policy
- Medical examinations are not required
- Cash values do not accumulate sufficiently to provide loans
- Settlement options do not apply because of limited cash value
- Suicide provisions are not included in the policy because of the small benefit amount
- Nonforfeiture provisions do not allow the cash option until premiums have been paid for five years (compared to three years for ordinary policies)
- Dividends are used to reduce the premium payment, or to purchase paid-up additions

Credit Life Policy Provisions

Some of the major provisions found in credit life insurance policies are those that provide the following:

- Insureds must be given a certificate of coverage under the creditor's group policy, including their rights and obligations under the policy
- The number of insureds under the policy must be maintained at a specified level (usually 100); if participation drops below that number, the insurer may not insure new debtors
- The debtor's coverage will terminate when the debt is paid off, transferred to another creditor, refinanced, or becomes significantly overdue

Unlike standard group insurance policies, the policy does not have a conversion privilege.

REVIEW QUESTIONS

24. An industrial policy is one usually written for a (small/large) ____________ face amount.
25. Premiums are paid frequently, usually ________ ____________________
26. Industrial insurance is characterized by the insured's need to show evidence of insurability. (True/False) __________
27. Group credit life insurance could be issued to a single individual who took out an installment loan to purchase an automobile. (True/False)________

☞ ***Answers to Review Questions are located at the back of the book.***

Basic Forms of Life Insurance

	Ordinary	Industrial	Group	Credit Life
Policy Types	Whole Life Term Endowments	Whole Life Endowments	Permanent Term Endowments	Term
Face Amounts	$1,000 or more	$1,000 or less	$1,000 or more	Equal to indebtedness
Premiums	Paid by the insured-policyowner	Collected by the agent	Employer paid or employer—employee paid	Paid by the debtor

Chart 5-18

LIFE INSURANCE POLICY RIDERS

Riders take their name from the concept that they have no independent existence. They have force and effect only when they are attached to a policy. A rider is a special provision or arrangement not in the basic policy contract but that has been attached to and made a part of the contract, sometimes for an extra premium. Riders can be used to enhance or add benefits to the policy or they can be used to take benefits away from the policy.

A **waiver** is a type of rider which is usually used to exclude benefits and for which no premium is charged. For example, for underwriting reasons, a waiver may be attached to a policy which excludes benefits for death by a specified cause such as a particularly hazardous hobby or occupation.

The other riders discussed in this section all require the payment of a relatively small additional premium for the benefits provided.

Accidental Death (Double Indemnity)

This rider provides an additional death benefit and a dismemberment benefit for loss of certain body members, if the death or the loss is due to an accident.

The accidental death benefit, usually referred to as the **principal sum** (the rider's face amount), pays an additional death benefit if the cause of death is due to an accident as defined by the policy. Usually, death must occur within 90 days of the accident for the benefit to be paid.

Accidental death is usually defined by the policy in terms of death which occurs while a fare paying passenger (taxi, airplane, train, bus, etc.), death in a burning building, death as the result of a natural disaster (earthquake, tornado, etc.) and generally death caused by other accidents such as drowning or possibly an automobile accident. Death resulting from involvement in illegal activities, or due to illness, war, or suicide is excluded.

The insurer may elect to have a very liberal definition of accidental death or a very strict, limited definition. Regardless, if a death claim is submitted, it must comply with the policy's definition if the additional, accidental death benefit is to be paid.

Typically, the accidental death benefit is provided as double or triple indemnity. Double indemnity has the effect of paying twice the policy's face amount as the total policy benefit. Triple indemnity pays triple the base policy's face amount if death occurs accidentally.

For example, John has a $10,000 whole life policy which contains the accidental death rider (double indemnity). If he is killed accidentally as defined by the policy, the total death benefit will be $20,000. However, it should be noted that the value of the accidental death rider is $10,000. It is an amount equal to the face amount of the policy. The basic whole life amount of $10,000 is increased by another $10,000 due to the rider.

The dismemberment portion of this rider provides for the payment of the **capital sum** (the face amount) in the event that, due to an accident, the insured loses two arms, two legs, two hands or the irrecoverable loss of vision in both eyes. Loss is generally defined as the actual severance or removal of the arm or leg as a result of the accident. Again, the loss usually must occur within 90 days of the accident.

Some companies will pay a reduced capital sum if the insured suffers the loss of only one arm for example. The full capital sum would be paid for the loss of both arms.

There is a small additional premium for this rider, usually less than $1.00 per one thousand dollars of coverage per year.

Waiver of Premium

This rider provides that in the event of total disability as defined by the policy, premiums for the policy will be waived for the duration of the disability. The rider is temporary in that it usually expires at the insured's age 65. However, if a total disability occurred prior to the expiration of the rider, the premiums are waived for the duration of the disability.

There is a six month waiting period before the rider's benefits are payable. This means that the insured must be totally disabled for six months (a few insurers only require three months) and then future premiums will be waived for the duration of the total disability. Once the six month waiting period has been satisfied, any premiums paid during the waiting period will also be refunded to the policyowner.

A small additional premium, usually about $1.00 annually per thousand dollars of insurance, is charged for this rider. This rider and the benefit it provides is very worthwhile to the insured.

A version of this rider is **Waiver of Premium with Disability Income**. The same concept applies as with waiver of premium but this rider will pay a weekly or monthly disability income benefit to the insured in addition to the life insurance premiums being waived.

Guaranteed Insurability

This rider guarantees that on specified dates in the future (or at specified ages or upon the event of specified occurrences such as marriage or birth of a child), the insured may purchase additional insurance without evidence of insurability. The rate for this additional coverage will be that for his or her attained age, not the age at which the policy was issued.

The amount of insurance which can be purchased on the option dates is usually limited to the amount and type of the base policy. Thus, if the insured had a $10,000 whole life policy with the guaranteed insurability rider, he or she could purchase up to an additional $10,000 of whole life coverage on the option dates.

The option dates are usually the policy anniversary nearest the insured's birthdays at ages 25, 28, 31, 34, 37, and 40. In addition, marriage and the birth of children between the ages of 25 and 40 also trigger additional options.

The biggest advantage offered by this rider is the opportunity to buy additional amounts of insurance as one's responsibilities and needs change, without proof of insurability.

The rider expires at the insured's age 40. There is an additional premium which is usually between one and two dollars per $1,000 of option amount.

Return of Premium

This rider was developed primarily as a sales tool to enable the agent to say, "In addition to the face amount payable at your death, we will return all premiums paid if you die within the first 20 years," for example. The rider is simply an increasing amount of term insurance that always equals the total of premiums paid at any point during the effective years. Correctly, the rider does not return premiums but pays an additional amount equal to premiums paid to date of death. The policyowner who purchases the rider is simply buying additional term insurance.

Return of Cash Value

This rider, not often used, was designed to offset the invalid complaint, "When I die, the company confiscates the cash value." Such a complaint is based on lack of understanding of the mathematics involved in a level face value life insurance policy. However, if the agent can say, "We can attach a rider returning the cash value in addition to the face amount," the objection is more easily answered than if it is necessary to explain the mathematics involved. The "return of cash value" rider is similar to the "return of premium" in that it is merely an additional amount of term insurance that is equal to the cash value at any point while effective. Buying it, the policyowner is simply getting additional term insurance. Correctly, the rider does not "return" the cash value: it pays an additional amount of insurance equal to the cash value.

The premium paid for either the return of premium or the return of cash value riders is actually equal to the cost of adding an increasing term insurance rider to the base policy. Accordingly, the term premium would take into account the age of the insured, amount and duration of the term insurance.

Cost of Living

Because of the high inflation years of the 1970s, many insureds were concerned that the face amounts of policies purchased would not be adequate to cover family expenses by the time the death benefit was paid. The cost of living rider changes the face amount of the policy each year by a stated percentage, such as 5%. This amount is compounded annually. This rider can be used to increase the face amount of the policy, depending on that year's cost of living. There are limits on the amount the face amount can be decreased, however.

Additional Insureds

Riders are also commonly attached to life insurance policies to provide coverage on the lives of one or more additional insureds. Usually these are term insurance riders covering a spouse, one or more children, or all family members in addition to the insured policyholder. Many companies will issue additional insured riders on request. Some companies actively market combination coverage policies for family members under the label "family protection policy."

Substitute Insured Rider

Although it seems unusual to allow for the substitution of "insureds" in life insurance, the "substitute insured rider" actually does permit a change of insureds. This would be desirable, for instance, in business-owned life insurance, when a key employee or business executive is insured for the benefit of the corporation. Should this employee terminate employment or retire, the insurance can be "switched" over to apply to the employee's replacement, subject to evidence of insurability. This way, the policy can continue (rather than be terminated and a new policy issued) with the same face amount, and with premiums calculated based on the new insured's age, sex, etc.

Living Need

The Living Need rider is a very recent development in life insurance. This rider allows a terminally ill individual to obtain part of the insurance proceeds prior to death. To be eligible for this benefit the individual must present medical proof of the terminal illness. Most companies offering this benefit will limit the amount of the insurance proceeds which may be paid in this manner.

The purpose of this benefit is to provide the terminally ill person with necessary cash with which to take care of expenses related to the terminal illness, i.e., medical expenses or nursing home expenses.

Most companies do not charge for this rider as it basically is an advance against the death proceeds for which the insured has been paying premiums.

LIVING BENEFIT PROVISIONS ATTACHED TO LIFE INSURANCE POLICIES (ACCELERATED BENEFITS)

Long term care insurance, which reimburses health and social service expenses incurred in a convalescent or nursing home facility, can be marketed as a rider to life insurance policies.

LTC rider benefits are similar to those found in a LTC policy. The benefit structure includes the following:

- Elimination periods of 10-100 days
- Benefit periods of 3-5 years or longer
- Prior hospitalization of at least three days may be required
- Benefits may be triggered by impaired activities of daily living
- Levels of care include skilled, intermediate, custodial, and home health care

In addition, certain optional benefits may also be provided such as adult day care, cost of living protection, hospice care, etc.

There are two approaches to the LTC rider concept. The generalized or independent approach recognizes the LTC rider as independent from the life policy, since the benefits paid to the insured will not affect the life policy's face amount or cash value. The integrated approach links the LTC benefits paid to the life policy's face amount and/or cash value.

The "living benefit" or "living needs" rider combines life insurance and LTC benefits, drawing on the life insurance benefits to generate LTC benefits. In a sense, it's like borrowing from the life insurance to pay LTC benefits. Under the LTC option, up to 70-80% of the policy's death benefit may be used to offset nursing home expenses. Under the Terminal Illness option, 90-95% of the death benefit may be used to offset medical expenses. Of course, payment of LTC benefits reduces the face amount of the life policy.

REVIEW QUESTIONS

Match the following numbered definitions with the lettered terms below.

____ 28. A rider that is actually increasing term insurance always equalling the total premiums paid during the time the policy is in effect

____ 29. A special provision attached to the policy deleting or limiting provisions in the policy

____ 30. Double payment because of this occurrence

____ 31. A waiver of all future premiums in the event of "total" and "permanent" disability

____ 32. A guarantee that at specified ages, dates, or events, the insured may buy additional insurance without a medical exam

A. Rider
B. Guaranteed Insurability
C. Return of Premium
D. Accidental Death
E. Waiver of Premium

33. Describe the difference between the generalized approach and the integrated approach to long term care riders. ________________

34. Discuss the major disadvantage to the "living needs" rider. ________________

☞ ***Answers to Review Questions are located at the back of the book.***

NOTES

6

LIFE INSURANCE POLICY PROVISIONS

An insurance policy is a legal contract. The validity of life insurance policies as such has been established in the United States since 1815 [Lord vs. Ball, 12 Mass. 115 (1815)]. As does any contract, it contains provisions setting forth the rights and duties of parties to the contract. While it is necessary to look beyond the actual wording of the policy contract and into the statutes and court decisions for a full interpretation of these provisions, they are, nevertheless, the basis of the agreement between the company and the policyholder (and the beneficiaries, heirs, and assignees of the policyholder).

There are no "standard" policies in life insurance in the sense that there are in the property and casualty insurance field. However, many states have provisions that are required in all life policies so that the following provisions have become more or less "standard" in such policies.

This chapter will discuss the standard provisions, restrictions and limitations and the beneficiary provisions. For added help, we have included a sample whole life insurance policy in the Sample Policy Section at the end of this manual.

STANDARD PROVISIONS

Insuring Clause

The Insuring Clause states that in consideration of the payment of premiums, the company agrees to pay the face amount to the named beneficiary, upon due proof of death of the insured, or to pay certain benefits if the insured lives to some specified age, such as 65. It sets forth the basic agreement between the company and the insured.

The insuring clause is the company's promise to pay the policy benefits in accordance with the contract's provisions.

The Consideration Clause

Part of the insuring clause states that the company promises to pay the policy benefits in consideration of the premium payments. The consideration clause identifies the fact that the policyowner must pay something of value for the insurer's promise to pay benefits. This valuable consideration is the premium.

Payment of Premium

This provision specifies when, where, and how premiums are to be paid. Usually premiums are to be paid in advance either at the company's home office or to the agent. The various modes of paying the premium will also be identified, such as monthly, quarterly, semi-annually and annually.

In addition, most insurers permit the premium to be paid by means of a monthly bank draft. This method is referred to as Monthly Bank or Automatic Check Plan. The insurer simply sends a monthly premium notice to the policyowner's bank and the bank sends the insurer a check for the monthly premium.

The least expensive way to pay the premium is annually or by a monthly bank plan. The other premium modes require the payment of a service charge added to the basic premium. For example, an annual policy premium may be $300. The monthly premium may be $25.50 which would total $306 of premium in a year.

Ownership Rights

The owner of a life insurance policy is entitled to certain valuable rights. These include the right to assign or transfer the policy, and the right to select and change the payment schedule, beneficiary and settlement option.

The owner also has the right to receive cash values, dividends and the right to borrow from the cash values. As previously discussed the owner and the insured may be two different parties. The policyowner must have an insurable interest in the insured such as would be the case of a father who is the owner of his minor son's policy or a corporation which owns a policy on the life of its president.

This third party ownership arrangement usually offers a tax advantage to the insured. Life insurance proceeds are generally received free of federal income tax but these proceeds are included in the deceased's gross estate for federal estate tax purposes. If the insured has no incidence of policy ownership, then the proceeds would not be included in the insured's estate thereby possibly reducing the federal estate tax liability.

Grace Period

The insured has a grace period of 30 or 31 days from the premium due date in which to make a premium payment. During the grace period coverage continues in force. Therefore, if the insured dies during this period the death benefit is payable. Any premium due to cover the grace period extension will be deducted from the final settlement. The purpose of this provision is protection of the policyholder against unintentional lapse. If this provision were not included and the insured's payment was even one day late, technically he or she would have to furnish evidence of insurability to continue coverage.

Reinstatement

If the premium has not been paid by the end of the grace period, this provision allows the policyowner/insured to apply for reinstatement within a specified period of time following the policy's lapse. In most states, this period of time is at least three years. Some states or companies allow up to five years.

Usually the reinstatement process includes the submission of a reinstatement request or application by the policyowner, evidence of continued insurability and the payment of all back premiums plus interest. In addition, any outstanding loans or other indebtedness against the policy will have to be paid.

The insurer has the right to decline the request for reinstatement if for example, the insured is unable to provide satisfactory evidence of continued insurability. Any statements made on the reinstatement application are subject to a new incontestable period (usually two years). Normally, the reinstatement request will be approved. If the policy has not been in force for some time, the policyowner may think it is better to simply purchase a new policy rather than pay back premiums plus interest to reinstate the lapsed policy. However, there are several reasons for considering reinstatement. These include:

- The lapsed policy may have more liberal policy provisions
- The older policy may offer lower interest rates on policy loans
- Suicide and incontestable clauses probably will no longer apply if the policy is three years old or older
- The lapsed policy probably has a lower premium than a new policy

This last point is especially true if the policyowner had purchased the lapsed policy 10 or 15 years earlier. Instead of paying attained age rates for a new policy, the policyowner could reinstate the lapsed policy at original issue age rates.

Policy Loan Provisions

The following provisions apply to any policy which has a cash value element.

After a policy has been in force for a specified period of time (usually three years), it must contain some cash value which may be borrowed by the policyowner.

The amount of money which may be borrowed is the current cash value less any outstanding and unpaid policy loans.

The insurance company may charge interest on cash value loans. The amount of interest is usually relatively nominal and regulated by state laws. Often, if the policyowner agrees to pay the interest in advance, the amount charged will be reduced. A slightly higher interest rate is charged if it is paid at the end of a loan year. Most states allow the insurer to use an adjustable rate of interest in lieu of a fixed loan rate.

If the loan amount and interest due are not paid, these amounts will be considered an indebtedness against the policy and will result in a reduced death benefit should the insured die while the indebtedness is outstanding. In most policies, after the policy has been in effect a certain number of years, failure to repay the loan or to pay interest on it will not void the policy unless or until the total amount of the loan and accrued interest equals or exceeds the cash value of the policy, and then only after 30 days notice has been mailed to the last known address of the policyholder, and his assignee, if any.

The insurer may defer a loan request for up to six months from the date of the loan application unless the reason for the loan is to pay premiums due.

Interest Sensitive Provision

Policy provisions on "interest sensitive" policies, like universal life were created to respond to competition from other investment opportunities provided by consumers. Typically, a life insurance interest guarantee is between 4% and 6%. The insurance company would take the insured's money and invest it, and as the economic climate improved the insurer's interest earnings improved. Consumers began to be aware of this fact, and determined that they could invest their own money and earn more than 4% or 6% interest on their investment.

To offset this, the insurance company made provisions for the insured to purchase life insurance and still take part in any increase in interest earnings. Today, most variable and flexible premium policies contain provisions that guarantee certain interest earnings, which will not ever be less than a certain percentage, for example, 4%.

Then, by actuarially calculated methods, the insurer will also guarantee that the insured will make a certain percentage of the current interest rate should that interest rate go above the 3% or 4% interest the insured needs to earn. This additional interest percentage is the **excess interest over the minimum guaranteed interest.** For example, if the insurer is earning 7% on an investment, the insured will earn the guaranteed 4%. But if the insurer earns 11%, the insured may earn an additional 3% on the current interest rate. Therefore, the combined interest earnings to the insured will be 7%. A typical policy provision may state that interest *will be the greater of the current interest rate or 6% per year.*

Incontestability

By this clause, the company agrees not to use as a defense against a claim for payment of benefits any error, concealment, misstatement or even fraud, on the part of the policyowner after the policy has been in effect a certain length of time, usually two years.

Thus the policy becomes incontestable after the two-year period (in a few states, one year). This provision makes the insurance contract a little different from other types of contracts. Usually, contract law specifies that if a fraudulent contract has been enacted, it may be voided or cancelled at any time. The incontestable period limits the period of time in which the insurer may contest the insurance contract as to any misrepresentations or fraud on the part of the applicant.

It should be noted that the incontestability provision is slightly different for health insurance policies. This concept will be addressed in a subsequent chapter.

Entire Contract and Representations

The policy, together with the attached application, constitutes the entire contract. This provision limits the use of evidence other than the contract and the attached application in a test of the contract's validity.

All statements made by the insured in the application are, in the absence of fraud, deemed representations, and not warranties.

In addition, the entire contract provision also specifies that the agent cannot alter or change the policy. Only company officers have the authority to change or amend the insurance contract. Further, any such changes or modifications must be in writing, signed and acknowledged by the policyowner and signed by a company official. These signed and witnessed changes then are attached to the policy and become part of the legal contract between the policyowner and the insurer.

Assignment

This is a transfer to another individual of all or a portion of the policyholder's rights, title or interest under an insurance contract.

There are two types of assignments of life insurance contracts. The **absolute** assignment gives the assignee every right in the policy the owner possessed before the assignment — all "incidents of ownership" are transferred. Of course, the assignee can receive only the rights the owner had himself. Thus, any assignment is subject to debts owed to the insurance company. Upon the completion of an absolute assignment, the prior owner retains no ownership interest whatsoever.

A more limited type of assignment is the **collateral** assignment. The collateral assignment is used to provide security (collateral) for some transaction between the owner of the policy and the assignee. For example, the policyholder may borrow money and make a collateral assignment of the policy to serve as security for repayment. If a collateral assignment is made, only some of the "incidents of ownership" are transferred to the assignee, generally for a limited period of time. The assignee receives only those rights necessary to provide security for the loan. Thus, the owner retains some ownership rights. For example, he retains the right to designate the beneficiary of the policy. The owner could not, however, cash in the policy or exercise any ownership right that would impair the security arrangement of the collateral assignment.

An absolute assignment is a permanent and complete assignment of the policy's ownership rights and privileges. A collateral assignment is a temporary and partial assignment of the ownership rights of the policy.

Misstatement of Age or Sex

If the insured's age or sex is misstated on the application, the insurer has the right to adjust the policy's benefits to reflect the amount that the premiums paid would have purchased based on the correct age or sex of the insured.

For example, let's assume that Cindy, age 37, applies for whole life insurance. By mistake, her age is recorded as 35 on the application. The policy is issued and the premium is based on age 35 rates. Forty years later, Cindy dies and the misstated age is then discovered. Cindy has paid a premium which was lower than it should have been. The death benefit will be decreased slightly to reflect the amount of insurance which should have been purchased (with the premium that was paid) had her correct age been stated.

This adjustment in the death benefit can be upward or downward depending on whether the insured was younger or older than the misstated age.

The same concept applies for misstatement of sex. Due to life expectancy (females have longer life expectancy), males pay more for life insurance than females. Therefore if the insured's sex has been misstated on the application, an adjustment in the death benefit will be made or if the mistake was found while the insured was alive, an adjustment in the premium would be made. The premium adjustment would include a new, higher premium for the future and a request for additional premium to take care of the amount which should have been paid by the policyowner in the past.

This provision allows the insurer to make a change in the policy even though the error is discovered beyond the incontestability period.

Medical Examinations and Autopsy

Some states require life insurance policies to include a provision that gives the insurer the right and opportunity at its own expense to conduct a medical examination of the insured as often as reasonably required when a claim is pending, and to make an autopsy in case of death where it is not forbidden by law.

Modifications

Modifications or changes in the policy, or any agreement in connection with the policy (such as changes in the beneficiaries, face amount, or additional coverage), must be endorsed on or attached to the policy in writing over the signature of a specified officer or officers of the company. No one else has any authority to make changes or agreements, to waive provisions, or to extend the time for premium payment.

Some modification clauses also specifically state that no agent has the right to waive policy provisions, make alterations or agreements, or extend the time for payments of premiums.

Policy Change Provision (Conversion Option)

The policy may contain a provision which permits the insured to exchange a policy for another type of policy form permitted by the company. This exchange is usually made from one policy type to another policy form with the **same face amount.**

If the exchange is to a policy with a higher premium, then the insured merely has to pay the higher premium and no proof of insurability would be required.

If the exchange is to a policy form with a lower premium, then proof of insurability may be required as this could result in adverse selection against the insurer. For example, if Charlie discovers that he only has six months to live, then he might decide to exchange his higher premium 20-pay life for one-year term insurance with the same face amount. The insurer's risk has increased while its premium income has decreased. Thus, Charlie will have to prove insurability.

Free Look

No policy of individual life insurance can legally be delivered or issued for delivery in most states unless it has printed on or attached to it a notice stating in substance that during a period of 10 days (some companies allow 20 days) from the date the policy is delivered to the policyholder, it may be surrendered to the insurer together with a written request for cancellation of the policy and in such event, the policy shall be void from the beginning and the insurer shall refund any premium paid.

This provision allows the policyholder an opportunity to review the entire contract and reevaluate the purchase decision.

REVIEW QUESTIONS

Match the following numbered definitions with the lettered terms below.

____ 1. An agreement by the company not to refuse to pay benefits because of a concealment or misstatement after the policy has been in effect for a stated period of time

____ 2. This provision specifically states that the agent does not have the right to waive or make alterations in the policy provisions

____ 3. The policy and the application

____ 4. To put the policy back in force after defaulting on premium payments generally requires evidence of insurability, payment of back premium and any other indebtedness to the company with interest

____ 5. Transfer of policyowner's rights, title or interest in an insurance contract

____ 6. Time period of not fewer than 30 days after the date when any premium (other than the first) is due during which the company will continue coverage

____ 7. Makes the provision that if a loan is not repaid and the insured dies, the loan amount will be deducted from the face amount which would have been paid to the beneficiaries

____ 8. Allows the policyholder a chance to look at the policy before being committed to his or her decision to buy

A. Reinstatement
B. Assignment
C. Policy Loans
D. Modifications
E. Aviation Restriction
F. Grace Period
G. Free Look
H. Incontestability
I. Entire Contract

☞ ***Answers to Review Questions are located at the back of the book.***

THE BENEFICIARY PROVISION

The beneficiary is the person or interest to whom payment of the life insurance proceeds will be made upon the death of the insured. The beneficiary provision allows the insured or the policyowner to direct the payment to any person he or she chooses.

A variety of different parties or interests may be designated as beneficiaries under the life insurance policy. The beneficiary can be a person or an institution, such as a foundation or charity. A specifically designated person, more than one person, or a class or classes of persons may be named as beneficiaries. The insured may name his or her estate, an institution, a corporation, a trust, or any other legal entity as a beneficiary.

As you should recall, to form an insurance contract, the policyowner must have an insurable interest in the insured at the time of application but not necessarily at the time of death. After a policy is in effect, the policy remains valid even if the insurable interest of the policyowner ceases to exist.

A beneficiary is not required to have an insurable interest, but often does. In many cases, a spouse, parent or child of the insured person is named as the beneficiary, so the beneficiary does happen to have a coincidental insurable interest in the life of the insured. Nonetheless, insurable interest on the part of the beneficiary is not required, and there is no need to change a beneficiary designation if the original family relationship changes.

For example, a couple is married and each spouse is the owner and beneficiary of a life insurance policy covering the other spouse's life. Insurable interest exists at the inception of the insurance contract. Later, this married couple divorces. Legally, the policies remain valid, even though insurable interest has ceased, and there is no obligation to change the beneficiary designations.

However, more than likely, there will be a change in ownership rights, or the beneficiary designations, or both, or the policies will be surrendered when a marriage terminates. If there are children from the marriage, ownership rights might be transferred to the children or the children may be designated as new beneficiaries. If there are no children, the policies will probably be surrendered, because people generally don't continue to pay life insurance premiums when financial and emotional interest in an insured has ceased.

Revocable vs. Irrevocable

One of the rights of the life insurance policyowner is the right to designate a beneficiary and to change that beneficiary designation at will. Almost all life insurance beneficiary designations are **revocable** (changeable). Usually the insured retains the right to change the beneficiary, unless he has specifically given up that right. Most policies have a revocable beneficiary.

It is possible, however, for the owner of the policy to give up the right to change the beneficiary designation at will. In such cases there is an **irrevocable** beneficiary and the designation cannot be changed without the consent of the beneficiary. An irrevocable designation might be used when a court orders a husband in a divorce settlement to continue payment on an insurance policy on his own life, with an irrevocable beneficiary designation on behalf of his wife (the primary beneficiary), and his children (the contingent beneficiaries). In the event that the irrevocable beneficiary dies before the insured, the right to select the beneficiary may revert to the policyowner on a "reversionary" basis.

There are two methods for naming and changing beneficiaries: the filing method and the endorsement method.

Filing Method. This method of effecting a beneficiary change is also known as the *recording method.* Under this method the request must be "filed" in writing to the insurer. The request is made effective by the insurance company "recording" the change in its records. Once recorded, the change takes effect as of the date the insured signed the request.

Endorsement Method. This method requires that the beneficiary change be typed or affixed directly to the policy. The insured must make a written request and mail the request along with the policy to the insurance company. The insurance company will then make sure that the beneficiary change is made to the policy.

Succession of Beneficiaries

The designation of a beneficiary is not a requirement to have a life insurance policy issued. However, it is better to name a beneficiary. It is customary in life insurance contracts to specify a **primary beneficiary** or beneficiaries and a **contingent** (secondary) **beneficiary** or beneficiaries. The primary beneficiary has first claim to the proceeds of the life insurance policy following the death of the insured. If the primary beneficiary dies before the insured, however, the contingent beneficiary is entitled to the benefits of the life insurance policy. (If the primary beneficiary predeceases the insured and there is no contingent beneficiary, the estate of the insured becomes the beneficiary and is subject to the claims of unsecured creditors.) In a family situation, a common primary and contingent designation is as follows:

Mary Jane Smith, wife, and as contingent beneficiaries, all children, adopted or born of this marriage, to share equally.

It is also possible to designate a **tertiary beneficiary.** A tertiary beneficiary occupies the third level in the succession of beneficiaries and is entitled to receive the life insurance proceeds following the death of the insured, provided that both the primary and contingent (secondary) beneficiaries have died before the insured.

After the death of the insured, the proceeds belong to the beneficiary. What is left after the beneficiary dies, of course, depends upon the settlement option selected to go into effect at the death of the insured. If a lump sum benefit is paid, the insurance company has no further obligation to the beneficiary. If an option other than a lump sum payment is selected, or an arrangement is made where benefits continue over a period of time, the beneficiary should name his or her own beneficiary.

Beneficiaries Must Be Clearly Named

Careless wording of beneficiary designations can result in undesirable consequences. A tremendous amount of time is spent each year in courtroom litigation attempting to determine the beneficiaries and heirs. For this reason the life insurance agent should insist that the applicant word his or her beneficiary designation carefully. For example, if the insured designates his "wife" (not specifically named) as the beneficiary, a problem may arise. If the insured has married several times, it may be difficult to identify the true beneficiary. In such case, does "wife" mean the insured's present wife or does it mean his wife at the time the beneficiary was designated? Or does it apply to a wife who is now caring for the insured's minor children? Who was the intended beneficiary in such a case? It is important that the beneficiary be designated by full name to avoid misunderstanding.

Or, if "children" are designated as a class to receive the proceeds, and if it is apparently the intention of the insured that an adopted child be included, a disposition of the proceeds will be made to follow that intention.

The insurer will make every effort to make a disposition of the proceeds of the policy in compliance with the wishes of the insured, as long as the insured makes it clear what his intention is. When the intention is not clear, the insurer must distribute the funds according to the apparent intent of the insured, or pay the funds into court and seek a judicial determination of the proper distribution.

Designation Options

A Minor as Beneficiary. It is common to name minor children as contingent beneficiaries under life insurance contracts. Insurance companies usually will not pay proceeds to a minor since any release or settlement signed by a minor can be legally rejected by the minor when he or she attains legal age. For this reason, it is necessary for a guardian to be appointed to receive the funds on behalf of the minor.

If a minor becomes eligible to receive life insurance proceeds due to the death of both parents, any of their estate left to the minor would have to be administered by a general guardian regardless of whether it includes life insurance proceeds. Thus the life insurance proceeds would be paid to that guardian. Also, some parents anticipate this problem by establishing a trust to administer the life insurance proceeds and all other property in the estate of the parents in the event that both parents die leaving minor children.

A Trust as Beneficiary. A trust is formed when the owner of property (the grantor) gives legal title of that property to another (the trustee) to be used for the benefit of a third individual (the trust beneficiary). This fiduciary relationship allows the trustee to manage the property in the trust for the benefit of the trust beneficiary only. The trustee legally must not benefit from the trust.

When a trust is designated as the beneficiary of a life insurance policy, the policy proceeds provide funds for the trust. Upon the death of the insured, the trustee administers the funds in accordance with the instructions set forth in the trust provisions.

While there are many benefits in naming a trust as beneficiary of an estate or a life insurance policy, particularly for minor children, there are drawbacks as well. A trustee will charge a fee for managing a trust. The way the trust property is managed is often left up to the trustee, leaving the trust beneficiary powerless to intervene if the trust is poorly managed. Also, the trustee may not provide resources for the trust beneficiary as he or she or even the grantor would have wanted; the trust beneficiary must request resources from the trustee, he or she cannot make free use of the property in the trust.

An **inter vivos trust** is one that takes effect during the lifetime of the grantor. A **testamentary trust** is a trust created after the grantor's death, according to the provisions of the grantor's will.

The Insured's Estate as Beneficiary. The insured's estate can be named as beneficiary. The insured may direct that the policy proceeds be payable to his or her executors, administrators or assignees. Such a designation might be made by an insured in order to provide funds to pay estate taxes, expenses of past illness, funeral expenses, and any other debts outstanding prior to the settlement of the estate. Designating the insured's estate as beneficiary aids in the settlement of the estate by avoiding the need to sell other assets of the estate to pay these last expenses. Frequently, it is not desirable to name the estate as beneficiary because the insurance proceeds then become assets of the estate and are subject to the claim's of creditors and this situation may not be what the insured intended when naming the estate as beneficiary. In addition, these proceeds increase the size of the estate and at the same time can increase the expenses, inheritance taxes and federal estate taxes involved in estate administration and settlement. If the primary beneficiary dies before the insured, and there is no contingent or tertiary beneficiary, the estate automatically becomes the beneficiary.

Class Designation. In naming children as beneficiaries, a class designation is desirable. Class designations should be used when individuals of a specific group (such as children of the insured) are to share the policy proceeds equally. For example, if an insured designates his children as beneficiaries by naming each child specifically, other children might be excluded from sharing in the proceeds of the policy. This might occur if the insured failed to update his beneficiary provision in his policy to include children who joined the family (household) since the date that the policy was obtained.

The wording of the class designation must carefully specify the insured's intentions. A designation of "my children" might include children of other marriages or other unions, when in fact the insured might prefer to exclude both. In addition, including the children of the insured as beneficiaries would allow all children living at the time of the insured's death to share in the proceeds, but a posthumous child (born after the father's death) would not be entitled to receive a portion of the proceeds.

If the insured wishes to restrict the designation to the children of his present marriage, he might designate his present wife "Carolyn Jones Bennett" as primary beneficiary and use the term "our children" or "children born of this marriage" as his contingent beneficiaries. By using the wife's given name, maiden name and married name, followed by the designation "my wife," no question can arise as to the intent of the insured to have his wife as the primary beneficiary. Likewise, his intent to restrict the contingent beneficiaries to children of his marriage to Carolyn Jones Bennett is made clear.

Per Capita and Per Stirpes Designations. In addition to the class designation, the per capita and per stirpes designations are used to benefit children. The per capita designation means "by heads," (individual) and per stirpes means "by stock" (family line or branch). Under a **per capita** designation each surviving child shares equally in the death benefit.

Under a **per stirpes** designation each child, grandchild, or great grandchild, etc., moves up in a representative place of a deceased beneficiary. A per stirpes designation can become quite involved and it is important to know how the line of representation works because of the manner in which courts interpret the per stirpes designation. The majority of courts hold that each child moves up to represent the closest relative (the parent). The child represents the deceased parent (insured), the grandchildren represent the child, great grandchildren represent the grandchildren, and so forth. Perhaps the following examples will help to clarify the per stirpes designation.

Example 1 — Mrs. Smith has three children, Faith, Hope, and Charity. At her death each child will share equally in the death benefit — one-third each.

Example 2 — If, at Mrs. Smith's death, Faith is no longer living and she has no dependents, Hope and Charity will share the death benefit equally — one-half each.

Example 3 — If, at Mrs. Smith's death Faith is no longer living but she is survived by two children, Jack and Jill (Mrs. Smith's grandchildren); Hope and Charity will each receive one-third of the benefit, and Faith's one-third will be divided equally between Jack and Jill — one-sixth each.

Example 4 — If, at Mrs. Smith's death, Faith (child) and both Jack and Jill (grandchildren) are also deceased, but Jack is survived by two children and Jill is survived by one child (Mrs. Smith's great grandchildren) Jill's child will get one-sixth benefit while, one-sixth of the benefit will be divided between Jack's two children — one-twelfth each.

Example 5 — If, of the three great grandchildren one of Jack's children is dead at the time of the distribution and has left two children (Mrs. Smith's great great grandchildren) those two children are only entitled to share Jack's child's one-twelfth — the great grandchildren receive one-twenty-fourth each.

Although the preceding examples represent the majority finding, some courts have held that, for example, a grandchild can move up and share in the benefits on the same percentage basis as the original children.

Equal Distribution Among Living Beneficiaries

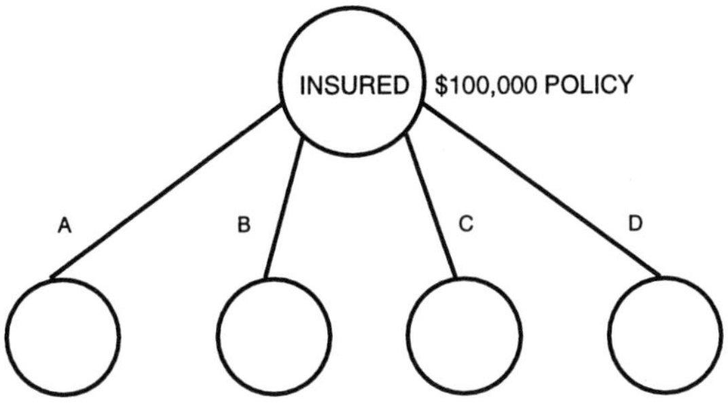

BENEFICIARIES EACH RECEIVE $25,000 ($100,000 ÷ 4)

PER CAPITA

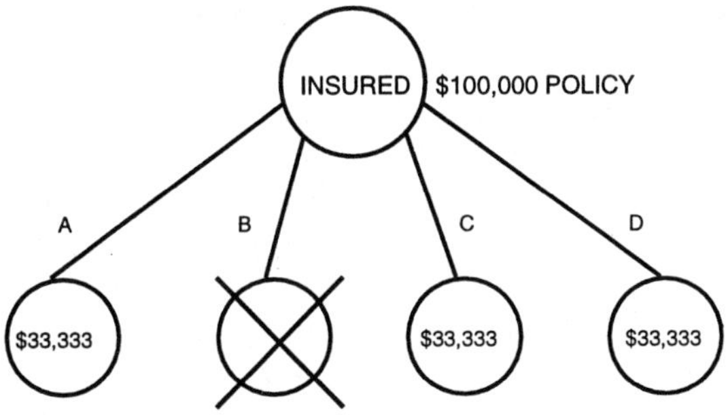

IF B HAS PREDECEASED THE INSURED, B's SHARE IS FORFEITED AND SURVIVING BENEFICIARIES EACH RECEIVE $33,333.

PER STIRPES

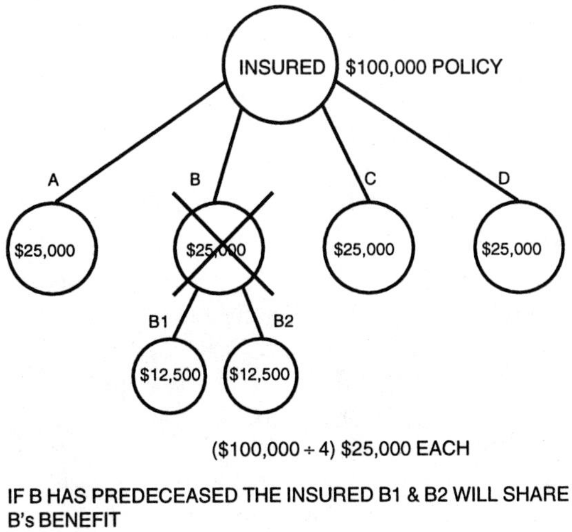

($100,000 ÷ 4) $25,000 EACH

IF B HAS PREDECEASED THE INSURED B1 & B2 WILL SHARE EQUALLY B's BENEFIT

The Uniform Simultaneous Death Act

A problem arises when the insured and the primary beneficiary die simultaneously with no evidence as to who died first. Many states have adopted the Uniform Simultaneous Death Law. Under it, if there is no evidence as to who died first, the policy will be settled as though the insured survived the beneficiary.

Accordingly, the life insurance proceeds would be paid to the estate of the insured, not the estate of the beneficiary. Of course, if contingent beneficiaries are designated, the proceeds would be payable to them. Or if there is clear evidence that the beneficiary survived the insured, then the proceeds are payable to the beneficiary's estate.

Let's assume that John, the insured, has designated his wife, Jane, as primary beneficiary on a $100,000 whole life policy. John's children from a previous marriage are named as contingent beneficiaries. John and Jane are killed in an auto accident and it is determined that Jane survived John by 15 minutes. The insurance proceeds would be payable to Jane's estate and may not benefit the children.

In accordance with the Uniform Simultaneous Death Act, if it could not be determined that Jane survived John, then the proceeds are payable to the children as contingent beneficiaries. If the children were not designated as contingent beneficiaries, then the proceeds are payable to John's estate.

To avoid the problem of the primary beneficiary living for a very short time following the death of the insured and thus receiving the insurance proceeds, many policies will include a **common disaster provision**. This provision places a time element on the survival period of the primary beneficiary by stipulating that the primary beneficiary must survive the insured by a specified period of time such as 30, 60 or 90 days

Thus, in the John and Jane example, if the policy contains a common disaster provision of 30 days and Jane only survived John by 15 minutes the proceeds are payable to the contingent beneficiaries.

Spendthrift Clause

One of the unique features of life insurance is that the life insurance proceeds are exempt from the claims of the insured's (deceased's) creditors as long as there is a named beneficiary other than the insured's estate. A similar provision with reference to the beneficiary is the spendthrift clause.

The spendthrift clause is designed to protect the beneficiary from losing the life insurance proceeds to creditors, assigning the proceeds to others, or spending large sums recklessly. The spendthrift clause is not applicable to lump sum settlements but is operative with installment settlement options. It only protects the portion of proceeds not yet paid (due, but still held by the insurer) from the claims of creditors to the extent permitted by law.

The insured normally elects to have this provision as part of the policy at the time of the application for insurance. As long as the proceeds are paid on one of several settlement options whereby the insurer keeps the proceeds and sends a monthly payment to the beneficiary, then the amounts received by the beneficiary are exempt from the claims of the beneficiary's creditors.

Facility of Payment Provision

This provision allows the insurer to select a beneficiary if the named beneficiaries cannot be found. This provision is most commonly found in group life insurance contracts and industrial life policies.

When a named beneficiary cannot be found (after a reasonable time), to facilitate the payment of the death proceeds, the insurer may select a beneficiary if this provision is in the policy. Typically, this provision is found in policies with relatively small death benefits, such as Industrial Life. Normally, the insurer would select someone who is in the family's immediate blood line (a brother, sister, aunt, uncle, etc).

REVIEW QUESTIONS

Match the following numbered definitions with the lettered terms below.

_____ 9. A person or interest to whom life insurance proceeds will be paid

_____ 10. Using the phrase "my children" as one's life insurance beneficiaries for example

_____ 11. The person or interest entitled to the insured's life insurance proceeds if the primary beneficiary predeceases the insured

_____ 12. Clause describing what happens if the insured and primary beneficiary die simultaneously with no evidence as to who died first

_____ 13. Beneficiary designation that can be changed

A. Revocable
B. Contingent Beneficiary
C. Class Designation
D. Common Disaster Clause
E. Beneficiary

Answers to Review Questions are located at the back of the book.

EXCLUSIONS & LIMITATIONS

Life insurance policies may contain certain exclusions or restrictions. The main exclusions are:

Suicide

Initially, life insurance contracts excluded the risk of suicide entirely. This exclusion left dependents without protection, defeating the purpose of purchasing insurance coverage. Also, it was incorrect to exclude suicide completely because death by suicide is included in the mortality tables upon which premiums are based.

The majority of life insurance policies issued today contain a provision restricting liability in the event of suicide. Usually the time limit on the restriction is two years, although occasionally it is only one year or less. A typical provision is that in the event of suicide within this period, the liability of the company shall be restricted to an amount equal to the total of premiums paid, without interest less any indebtedness. Excluded from payment in event of suicide is any accidental death benefit, since suicide is not considered an accident.

Aviation Restriction

In the past, aviation exclusions were very common. Today, this type of exclusion is rarely found in life insurance policies. Among the types of aviation restrictions still found are these:

- Exclusion of all aviation caused or related deaths except those of fare-paying passengers on regularly scheduled airlines. Some policies do not include the phrase, "regularly scheduled airlines," thus covering nonscheduled flights also, but only for a fare-paying passenger.
- Exclusion of deaths in military aircraft only or death while on military maneuvers.
- Exclusion of pilots, crew members, student pilots, and (sometimes) anyone with duties in flight or while descending from an aircraft, e.g., parachuting.

Companies using any or all of these restrictions will afford coverage of civil aviation deaths for an extra premium. The exclusions or restrictions apply only to those unwilling to pay the extra premium required and to military duties.

War and Military Service

In wartime, it has been common for companies to include restrictions which limit the death benefit paid to usually a refund of premium plus interest or possibly an amount equal to the policy's cash value. Often in the past, the policy's benefits were suspended during a war or an act of war. The term, "act of war" has been used to describe the Korean and Vietnam conflicts.

Today, most insurers will provide some form of life insurance coverage for those on military duty. Traditionally, there are usually two types of restrictions or clauses which may be used. The **status clause** excludes the payment of the death benefit while the insured is serving in the military. The **results clause** excludes the payment of the death benefit if the insured is killed as a result of war.

Most insurers today do not use a war exclusion or clause. Instead they may limit the amount of insurance that a person may apply for if military service is contemplated or a higher premium may be charged to cover the slightly higher risk involved.

Hazardous Occupations and Avocations

By today's underwriting standards, few applicants are declined life insurance because of their occupations. For example, firefighters and police personnel can purchase life insurance at standard rates. Even commercial airline pilots can usually purchase life insurance (although possibly at higher than standard rates).

Much of the underwriting attention is focused on the applicant's avocations or hobbies. If an applicant participates in a hazardous hobby such as auto racing, sky diving, scuba diving, etc., then the amount of insurance which may be purchased may be limited or an extra premium may be charged due to the additional risk. Depending on the hobby, the death benefit may be excluded if death was caused as a result of the hazardous avocation.

PROHIBITED PROVISIONS

By law in most states, life insurance policies are **not** permitted to contain the following provisions:

- A provision that limits the time for bringing any lawsuit against the insurance company to less than one year after the reason for the lawsuit occurs.
- A provision that allows a settlement at maturity of *less* than the face amount plus any dividend additions, less any indebtedness to the company and any premium deductible under the policy.
- A provision that allows forfeiture of the policy because of the failure to repay any policy loan or interest on the loan if the total owed is less than the loan value of the policy.
- A provision making the soliciting agent the agent of the person insured under the policy or making the acts or representations of the agent binding on the insured. (The agent must only be an agent of the company, not the insured.)

The law of the state in which the policy is sold governs the contract. The policy may not contain a provision by which the laws of the home state of the insurer govern the policy provisions.

REVIEW QUESTIONS

14. What are the two types of military restrictions? ______________________ and ______________________.
15. How long is the usual suicide restriction? ______ ______________________.

☞ ***Answers to Review Questions are located at the back of the book.***

NOTES

7

LIFE INSURANCE POLICY OPTIONS

The life insurance policy provides important policy options. These options give the life insurance contract flexibility to meet the needs of the insuring public. Of particular value are the settlement, nonforfeiture, and dividend options available under a life insurance contract. A life and health agent must have an understanding of the general nature of the options in each of these areas.

SETTLEMENT OPTIONS

Probably the most common reason for the purchase of life insurance is to provide money for beneficiaries on the death of the insured or for the insured during retirement. The usual life insurance policy is written as an agreement to pay a stated sum in cash on the death of the insured. However, the need of beneficiaries is more often for a stream of future payments than for a lump sum of money. Similarly, the need in retirement is less often for a lump sum of cash than it is for a steady income. As a result of these and other varying needs, optional modes of settlement have been developed.

There are five frequently used optional modes of settlement:

- Interest only
- Fixed-period installments
- Fixed-amount installments
- Life income
- Joint and survivor

In addition, most companies will agree to distribute the proceeds under any reasonable and actuarially sound mode. Settlement options may be elected by the policyowner for the beneficiary or for himself or herself. If he or she has made no election prior to death, the beneficiary will usually be allowed to select an option.

If a death claim is made while there is a loan against the policy, the loan plus any accrued interest will be deducted from the death benefit. The death proceeds include the death benefit plus any accumulated dividends, paid-up insurance additions or one-year term insurance additions. The net death proceeds will then be used to determine the amount payable under any one of the following options.

Interest Only. Under this option, the proceeds are held by the company, and the interest earned on the proceeds is paid to the beneficiary at least annually. The minimum interest rate that will be paid is guaranteed in the policy. Usually the policy also provides that if the company earns interest in excess of the minimum guaranteed, it will pay excess interest on the proceeds, usually on an installment basis.

The policyowner may specify that no part of the principal is ever to be paid to the beneficiary but that it will be paid to a contingent beneficiary on the death of the primary beneficiary, or to the estate of the policyowner. On the other hand, the policyowner may specify that the beneficiary may withdraw the principal in whole or in part or elect another option in the policy. The policyowner may also specify that the proceeds will remain on an interest only basis for a stated period of time or to a stated date and then be paid in cash or under one of the options.

Fixed-Period Installments. This option is also referred to as "installments certain" and as the "time option." The proceeds are retained by the insurer and paid in equal installments over a specified period of months or years. The payments are comprised of both principal and interest. The payments are established without regard to the length of life of the primary beneficiary. If the primary beneficiary dies, they are continued to the contingent beneficiary as long as the payments last. If no contingent beneficiary is surviving, or none were named, the commuted value (an amount reflecting the current value of a number of payments) of the remaining payments is paid to the estate of the last beneficiary. The amount of each installment will be increased by any excess interest earned.

Fixed-Amount Installments. This option is sometimes called the "amount option" and sometimes, "principal and interest to exhaustion." It calls for the payment of a fixed, periodic (annual, semiannual, quarterly, monthly) benefit of a predetermined amount until the proceeds (principal) and interest thereon are exhausted. The size of each installment determines the duration of the payments in contrast to the fixed-period option where the length of the income period selected determines the size of the installment. Excess interest will increase the duration of the installments rather than the size of the installment. Fractional amounts are paid in full with the last full installment.

Life Income. Under the life income option, the proceeds are retained by the insurer and paid in equal installments (monthly, quarterly, semiannually, or annually) as long as the beneficiary lives, even if the total paid exceeds the amount of principal plus interest. When a life income only option is elected, there is no refund when the beneficiary dies even if only one installment has been paid. Beneficiaries who do not live to draw all their proceeds make it possible to continue payments to those who outlive their proceeds and the interest earned on them. The benefits are calculated on a basis of the beneficiary's life expectancy at the time payments begin. The older the beneficiary at the beginning of the payment period the larger the payments per $1,000 of proceeds.

When this option is used to settle a death claim, the face value becomes the principal. When it is used to provide income for a living insured, the cash or endowment value becomes the principal. The greatest risk with a "life income only" option is that premature death will end all benefits, even if only a small portion of the principal has been received, and any principal which has not been paid out will be lost. To reduce or eliminate this risk, many recipients want to have payments guaranteed for a specified period of time. This can be arranged by electing a **life income with period certain** option. Under this option, the benefits are guaranteed for a "period certain" (usually 5, 10, or 20 years). If the primary recipient dies before the end of the period certain, benefits will continue to be paid to another person for the remainder of the period certain (or the commuted value may be paid to the estate of the insured or last beneficiary to die). If the original recipient lives beyond the period certain, the benefit payments continue for as long as he or she lives. However, the longer the period certain, the smaller the periodic benefit payments, because funds have to be set aside to cover the possibility that benefits will continue to be paid after a person's death.

Joint and Survivor. Some policies contain a joint and survivor option. Most companies that do not include it in the contract will grant it as a special settlement agreement. This option can be used to provide for two beneficiaries upon the death of the insured. Under this mode of settlement, two beneficiaries receive the proceeds of a life insurance policy. When the first beneficiary dies, the second beneficiary (if he or she is still living) continues to receive the proceeds of the policy, in installments, for his or her lifetime (or for a specified period).

The option can also be written as "joint and two-thirds" survivor, "joint and one-half" survivor, or with other reduced installment methods. Under the "joint and two-thirds" survivor option, the income for the survivor of the two recipients is two-thirds of the amount paid while both were still alive.

Withdrawal Provisions. The withdrawal provision is used in connection with settlement options. Under this provision the proceeds of a policy are held by the insurance company and earn interest. The insured has the right to withdraw the funds left on "deposit" with the insurer at any time. The beneficiary may only withdraw a limited amount each year. Quite often this withdrawal provision is used to pay for college.

Other Settlement Arrangements. Many policies are written with no provision for any special arrangements in the settlement of proceeds. However, a large number of companies will permit other settlement arrangements. Special settlement arrangements are sometimes desirable in order to accomplish the estate planning objectives of some insureds, and insurance companies will cooperate with almost any arrangement that is reasonable. Whatever plan is selected, however, must be of such nature that it can be administered by the insurance company and with regard to proper actuarial principles. In other words, any installments received under the special arrangement must be the actuarial equivalent of the other settlement options available under the contract.

Administration of the special arrangement must strictly follow the terms of the contract. An insurance company does not provide trustee services. If an insured, for example, requested a settlement arrangement whereby the insurance company would make payment of the proceeds to two beneficiaries "according to their needs," the insurance company would not accept such a settlement arrangement, since it would require that the insurance company make a judgment determination. The insurer will provide administrative services but will not provide judgment services. Insurance companies will handle settlement option elections by individually drafting such agreements and applying them to individual policies. The companies do, however, have rules to avoid arrangements which are uneconomical to administer. For example, a company may specify that a minimum of $1,000, or in some cases $2,000, may be placed under a settlement option. It may prescribe that minimum installments payable shall be not less than a certain amount per installment. It is not a good business practice and might not be legal to hold proceeds for an indefinite period of time. Consequently, a company may set a time limit for holding proceeds at interest, such as for the lifetime of the primary beneficiary or the lifetime of a contingent beneficiary.

Third-Party Rights and Creditor's Rights

Although the life insurance contract is between the policyowner and the insurer, once the insured has died, a contractual arrangement exists between the insurer and the beneficiary. The beneficiary may sue the insurer if payment is not received upon proper proof of death.

Likewise, once the insured dies the proceeds of a life insurance policy belong to the beneficiary, and the insured's creditors have no right to them. The beneficiary's creditors, however, may have a right to the life insurance proceeds.

Even the cash value of life insurance is generally protected from creditors.

The only exception to these statements is if the premiums which paid for the insurance were from embezzled funds.

Advantages of Settlement Options

One of the principal advantages for the insured or beneficiary for selecting one of the various settlement options is freedom from investment concerns. If a beneficiary elects a lump sum settlement of the death benefit, then he or she must decide how to use or invest the money. In essence, by electing a settlement option other than a lump sum, the beneficiary is trusting in the expertise and knowledge of the insurance company to administer these proceeds and provide some form of income.

Another advantage of settlement options is the fact that any of the options will guarantee a greater return than simply taking the face amount of the policy. A $100,000 policy will generate a greater death benefit than $100,000 if these proceeds, consisting of principal and interest, are paid to a beneficiary over a period of time. For example, if a beneficiary elected an interest only option, he or she would receive interest payments over a period of time and then possibly at some future date, the principal. This could result in a total sum of money many times greater than just the face amount of the policy.

REVIEW QUESTIONS

1. What are the optional modes of settlement of proceeds found in most policies? ______________
2. How does the "interest only" option work? ______________
3. When should fixed-period be elected and when fixed-amounts? ______________
4. What is the difference between life income and life income with period certain? ______________
5. How does "joint and survivor" work? ______________

Answers to Review Questions are located at the back of the book.

NONFORFEITURE OPTIONS (GUARANTEED VALUES)

The nonforfeiture options (or provisions) of the life insurance policy are designed to protect the policyowner against total forfeiture or loss of benefits when a policy contains cash values and for whatever reason, premium payments cease. Nonforfeiture values are thus factors of the policy's cash value. If a policy has no cash value (such as term insurance), then there are no nonforfeiture values.

The following are common nonforfeiture options in cash value policies:

- Cash surrender value
- Extended term insurance
- Paid-up insurance

Cash Surrender Value. The cash value of a life insurance policy is the amount a policyowner is entitled to when the policy has been surrendered before maturity. The minimum cash value is determined by a formula established by law. A portion of each premium paid is allocated to the policy reserve which is a fixed liability of the insurance company. The balance of the premium is used to cover certain expenses (acquisition costs, administrative expenses, agents' commission, etc.). In the early years of the policy (the first two or three), all of the premium is used for the reserve requirement and other liabilities and expenses. The life insurance contract is a heavily loaded with expenses initially, thus, there is no cash value in the early years of the policy.

Usually about the third year of the policy, these initial expenses are covered and the policy's guaranteed cash value begins to grow. As the cash value grows so too do the values associated with the nonforfeiture options. If the policyowner elects to "cash in" the policy, that is, surrender it for its available cash, he or she may do so. This concept can easily be seen in the nonforfeiture table illustrated in chart 7-1. The longer the policy is in force, the higher is the cash surrender or loan value and the higher are the other nonforfeiture values.

Extended Term Insurance. Under this option, the company uses the cash surrender value to buy term insurance in the same face amount as the current policy, the term period being for however long the cash value will pay the new policy premium. Many policies state that in the event of a lapse, this option will take effect unless another option is chosen.

In the case of endowment policies, if the cash value available extends the policy term beyond the endowment date, the excess is used to buy a pure endowment, which is an amount payable only if the insured lives to the endowment date.

If the policy dividends have been allowed to accumulate or have been used to buy paid-up additions to the policy, the amount of the accumulated dividends or the cash value of the paid-up additions will also be used as part of the cash value in "buying" the extended term insurance.

The extended term option buys time for the insured. Unlike the cash surrender option which leaves the insured with no life insurance, the extended term option provides the insured with the full face amount of the policy for a specified period of time and of course, no further premium payments are required.

Reduced Paid-Up Insurance. The cash value of the policy is used as a single premium to provide life insurance on the same plan as the current policy itself, for as large an amount as the cash value will purchase at the insured's age when the option becomes effective. The purchase is on a single premium basis and the insurance purchased is fully paid up. The policyowner has the same plan of insurance but in a reduced amount from the current face amount.

Under the paid-up option, a reduced amount of insurance remains in force for the duration of the policy period. Under the extended term option, the full amount remains in force for a reduced amount of time.

As a "new" single premium policy, this reduced paid up contract will also begin to grow in cash value over the life of the policy.

Automatic Premium Loan

Although not part of the policy's nonforfeiture values or options, the automatic premium loan (APL) option or provision is discussed here because it too is related to the policy's available cash value.

This option, usually elected at the time of the application, provides that in case of a possible policy lapse, the premium will be automatically paid from the contract's guaranteed cash value. This option naturally protects the policyowner/insured from an unintentional lapse. There is no charge for this option as the premium is being paid by the policy's cash value.

Since this option is dependent upon guaranteed cash values, APL is not available with term insurance as term does not have cash value.

$100,000 WHOLE LIFE POLICY
MALE, AGE 35, NONSMOKER

Sample Table of Guaranteed Nonforfeiture Values

End of Policy Year	Cash Surrender Or Loan Value	Reduced Paid-Up Insurance	Extended Term Insurance Years	Extended Term Insurance Days
1	$ .00	$ 0	0	0
2	.00	0	0	0
3	641.00	3,658	2	169
4	1,632.00	8,927	5	312
5	2,659.00	13,944	8	246
6	3,727.00	18,741	11	4
7	4,832.00	23,304	12	316
8	5,978.00	27,656	14	116
9	7,165.00	31,803	15	174
10	8,395.00	35,759	16	146
11	9,657.00	39,483	17	40
12	10,965.00	43,042	17	236
13	12,320.00	46,442	18	18
14	13,727.00	49,705	18	123
15	15,183.00	52,822	18	197
16	16,691.00	55,807	18	244
17	18,251.00	58,666	18	268
18	19,860.00	61,397	18	271
19	21,519.00	64,010	18	256
20	23,225.00	66,506	18	222
25	31,461.00	75,080	17	29
27	34,993.00	77,940	16	124
30	40,464.00	81,688	15	59
35	49,800.00	86,687	13	42

Chart 7-1

REVIEW QUESTIONS

6. What nonforfeiture options are usually found in cash value policies? ______________________

____

____

7. If the policyowner withdraws the cash value, what happens to the policy? ______________________

____

____

8. When should a person elect paid-up insurance and when should he or she select extended term insurance? ______________________

____

____

____

Answers to Review Questions are located at the back of the book.

DIVIDEND OPTIONS

Life and health policies may be issued on either a **nonparticipating** or **participating** basis. A nonparticipating plan requires the policyowner to pay a fixed premium and no dividends are payable. Under a participating plan, the policyowner pays a somewhat higher "gross" premium and is entitled to policy dividends as declared by the insurer. These dividends represent the difference between the premium charged based on predicted experience for a given class of policies and the actual cost of these policies as experienced by the company. These dividends are not a profit in a legal sense but a return of excess premium.

As a matter of practice, many companies declare and pay dividends annually. The policyowner is usually offered several options for the settlement of these dividends. The following represents a list of possible dividend payment options. Although these are the most frequently used options, the list is not all inclusive:

- Cash
- Application to Reduce Premium
- Accumulation at Interest
- Paid-up Additions
- Accelerated Endowment
- Paid-up Option
- One-year Term Option

The agent should understand the dividend options in order to advise policyowners as to the best one to select for their particular purposes from the range of possible choices.

Cash. Dividends are simply paid to the policyowner as declared by the insurer. Again, due to various expense factors, there is often no dividend available in the first year or two of the policy. The "excess premium" paid is used to cover expenses.

Application to Reduce Premium. Many policyowners use dividends to pay part of the premium due at the time the dividend is declared. Usually if this option has been elected on the application (or later), the premium notice will show the gross premium minus the dividend; and the policyowner has merely to send his or her check for the net amount. If the dividend equals or exceeds the premium amount, the premium payment may be suspended.

Accumulation at Interest. Dividends are allowed to accumulate, and interest is paid on them at a rate specified in the policy and compounded annually. The interest rate specified is usually a guaranteed minimum. If the insurer earns more than the minimum, the payment of "excess interest" on the accumulations may result. This option also permits the withdrawal of the accumulations at any time, provided they have not been used under a nonforfeiture provision.

It should be noted that life insurance policy dividends paid or credited to the policyowner are not taxable as they are viewed as a return of excess premium (which has already been taxed). However, if the dividends are left to accumulate at interest, the interest paid or credited is taxable to the policyowner.

Paid-Up Additions. Most policies provide the policyowner an option to use policy dividends to buy additional, paid-up participating insurance of the same type as the policy, often referred to as "dividend additions" or "paid-up ads". The "paid-up adds" are actually small single premium policies with the single premium being generated from the dividend. Of course no new policies are issued. The base policy is simply amended to reflect the additional paid-up values. Each of these additions will also develop cash value. The face amount and the additions make up the total death benefit if the policy matures as a death claim. Should the policyowner elect to surrender the policy for its cash value prior to that time, both the cash value of the policy and the additions would be paid.

When this option is elected at the time of the policy application, the additional paid-up insurance is provided without proof of insurability. The company may require proof of insurability if this option is elected several years after issue.

Accelerated Endowment. Dividends may be applied to convert the policy into an endowment, or in the case of endowment insurance, to shorten the endowment term. The usual methods are described below:

- Dividends remain as accumulations until they, together with the cash value, equal the face amount of the policy, at which time the face amount will be paid as an endowment, if so requested.
- The dividends are used each year to shorten the endowment period. The effect is to change the policy form each year by reducing its term. Under this option, a policy will mature more quickly because its cash value will reach the desired face amount of the insurance in a shorter period of time. This is because the annual application of the dividend reduces the amount at risk. With less at risk, a smaller proportion of future premiums to be collected will be needed than originally anticipated to pay the cost of the insurance. This form of the endowment option endows the policy more quickly than the one in the first method described.

Paid-Up Option. This option actually allows the policyowner to pay the policy up early. For example, the insured has a 20-pay life. By using the dividends over the life of the policy, it may be paid up after 16 or 17 years instead of the full 20 years. If the insured owned a whole life contract, by using the dividends in this manner, he or she would not have to pay on the policy to age 100.

One-Year Term Option. This option permits the use of dividends to buy one-year term insurance, usually up to the amount of the cash value of the policy. If the option is not selected at the time the policy is issued, evidence of insurability will usually be required when it is requested later. Any excess of the total dividend over the term premium may be applied to any other dividend option in the policy.

The primary purpose of this option is to keep the total amount of insurance payable equal to the face amount of the policy when there is a loan outstanding against the policy, otherwise, the outstanding loan balance would be deducted from the face amount if the policy became a death claim. This option is sometimes referred to as the "5th dividend option".

REVIEW QUESTIONS

9. Dividends are payable under a (participating/nonparticipating) ________________ plan.
10. The option in which policy dividends are used to buy more insurance of the same type as the policy is called ________________

    ____
11. What dividend option is used most frequently when the policy is paid up?________________

    ____

☞ ***Answers to Review Questions are located at the back of the book.***

8

ANNUITIES & RETIREMENT PLANS

ANNUITIES

Nature of Annuities

Annuities are not "life insurance," but inasmuch as annuities are sold by life insurance agents, a basic understanding of the types of annuity policies available is necessary to qualify for a life and health agents license. Life insurance is designed to protect against the risk of premature death. Annuities are designed to protect against the risk of living too long.

Annuities have been called "upside down" life insurance. The purpose of life insurance is the creation of an estate triggered by the death of the insured. The insurer's obligation is to pay a benefit upon the death of the insured. The basic function of an annuity is to systematically liquidate a principal sum over a specified period of time. An annuity contract provides for a series of periodic payments that begin on a specific date (such as the annuitant reaching a stated age) or a contingent date (such as the death of another person), and continue for the duration of a person's life or for a fixed period. Usually, but not always, an annuity guarantees a lifetime income for the recipient.

The **annuitant** is the "insured", the person on whose life the annuity policy has been issued. As is the case with life insurance, the owner of the contract may or may not be the annuitant. In most cases, the annuitant is the intended recipient of the annuity payments.

Depending on the type of annuity and the method of benefit payment selected, a **beneficiary** may also be named in an annuity contract. In such cases, annuity payments may continue after the death of the annuitant for the lifetime of the beneficiary or for a specified number of years.

Life insurance is designed to protect the insured against premature death. An annuity is designed to protect the annuitant against the risk of living too long and possibly outliving his or her financial resources during retirement. Thus, most often, the primary purpose of an annuity is to provide retirement income. Like life insurance policies, annuity contracts may include nonforfeiture provisions to protect the contract holder from total forfeiture or loss of benefits if he or she stops making the required periodic payments, and surrender charges, or penalties for "cashing in" the annuity before the payout period begins.

Annuities may be purchased on an individual basis to help solve individual retirement needs. In this case, the annuitant is the owner of the annuity. Often, annuities are purchased on a group basis covering a number of annuitants typically in an employer-employee situation. Group annuities are often used to fund an employer-sponsored retirement plan, with the employer as the contract owner.

Types of Annuities

There are two principal types of annuities: fixed and variable. A **fixed annuity** is a fully guaranteed contract. Principal, interest and the amount of the benefit payments are guaranteed. Fixed annuity payments are considered part of the insurer's general account assets, the conservative investment portfolio used by the insurance company for investing premium income. There are two levels of guaranteed interest; current and minimum. The current guarantee reflects current interest rates and is guaranteed at the beginning of each calendar year. The policy will also have a minimum guaranteed interest rate, such as 3% or 4%, which will be paid even if the current rate falls below the policy's guaranteed rate.

A **variable annuity**, like variable life insurance, is designed to provide a hedge against inflation through investments in a separate account of the insurer consisting primarily of common stock. A variable annuity is not a fully guaranteed contract. However, both a fixed and variable annuity guarantee expenses and mortality.

Any expense deductions made are guaranteed not to exceed a specific amount or percentage of the payments made by the annuitant. The guarantee of mortality provides for the payment of annuity benefits for life.

Occasionally, an annuitant may decide that it is in his or her best interests to purchase an annuity which offers some guarantees but also offers protection against inflation. This type of annuity is usually identified as a **combination or balanced annuity.** It is a combination of a fixed and variable annuity.

Method of Premium Payment

A **single premium** or **single payment** annuity is purchased by making one lump sum payment. For example, a life insurance policy could be cashed in at the date of retirement and the cash value used to buy a single premium annuity.

A **periodic premium or periodic payment** annuity consists of a series of periodic payments over a period of time. These payments may be made annually, semi-annually, quarterly or monthly. These periodic payments are not mandatory. Often, this type of purchase may be identified as a flexible premium annuity in that the frequency and amount of these payments are flexible.

Time When Benefits Begin

In addition to identifying an annuity by the method of purchase, it can further be described in terms of when the benefit payments to the annuitant will begin.

Benefits may be **immediate** or they may be **deferred** until a later date. If an annuitant purchases an annuity with a single payment, the benefits may begin immediately or they may be deferred. We would refer to this annuity as a single payment (premium) immediate or deferred annuity. If the annuity is purchased with a series of periodic payments, then the benefits will be deferred until all payments have been made. This annuity would be referred to as a periodic payment deferred annuity.

THE ANNUITY PROCESS

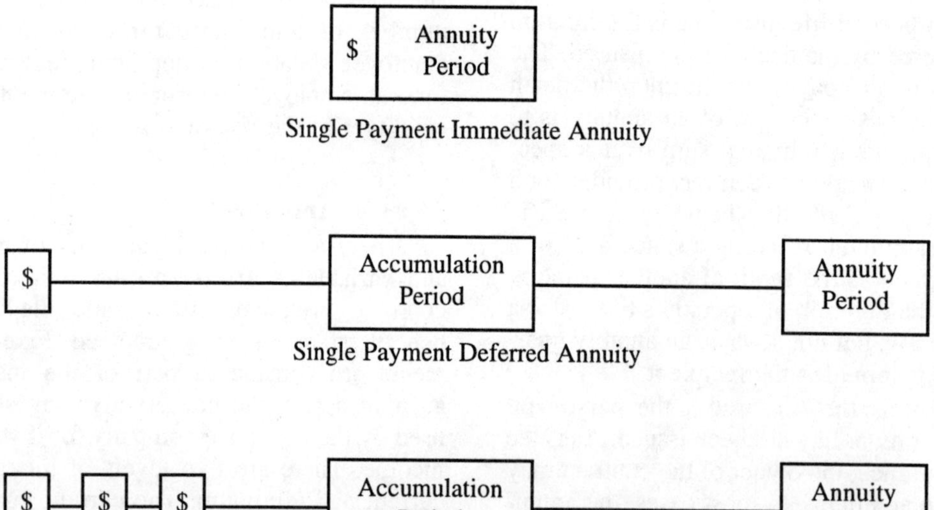

Chart 8-1

Periods of Time

There are two periods of time associated with an annuity; the accumulation period and the annuity or benefit period. The **accumulation period** is the "putting in" time. It is that period during which the annuitant is making the contributions or payments to the annuity. A unique feature of this period of time is the fact that the interest paid on the amounts contributed will grow tax deferred. The interest earned will be taxed but not until the annuitant begins to receive the benefits.

The **annuity period** is the "taking out" time. This is the period following the accumulation of the annuitant's payments (principal and interest) during which annuity benefits are received.

Annuity Settlement Options

Annuity settlement options are the settlement provisions of the annuity. Generally, when the annuitant decides to take money from the annuity (the annuity period), an annuity option will be selected as a method of disposing of the annuity's proceeds. It is not unusual for an annuity option to be elected at the time of application. Thus, if an annuitant purchased a single payment deferred straight life annuity, this person owns an annuity, purchased with a single payment, which will provide a payout for life. Even if an annuity option is elected at the time of purchase, it may (and probably will) be changed at the annuity period to reflect the annuitant's needs at retirement.

The amount of money available during the annuity period is determined by the annuity option selected, the amount of money accumulated by the annuitant and the life expectancy of the annuitant. Annuity options include the following types.

A **Life Only** (straight life) option provides for the payment of annuity benefits for the life of the annuitant with no further payment following the death of the annuitant. There is a risk to the annuitant in the fact that he or she must live long enough once the annuity period begins to collect the full value of the annuity. If an annuitant dies shortly after benefits begin, the insurer keeps the balance of the unpaid benefits. This option will pay the highest amount of monthly income to the annuitant because it is based only on life expectancy with no further payments after the death of the annuitant.

A **Refund Annuity** option will pay the annuitant for life but if he or she dies too soon after the annuity period begins, there may be a refund of any undistributed principal or cost of the annuity. This option assures the annuitant that the full purchase price of the annuity will be paid out to someone. Depending on when the annuitant's death occurs, there may or may not be a refund.

If the annuitant lives well beyond average life expectancy, then all of the annuitant's investment in the annuity will have been paid and thus there would be no refund. But if the annuitant died just a few years after retiring, then a refund of the total payments made by the annuitant, less any distributed amounts would be made to the annuitant's survivor. This refund may be in the form of continued monthly installments (an **installment refund annuity**) or it may be in one lump sum (a **cash refund annuity**), whichever has been elected by the annuitant.

Life with Period Certain is basically a straight life annuity with an extra guarantee for a certain period of time. This option provides for the payment of annuity benefits for the life of the annuitant but if death occurs within the period certain, annuity payments will be continued to a survivor for the balance of the period certain.

The period certain can be for just about any length of time — 5, 10, 15, 20 years. Most often, the period selected is 10 years because 10 years is approximately the average life expectancy of a male who retires at age 65. Thus, if Archie, the annuitant, retires at age 65 and selects life with 10 years certain and dies at age 70, his survivor will continue to receive the monthly annuity payments for the balance of the period certain (five more years).

The **Joint-Survivor** option provides benefits for the life of the annuitant and the life of the survivor. A stated monthly amount is paid to the annuitant and upon the annuitant's death, the same or a lesser amount is paid for the lifetime of the survivor. The joint-survivor option is usually classified as a joint and 100% survivor, joint and two-thirds survivor or joint and 50% survivor.

For example, if the annuitant was receiving $1,000 monthly under a joint and 50% survivor option, the survivor would receive $500 (50% of $1,000) upon the death of the annuitant.

The joint-survivor annuity option should be distinguished from a **joint life annuity**, which covers two or more annuitants and provides monthly income to each annuitant until one of them dies. Following the first annuitant's death, all income benefits cease.

The above mentioned annuity options all have one concept in common, they guaranteed an income for the life of the annuitant. Some of them may also provide continued payments following the death of the annuitant. The final annuity option to be discussed is an annuity certain.

An **Annuity Certain** is not an option which guarantees a lifetime income to the annuitant. It does provide an income for a guaranteed period of time whether the annuitant is alive or not. The guaranteed period could be 5, 10, 15 or 20 years. If the annuitant outlives the guaranteed period, the annuity payments cease. If the annuitant dies during the guaranteed period, the payments continue to the survivor until the guaranteed period of time ends.

Chart 8-2 summarizes the various annuity options.

Temporary Annuity

A temporary annuity provides annuity payments for a specified period of time (such as 5 years or 10 years), or until the death of the annuitant — *whichever occurs first*. A temporary annuity does not necessarily guarantee payment for life or the specified period of time. Unlike all forms of life annuities, there is no guarantee that an annuitant will receive payments for life because payments end when the specified period expires. Unlike an annuity certain, the period of time for a temporary annuity is not guaranteed and could be terminated by early death. The key concept is that the *earlier* event will terminate benefits.

For example, an annuitant purchases a 10-year temporary annuity to distribute an inheritance in monthly installments. If the annuitant dies three months into the annuity period, all benefits stop. If the annuitant lives for 20 years, all annuity payments stop at the end of the 10-year period.

Calculating Guaranteed Interest Rates

Premiums or payments made during the accumulation period earn a guaranteed return on a tax-deferred basis. There are two ways to calculate guaranteed interest paid on these contributions.

The **current purchase rate** reflects the current interest rates relevant to current economic conditions. This rate is guaranteed at the beginning of each calendar year, and could fluctuate from year to year. Increasing or decreasing interest rates will mirror present investment, banking, and market rates available in the marketplace.

The **guaranteed purchase rate** is the "minimum" interest rate that is guaranteed for the life of the contract. This will be a fairly modest amount such as 4-5%. This is the minimum return which will be paid even if the current annual rate falls below the guaranteed rate.

Thus, deferred annuities guarantee a minimum interest rate which contributions will earn. Since the guaranteed rate is less than prevailing interest rates, the insurer will often credit excess interest on the contract.

Excess interest is calculated based on how much the insurer has earned through its investments. If the insurer considers all of its invested reserves and net investment earnings over a relatively long period of time, the interest rate calculation is said to be made based on the **portfolio method.** If the insurer instead considers portions of its invested reserves over a shorter period of time the interest rate calculation is based on the **tier method**.

Most Common Uses of Annuities

Annuities are primarily used as retirement vehicles due to their guarantee of income for the life of the annuitant. During the accumulation period, the investment income realized on the payments made by the annuitant are tax deferred until taken at retirement. If the annuitant dies during the accumulation period, the money accumulated will be paid to a survivor. A

Annuity Options

Annuity Option	Payments to the Annuitant	Payments to the Survivor
Life Only	Guaranteed for life	None
Refund Options	Guaranteed for life	Unpaid principal upon annuitant's death cash or installments
Life with Period Certain	Guaranteed for life	Upon annuitant's death for the balance of the period certain
Joint-Survivor	Guaranteed for the life of the annuitant and the survivor	Benefits continue upon annuitant's death for life, at 50-100% of the annuitant's benefit
Annuity Certain	Guaranteed for a specific period of time	Benefits continue upon the annuitant's death for the balance of the guaranteed period

Chart 8-2

common illustration is the annual premium retirement annuity contract, where the total accumulation is calculated based on an annual premium, an assumed interest rate and retirement age (usually 65).

During the accumulation period, the annuity contract is very flexible in that the annuitant may make payments or not make payments. In addition, the annuitant has withdrawal options whereby the money accumulated can be withdrawn totally, or in part, during the accumulation period.

Annuities may be used to fund individual retirement accounts (IRAs), in which case premium payments may be tax deductible, but there are more restrictions on withdrawals (including tax penalties for withdrawals before age 59 ½).

Although most commonly used to build retirement funds, annuities may be used for many other purposes where there is a need to accumulate funds over a period of time and/or to provide periodic payments for a specific need. For example, annuities may be used to accumulate funds for children's education or to bestow a charitable gift.

Another common use for an annuity is to liquidate large cash settlements such as lawsuits or lottery winnings. These large sums of money can be used to purchase a single payment annuity and thus provide the annuitant with a guaranteed lifetime income.

Occasionally, an annuity may be used when an individual is uninsurable. Applicants for annuities do not have to prove insurability since the risk involved is outliving your retirement resources by living too long. If for example, a businessowner was uninsurable and there is a need to provide cash for funding a business agreement, an annuity might be an alternative method for funding the business obligation.

REVIEW QUESTIONS

1. What is an annuity? ______________________
2. What is the basic difference between an annuity and a life insurance policy? ______________________
3. What is the difference between an "annuity certain" and a "life annuity"? ______________________
4. What is a "refund" annuity? ______________________

> ☞ ***Answers to Review Questions are located at the back of the book.***

VARIABLE ANNUITIES

Purpose of Variable Annuities

Variable annuity premiums are invested in securities and the annuity income varies according to the market value of the securities. The insurer invests the annuity premiums or payments in a separate account which consists primarily of a portfolio of common stock. Because of the equity element, there is investment risk to the annuitant.

The primary purpose of the variable annuity is to provide a hedge against inflation. Historically, the stock market has kept pace with inflation and thus preserved the purchasing power of the dollar. The separate accounts of the insurer which hold primarily common stock (also some preferred stock, bonds and other equity-type products) should thus keep pace with inflation. Accordingly, the annuitant investing in a variable annuity has the opportunity to preserve the purchasing power of his or her retirement dollars.

The General Account

An insurer's general account is an investment portfolio used by the insurance company for investing its premium income. It generally consists of safe, conservative, guaranteed investments, such as real estate and mortgages. Funds which are invested for insureds or annuitants who hold variable contracts must be held in a separate account.

The Separate Account

In accordance with the Investment Company Act of 1940, the separate account funding a variable annuity must be registered with the Securities and Exchange Commission (SEC) as an investment company. Most often the separate account will be registered as a unit investment trust (UIT). As a UIT, the separate account management will purchase and hold assets (common stock and other securities) for the benefit of plan participants.

If the portfolio of securities performs well then the separate account performs well and the variable annuity, backed by the separate account, will also do well. Thus, it can be said, that the performance of the variable annuity is dependent upon the performance of the separate account. Due to this fact, there is investment risk to the annuitant since there is no guarantee of principal, interest or investment income associated with the separate account. The securities held in the separate account are valued each business day at the close of the New York Stock Exchange.

As evidence of the annuitant's participation in the separate account, units of the trust are issued. This is very similar to shares of a mutual fund which are issued to mutual fund investors. During the accumulation period, these units are identified as **accumulation units**. Both the number of the units and the value of these units will vary in accordance with the amount of premium payments made and the subsequent performance of the separate account.

For example, Jan invests $100 per month in her variable annuity. On the day the insurer received her $100 payment, the value of an accumulation unit was $10. Thus, Jan is credited with 10 additional accumulation units.

When the annuitant reaches the annuity period, these accumulation units are converted to **annuity units**. The number of annuity units remains constant. No further money is being contributed to the annuity, thus, there is no further increase in the number of annuity units. However, the value of the annuity units will vary in accordance with the daily performance of the separate account. Accordingly, during the annuity period, benefit checks issued to the annuitant will vary depending on the value of the annuity units at the time the monthly check is issued.

There are few guarantees associated with a variable annuity. The variable annuity contract will guarantee that expenses chargeable to the annuity will not exceed a specific amount or percentage. In addition, the policy will also guarantee mortality which means a benefit check will be guaranteed for the life of the annuitant. However, the variable annuity does not guarantee the amount of the benefits at retirement nor does it guarantee principal or interest.

Regulation of Variable Annuities

Considerable controversy has raged over the regulatory issue of whether a variable annuity is really an insurance product or an equity investment. Both the federal Securities and Exchange Commission (SEC) and state Insurance Departments regulate variable annuities. They are considered securities and have to comply with federal securities laws and regulations with certain limited exemptions. Regulation by state Insurance Departments includes licensing companies and agents to sell variable annuities and approving variable annuity contracts.

Due to this dual regulation, to sell variable annuities (and variable life products), an agent must pass a test and be registered with the National Association of Securities Dealers (NASD). In addition, the agent must also be licensed to sell life insurance by the state. Some states also have specific variable contract requirements which require a separate variable contracts license in addition to the other licenses.

Characteristics of Annuities

Fixed Annuities	Variable Annuities
Guaranteed expenses	Guaranteed expenses
Guaranteed mortality	Guaranteed mortality
Guaranteed payout	Variable payout
Guaranteed interest	No guarantee of interest
Guarantee of principal	No guarantee of principal
Investment risk assumed by the insurer	Investment risk assumed by the annuitant
Performance based on the general account	Performance based on the separate account
No protection against inflation	Provides a hedge against inflation
Insurance regulation only	Insurance and federal regulation

Chart 8-3

Summary of Annuity Characteristics

Variable annuities may be purchased in the same way as fixed annuities — single premium immediate or deferred and periodic payment deferred contracts. Also, variable annuities include a variable premium feature, known as a flexible premium deferred annuity (FPDA) contract. Variable annuities offer the same annuity options for settlement of the contract as fixed annuities. Both types of annuities are primarily used as retirement vehicles. Other characteristics are illustrated in chart 8-3.

REVIEW QUESTIONS

5. What is a "variable" annuity? ____________

6. Name three types of variable annuities. ____________

☞ ***Answers to Review Questions are located at the back of the book.***

QUALIFIED & NON-QUALIFIED RETIREMENT PLANS

Life insurance and annuity products are frequently used to provide the funding for retirement plans and other types of plans. Some of these plans may also be funded with other products such as mutual funds, certificates of deposit (CDs), stocks and bonds, cash held in bank accounts, etc.

GENERAL REQUIREMENTS

Retirement plans and other corporate and individual plans may be described as qualified or nonqualified. Some of the characteristics of **qualified plans** include:

- The plan must be in writing and be communicated to the plan participants
- The plan must be filed and approved by the IRS
- The plan cannot discriminate as to participation (all eligible employees must be included)
- The plan is usually established by an employer for the benefit of employees (there are a few exceptions)
- The employer will receive a tax deduction for plan contributions
- Employer contributions on behalf of the employee are generally excluded from the employee's gross income; no tax is due until benefits are actually distributed to the employee
- Investment income realized by the plan is tax deferred until it is received by the plan participants

A **nonqualified plan** has the following features:

- The plan must be in writing and be communicated to the participants
- The plan is not filed with the IRS
- The plan may discriminate as to participation (the plan may be selective as to who is covered)
- The employer does not receive a current tax deduction for any contributions made

The fact that a nonqualified plan is not approved by the IRS does not imply that is illegal or unethical. A nonqualified plan is a legal method of accumulating money for retirement funds and other purposes.

NONQUALIFIED PLANS

An example of a nonqualified plan would be the situation where a person buys an **individual annuity** for the purpose of accumulating his or her own retirement benefits. When the annuitant pays the annuity premium or payment, there is no tax deduction for the payment of the premium. The annuity is not filed with the IRS.

Deferred compensation is a typical example of a nonqualified plan which is provided by many corporations for the benefit of key employees or corporate executives. Under these plans, the key people or executives who may participate are selected by the corporation, and all others are excluded. As a nonqualified plan, a deferred compensation arrangement may be discriminatory with regard to participation. These plans are not filed with the IRS, but they must be in writing in the form of an agreement between the employer and each key executive who participates.

Under this plan, the employee agrees to defer receipt of current compensation until retirement, death or disability. The employer promises to pay this deferred amount when any of these contingencies occur. The plan may be funded or unfunded. If funded, a fixed or variable annuity could be used as the funding mechanism. If unfunded, the deferred compensation plan amounts to an unsecured promise by the employer to provide the compensation at a later date. The employer receives no current tax deductions. The employee is not currently taxed. Upon receipt of the deferred compensation at a later date, the employee will be taxed on the amounts received as current income and the employer is allowed to deduct these amounts as current compensation paid to the employee.

QUALIFIED PLANS

Types of Plans

Corporate Pension Plans. Pension plans comprise a large portion of existing qualified plans. Typically, an employer will install a pension plan as an employee benefit for all eligible employees. These plans may be described in terms of the contributions made to the plan or the benefits to be received from the plan.

A **defined contribution plan** is a qualified retirement plan in which the employer agrees to make a specific contribution on behalf of all eligible employees. This contribution is usually expressed as a percentage, such as, 5 or 10% of compensation. The amount of the contribution is clearly identified. The amount of retirement benefits to be received is not specified. The plan participants will receive the contributions made and the interest earned on those contributions as a retirement benefit.

A **defined benefit plan** is a qualified plan in which the employer agrees to make necessary contributions on behalf of all eligible employees in order to provide a specific retirement benefit, such as 10% of compensation. The amount of the employer's contribution is not specifically known but the amount of the retirement benefit is clearly defined.

Generally, a pension plan represents a fixed liability for the employer.

Benefits paid to employees from pension plans are taxed as regular income at the time the benefits are received. Since this is generally at the time of retirement, when the retiree has a lower income, the recipient usually falls into a lower income tax bracket at that time.

Profit Sharing Plan. An employer may elect to establish a qualified profit sharing plan, under which contributions to the plan are made only if profits are realized. Generally, the amount of the contribution will be expressed as a specified share of company profits (perhaps 30%) up to a percentage of each employee's compensation (such as 10% of salary). However, this contribution is contingent on profitability. If profits are inadequate in a given year, the specified share might only fund a lesser proportion of employee compensation (such as 6%). If there are no profits at all, there would be no contribution for that year. In contrast to pension plan obligations, a profit sharing plan is not a fixed liability.

Profit sharing plans frequently require an immediate distribution of each employee's share on an annual basis. These plans are not necessarily designed to provide retirement benefits — it is not a requirement. But in some cases they are set up to accumulate the profit sharing proceeds for the purposes of paying benefits at retirement. When the payment of profit sharing proceeds is deferred, life insurance policies or services are often used to accumulate funds and make disbursements as required.

Keogh Plans. The Self-Employed Individuals Tax Retirement Act of 1962, known popularly as the "Keogh Act," makes a special type of retirement plan available for non-incorporated businesses. A Keogh Plan (or an HR-10) is a qualified retirement plan for self employed individuals and their eligible employees. Keogh plans are similar to corporate pension plans in that they provide tax benefits. The primary difference is simply that a Keogh plan is for a non-incorporated form of business. The advantages of a Keogh plan are that:

- Contributions to the plan are treated as income tax deductions for the employer
- Plan contributions are not taxable as income to the individual for whom they are made in the year in which they are made
- Interest accumulating in the plan is not taxed until withdrawn
- All distributions (principal and interest) are taxed as current income in the year withdrawn

A Keogh plan must cover all full-time employees (as defined by the IRS) who are at least 21 years of age and who satisfy the minimum service requirements (hours and years of service as specified in the tax laws). Keoghs can be funded by life insurance (when incidental to the plan), fixed or variable annuities, mutual funds, trust accounts, or other financial institution accounts.

Like corporate pension plans, Keogh plans may also take the form of defined contribution or defined benefit plans. With either plan, there are annual limits to the amounts that can be contributed to the plan: 25% of compensation for defined contribution plans, and 15% of compensation for defined benefit plans. The maximum dollar contibution is limited to $30,000 per year. However, the maximum compensation used in this calculation is currently limited to $150,000 per year, which in effect puts a $22,500 cap on the amount that can be contributed to a defined benefit plan.

Individual Retirement Accounts (IRAs). These are qualified retirement plans available to individuals. Almost any individual with earned income who is under the age of 70 ½ is eligible to open an IRA. IRAs help individuals to save money to finance their retirement by allowing them to deduct contributions to these accounts from their pre-tax incomes for income tax purposes. These deductible contributions are a form of deferred compensation, and will only be taxed when the individual withdraws them from the account at retirement — usually a time when the individual is in a lower tax bracket.

Deductible yearly contributions to regular IRAs are limited to **100%** of earned income or **$2,000**, *whichever is less*. Additional nondeductible contributions may also be made. For a married couple, an account can be set up for each person, even if only one spouse is working. Married couples may contribute up to $4,000 annually, or $2,000 per person.

The maximum IRA deduction may be reduced or eliminated if an individual is a participant in another qualified plan, such as an employer's pension plan, and earns a specific amount of compensation. However, an individual may still make non-deductible contributions to an IRA account (either in excess of or in lieu of any allowed deduction) and enjoy tax deferred growth on the money.

IRAs can be funded by individual retirement annuities, mutual funds, trust accounts, or other financial institution accounts.

Simplified Employee Pension Plan (SEP). Under a SEP, an employer contributes specific amounts directly into IRA accounts on behalf of eligible employees. This is a simplified method of establishing a pension plan, since an IRA is already a qualified plan, and it is easier for an employer to establish and administer. Contributions to the plan are not included in the employee's taxable income for the year made, to the extent that the contribution does not exceed 15% of the employee's compensation or $30,000. (The permitted contribution is actually capped at $22,500 under current tax law due to a $150,000 maximum on the amount of earned income upon which the contribution may be based.)

For example, Richard has annual compensation of $175,000. His employer may contribute up to 15% of Richard's compensation to the simplified employee pension plan. But current tax law places a $150,000 limit on the amount of compensation that may be included in this calculation. In effect, this creates a $22,500 cap on the maximum contribution (15% of $150,000).

Distributions from the plan will be taxable as current income when received after retirement. Once a SEP is established, the employer must make contributions for each employee who is at least 21 years of age, who has performed services for the employer during the year in which the contribution is made, and has performed services for at least three of the previous five years. In other words, three years of recent service, current year service, and age 21 are the minimum eligibility requirements.

Tax Sheltered Annuity (TSA). A TSA is a pension plan for employees of non-profit organizations as specified by the IRS, in accordance with section 501(c)(3) and 403(b) of the Internal Revenue Code. The tax deferment allowed is much like that allowed for contributions a corporate employer makes to a qualified pension or profit-sharing plan. Under a 403(b) plan, employees of organizations such as school systems, churches and hospitals are eligible to set aside portions of their current income by means of a **salary reduction** or an **elective deferral**. Like a qualified plan, this elective deferral is not currently taxed, will grow tax deferred and will be totally taxed when received usually at retirement. Employers may also contribute to the TSA but generally, TSAs are employee-pay plans. Employer contributions cannot exceed 25% of the participant's compensation up to a maximum contribution of $30,000. Salary reduction deferrals by an individual may not exceed $9,500 per year.

401(k) Plans. Another type of elective deferral (salary reduction) plan is known as a 401(k) plan. The name comes from the section of the tax code which applies. This plan allows an employee to reduce his or her compensation by a stated percentage and have this amount placed in the 401(k) plan on a tax deductible and tax deferred basis. Often the employer may "match" employee contributions by contributing a percentage or dollar amount, such as 50 cents for each dollar contributed by an employee.

Employee Stock Ownership Plan (ESOP). An ESOP is a qualified employee benefit plan which gives employees part ownership in the company for which they work. Stock in the company is issued and held in trust for the benefit of eligible employees. An ESOP can borrow money to purchase the stock on behalf of the employees. As a qualified plan, an ESOP enjoys most of the tax advantages of other qualified plans. There are tax incentives for starting an ESOP: company contributions to the ESOP are tax-deductible to the company, any dividends paid may be tax deductible, and special loan rates are available for borrowing money by ESOPs.

Rollover Provisions

There is one major exception to the various annual contribution limitations that have been discussed with respect to qualified plans — permitted rollovers from one plan to another.

A **rollover** is a tax free withdrawal of cash or other assets from one retirement program and its reinvestment in another retirement program. The amount rolled over is not counted as current income and is not taxable until later withdrawn. However, the rollover must be completed within **60 days** after the distribution is received, or else the full amount becomes taxable as current income.

Rollovers are permitted from pension plans, Keogh plans, 401(k) plans and other plans. Usually, the funds are rolled over into an IRA, but this is not always the only choice.

For example, Bud is terminating employment with IBM and taking a new position with General Motors. Upon termination, the entire vested portion of the funds in Bud's IBM pension plan ($10,000) is released to him as a distribution from the plan. If Bud elects to keep the distribution, the entire $10,000 becomes taxable as additional income in the year received. But if Bud establishes an IRA rollover account and contributes the entire amount within 60 days, the money is not taxable and will continue to grow on a tax deferred basis until retirement (the normal $2,000 annual contribution limit does not apply to a rollover).

A distinction should be made between an IRA rollover and an IRA transfer. With an IRA transfer, the IRA owner is never in possession of the funds. There

TAX TREATMENT OF QUALIFIED PLANS

CONTRIBUTIONS:	Annual Contribution Limits	Distributions
Corporate Pension Plan	Subject to top-heavy and non-discrimination rules	Taxed as income when received
Keogh Plan:		
Defined Contribution	25% of compensation; $30,000 maximum	Taxed as income when received
Defined Benefit	15% of compensation; $22,500 maximum	Taxed as income when received
IRA:		
Individual	Lesser of $2,000 or 100% of earned income	Taxed as income when received
Married couple	$4,000 (up to $2,000 each)	Taxed as income when received
SEP	15% of compensation; $22,500 maximum	Taxed as income when received
Tax Sheltered Annuities		
Employer Contributions	15% of compensation; $30,000 maximum	Taxed as income when received
Individual Salary Reduction Deferrals	$9,500	Taxed as income when received
401(k) Individual Salary Reduction Deferrals	$9,500	Taxed as income when received

TAX PENALTIES:

Excess IRA Contributions	6% tax penalty on excess
Early Withdrawals before age 59½ (all plans)	10% tax penalty plus taxed as current income
Late Withdrawals after age 70½ (all plans)	50% penalty on amount which should have been received

ROLLOVER PROVISIONS:

All Plans	No tax consequences if rolled over within 60 days; otherwise, amount received taxed as current income

Chart 8-4

is no constructive receipt. Transfers are made directly from one IRA custodian or plan to another.

Contribution and Withdrawal Penalties

There is a 6% **excess contribution** penalty that applies to IRAs. For example, if an individual contributed $3,000 to an IRA, this would represent an excess contribution of $1,000, which would be subject to a tax penalty of 6%.

Since qualified plans are designed as retirement plans, a tax penalty is imposed for **early withdrawals** by an individual — all withdrawals are taxable as current income, but any withdrawal before age 59 ½ is subject to an additional **tax penalty of 10%** of the amount withdrawn.

There are some exceptions to the 10% penalty for early withdrawal:

- Distributions due to death or disability of the participant
- Distributions received by a participant who is at least age 55 and has satisfied the plan's early retirement rules
- Distributions to a former spouse or dependent child as a result of a divorce decree
- Distributions which are part of a series of periodic payments which are made for the life of the individual or joint lives of the individual and his or her survivor (life annuity)
- Distributions which are due to removal of excess contributions
- Allowable plan loans

There is also a requirement that distributions from any qualified plan must begin by a certain age. By April 1 of the year following the year the individual becomes 70 ½, the individual must take a distribution from the account or at least begin a plan of distribution. Failure to do so results in a **late withdrawal** penalty equal to 50% of the amount which should have been received by the participant.

Regulation of Qualified Plans

The Employee Retirement Income Security Act (ERISA) of 1974 provides much of the regulation for qualified plans. ERISA establishes certain reporting and disclosure requirements for employer sponsored plans. The reporting provisions apply to specific requirements with regard to the Department of Labor and the IRS. In addition, specific disclosure information is required to be provided to plan participants.

These regulations specify eligibility requirements, contribution limitations, tax rules, vesting considerations and penalties for non-compliance with qualified plan requirements. It should be remembered that laws, especially the tax laws, change periodically. Thus, eligibility or contribution requirements and limitations sometimes change as does the tax status of some of these qualified plans.

Other Employee Plans

Employee Benefits. Life insurance is a commonly offered employee benefit, provided in the form of group life insurance for employees and dependents. Life insurance products may also be used to partially fund pension and profit sharing plans and to fund salary continuation plans for the dependents of deceased employees. Many employers also offer disability insurance, medical insurance, and other insurance benefits.

Special Rules for Life Insurance

Pension plans and other qualified plans may include **incidental life insurance** and health insurance benefits, but these must be *incidental to the purpose of the plan* — the primary purpose of the plan must be to provide retirement benefits. In order to stay within the requirements established by the IRS, qualified plans must satisfy the **incidental limitation** rule, which requires that the cost for life insurance benefits provided by a pension plan, or life and health insurance benefits provided by a profit sharing plan, must be **less than 25%** of the cost of providing all benefits under the plan.

The cost for life insurance provided under a qualified pension or profit sharing plan is included as part of an employees taxable income for the year. However, the employee only pays tax on the cost of that portion of insurance protection which provided an **economic benefit** to the employee. Generally, the cost for insurance protection under a pension or profit sharing plan is taxable as income to the employee to the extent that any death benefit is payable to the employee's beneficiary or estate. The cost for any protection for which the proceeds are payable to and may be retained by the plan, trustee or employer is not taxable as income to the employee (thus the employee would not pay tax on the cost of key person insurance).

To the extent that an employee is taxed on the cost for incidental life insurance protection, the employee only pays a tax on the cost for pure protection. For cash value insurance, the taxable cost would be the one year term rate for the amount of protection at risk (face value minus accumulated cash value), regardless of the premium actually being paid by the plan. For term insurance protection, the entire actual cost for protection would be taxable to the employee, because that is the cost for pure protection.

REVIEW QUESTIONS

Match the following numbered definitions with the lettered terms below.

_____ 7. A qualified IRS retirement plan for self-employed persons and their employees with favorable tax benefits

_____ 8. Retirement Plan which currently allows a $2,000 yearly contribution for individuals with earned income

_____ 9. Set up by a company to provide retirement benefits for its employees who have been employed a certain length of time

_____ 10. May or may not be used to provide retirement benefits

A. Keogh Plan
B. Pension Plan
C. IRA
D. Profit Sharing Plan

☞ ***Answers to Review Questions are located at the back of the book.***

NOTES

9

HEALTH INSURANCE BASICS

While it is not often recognized, the financial impact of total disability may be greater than the financial impact of death. A person may live for many years totally disabled and, therefore, be unable to generate an income to pay for the higher medical and living expenses caused by the disability.

Health insurance provides payment of benefits for the loss of income and/or the medical expenses arising from illness or injury. Health insurance is often called accident and sickness insurance or accident and health insurance. Many different kinds of health insurance coverages are available. Health insurance varies according to the methods of underwriting, the injury or illness covered, the types of insurers, the types of benefits and services provided, the types of losses covered, and the amount of benefits available.

Health insurance originated in the United States in the mid-1800s. It was first provided by casualty insurance companies and then by riders to life insurance products. The earliest policies were to provide benefits for losses due to accidental injuries and to protect railroad travellers. Later coverage provided benefits due to illness as well as accidents.

TYPES OF LOSSES & BENEFITS

Loss of Income from Disability

Disability income insurance, also referred to as loss of time insurance, pays a weekly or monthly benefit for disabilities due to accident or sickness. The primary purpose of disability income coverage is to replace loss of personal income due to a disability.

Disability income policies are issued on an individual basis or on a group basis through an employer-sponsored plan, labor union or association. Benefits paid are in accordance with the policy's provisions and to a degree, the insured's loss of income.

Accidental Death and Dismemberment (AD&D)

Although a health insurance product, AD&D benefits are frequently provided as riders to individual and group life insurance contracts. This product was discussed in the life insurance section of this text.

AD&D policies (or riders) pay the policy's **principal sum** for accidental death in accordance with the policy's provisions and definition of accidental death. The principal sum is similar in meaning to a policy's face amount. This same amount is paid if the insured suffers the actual severance of two arms, two legs, or the loss of vision in two eyes due to an accident. This amount is usually identified as the **capital sum** if the policy is paying an accidental dismemberment benefit.

AD&D benefits may be included as riders on life insurance policies, as part of disability income insurance, as part of health insurance, or as a separate policy (a type of limited coverage).

Medical Expense Benefits

Medical expense insurance, commonly referred to as hospitalization insurance, provides benefits for expenses incurred due to in-hospital medical treatment and surgery as well as certain outpatient expenses such as doctor's visits, lab tests and diagnostic services. Hospitalization insurance may be issued as an individual policy covering all family members or as a group insurance policy provided through an employer-sponsored program.

When medical expense coverage provided for proprietors and partners is paid for by the business, the premiums have traditionally been considered tax deductible to the business but includable as income to the individual. There is no limit to the amount of tax free medical expense benefits the individual can receive, however.

Dental Expense Benefits

Dental expense benefits are generally sold as part of group hospitalization coverage. Most insurers do not provide individual dental coverage. Dental benefits are provided for preventive maintenance (cleanings and x-rays), repair (fillings, root canals, etc.) and replacement of teeth.

Long-Term Care Insurance

Long-term care (LTC) insurance pays for the care of persons with chronic diseases or disabilities, and may include a wide range of health and social services provided under the supervision of medical professionals. LTC often covers nursing home care, home-based care, and respite care.

Limited Health Exposures and Insurance Contracts

There are a variety of special health insurance policies providing limited coverage. To ensure that the insured has sufficient notice that the coverage is limited, every policy that provides limited coverage must, by law, state plainly on the first page of the policy: "THIS IS A LIMITED POLICY."

Travel accident insurance provides coverage for death or injury resulting from accidents occurring while the insured is a fare-paying passenger on a common carrier.

Specified disease or **dread disease insurance** provides a variety of benefits for only certain diseases, usually cancer or heart disease.

Hospital income insurance pays a specified sum on a daily, weekly or monthly basis while the insured is confined to a hospital. The amount of the benefit is not related to expenses incurred or to wages lost while the insured is hospitalized.

Accident only insurance provides coverage for injury from accident, and excludes sickness. Benefits may be paid for all or any of the following: death, disability, dismemberment, or hospital and medical expenses.

Credit insurance is listed here because of the limited nature of its coverage. This policy is issued only to those who are in debt to a creditor. The coverage is limited to the total amount of the debtor's indebtedness.

Blanket insurance is a form of group insurance. Often the individual's name is not known because the individuals come and go. Such groups include students, campers, passengers of a common carrier, volunteer groups, and sports teams. Unlike group insurance the individuals are automatically covered under the blanket policy, and they do not receive certificates of insurance.

Prescription Coverage

Prescription medication coverage is normally provided as an optional benefit under a group medical expense policy. The insured and eligible dependents are provided with a stated cost for any prescription medication required. This specific cost is usually, two, three, or five dollars per prescription. Thus, regardless of the cost of the medication, the insured only pays the stated amount and the balance of the prescription cost is paid by the insurance company.

DETERMINING INSURANCE NEEDS

Life insurance is designed to protect the individual and his or her family from the risk of premature death by providing specific amounts of money exactly when needed to cover necessary expenses. Health insurance is designed to protect the insured from the risk of medical and disability expenses.

Similar to life insurance, health insurance benefits provide benefits exactly when needed. Disability income insurance can enable the insured to pay a mortgage and other necessary family expenses when total disability due to an accident or sickness cuts off the insured's income.

Medical expense insurance provides the insured with necessary funds to cover hospital and physician expenses associated with a serious illness, thus preserving the family's savings and other assets.

Basically, the process of determining health insurance needs is similar to identifying an individual's life insurance requirements. The principal difference is the risk being insured — premature death or health insurance expenses.

The individual's and family's health insurance needs must be identified. These needs are then prioritized in terms of their importance to the family. Other forms of health insurance should be reviewed with regard to this needs analysis. These benefits include:

- Workers compensation benefits for job-related disabilities
- Social Security disability benefits
- Medicare, if the individual is eligible
- Work-related benefits through employer-sponsored plans
- Health coverage under any statutory plans

Once the individual's total health insurance needs analysis has been completed, then meaningful recommendations can be made as to the type and amounts of health insurance required.

REVIEW QUESTIONS

1. Who is covered by a disability income policy? ____________________

2. Why is a cancer policy called a limited policy? ____________________

3. AD&D stands for ____________________

4. Hospitalization insurance may provide benefits for both inpatient and outpatient expenses under either individual or group policies. (True/False) ________

5. When might someone want to buy a blanket accident policy? ____________________

6. What types of expenses would need to be covered when an individual suffers a disability, and what types of insurance could be used to cover those expenses? ____________________

> ☞ ***Answers to Review Questions are located at the back of the book.***

TYPES OF PROVIDERS & PLANS

HEALTH CARE PROVIDERS

Patients have traditionally been seen by physicians in office or hospital environments. Today physicians also see patients in surgicenters, urgent care centers, and at skilled nursing facilities. **Surgicenters** provide a site for outpatient surgery where general anesthesia must be used, but a patient does not need to stay overnight. **Urgent care centers** see patients often without an appointment during the daytime, as well as evening and weekend hours. **Skilled nursing facilities** provide medical care for patients who no longer require hospitalization, but cannot yet care for themselves at home. **Home health care** is also provided by nurses and others for patients ready to be at home, but who cannot yet fully provide for all of their own needs.

The traditional broad health coverage provided by insurance plans provides little incentive for efficient, cost-effective health care delivery. In the past decade it has become clear that too much money is being spent on health care. One response from insurers and providers has been to reorganize the health care delivery system into a form of **managed care**. Managed care imposes controls on the use of health care services, the providers of health care services, and the amount charged for these services, usually through health maintenance organizations or preferred provider arrangements, all discussed below. Of all workers covered by employer-sponsored health plans in 1994, 63% were enrolled in managed care plans.

HEALTH CARE PLANS

The insurers of health care are not only the traditional stock and mutual companies, and Blue Cross and Blue Shield, but also the health maintenance organizations and preferred provider organizations formed by hospitals and physicians to deliver health care directly to enrollees in their plans.

Commercial Insurers

Commercial insurers are stock and mutual life insurers, and sometimes casualty companies. Commercial insurers have traditionally provided coverage on a reimbursement basis but have also begun to embrace alternative approaches. **Reimbursement** plans pay benefits directly to the insured. Once the insured receives the benefits, it is his or her responsibility to pay the providers of the medical services.

Commercial insurers offer both individual and group health insurance products. These products include, basic medical expense coverage, major medical plans, comprehensive medical plans, disability income policies and other types of health products.

Recent developments from commercial insurers in response to the need for cost control include the Preferred Provider Organizations (PPOs) and Health Maintenance Organizations (HMOs). These organizations will be discussed in more detail later in this chapter.

Blue Cross and Blue Shield

The 63 Blue Cross and Blue Shield plans nationwide provide coverage to 64 million people. When considered in combination, they are the dominant health insurer of the United States. The nation's Blue Cross and Blue Shield Plans are loosely affiliated through the national Blue Cross & Blue Shield Association but are independently managed.

Differences from Commercial Insurers. Blue Cross and Blue Shield (the blues) are different from traditional commercial insurers in the following important areas:

- The blues provide the majority of their benefits on a **service** basis rather than on a reimbursement basis. This means that the insurer pays the provider directly for the medical treatment given the insured, instead of reimbursing the insured.
- The blues have contractual relationships with the hospitals and doctors. As participating providers, the doctors and hospitals contractually agree to specific costs for the medical services provided to subscribers. Thus, there is no contractual arrangement between the blues and the subscribers as there would be between the insurer and the insured.

Corporate Structure. Traditionally, the blues have operated as nonprofit organizations, which means any net gain realized from company operations is eventually returned to the policyholders in the form of reduced premiums or increased benefits. More and more frequently, plans have been allowed to become for-profit companies, or form for-profit subsidiaries, to allow them to raise money for expansion and compete in the health care marketplace.

Blue Cross traditionally has been a hospital service plan and Blue Shield a physicians service plan but these distinctions are becoming blurred. In some states both Blue Cross and Blue Shield serve as hospital and physician service plans. Under the hospital plan the contract is between Blue Cross and the hospital providing the hospital care. Under the medical plan the contract is between Blue Shield and the physicians providing the service. The contract is evidence of their joint cooperation in providing health care to the public.

Enrollment and Premium Rates. Members of Blue Cross and Blue Shield are known as **subscribers.** Subscribers in either plan can transfer their membership from one blues organization to another in other areas of town, or to other cities or states. Subscribers may also change their coverage from individual to family, from family to group, or any combination of change they need to make. When transfers or changes are made, the subscriber's coverage continues without interruption.

Blue Cross and Blue Shield plans are called **prepaid** plans because the plan subscribers pay a set fee, usually each month, for medical services covered under the plan.

Types of Coverage and Benefits. Blue Cross offers broad coverages and pays claims on a service basis. The plan covers hospital daily room and board, outpatient services for minor surgery, or accidental injury, medical emergencies, diagnostic testing, physical therapy, kidney dialysis, chemotherapy, and in some cases preadmission testing. Family plans may also include coverage for dependent handicapped children. Maternity benefits are also made available the "same as for any other disability."

Blue Cross also has a supplemental coverage, for catastrophic loss, which is similar to commercial major medical plans. This supplement has a deductible and an 80%-20% coinsurance feature.

Blue Shield offers medical coverage to cover the physician expenses incurred by plan subscribers. Again, through the contractual arrangement with the providers, Blue Shield will normally pay the participating physician a predetermined amount for the specific service provided. Usually, this amount will be based on a usual, customary and reasonable (UCR) basis depending on the charges made by other physicians in the same geographical area for the same or similar medical procedure.

It is also possible to obtain dental coverage through Blue Cross/Blue Shield, which contracts with dental providers and pays fees on a service basis. An estimated 15% of people with dental insurance have their coverage through Blue Cross/Blue Shield plans.

Special Requirements for Consolidated Plans. Jointly-operated (consolidated) Blue Cross/Blue Shield plans are often so comprehensive that supplementing them with major medical coverage is not necessary. Plan provisions applying to consolidated Blue Cross/Blue Shield plans are similar to plan provisions applying to comprehensive major medical plans.

Health Maintenance Organizations

History and Development. Health maintenance organizations (HMOs) are a relatively recent service approach to providing prepaid doctor and hospital care. Their growth has been encouraged by rising health care costs, and federal legislation. The law requires employers with 25 or more employees who offer health care benefits to offer enrollment in an HMO if an HMO is located nearby. HMOs are sometimes owned and controlled by commercial insurers, however, many are independently owned. Blue Cross and Blue Shield plans own or operate almost 100 HMOs. Other organizers of HMOs include governments, hospitals, employers, unions, consumer groups, and local communities.

The principal objectives of HMOs are to reduce medical expenses by:

- Stressing preventive medicine through physical exams and diagnostic procedures
- Reducing the number of unnecessary hospital admissions
- Reducing the average number of days per hospital visit
- Reducing duplication of benefits
- Saving on administrative costs

Dual Choice. The HMO Act of 1973 required that employers with certain characteristics are required to offer HMO coverage by a federally qualified HMO as an alternative to an indemnity plan. Employers falling under this act are those which:

- Have 25 or more employees and are within the service area of a federally qualified HMO
- Are paying at least minimum wage
- Offer a health plan to their employees

Corporate and Structural Characteristics. HMOs can be organized as for-profit (commercial) corporations or nonprofit corporations. The majority of HMOs, however, are for-profit corporations. HMOs must operate within a specified geographical area known as the **service area**. The service area must be approved by the Department of Insurance and all members of the HMO must reside in the prescribed service area. The service area is usually a city, or part of a city and occasionally an entire state. HMOs may be state qualified (able to provide services within a single state or states) and/or federally qualified (able to provide services in specified areas throughout the nation for national contracts like the United Auto Workers, Teamsters, or government employees). If an HMO is federally qualified, it must also be state qualified in the states where it serves members obtained through a national contract. HMOs provide service to their members through one or more of three "models" of operation. These models of operation are as follows:

- A **Group Practice Model (GPM),** also known as the Medical Group Model, is composed of a group of physicians of varying specializations practicing in one facility. This is similar to a clinic type operation. The HMO contracts with the medical group to provide health care services to the HMO's members. If the medical group provides services to HMO members only it is called a **closed panel** medical group. Under a closed panel HMO, physicians are usually salaried employees of the HMO and work at a clinic owned by the HMO. If the medical group provides services to HMO members in addition to other, nonmember patients, it is called an **open panel** medical group. Under the open panel, physicians are not salaried and treat HMO subscribers in their own offices. Generally, a member need go no farther than the medical group for the health care required, unless hospitalization is needed. The medical group refers HMO members internally, within the medical group to physicians of differing specializations as needed (i.e. pediatrician, surgeon etc.). Special arrangements are made for the member if a specialist of a particular type of medicine is not a part of the medical group. The HMO also contracts with hospitals in the area to provide services to members not available through the medical group, or in the case of surgery, etc.
- A **Staff Model** health care delivery system is actually owned, operated, staffed etc., by the HMO. In this case the HMO would control the physician group, and the physicians and other health care professionals working in it would be employees of the HMO. The HMO could also build a medical group facility and hire physicians to staff it and provide health care services to members. In any event, the key element of a Staff Model is that the HMO's own employees and facilities are being used to provide health care services to the HMO's members.
- The **Independent Practice Association Model (IPA)** is a network of individually practicing physicians who contract with the HMO to provide health care services to its members. Unlike the Group Practice Model, an IPA's physicians are located throughout a geographic area and are operated independently of each other. An HMO member selecting an IPA would have a list of physicians of varying specializations to choose from when seeking health care services. Initially, the member chooses his or her **primary care physician** (usually a general practitioner, or if for a child oftentimes a pediatrician). When in need of health care services, the member will visit his or her primary care physician for treatment. If the primary care physician cannot render treatment, then he or she will refer the member to an appropriate specialist within the IPA network. Like the Group Practice Model, the physicians of an IPA may utilize hospitals affiliated (contracted) with the HMO to render services not available at their independent practices. Physicians who are part of an IPA treat patients on an open panel (HMO members and nonmembers) or closed panel (HMO members only) basis, depending on their contract with the HMO.

Benefit Structure. The emphasis of HMOs is prevention, as the benefits offered are broader than those provided by commercial insurers or the blues. HMO benefits are not limited to treatment resulting from illness or injury as they also include preventive health care measures like routine physical examinations. HMO members pay a set fee, usually on a monthly basis which entitles them to all necessary health care. Most HMOs accept enrollments only from clearly designated groups, although individuals may be allowed to enroll.

HMOs — Benefits Provided. Health maintenance organizations are required to provide a wide range of health care services. The required services that must be provided are referred to as **basic health care services.** Any services or benefits provided by the HMO to members in excess of the basic health care services are referred to as **supplemental health care services.** The basic health care services that must be provided are as follows:

- **Inpatient hospital and physician services** for a period of at least 90 days per calendar year for treatment of illness or injury. If inpatient treatment is for mental, emotional or nervous disorders, including alcohol and drug rehabilitation and treatment, then services may be limited to 30 days per calendar year. Treatment for alcohol and drug rehabilitation and treatment may be restricted to a 90-day lifetime limit. A partial list of the hospital services provided include room and board; maternity care; general nursing care; use of operating room and facilities; use of intensive care unit; X-rays, laboratory, and other diagnostic tests; drugs, medications and anesthesia; physical, radiation and inhalation therapy.
- **Outpatient medical services** when prescribed or supervised by a physician and rendered in a non-hospital based health care facility (i.e. physician's office, member's home, etc.). Outpatient medical services shall include diagnostic services, treat-

ment services, short term physical therapy and rehabilitation services, laboratory and X-ray services and outpatient surgery.

- **Preventive health services** with the goal of protection against and early detection and minimization of the ill effects and causes of disease or disability. Specifically, this will include well child care from birth, eye and ear examinations for children age 17 and under, periodic health evaluations and immunizations.
- **In and out of area emergency services,** including medically necessary ambulance services, available on an inpatient or an outpatient basis 24-hours per day, 7-days per week.

Supplemental health care services may take the form of additional coverages over and above those provided as basic, or additional amounts of the basic benefits already provided.

Copayments. A copayment is a specific dollar amount, or percentage of the cost of a service that must be paid by the HMO member in order to receive a basic health care service. For example, a $5 copayment might be required for an office visit to a member's physician, or a member might be required to pay a 30% copayment (30% of the cost of the services) for alcohol and drug rehabilitation. Generally, copayments are quite minimal for most services, usually under $10. Many HMOs don't require any copayment for a considerable amount of their services. Copayments for alcohol and drug rehabilitation, and services for mental and emotional disorders are usually expressed as a percentage of the cost of the service and are therefore more costly to the member. Copayments for supplemental services are often considerably more than for basic services.

Exclusions and Limitations. Exclusions and limitations are used to either limit a benefit provided or specifically exclude a type of coverage, benefit, medical procedure etc. HMOs may not exclude and limit benefits as readily as commercial insurers. This is because the rationale of an HMO is to provide comprehensive health care coverage. Some of the benefits an HMO may exclude from coverage, and often do, include: eye examinations and refractions for persons *over* age 17, eyeglasses or contact lenses resulting from an eye examination, dental services, prescription drugs (other than those administered in a hospital), long-term physical therapy (over 90 days) and out-of-area benefits (other than emergency services).

Complaint System. All HMOs are required to have a complaint system, often called a **grievance procedure,** to resolve written complaints by members. The HMO is required to provide forms for written complaints, including the address and telephone number of where complaints should be directed. Additionally, upon providing the necessary forms for a complaint to a member, the HMO must notify the member of any time limits applying to a complaint. Complaints must be resolved within 180 days of being filed with the HMO (with a few exceptions). Complaints may be resolved through binding arbitration if so specified by the HMO and agreed to by the member.

Evidence of Coverage. An evidence of coverage is required to be provided by an HMO to members within 60 days of their enrollment. It is the equivalent of a Certificate of Insurance, for standard insurance policies. In it, the member's coverages and benefits (including required copayments), benefit limits, exclusions, and conversion privileges are specified. The evidence of coverage will also include the name, address, and telephone number of the HMO, the effective date and term of coverage, a list of providers and a description of the service area, terms and conditions for termination, a complaint system, a 31-day grace period for premium payment provision, a coordination of benefits provision, incontestability clause, and a provision on eligibility requirements for membership in the HMO. Other provisions may also be found in the evidence of coverage, but those outlined above must be included.

Prohibited Practices. HMOs, like traditional commercial insurers, are not allowed to engage in certain types of business practices, policies, etc. Specifically, HMOs are prohibited from excluding a member's preexisting conditions from coverage, from unfairly discriminating against a member based on age, sex, health status, race, color, creed, national origin, or marital status. HMOs are also prohibited from terminating a member's coverage for reasons other than: nonpayment of premiums or copayments, fraud or deception in the member's use of services, a violation of the terms of the contract, failure to meet or continue to meet eligibility requirements prescribed by the HMO, or a termination of the group contract under which the member was covered.

Quality Assurance. Because HMOs provide service benefits rather than reimbursement benefits, they are required to follow guidelines prescribed by the Insurance Department to assure quality service to members. These guidelines specify the requirements for reasonable hours of operation and after-hours emergency health care and standards to insure that sufficient personnel will be available to attend to members' needs. The guidelines also require adequate arrangements to provide inpatient hospital services for basic health care and a requirement that the services of specialists be provided as a basic health care service.

Open Ended Plans. An open ended HMO (also known as a "leaky HMO" and "point of service HMO") is a hybrid arrangement whereby participants may use non-HMO providers at any time and receive indemnity benefits which are subject to higher deductible and coinsurance amounts. The out-of-pocket cost to the participant (and probably the employer, too) is higher, but the arrangement allows participants to remain in control in choosing a health care provider.

Preferred Provider Organizations (PPOs)

Development and Characteristics. Preferred Provider Organizations developed as a compromise between the benefits of an HMO and a traditional reimbursement insurance plan offered by commercial insurers. Commercial insurers implemented PPOs as an answer to some of the negative aspects of HMOs, such as a the limited choice of physicians. Like HMOs, PPOs may operate as open panel or closed panel networks, and the services provided may range from basic to comprehensive care. A PPO is made up of various hospitals and private physicians in an area, who agree to provide services to the insurer's clients at a predetermined price. In return, the insurer designates these doctors and hospitals as **preferred providers.** If an insured seeks treatment from a preferred provider the coverage for the services rendered is 100% minus a nominal copayment for each office visit or hospital stay. If the insured elects to receive treatment from a nonpreferred provider then the reimbursement benefits will be reduced to the usual 80%. This type of plan allows the insured to choose between cost savings and freedom of choice in selecting a health care professional.

PPOs are considered to be closer to indemnity plans than managed care, since the insurer pays discounted rates for medical services without becoming overly involved in health care decisions about the treatments rendererd.

Exclusive Provider Organizations (EPOs)

Exclusive provider organizations are a type of PPO in which individual members use particular preferred providers, instead of having a choice of a variety of preferred providers. Providers are not paid a salary, but are paid on a fee-for-service basis.

EPOs are characterized by a primary physician who monitors care and makes referrals to a network of providers (this is known as the gatekeeper concept), strong utilization management, experience rating, and simplified claims processing. EPOs can serve as an alternative to or companion to HMOs and PPOs.

Emerging Variations

Today there are many variations of managed health care providers, including point of service plans (POSs), physician hospital organizations (PHOs), practice management organizations (PMOs), and provider sponsored networks (PSNs).

The principal differences between these organizations are the parties to the contracts and their basic structure and organization. For example, with the physician hospital organization, the physicians and hospitals contract directly with employers to provide health care services. Most of these arrangements are funded through capitation fees much like HMOs.

Multiple Option Plans

A multiple option plan is an integrated health plan which may include services of an HMO, PPO, EPO, and/or indemnity plan, all of which are administered by a single vendor (usually an insurance company).

EMPLOYER ADMINISTERED PLANS

Self-Funding

If claim costs are fairly predictable, an employer may consider a self-funded health care plan. With a self-funded plan an employer, not an insurance company, provides the funds to make claim payments for company employees and their dependents. In the event that claims are higher than predicted, a self-funded health insurance plan can be backed-up by a "stop-loss" contract. A **stop-loss contract** is designed to limit the employer's liability for claims. There are two variations of this coverage. Specific stop-loss coverage begins to apply after an individual's medical expenses exceed a predetermined threshold such as $5,000. Aggregate stop-loss coverage applies when the employer's liability for group insurance claims exceeds a specified amount. The insurer pays all claims once the specified amount is reached.

An employer self-funded plan may be an indemnity program which reimburses covered employees for medical care they have received. Or, the employer may provide benefits through the service plan offered under an HMO, or through an insurer's PPO network.

An insurer may also be used for a self-funded employer under an "administrative services only" (ASO) contract. Under the **ASO contractual agreement** the insurer provides claim forms, administers claims, and makes payments to health care providers, but the employer still provides the funds to make claims payments.

Advantages of Self-Insurance. Self-insurance has four major advantages:

- The company can save money if actual losses are less than those predicted.

- The expense of carrying insurance may be reduced because of the elimination of administrative costs, agent commissions, brokerage fees, and premium tax.
- Because the company has assumed the entire risk, there may be a greater effort on its part to seek ways to reduce claims, and encourage employees to actively participate in "wellness" programs and improved lifestyles.
- The company has use of the money that would normally be held by the insurance company.

Disadvantages of Self-Insurance. The main disadvantages of self-insurance are the following:

- Actual losses may be more than predicted, causing the unexpected loss of funds that were to be used for other purposes.
- Expenses could be higher than expected if additional personnel have to be hired to administer claims, manage risk, or offer employee information.
- Income taxes could be higher because the company will not be able to take premiums paid as a deduction; only the claims paid, and operating expenses may be taken as a tax deduction.
- Contracts are usually not regulated by the Insurance Department, and therefore the Department cannot assist consumers with problems.
- Contracts are not subject to mandated benefits laws.

Small Employers

Small employers (usually defined as those with fewer than 20-25 employees) have been especially hard hit by increases in health care insurance premiums. Because many group plans are "experience rated," small employers see an immediate premium increase whenever claims are particularly high. If the average age of the participants is particularly high, or if claims experience is high, or if there has been even one long or catastrophic illness in a small employer plan, it can have a devastating effect, making health insurance unaffordable for the whole group. Recent surveys by the Health Insurance Association of America (HIAA) indicate a substantial decline in the number of small firms that are able to offer health coverage to their employees.

Several states have acted to ensure that health insurance coverages are available at a reasonable cost and under reasonable conditions for small employers. Among the new requirements:

- Standard benefit plans that must be offered to small employers
- Maximum waiting periods for preexisting conditions
- The insurer may not exclude particular individuals or medical conditions from coverage
- Carriers may only cancel or nonrenew small employer plans for nonpayment of premium, fraud, misrepresentation, or noncompliance with plan provisions

Cafeteria Plans

A cafeteria plan could be defined as a plan in which employees select health benefits from a variety of coverage options, based on their individual and family needs. Cafeteria plans tend to be more complex (and more expensive) than traditional plans, especially with regard to plan administration, and usually make the most sense for larger employers. Benefits are elected in advance of the year in which they will be used (benefits to be used in 1996 will be elected at the end of 1995). Taxation of cafeteria plans is regulated by Section 125 of the Internal Revenue Code.

Medical Savings Accounts (MSAs)

A medical savings account (MSA) is an employer-funded account linked to a high deductible medical indemnity plan. Usually, the employer raises the existing plan deductible (usually by 300% to 400%) and in turn returns a portion of the premium savings to employees as contributions to the medical savings account. Employees can use the contributions to pay for health care expenses throughout the year, and at the end of the year may withdraw whatever remains in the account as (taxable) cash.

Multiple Employer Trusts (METs)

Multiple employer trusts provide health insurance benefits to small businesses through a series of trusts usually established based on specific industries such as manufacturing, sales and service, real estate, etc. Most states have group size eligibility requirements for employer groups to qualify for group insurance.

Generally, states may require a minimum of five to ten participants for a group to be eligible for group benefits. METs typically have no such requirements and in reality a group of one could be eligible for group benefits.

METs are formed by insurers or third-party administrators who are called sponsors. The sponsor develops the plan, sets the underwriting rules, and administers the plan. To help prevent the possibility of adverse selection, the underwriter must make sure that the sponsor's underwriting rules are adequate and that he or she adheres to them. This is necessary because an employer with only two, three or five employees could elect to join an MET because they know of the poor health condition of one of the employees. The underwriting standards must be able to prevent this from happening.

If state law allows, METs may be noninsured. A **noninsured** plan is a self-funded plan; that is, a plan that operates without the services and funds of an insurance company. The trustee has charge of the funds and the policies and all financial activities occur through the trust.

As with a traditional group insurance plan, a master policy is issued to a trustee who is operating under a trust agreement. The master contract has its own policy effective date and renewal dates which the insurer may use for changing rates on the MET's entire block of business. Also, each individual employer under the MET has its own effective dates and anniversary dates. Rates are generally changed on the employer's anniversary date, but usually not more than once in 12 months.

Multiple Employer Welfare Arrangements

Multiple Employer Welfare Arrangements (MEWAs) are employer funds and trusts providing health care benefits (among other benefits) to employees of two or more employers.

ERISA, the federal Employee Retirement Income Security Act which is designed to protect group health insurance plan participants, restricts states' ability to regulate employee welfare benefit plans while preserving state insurance laws having to do with reserve requirements. A state may regulate insurance, but may or may not consider an employee welfare benefit plan an "insurance plan" for the purpose of regulation.

Some self-funded MEWAs claim they are not subject to Insurance Department regulation and operate under a supposed preemption under ERISA. As a result, many have gone unregulated, and have fraudulently collected premiums from small business only to fold and leave millions of dollars of unpaid claims.

State and federal regulators are attempting to resolve the question of jurisdiction. Meanwhile, in most states MEWAs need to obtain a Certificate of Authority in order to transact insurance business, and must be fully insured by a licensed insurer. Usually, agents and brokers are prohibited from assisting MEWAs to transact insurance until and unless the agent or broker files a report with the Department of Insurance outlining the MEWA's organization, insurance contracts, benefit plan description, and the designated third party administrator.

Third-Party Administrators (TPAs)

A third-party administrator is a firm which provides administrative services for employers and other associations having group insurance policies. The third-party administrator acts as a liaison between the insurer and the employer in matters such as certifying eligibility, preparing reports required by the state and processing claims. The use of third-party administrators has become common as a result of employers self-funding health benefits.

GOVERNMENT HEALTH INSURANCE

Both the federal and state government offer statutory health insurance programs. On the federal level, Social Security provides disability income benefits and administers the Medicare program. Medicare will be discussed in a later chapter of this text.

SOCIAL SECURITY

Social Security pays four types of benefits:

- Disability income benefits to workers
- Medicare benefits
- Retirement benefits to workers and their dependents
- Survivors benefits to a worker's family

A special insured status is required if a worker is eligible for disability benefits under Social Security. This status requires that the worker be fully insured and to have earned at least 20 quarters of coverage in the 40 calendar quarter period ending with the calendar quarter in which the disability begins. This requirement is modified slightly if a covered worker is disabled prior to age 31.

A covered worker may be eligible for disability income benefits if the required insured status is achieved, the worker is under age 65, and can satisfy the Social Security definition of total disability.

Social Security defines total disability as the inability to engage in any substantial gainful activity due to physical or mental disability which is expected to last for at least 12 months or end in death. Substantial work activity means significant mental and/or physical duties for which a person is compensated.

This definition does not refer to the individual's occupation prior to disability or to the level of predisability compensation. A surgeon earning $200,000 annually may be disabled to the degree that he or she could no longer perform surgery. However, if this person *could perform other meaningful* work duties (bank employee, school teacher, salesperson, etc.), he or she would probably not be eligible for disability benefits since they could not meet the Social Security definition of total disability.

The amount of the disability benefit is equal to the worker's PIA (Primary Insurance Amount) which in essence is the same as the individual's monthly retirement benefit. Disability benefits are only payable for total disabilities. Disability benefits begin with the sixth full month of disability. This waiting period begins with the first full month of disability. No benefit is paid for a partial disability.

Family members such as the following may also receive disability benefits as a result of the disabled person's work record:

- An unmarried child under 18, or under 19, if in high school full time
- An unmarried child disabled before age 22
- A spouse caring for a child under 16 or disabled
- A spouse age 62 or older
- A disabled widow or widower age 50 or older
- A disabled surviving divorced spouse age 50 or older, if the marriage lasted at least 10 years

On the state level, all states have workers compensation laws and Medicaid or some similar form of state subsidized health care.

WORKERS COMPENSATION

Most states require employers to provide workers compensation benefits for their employees. Workers compensation is designed to help the person who suffers from loss of income due to injury or sickness which occurs as a result of his or her occupation.

Eligibility. In order to be **eligible** for workers compensation benefits the disabled worker must:

- Work in an occupation that is covered by workers compensation
- Have had an accident or sickness that is work-related

Benefits. Workers compensation laws provide for the payment of four types of benefits:

- Medical benefits
- Income benefits
- Death benefits
- Rehabilitation benefits

Medical benefits are provided without limit. An injured or diseased employee is entitled to receive all necessary medical and surgical treatment to cure or relieve the condition. Certain maximums or limits may apply to a type of care or a particular medical item, but overall benefits are unlimited.

Income benefits are paid to employees who suffer work-related disabilities. An **elimination period** applies before benefits for loss of wages begin. If the disability continues beyond a certain period, retroactive benefits will be paid for the initial waiting period. A disability may be total (making employment impossible) or partial (resulting in a reduced ability to work). Either type of disability may be temporary or permanent. For **permanent total disability** or **temporary total disability**, the benefit is 66⅔% of weekly wages, subject to minimum and maximum weekly limits. However, for permanent total disability the dollar maximum and the benefit period are greater (benefits for permanent total disability often continue for life, while benefits for a temporary total disability are limited. People with **partial disabilities** are able to perform some work, so the laws provide a benefit equal to a percentage of the wage loss (difference between earnings before and after the accident). In addition to benefits for lost wages, the state provides scheduled benefits for specific **permanent partial disabilities**, such as loss of limbs, sight, or hearing. Usually these benefits are paid in addition to any other income benefits.

Death benefits provide two types of payments. Up to a certain dollar amount is provided as a burial allowance, and the state also provides weekly income payments for a surviving spouse and/or children. Weekly benefits are 66⅔% of the deceased worker's wages, subject to minimum and maximum dollar amounts, and a maximum time limit, and an aggregate payment limit. Surviving children generally receive benefits until a certain age.

Rehabilitation benefits are now recognized as a valuable tool for reducing workers compensation costs and returning disabled employees to their jobs, as soon as possible. Rehabilitation may include therapy, vocational training, devices such as wheelchairs, and the costs of travel, lodging, and living expenses while being rehabilitated.

MEDICAID

Medicaid provides health care benefits for the financially needy. It is basically a state program with some federal financial support. Medicaid is designed to provide increased assistance to those who are unable to pay for their medical needs. For those persons aged 65 or over, Medicaid principally supplements Medicare for those who cannot pay the expenses not covered by Medicare. For those not eligible for Medicare, it provides medical assistance for certain categories of people who are medically needy — the blind, the disabled, families with dependent children, or medically needy children under age 21.

Medicaid is a federal-state program. The federal government encourages states to increase medical assistance to the indigent, regardless of age, by paying one-half of the administration cost of state medical assistance programs and 50% to 80% of the fees to the providers of services to the needy. The actual federal matching proposition varies inversely with the state average per capita income; therefore the poorer states receive the larger federal grants.

Generally, Medicaid helps to pay for medical services which the patient cannot pay for. Thus, Medicaid will cover such services as hospitalizations, physician's services, diagnostic testing, pregnancies, etc.

In addition, Medicaid also serves as a "supplement" to Medicare in some situations. For example, Medicare currently offers extremely limited coverage for nursing home care. Often Medicaid will supplement these limited benefits by paying for nursing home expenses. Other health care expenses not completely covered by Medicare may be paid for by Medicaid.

U.S. GOVERNMENT PLANS — CHAMPUS

CHAMPUS stands for the Civilian Health and Medical Program of the Uniformed Services. CHAMPUS is part of the overall Uniformed Services Health Benefits Program which supplements the medical care available for families of active, deceased, and retired military personnel in uniformed services medical treatment facilities. It is not designed to be a substitute program, but under some circumstances CHAMPUS will share in the cost of medical care provided in civilian facilities (off-base hospitals), when care is not available at a military hospital or clinic. CHAMPUS coverage is secondary to any other health insurance covering the insured. CHAMPUS helps pay most doctor bills for inpatient and outpatient care, hospital bills, and medical supplies, and will help pay for covered care at health care centers other than hospitals such as residential treatment centers or drug and alcohol rehabilitation centers.

CHAMPUS is a cost sharing program. The government pays a significant portion of the charges and the beneficiary pays the remainder.

REVIEW QUESTIONS

7. Blue Cross/Blue Shield organizations are called "service insurers" because they pay benefits to doctors and hospitals for the delivery of services to their subscribers. (True/False) ____________
8. Commercial insurers are called "reimbursement insurers" because they reimburse their insureds for the cost of services they have received from doctors and hospitals. (True/False) ____________
9. Define a "stop-loss" contract. ____________

____

10. What is the purpose of an MET? ____________

____

____

11. The possibility of adverse selection in METs is increased because small employers have a greater likelihood of purchasing insurance when they have a sick employee. (True/False) ____________

Match the numbered definitions with the lettered terms below.

____ 12. Medical care system for the financially needy paid for by the states and the federal government.

____ 13. Coverage available to supplement medical care for families of active, deceased, and retired military personnel in uniformed services medical treatment facilities.

____ 14. A plan which offers the insured freedom of choice in selecting a health care professional by providing differing levels of reimbursement depending on whether the insured selects a provider designated by the plan or not.

____ 15. An organization providing for prepaid doctor and hospital care within a specified service area and stressing preventive medicine.

____ 16. A firm acting as a liaison between the insurer and employer in processing claims, certifying eligibility, and preparing required reports for group insurance policies.

____ 17. A type of PPO where the individual members must use a particular preferred provider.

A. Exclusive Provider Organization (EPO)
B. Medicaid
C. Health Maintenance Organization (HMO)
D. CHAMPUS
E. Third-Party Administrator (TPA)
F. Preferred Provider Organization (PPO)

18. What are the four benefit areas provided under workers compensation?

(1) ____________________________

(2) ____________________________

(3) ____________________________

(4) ____________________________

Answers to Review Questions are located at the back of the book.

TAXATION

INDIVIDUAL HEALTH INSURANCE

As a rule, premiums paid for individually-owned medical care insurance (but not disability income insurance) are tax deductible to the individual, to the extent that the combination of premiums paid plus other unreimbursed medical expenses exceeds 7.5% of adjusted gross income. Examples of individually-owned medical care insurance would be Blue Cross/ Blue Shield coverage, major medical insurance, long-term care insurance, and Medicare supplement insurance coverage. Thanks to the 1996 federal tax law changes, long-term care insurance premiums are tax-deductible. The deduction is subject to age-related limits of between $200 per year for taxpayers under age 40 up to $2,500 per year for taxpayers age 71 and older.

Premiums paid for individually-owned disability income insurance are not tax deductible, since they are not considered premiums for medical care insurance. Disability income benefits under individual policies are received tax-free.

Beginning in 1997, long term care benefits are received tax free up to $175 per day. (After 1997, the $175 figure will be indexed for inflation.)

EMPLOYER-PROVIDED HEALTH INSURANCE

Medical Expense Premiums

An employer can deduct all premums paid for group or franchise health insurance on employees as a business expense, provided the employer is not the beneficiary of the policy (benefits are payable to the employees, not the employer). The value of the coverage provided by the employer is not considered taxable income to the employee.

Payments for permanent losses under accidental death and dismemberment coverage (such as loss of a limb or bodily function, loss of sight or hearing, or permanent disfigurement) are not included as taxable income to the employee, regardless of who paid the premium.

Accidental death benefits are considered life insurance benefits and are received income tax free by the beneficiary, provided the contract meets the IRS statutory definition of life insurance (this means the policy's cash surrender value cannot exceed the net single premium necessary to fund future benefits, and the policy must meet other minimum requirements).

Effective in 1997, long-term care insurance provided on a group basis now enjoys the same tax status as group life and health insurance, meaning premiums paid by the employer are tax deductible and benefits are received tax free up to specified limits.

Medical Expense Benefits

Medical expense benefits are generally considered to be reimbursements for medical expenses already incurred, and therefore are not taxable as income. It should be noted that a taxpayer cannot deduct medical expenses from income for tax purposes that have been reimbursed by the insurance company. This is true whether premiums for the policy were paid for by an employer or by the individual.

Disability Income Premiums

Disability income premiums paid by an individual are not tax deductible. Premiums paid by an employer are deductible for the employer provided the premium is a necessary business expense and the employer is not the recipient of any other of the employee's benefits.

The employer may be a covered employee under the plan and receive benefits as an employee.

Basically, the concept is that if one party receives a tax deduction for the premium, the other party will be taxed. Either the premium or the benefit will be taxed. If the benefit is received tax free, the premium was taxed.

Disability Income Benefits

Whether disability income "wage continuation" benefits are taxable or not depends on who paid the premiums for the policy. If the employee paid the premiums, then any disability income benefit received is tax free. If the employer paid the premiums, income benefits received are subject to income tax.

Any benefits paid under a disability policy for a permanent loss, are not subject to income taxes *regardless of who paid the premium.*

PARTNERS & SOLE PROPRIETORS

As a rule, partners and sole proprietors are considered self-employed individuals, not employees, so the rules for personally-owned health insurance apply. The federal government allows self-employed individuals to deduct a portion of their health insurance premiums. The deduction was 30% for tax years 1994 through 1996. Under new tax laws this deduction will be gradually increased to 80% by the year 2002.

If the partnership pays the premiums for medical care insurance on the partners without regard to partnership income, premiums are deductible by the partnership but are included in the partners' taxable income.

TAXATION OF HEALTH INSURANCE

	Premiums	Benefits
Individual Disability Income	Not deductible	Not taxable
Group Disability Income	Deductible for employer	Taxable#
Individual Medical	Deductible*	Not taxable
Group Medical	Deductible for employer	Not taxable
Individual Long-Term Care	Deductible*	Not taxable†
Group Long-Term Care	Deductible for employer	Not taxable
Individual Medicare Supplement	Deductible*	Not taxable
Group Medicare Supplement	Deductible for employer	Not taxable
*To the extent that combined premiums and unreimbursed medical expenses exceed 7.5% of adjusted gross income.	†In 1997, the first $175 of daily benefit is tax free.	#Benefits for permanent loss are not taxable

Chart 9-1

REVIEW QUESTIONS

19. If disability income is received from a plan where premiums were paid by an employer, the disability income is taxable as income to the insured. (True/False) ___________

20. For permanent or temporary total disability, workers compensation benefits are usually ____% of weekly wages subject to ______________________________

____

Answers to Review Questions are located at the back of the book.

GROUP HEALTH INSURANCE

GROUP VS. INDIVIDUAL HEALTH INSURANCE

Although group and individual health insurance policies share many of the same policy provisions, there are many differences.

For an individual policy, the contract is between the insurer and the covered individual. For a group policy, the contract is between the insurer and the employer, union, trust or other sponsoring organization. Family members may generally be covered under both group and individual policies.

While group policies may have fewer limitations, they do have one important drawback. If an insured changes jobs, he or she may no longer be covered under his or her past employer's group policy. Individual health insurance contracts continue regardless of change of employment.

GROUP INSURANCE CONTRACT

The group insurance policy is called a **master policy** and is issued to the policyowner — usually the employer, association, union, or trust, etc. The individuals covered under the group policy are issued **certificates** of insurance. The certificate lists what the policy covers, and explains to the insured such things as how to file a claim, the term of insurance, and the right to convert from group coverage to an individual policy. Many of the group health insurance contracts features are similar to the contract features of group life insurance.

Group health insurance is generally subject to **experience rating**, under which the premium modification factor is determined by the experience of the group as a whole. In contrast, individual policies may be subject to **community rating**, under which the insurer's overall experience is adjusted in different areas to reflect variations in local costs for doctor and hospital services.

TYPES OF GROUPS

Employee Group

An employee group policy may be issued to an employer (or to the trustee of a fund established by an employer) where insurance is secured for the benefit of the employees, or for persons other than the employer. The employer is the policyowner, and establishes the eligible class of employees to be covered under the group policy.

Usually, this classification will include all full-time employees (including the employer). Further, the classification can also specify full-time, salaried, non-union employees. By classifying the employee group in this manner, the employer is legally able to exclude certain groups of employees (part-time, union, etc.) from the eligible class of covered employees. The eligible class of employees may also include retired employees.

Labor Union or Association Group

An association, including a labor union, must have the following characteristics to be considered an authorized group:

- Have a constitution and bylaws
- Be organized and maintained in good faith for purposes other than obtaining insurance
- Have insurance for the purpose of covering members, employees, or the employees of members for the benefit of persons other than the association or its officers or trustees

In this section the term "employee" may include retired employees.

Trustee Group

A policy may be issued to the trustees of a "trust group" if the fund has been:

- Established by two or more employers in the same or related field
- Established by one or more labor unions or associations (this is also known as a "Taft-Hartley Trust")

The trustees are the policyholder of the plan which covers the eligible employees. Such plan must not be for the benefit of the employer, union or association. The individuals who may be considered "employees" as defined by this section are the same as those previously listed under *Employee Group*.

Credit Health Insurance

Credit health insurance is usually written as a group disability income contract although it could also be an individual policy. The purpose of credit health is to provide payment of the insured's debt when he or she is disabled due to accident or sickness.

The creditor is the policyowner and the debtor the insured. Disability benefits equal to the insured's indebtedness are paid directly to the creditor in the event that the insured is totally disabled in accordance with policy provisions. These benefits are usually paid on a monthly basis as long as the debt remains and the insured is totally disabled.

REVIEW QUESTIONS

21. For an individual policy, the contract is between the insurer and the ______________. For a group policy, the contract is between the insurer and the ______________________________
____
____

22. Insurance designed to pay an insured's indebtedness if the insured becomes totally disabled is known as ______________________________.

23. Name the three characteristics a labor union must have to be considered an authorized group.
(1) ______________________________
(2) ______________________________
(3) ______________________________

☞ ***Answers to Review Questions are located at the back of the book.***

TYPES OF GROUP COVERAGE

Group health coverages track closely with benefits available under individual coverages. We will discuss them under the headings of disability income, accidental death and dismemberment, and medical expense benefits.

Disability Income

Group disability income coverage provides for loss of income benefits due to the disability of the employee caused by an accident or sickness. The amount of benefits to be paid is usually a percentage of the employee's weekly or monthly compensation; such as 60% or 70%. This is intended to encourage the disabled employee to recover and return to work. If 100% of compensation were provided, there would be no such incentive.

Benefits are payable following the policy's elimination period (EP). The EP is a waiting period during which the insured must be totally disabled as defined by the policy. The EP could be 7, 15, 30 days or longer. Group benefits may be short-term or long-term. Short-term benefits are usually payable for up to one or two years. Most frequently the short-term benefit period is one year. Short-term policies usually have short elimination periods such as 15 or 30 days.

Long-term disability (LTD) benefits are usually payable for longer benefit periods such as five years or until age 65. Generally, LTD policies will have longer elimination periods, such as 90 or 180 days.

Accidental Death and Dismemberment

Accidental death and dismemberment coverage pays specified amounts for specific injuries or for death. Benefits are only payable if the injury or death is caused by accident. Injuries must result in specific losses such as loss of sight, arms, legs, or feet. This coverage can be written as a separate policy or as part of a policy providing other group health insurance benefits.

Medical Expense

Basic group medical expense policies usually provide benefits for inpatient services such as hospital room and board costs, surgical expenses and miscellaneous charges. Outpatient (out of the hospital) expenses are usually not covered.

Basic group plans have limitations. Usually, benefits are limited to a specified amount. Room and board charges may be limited to $300 or $400 per day for example. Surgical benefits are usually factors of a surgical schedule which specifies the maximum surgical benefit to be paid. Miscellaneous benefits (private duty nurses, bandages, medication, in-hospital X-rays, lab work, etc.) are usually limited by an amount equal to 10 or 20 times the daily room and board rate.

Basic plans are also limited in terms of time. Most plans will specify that policy benefits will be paid for 30 days or possibly up to 365 days.

Because of these limitations, basic medical expense plans usually do not cover the insured's medical expenses in full. As a result, the insured will be responsible for certain out-of-pocket expenses.

In contrast to basic group medical plans, **group major medical** policies provide more comprehensive benefits. Group major medical will "limit" benefits normally to what is reasonable and customary as opposed to a specific dollar amount. In essence, the insured is provided with a sum of money to cover medical expenses. This sum is usually $1 million or more. These dollars are then used to cover medical expenses — both inpatient and outpatient expenses.

Group major medical plans have deductibles and coinsurance features. Generally, the deductible may be $250 or $500 per calendar year. After the insured has satisfied the deductible, major medical benefits are then payable. Usually, the initial policy benefits are subject to the coinsurance features of the policy whereby the insured "co-insures" his or her claim by paying a portion of the charges, such as 20%. The insurer would pay 80% of the claim. Usually this coinsurance feature only applies to the first $2,500 or $5,000 of a claim. If the claim exceeds this amount, the insurer pays 100% of the covered expenses.

These features will be discussed in more detail in a subsequent chapter of this text.

Other Forms of Group Insurance

Two variations of group health insurance are worthy of mention.

Blanket health insurance operates on the same principles as group health insurance. The only difference is that the insured members are not named. The insurance company has no record of them. The policy was designed for groups where the membership changes frequently. Some examples are:

- All students at a particular school
- All youths attending Boy or Girl Scout Camp
- All members of volunteer charitable organizations

Franchise health insurance can be used for insureds who don't meet the minimum number requirements for regular group health insurance. Franchise, or wholesale insurance as it is sometimes called, is different from group insurance in the following ways:

- Each individual is usually underwritten separately and receives a separate policy

- There is no master policy
- There may be some choice of benefits by each individual

GROUP INSURANCE PREMIUMS

Under a **contributory plan** both the employer and eligible members of the group each pay a portion of the premium. Most insurers require 75% or more of the eligible members to participate. Under a **non-contributory plan**, the employer pays the entire premium. The insurers in this case require 100% participation.

The minimum participation requirement is to help guard against adverse selection. If a free choice were given, many people in good health might not choose the insurance, whereas many in poor health most certainly would.

Group medical coverage may cost less than individual policies depending on the ages and dependent status of the participants. Often, a single person can purchase individual coverage for less premium than if comparable coverage was obtained under a group policy.

When a group policy is rated, the premium may be higher or lower than individual coverage because in a sense, everyone in the group is paying for every other group member. For example, if the ages of the participants are relatively high, the premiums will be high. A single employee, age 21, will consequently pay a relatively higher rate (due to the age of the group) than he or she might pay on an individual policy basis. An individual policy is rated on the age and insurability of the applicant, not an entire group.

On the other hand, a married individual with several children would probably find that the group premium would be less than an individual family premium. On an individual basis, this person must "pay by the head"; must pay a premium for each covered family member. Usually, a group policy will charge a family rate regardless of the number of dependents the participant may have.

REVIEW QUESTIONS

Please answer each of the following questions True or False.

24. Long-term coverage provides benefits for one year or more. (True/False) __________
25. Blanket health insurance covers all named members of an association. (True/False) __________
26. Franchise policies are individually underwritten for each member of the group. (True/False) __________
27. Under a noncontributory plan at least 75% of eligible members must be covered. (True/False) __________
28. Group health insurance premiums for associations are generally higher than comparable individual policies. (True/False) __________

☞ ***Answers to Review Questions are located at the back of the book.***

10

HEALTH INSURANCE POLICY UNDERWRITING, ISSUANCE, & DELIVERY

UNDERWRITING

OBJECTIVES

Like life insurance, health insurance underwriting is the process of selection, classification, and rating of risks. Most companies offering health policies have a variety of policies available and underwriting standards for each policy are usually established. Low limit policies with limited coverages do not require the underwriting that broad coverage policies with high limits do; the greater the company's exposure the more careful the underwriter has to be. Underwriting is generally more restrictive for individual than for group policies. The underwriter's principal functions are to review applications to eliminate those that do not meet underwriting standards, thus reducing **adverse selection**, and to **classify risks** to establish benefits and corresponding premium.

You will find this section of the manual very similar to the life insurance portion of the study manual. Completing the application, collecting premiums, investigating the application, delivering the policy, and explaining its provisions — all these activities are nearly identical for both health insurance and life insurance. Therefore, some of the following material will be remarkably similar to what you have previously studied.

Any differences which may exist are primarily due to the fact that certain underwriting factors for health insurance may be more or less important than for the underwriting of life insurance.

For example, an individual with a serious back ailment presents a major risk for the health insurance underwriter because of the danger of such a chronic condition creating several expensive claim situations. However, for the life insurance underwriter, this same condition may be of little significance as a bad back is not likely to affect the individual's mortality.

SOURCES OF UNDERWRITING INFORMATION

The Application

The health insurance application is a vital document because it is usually attached to and made part of the contract. The agent must take special care with the accuracy of the application in the interest of both the company and the insured.

Application forms vary as to the type and amount of information required to complete the form. Insurers may use different forms for different health insurance coverages or they may use a multipurpose form.

The application is divided into sections or parts. Each section is designed to obtain specific types of information. Section 1 usually asks for personal information regarding the applicant, such as: name, address, Social Security number, dependent status, date of birth, work address and specific occupational duties. In addition, questions regarding the applicant's earned and unearned income may be included.

Another section of the application will request information regarding other health insurance coverage that the applicant may own. This part of the application will specify the type of coverage, benefit amounts and the name of the insurer(s).

If the insurance is to cover family members, a section of the application will be devoted to obtaining information regarding each family member, such as: name, date of birth, relationship to the insured, height and weight.

A major part of the application, usually entitled, part II, deals with medical information regarding the applicant and any family members to be covered. Part II will pose many questions designed to provide specific information regarding the individual's past medical history, current physical condition, moral habits and avocations (hobbies). This part of the application will usually be completed by the agent. Medical personnel may complete this part of the application if a physical exam is required. However, rarely is a physical exam required for health insurance.

The application must be signed by the proposed insured, and the policyowner, if different from the insured. (Note: if the policyowner is a business, a duly authorized representative, other than the proposed insured, must sign.) Finally, the insurance company's agent signs the application. The agent should make sure that all required persons properly sign the application — this eliminates potential delays in issuing the policy.

Questionnaires required because of extra hazardous hobbies or avocations must be signed by both the proposed insured and the agent. In addition, forms signed by the proposed insured are needed to obtain pertinent information from investigative agencies, hospitals, doctors, credit bureaus, and the like. Finally, if a conditional receipt for the premium is given, it must, of course, be signed by the agent representing the company.

Finally, it should be remembered that responses to questions on the application are considered representations, that is, statements believed to be true to the best of one's knowledge.

A sample application appears in the Sample Policy Section at the end of this manual.

REVIEW QUESTIONS

1. As in life insurance, an underwriter makes the decision of whether to __________ or __________ the application.
2. Medical information is needed to determine eligibility for health insurance. (True/False)________
3. Which of the following statements is true about proper signatures?
   a. The basic application requires the signature of the applicant.
   b. The applicant must sign the conditional receipt.
   c. Only the proposed insured must sign questionnaires relating to extra hazardous hobbies.
   d. Other forms for getting information from doctors, hospital, etc., need no signature.

☞ ***Answers to Review Questions are located at the back of the book.***

Other Sources of Information

The Agent. In health insurance, field underwriting is much more important than in life insurance. Moral hazard is a heavy factor in health insurance underwriting because of the possibility of malingering, and it is the agent, not the home office underwriter, who has personal contact with the applicant. It is the responsibility of the agent to be sure to ask the applicant questions clearly and precisely and to record the answers the same way. If the agent has any suspicions whatsoever, he or she should probe when taking the application, or, if the matter is not one he or she can probe, any suspicions should be stated to the underwriting department in the space provided on most applications for agent's comments. The goals of the agent are to get complete and accurate information from the applicant and to detect the possibility of moral hazard.

State law usually requires the agent and the applicant to certify in writing that the applicant has read, or had read to him, the completed application and that the applicant realizes that any false statement or misrepresentation may result in loss of coverage. Failure to complete an application accurately and honestly could subject the agent to disciplinary action.

As with the life insurance contract, the agent may be the insured's sole personal contact in the insurance process. It is the agent's job to explain all aspects of coverage. Also, on any matters pertaining to the insurance contract, notice to the agent is the same as notice to the company.

Attending Physician Statement. In individual underwriting a physical examination may be required and a statement from the attending physician or the hospital may be requested. This source of information is best for accurate information on the prospect's medical history. The physician can explain exactly what the prospect was treated for, the treatment required, the length of treatment and recovery, and the prognosis.

Medical Examination. Medical examinations, when required, are conducted by physicians or paramedics. Usually such exams are not required with regard to health insurance, thus the importance of the agent in recording medical information on the application. The medical exam requirement is much more common with life insurance underwriting.

Investigative Consumer Report. An "investigative consumer report" includes information on a consumer's character, general reputation, personal habits, and mode of living that is obtained through investigation, i.e., interviews with associates and friends and neighbors of the consumer. Such reports may not be made unless the consumer is clearly and accurately told about the report in writing.

This consumer report notification is usually part of the application. At the time the application is completed, the agent will separate the notification and give it to the applicant.

The MIB. Reports on previous insurance information can be obtained from the *Medical Information Bureau (MIB).* Members of MIB can request a report on an applicant and receive coded information from any other applications for insurance submitted to other MIB members. MIB information cannot be used to decline a risk, but can give the underwriter important additional information.

Underwriting Criteria

The underwriter's function is to select risks which are acceptable to the insurer, and at an acceptable premium. But the selection criteria used in this process, by law, must be only those items which are based on sound actuarial principles or expected experience. The underwriter cannot decline a risk based on sex, blindness or deafness, genetic characteristics (such as sickle cell), marital status, and sexual preference.

When underwriting health insurance policies, the prime considerations are: age, sex, occupation, physical condition, avocations, moral and morale hazards, and financial status of the applicant.

Age. Age is a factor in health insurance because people at older ages are more likely to have accidents and become sick, and they do not recover as quickly as younger people.

Sex. Some insurers have unisex rates for health insurance which results in both male and female insureds paying the same premium. Accordingly, the sex of the applicant is a less important underwriting factor.

However, many insurers do not offer unisex rates and thus this factor is an important underwriting consideration. Statistically, females offer a higher health insurance risk as they usually have more health problems than males. Accordingly, more health problems means more insurance usage and increased claims. Typically, this results in higher health insurance premiums for females.

Ironically, it could be that as a result of more frequent health care, the female's life expectancy is longer than males. Accordingly, female life insurance rates are typically lower than a male of comparable age. It is not that unusual for a male, age 35, to suddenly drop dead from a heart attack. It is unusual for a female, age 35, to die suddenly as the result of a heart attack. This fact could be the result of more frequent health care by the female and less care for the male.

However, it might be noted that as occupational roles change and more females achieve higher stress related jobs, it might well be that in the future, sudden stress related deaths among females may occur with the same incidence as with males.

Occupation. Occupation is an important factor in underwriting disability income insurance. A person's occupation affects his risk of becoming disabled, especially by accidental injury. Occupations are classified into broad groups having approximately the same claims experience. Classifications are based on frequency and severity of injury, exposure to hazards, moral hazards, nature of work, and length of disability by occupation. For example, a factory worker is more likely to injure his back than an office worker.

Most companies have accident insurance manuals which list hundreds of different occupations and a grading is assigned to each occupation depending on how hazardous it is. A clerical office worker (with a minimal occupational hazard) might be Class 1, or Class A and the rates would be low. On the other hand a deep sea diver might be assigned to Class 10, or Class J (severe occupational hazard) and the rates would be high.

Physical Condition. Physical condition refers to the applicant's current state of health and past medical history. Applicants who are in good physical health presently and who have had few, if any, health problems in the past, present the best risk to the underwriter.

Conversely, applicants who are currently being treated for health problems such as high blood pressure, ulcers, heart problems, and chronic back conditions, present a serious risk factor for the underwriter.

Chronic medical conditions which reflect a history of treatment and medical advice, reflect negatively on a health insurance applicant. The underwriter is concerned about what has medically happened to the applicant which could result in higher than average usage and claims experience.

Underwriting considerations are based on what has been, what is and what will be the medical condition of the applicant in the future.

Moral and Morale Hazards. A moral hazard is a condition of morals and habits that increases the probability of a loss. A morale hazard is an indifferent attitude which increases the probability of a loss or extends a claim beyond average expectations. A morale hazard exists when this is not the insured's attitude, and instead the insured is inclined to malinger, collect benefits, and not return to work. The underwriter wants to insure people with satisfactory social environments and stable financial conditions who are not excessive in their habits and who do not have long claims histories with other companies. Most people lead normal lives in a satisfactory environment and are financially stable. It is the underwriter's responsibility to assure that standard risks do not present any moral or morale hazards.

Personal Habits. Habits, including personal avocations are of particular interest to the underwriter. The underwriter would like to know about personal habits, such as the use of drugs and alcohol, and whether or not the insured smokes. Avocations would be the prospect's interest and participation in hazardous activities, such as sky diving, motor cycle racing, or mountain climbing.

Financial Status. The amount of earned and unearned income of the applicant is an important underwriting factor with regard to disability income insurance. Because of the risk of a moral or morale hazard associated with disabilities, the insurer will usually only allow an individual to insure 60-70% of gross earned income with a disability income policy. Unearned income, such as dividends, interests, rents, etc, may not be covered by a disability income policy.

To allow excessive amounts of disability income coverage could result in a situation whereby the insured might malinger following a disability. Any incentive to return to work could be lost if the insured is "making more money by being sick".

INDIVIDUAL UNDERWRITING ACTIONS

Underwriting is important because the class of risks the underwriter selects affects the ratio of claims paid to adequate rates. The major function of the underwriting department is to select risks that will fall into the "normal range" of expected losses as predicted on morbidity tables. A **morbidity table** provides statistical data related to the probability of a disability occurring in much the same way that a mortality table provides data relative to the possibility of death occurring at a specific age. If the risks selected fall above the normal range, the rates charged will not be adequate to cover claims, which will create a drain on reserves when this surplus is used to pay excess claims. If the risks selected fall below the normal range, the Commissioner of Insurance may request that the insurance company file revised rate forms because of the premium coverage.

Once a company underwriter has all of the information on an applicant, he or she may take one of four underwriting actions — accept the applicant on a standard basis, reject the applicant, accept the applicant at a higher premium charge, or accept the applicant by issuing the policy with a restrictive rider attached.

Generally, an underwriter will accept **standard** and **preferred** risks. Standard risks reflect average exposures and may be insured at standard rates and premiums. Preferred risks reflect a reduced risk of loss and are often insured at a discounted premium rate. For example, a physically active nonsmoker who works in a nonhazardous occupation would be a preferred risk, and might obtain coverage at a lower cost than a standard risk.

Substandard risks are those that reflect an increased risk of loss. For example, a physically inactive, overweight smoker who works in a hazardous occupation would be a substandard risk. If a substandard risk is acceptable, an underwriter will usually charge a higher premium, make use of a restrictive rider, or both.

A **rider** is an amendment attached to the policy contract which modifies the conditions of the policy by decreasing (or expanding) its benefits or excluding certain conditions from coverage.

GROUP UNDERWRITING

General Underwriting Characteristics

Group underwriting is different from individual underwriting in that usually there is no medical information required regarding plan participants. No proof of insurability is required. The underwriter focuses on the group as a whole, rather than individual members.

The following factors and requirements represent the underwriting process for group health insurance.

Statutory Requirements

Nondiscriminatory Classifications. An eligible group must not discriminate in favor of individuals in a manner that increases the opportunity for adverse selection against the insurance company. For instance, if an employer has five typists in the same job classification (job title and salary range) the employer cannot single out one typist to receive benefits greater than the other four typists. Therefore, employees will be grouped under "classifications," such as, "all eligible full-time employees," "all clerical workers," "all hourly employees," "all salaried employees," "all executives," "employees working one year or more," or "employees earning not less than $10,000 but not more than $15,000."

Optional Insurer Requirements

Employer Control. The employer should be in charge of enrollment, premium payment, benefit selection and all other areas of administration that are not an insurance company function. Because the contract is between the insurer and the policyowner, it is the employer's duty to see that plan administration is conducted in a confidential, legal and objective manner that precludes the individual insured's active participation in the business end of the insurance administration.

Group Size. Most insurers require a minimum number of employees or plan participants before a group health insurance plan may be written. This requirement may vary depending on state laws. Typically, the minimum group size for health insurance is 10 but it could be as low as five or some other number. The larger the group, the more predictable will be the loss experience.

Relatively small groups (25 employees or less) may require some form of individual underwriting whereby each plan participant may be required to prove insurability. Generally, larger groups do not need to prove insurability.

Predetermined Coverage Amount. The underwriter should determine that individual coverage is based on some plan other than individual selection. Individual members of the group cannot select the level of benefits for their own coverage. Coverage can be based on such things as the number of years with the company, occupation, or salary. Coverage must be uniform for plan participants.

Enrollment Percentage (Employer Shares In Cost). The underwriter should determine that individual participation meets his or her company's guidelines in order to prevent adverse selection. The insurance company requires that a majority of eligible individuals be members of the group of insureds. For example, under a plan of insurance where an employer pays the entire premium, and the employee does not contribute to the premium payment (noncontributory plan) 100% of all eligible employees must be covered. Under a plan where both the employer and the employee contribute toward the premium payment (contributory plan) 75% of all eligible employees must be covered.

Insurance Incidental to Group. The underwriter should determine that the group has not been formed only for the purpose of purchasing insurance. If individuals could form a group for the purpose of obtaining insurance the chance of adverse selection would increase dramatically.

Eligibility. The underwriter should first determine that the business is one that the insurer will cover. There was a period of time when certain occupations were of such a high risk or instable nature that employees could not get insurance. Today, virtually all occupations can get insurance coverage. However, the higher the risk or instability of the occupation the higher the premium.

Since death and illness rates differ in different parts of the country, underwriters may take geographic *location* into account. Also, certain parts of the country are more prone to catastrophic loss from natural disasters.

A newly established group plan must cover all eligible employees as of the effective date of the plan. A waiting or probationary period may be established for all new employees who will join the plan after the initial effective date.

For example, an employer may specify a 30, 60 or 90 day waiting period for new employees. This means that a newly hired employee must satisfy a specified period of time such as 30 days, called a **probationary period**, before being enrolled in the plan.

Under a contributory plan employees become insured only after signing a **participation form** acknowledging their participation in the plan and their agreement to pay premium (usually through payroll deduction). Under a contributory plan the employee does not automatically become insured as under the noncontributory plan. Under this plan, the employee usually has an additional period of 31 days following the end of probation to enroll in the plan. This period is called the **eligibility period** or **enrollment period.**

Composition of Group. The underwriter should determine that the group is of such nature that there is a reasonably steady flow of new members into the group. Many states have regulations that specify the number of members that must join the group in order for the group to remain eligible. If a group were to keep the same individuals in the group the chance of accident, illness, or death would increase as the group became older. Because of this increase in risk, rates would also increase.

The group underwriter must also be concerned about currently disabled employees or their dependents. A new insurer may decide to decline the entire group because of a large number of current claims unless the existing insurer agrees by contract to continue to honor these claims.

Also a new insurer may establish a preexisting condition provision in the group contract which excludes coverage for any condition which exists before the effective date of coverage. This provision will normally exclude these conditions for a period of 6 or 12 months after the effective date of coverage.

Generally, there will also be a requirement that only employees currently working at least 25 hours per week are eligible for coverage. Employees not actively at work are usually eliminated from coverage.

Although there have been changes to underwriting standards due to the passing of unisex laws, there are still instances where a group composed largely of women in general, young women, or older employees pay higher premiums.

Funding of Group Insurance

Several mechanisms for funding group health insurance have been developed. Alternative funding allows employers to absorb some of the risk and save premium dollars (and increase cash flow).

For example, a shared funding arrangement allows the employer to self-fund health care expenses up to a certain limit. The employer can select a deductible and pay covered expenses for any individual incurring claim up to that maximum, at which point the insurer assumes the risk.

Under a **retrospective premium** arrangement, the insurer agrees to collect less than the usual premium but may collect additional premium at the end of the year if the actual loss ratio exceeds a loss ratio determined at the beginning of the agreement period.

A **minimum premium** plan is where the employer agrees to fund expected claims and the insurer funds excess claims. The employer and insurer agree to a "trigger" beyond which the insurer is liable. The employer is responsible for a minimum premium consisting of administrative expenses, reserves, and a premium for stop-loss to fund claims over the "trigger".

A large employer may elect to fully self-fund, or may self-fund a plan but contract for **administrative services only (ASO)**.

REVIEW QUESTIONS

4. The party responsible for field underwriting because of his or her personal contact with the insured/applicant is the ____________.
5. If the application is inaccurate or misleading, the agent may be subject to ____________.
6. The ____________ is the document attached to the policy and made part of the contract.
7. Medical examiners are considered agents of the insurance company. (True/False) ____________
8. Name the five areas of consideration for underwriting health insurance.
   (1) ____________
   (2) ____________
   (3) ____________
   (4) ____________
   (5) ____________
9. An amendment attached to a health contract which modifies the policy conditions by decreasing or expanding benefits, or excluding certain conditions from coverage, is known as a(n) ____________.

☞ ***Answers to Review Questions are located at the back of the book.***

PREMIUM DETERMINATION & RESERVES

There are three factors used in the computation of health insurance premiums. The first of these is the **experience** factor. Unlike life insurance where accurate statistics are maintained in mortality tables, health insurance premiums must be based on each individual insurer's actual claims experience.

Added to this experience factor is the loading for expenses. **Expense loading** includes amounts for taxes, profit margin, sales charges, etc.

Thus, the health insurance premium will be based on experience plus expenses. Naturally, these premiums will earn interest just as life insurance premiums earn interest. Thus, the third premium factor is **interest.**

A certain part of every premium must be set aside as a reserve against the insurer's contractual obligations, meaning its obligation to pay claims. The reserves are used to pay current and future claims.

PAYMENT OF INITIAL PREMIUM

Under normal conditions, payment of initial premium is made at the time the application is completed. At that time, the agent may issue a **conditional receipt**.

Similar to life insurance, the conditional receipt may indicate that the health insurance coverage is effective as of the date of the receipt provided that the applicant is insurable at standard rates. However, the receipt may also specify that the coverage is effective upon the date that the application is approved by the insurer, rather than the date of the receipt.

It is important for the agent to submit the application, initial premium, and any other required forms to the home office underwriter promptly. In addition, all forms should be reviewed for completeness and to make sure they are properly signed. Not only does this make for good relationships with the home office underwriter, but it is extremely important to the applicant. Unnecessary delays in transmitting the application will cause a delay in delivering the policy. This can cause the applicant undue anxiety and may result in a loss of confidence in the agent.

When the initial premium is not **paid** with the application some insurers require that the agent send a transmittal notice verifying the date he or she received the first premium. Also, because the policy is not effective until the first premium has been paid and the policy has been delivered, the agent must get a statement at the time the policy is delivered. This statement verifies, basically, two things; one, that the insured has not suffered injury or illness since the time of the application to the date of policy delivery, and two, that the insured has not seen a physician with regard to any interim injury or illness.

Since agents are holding money belonging to their clients, it is extremely important that an accurate record of such transactions be kept. It is also wise for the agent to keep copies of applications and other forms in case the originals are lost.

DELIVERING & SERVICING THE POLICY

DELIVERING THE POLICY

The surest way to be certain the policy is delivered is to do it personally. In addition to knowing the policy has been delivered, the agent has the following opportunities:

- To explain the policy. It is important in health insurance for the policyowner to have basic understanding of what is and isn't covered. With today's high health costs, it is extremely important for the insured to know what the policy limitations are on the different types of medical expenses covered. Sometimes policy premiums are higher than standard (rated up) because the insured does not meet certain basic health requirements or is involved in extra hazardous hobbies or avocations. These facts should be explained to avoid future misunderstandings and/or dissatisfaction. Finally, if the premium was not collected with the application, the company may require the agent to obtain a statement of good health from the insured at the time the policy is delivered and the premium paid.
- To reinforce the relationship and goodwill which have been established with the client
- To explain the possible need for additional health or other coverages

Legally, the policy is considered "delivered" when it is mailed or turned over to the policyowner or someone acting on his or her behalf. Some companies do mail policies directly to policyowners. However, many prefer to have the agent make a personal delivery.

In some cases, a **constructive delivery** is deemed to occur when the insurer mails a policy to its agent for actual delivery to the policyowner, because the insurer has issued the policy and released it for delivery. However, a legal delivery has not yet occurred if the insurer requires personal delivery for verification of good health at the time of delivery, or if the policy is being provided to the applicant merely to review and inspect at that time, and not necessarily to buy.

SERVICING THE POLICY

In many industries, closing the sale means the end of the producer/consumer transaction. However, this is not so in insurance. Insurance policies require ongoing customer service throughout the policy period. Competition in the industry is another incentive to provide good customer service, since it can make all the difference at renewal time. Good customer service makes insureds feel more comfortable doing business with you and makes them more likely to renew with your agency. Proper service of insurance policies also results in referrals, additional coverage, good public relations, and reduced E&O exposure.

REPLACEMENT

Agents attempting to replace the insured's current policy with a new policy need to take special care not to mislead the insured or provide coverage which is to the insured's detriment. Of particular concern is the fact that health conditions covered under an insured's existing policy may not be covered under a replacement policy because of the exclusion of **preexisting conditions**, or new **waiting periods** may be established.

An agent recommending replacement should give special attention to the **exclusions** and **limitations** in the proposed policy as compared to the existing policy. Not all policies cover the same things. If the contracts are different, the replacement policy might not provide the same coverages or the same level of benefits as the existing policy.

An agent should consider the **underwriting requirements** of the replacing insurer. Will the insurer cover the insured on a basis as favorable to the applicant as the present insurer? Will the underwriter accept the risk at a similar rate, or will differencves in the insured's health or the underwriter's requirements result in a higher premium rate?

Some states have passed **"no loss-no gain"** legislation which requires that when health insurance is replaced, ongoing claims under the former policy must continue to be paid under the new policy, thereby overriding any **preexisting conditions exclusion**. In replacing group health coverage, a **transfer of benefits** statement assures that benefits provided under the old policy continue under the new policy.

One would assume there is no benefit to the insured (and great benefit to the agent) when an insurance policy undergoes *intracompany replacement* (is replaced by a similar policy with the same insurer). Therefore, most general agency and agent contracts specify that the agent's commission will be limited to a percentage of the increase in premium only when a policy is replaced within the same company. This discourages the agent from replacing existing policies with new policies from the same insurer unless the amounts of coverage (and thus the premium) are substantially increased.

Because the elderly are extremely vulnerable and often victimized insurance prospects, and are most susceptible to being penalized by preexisting conditions limitations, agents should be aware that there are often more restrictive regulations for replacing Medicare supplement policies.

Certainly, there are legitimate circumstances when replacement of a policy makes sense and should be recommended — for example, when broader coverage or higher benefits can be obtained at a lower rate, and preexisting conditions and waiting periods are not issues.

However, an agent needs to be very careful in recommending a change in policies or carriers when any potential factors could lead to an uninsured loss which might otherwise have been covered. The agent needs to be aware of his or her own errors and omissions liability, particularly in the area of replacement. Replacement is not illegal, but it is heavily regulated.

REVIEW QUESTIONS

10. Reserves are established to:
    a. earn interest.
    b. form a solid credit standing for the insurer.
    c. cover all the insurer's policy payment obligations.
    d. pay the insurer's operating costs.
11. Which of the following statements is true about submitting the application, premium and other forms to the underwriter?
    a. The agent is required to keep accurate records of all transactions involving the applicant's money.
    b. Since coverage is effective immediately, it is not necessary to send the forms to the home office underwriters more than once a week.
12. Legislation requiring that ongoing claims that were paid under an old policy continue to be paid under a new policy is called:
    a. stop-loss
    b. waiting period
    c. no loss - no gain
    d. preexisting conditions

☞ ***Answers to Review Questions are located at the back of the book.***

11

HEALTH INSURANCE POLICY PROVISIONS

All 50 states have enacted the provisions of the Uniform Policy Provisions Law, developed by the National Association of Insurance Commissioners. The law includes 12 mandatory provisions that must be included in individual health insurance policies and 11 optional provisions. The optional provisions are not required to be included in the policy, but if the subject of any of them is contained in the policy, it must be worded in accordance with the wording of the appropriate optional provision. An insurer may reword any of the mandatory or optional provisions so long as the new wording is not less favorable to the insured or the beneficiary. The mandatory provisions are usually in a section of the policy entitled Mandatory or Required Provisions.

UNIFORM MANDATORY PROVISIONS

Entire Contract; Changes

The first of these mandatory provisions is the entire contract and changes clause. This provision states that the policy, including riders and attached papers (such as the application) constitutes the entire contract. This is to ensure that the policyowner has a copy of the entire contract. The provision also states that the contract cannot be modified unless the change is authorized by an officer of the insurance company and attached to the contract. An agent cannot change any of the policy provisions.

Time Limit on Certain Defenses

The purpose of the time limit on certain defenses provision is to limit the period of time in which an insurer may challenge the contract or deny a claim on grounds of material misrepresentation in the application. This provision is similar to an incontestable provision in an individual life insurance contract.

The time limit on certain defenses provision consists of two paragraphs, paragraphs (a) and (b).

Paragraph (a) provides that the health insurance policy may not be contested regarding any statement on the application nor may a claim be denied, after the contract has been in force for two years (three years in some states). No material misrepresentation can void the health insurance contract after it has been in force for two years except for fraud. Fraud can void the health insurance contract whenever it is found and can be proven by the health insurer.

Paragraph (b) provides that the insurer cannot deny a claim on the basis of preexisting conditions after expiration of a two-year time limit, unless the condition was excluded from coverage under the policy by name or specific description. A preexisting condition is one that existed before the effective date of the policy, such as heart disease.

Grace Period

The grace period provision gives the policyholder additional time in which to pay the premium, keeping the insurance in force for a certain period of time after the premium is due but unpaid. The extra time allowed is 7 days for weekly premium policies, 10 days for monthly premium policies and 30 or 31 days for all other policies.

If a policy contains a cancellation provision, a reference to the cancellation provision may be made in the grace period provision. If a policy provides that the insurer reserves the right to refuse renewal of a policy, an additional provision allows the insurer to avoid the grace period provision by giving notice of its intention not to renew.

Reinstatement

The reinstatement provision provides for putting a policy that has lapsed for nonpayment of premiums back in force. If no application for reinstatement is required, usually acceptance of the past due premium by the insurer will reinstate the policy.

If an application for reinstatement is required, the insured must prove insurability and pay all past due premiums plus interest and submit the application and premiums to the insurer. Reinstatement is effective when the insurer notifies the insured. However, if no such approval or disapproval is offered by the insurer within 45 days of the date of the application for reinstatement, the policy will be automatically reinstated after the 45th day. A reinstated policy covers accidents immediately. However, there is a 10-day probationary (waiting) period for coverage of any sickness under a reinstated policy. This means that any sickness must begin after the policy has been in force for 10 days.

Notice of Claim

The policyholder must give the insurer or its agent written notice of a claim within 20 days of the loss or as soon as reasonably possible. Notice to the insurer or its agent with information sufficient to identify the insured shall be sufficient. In the case of a disability income benefit payable for at least two years, notice of claim regarding the continuance of the disability may be required every six months. If the nature of the disability is such that the insured is legally incapacitated, that is, unable to satisfy this requirement due to physical or mental disability, then the continued notice of claim requirement is waived.

Claim Forms

The claim forms provision requires the insurer, after it has been notified of the claim, to furnish claim forms within 15 days. If the forms are not furnished, then the insured will be deemed to have complied with the requirements of filing proof of loss upon submitting written proof of the occurrence, character, and extent of the loss.

Proof of Loss

The proof of loss provision limits the time within which the insured may file a written proof of loss. A proof of loss is a formal statement given to the insurer regarding a loss. It may include a doctor's statement or death certificate. Proof of loss must be filed within 90 days of loss or, in the case of a continuing loss, within 90 days after the end of a period for which the insurer is liable. If the insured cannot comply with these requirements proof of loss must be filed within a reasonable time not exceeding one year. In the event of legal incapacity there is no time limit on filing a proof of loss.

Time of Payment of Claims

The time of payment of claims provision requires that claims will be paid immediately upon receipt of proofs of loss except for periodic payments, which are to be made as specified in the policy or made at least monthly. Balances unpaid when the claim terminates shall be paid immediately upon receipt of due proof of loss.

Some states have substituted a specific number of days in place of the word, "immediately". In some locations, "claims will be paid immediately", means within 30 or 60 days of receipt of the proof of loss.

Payment of Claims

The payment of claims provision specifies to whom the policy's benefits will be paid. Benefits may be paid to a named beneficiary or to the insured's estate if there is a death benefit to be paid under the health insurance policy. For example, this would be true in the case of an accidental death benefit.

Normally, the health insurance benefits are paid to the insured who may also be identified as the loss payee; that is, the person who has experienced the loss. Often medical expense benefits payable under a health insurance policy may be paid to the provider of the medical care if the insured has executed an assignment form. The assignment authorizes the insurer to pay benefits directly to the provider of the medical services, such as a physician or a hospital.

Insurers may add either or both of two optional provisions. The first optional provision provides that if no beneficiary is named or if the named beneficiary is legally incapable of signing a valid release (such as a minor or legally incompetent person), the insurer may pay an amount specified in the provision not to exceed $1,000 to any relative by blood or marriage of the insured or to the beneficiary who is deemed by the insurer to be equitably entitled thereto. This is usually referred to as a **facility of payment** clause.

The second optional provision gives the insurer the option of making payments for medical, surgical and nursing expenses to the person or hospital rendering the services.

Physical Examination and Autopsy

The physical examination and autopsy provision allows the insurer, at its own expense, to examine the insured while a claim is pending, and in the event of death to perform an autopsy, at its own expense, where not prohibited by law.

Legal Actions

The legal actions provision restricts the time period during which an insured may bring a legal action against his or her own insurance company. This provision requires that no legal action to collect benefits may be started sooner than 60 days after the proof of loss is filed with the insurer. This waiting period allows the insurer time to evaluate the claim. The insurer may also not be sued later than three years after the time that the proof of loss is required to be filed.

Change of Beneficiary

If an individual health insurance policy provides a death benefit (as would an AD&D policy), it must also provide a change of beneficiary provision. This provision gives the policyowner, unless he or she has made an irrevocable designation of a beneficiary, the right to change beneficiaries or make any other change without the consent of the beneficiary or beneficiaries.

REVIEW QUESTIONS

Match the numbered definitions with the lettered terms below.

____ 1. Provision limiting the period during which the insurer may deny a claim on grounds of material misrepresentation in the application

____ 2. Provision limiting the time within which the insured may file a formal statement with the insurer regarding a loss

____ 3. Time period after the premium is due, but remains unpaid, during which the insurance will remain in force

____ 4. The 12 provisions mandatory for individual health insurance policies

____ 5. Provision stating that death proceeds will be paid to a named beneficiary, or if none, to the estate of the insured

____ 6. Provision allowing a policy to be put back into force under certain circumstances if the policy lapsed due to nonpayment of premium

____ 7. Restricts the time period during which an insured may sue the insurer, usually to within three years

A. Grace Period
B. Legal Actions
C. Uniform Mandatory Provisions
D. Reinstatement
E. Time Limit on Certain Defenses
F. Payment of Claims
G. Proof of Loss

☞ ***Answers to Review Questions are located at the back of the book.***

UNIFORM OPTIONAL PROVISIONS

In addition to requiring the inclusion of the 12 provisions just summarized, the Uniform Policy Provision Law sets forth 11 other provisions. These are not required to be inserted in the policy, but if the subject of any of them is contained in the policy, it must be worded in accordance with the wording specified in the law. An insurer may use other wording not less favorable to the policyowner, subject to approval by the state Insurance Department. Again, explanations and summaries of the provisions are provided.

Change of Occupation

The occupation of the insured is an important health underwriting factor especially as it would pertain to disability income insurance. Disability income policies are partially rated on the degree of risk inherent in the insured's occupation. For example, a police officer would pay a higher premium than a doctor because of the more hazardous nature of the police officer's occupation.

If this provision is contained in the policy (it is optional), it allows the insurer to adjust policy benefits if the insured has changed to a more hazardous occupation.

Let's assume that an attorney is paying $500 in annual premium for a disability income policy which will provide $1,000 per month in benefits if the attorney is disabled due to accident or sickness. After the policy is issued, the attorney decides to become a bartender, a more hazardous occupation. Subsequently a claim is filed for the $1,000 monthly benefit but now the insured has been disabled as a bartender, not as a member of the bar. In accordance with the change of occupation provision, the insurer will adjust the monthly benefit to reflect the benefit amount that a $500 premium would purchase for a bartender.

Conversely, this provision will also allow the insured to notify the insurer if he or she changes to a less hazardous occupation in which case the insured's premium would be reduced.

Misstatement of Age

This provision allows for an adjustment of the benefit payable when the insured's age is misstated on the application. If the insured's age has been misstated, all amounts payable under the policy will be adjusted to the amount that the premium would have purchased at the insured's correct age. This provision is similar to the misstatement of age provision found in life insurance policies.

Other Insurance with This Insurer

This provision is designed to limit problems of overinsurance with the **same insurer**. This provision permits the insurer to limit or control overinsurance through its own policies. Most often, this optional provision will be found in disability income policies in order to discourage a person from purchasing several disability income policies (with the same insurer) which could make a disability very profitable to the insured if indeed, the individual were overinsured. Remember most insurers limit the amount of disability income which may be purchased to 60-70% of the insured's gross earned income.

There are two versions of this provision. The first enables the insurer to place a maximum or cap on benefits received from all similar policies with the same insurer. For example, Charlie earns $1,000 per month and purchases several disability income policies with ABC Mutual Life Insurance Company, totaling $1,200 in monthly benefits. The policy maximum imposed by this provision caps monthly disability benefits at $700. Accordingly, the excess benefits will be void and all premiums paid for the excess will be refunded to the insured.

The second version of this option allows the insured (or the insured's estate) to select which policy or policies to be kept in force. The remaining policies will be voided and the premium refunded.

Insurance with Other Insurers (1)

This provision also covers the possibility of overinsurance except the concept applies to all similar coverage with all **other insurers**. There are also two versions of this provision. Version one states that if the insured has other valid policies with other insurers, providing coverage on an actual expense-incurred or service-incurred basis (such as a medical expense policy), and if the insurance company is unaware of other policies before a claim occurs, benefits to be paid will be limited to a proportion of the total loss or claim. The amount payable will be determined by dividing the amount of coverage that the insurer had prior notice of by the total of all available benefits (both known and previously unknown).

Insurance with Other Insurers (2)

Version two is identical to the first version except that it pertains to policies where benefits are paid directly to the insured, such as disability income policies.

Regardless of which version of this provision applies, the intent is the same. When an insured has two or more policies from various insurers which cover the same losses or expenses, and if the respective insurers were not informed of these other policies, then each insurer will only be liable for a proportionate share of any claim submitted. This is designed to prevent an insured from making money on an insurance claim.

For example, let's assume that Jan has three hospital expense policies. The policy issued by Company X provides a total benefit of $5,000; the policy issued by Company Y provides $2,500 of coverage; the policy issued by Company Z also provides $2,500 of coverage. Jan submits a claim for $4,000 of covered expenses to Company X, which just learns for the first time about the other policies. Since the company had no prior notice of the other coverage, it will reduce its claim proportionally and only pay $2,000 of Jan's claim (the $5,000 of coverage it knew about is 50% of the total available coverage of $10,000).

This proportional reduction of benefits only applies when other insurance has not been disclosed to the insurance company. If Company X knew about both other policies when it issued its own policy, the penalty would not apply. It would still provide up to $5,000 of coverage under its policy, subject to any other policy provisions about coordinating benefits or the order of payment when other benefits are available.

Relation of Earnings to Insurance

The relation of earnings to insurance provision is concerned with overinsurance for disability income benefits, so that an insured will not receive more money from disability insurance than he would receive from working. The provision may only be used in noncancellable and guaranteed renewable contracts. The provision states that if at the time the disability begins, the insured's total disability income exceeds his or her earned income, or average earned income for the preceding two years, the disability income benefits will be reduced proportionally. Premiums for any excess coverage will be refunded to the insured.

Bud earns $1,500 per month and has a disability income policy which provides $1,000 in monthly benefits (67% of his earned income). The insurer specifies that at no time may the disability benefit exceed 70% of earned income. Bud files a claim and at the time of the claim his earned income is only $1,000 per month. Bud now has 100% of his earned income insured. In accordance with the relation of earnings to insurance provision, Bud's monthly benefit will be reduced to $700 and he will receive a refund of premium for the excess coverage.

Unpaid Premium

This provision allows deduction of unpaid premiums from claim payments. Upon the payment of a claim, any premium then due and unpaid may be deducted therefrom.

Cancellation

This provision allows the insurer or the insured to cancel the policy with proper written notice. If the insurer cancels the policy, the notice of cancellation cannot take effect until at least five days from receipt of the notice. In reality, most insurers will provide for cancellation of the policy 30 days after receipt of the cancellation notice. If the insurer cancels the policy, the insured is entitled to a pro rata return of the unearned premium. Since premiums are paid in advance, the actual premium earned by the insurer may be retained but any unearned premium must be returned to the insured.

For example, the insured has paid a monthly premium of $100 and the insurer cancels the policy effective half way through the month. The insurer may keep one-half of the premium and the balance ($50) which is not yet earned, must be refunded.

The insured may also cancel the policy with proper written notice. The effective date of such cancellation will be the date the notice is received by the company or the date specified in the cancellation notice. When the insured cancels the policy, the insurer may keep any earned premium plus a portion of unearned premium. Since the insurer can keep part of the unearned premium, the refund to the insured is referred to as a short rate return.

Conformity with State Statutes

This provision amends the policy to conform to minimum requirements of state law, if necessary. Any provision of a policy which, on its effective date, is in conflict with the statutes of the state in which the insured resides is amended to conform to the minimum requirement of such statutes.

Illegal Occupations

Under this provision, liability is denied if loss results from the insured's committing or attempting to commit a felony or from the insured's engaging in an illegal occupation.

As an example, Sean operates a gas station which is actually a front for a stolen car ring. Sean is injured while stripping a stolen car at the gas station. This illegal occupation provision enables the insurer to deny the claim.

Intoxicants and Narcotics

This provision states that the insurer is not liable for any loss resulting from the insured's being intoxicated or under the influence of any narcotic unless administered on the advice of a physician.

It should be noted that *treatment for* substance abuse is a covered expense under a health insurance policy. The optional exclusion only relieves the insurer of responsibility for a loss caused by drug or alcohol use.

For example, if the insured is severely injured as the result of drunk driving, the claim can be denied. If as a result of the drunk driving charge, a judge orders the insured to undergo treatment for the drinking problem, this type of claim will be paid by the insurer in accordance with the provisions of the policy.

REVIEW QUESTIONS

Match the numbered definitions with the lettered terms below.

_____ 8. Provision explaining what happens to the insured's coverage if he or she switches to a more dangerous type of employment

_____ 9. Provision excluding payment for loss occurring out of an insured's committing or attempting to commit a felony

_____ 10. Provision limiting the payment under the policy to a proportion of the total loss if more than one policy provided coverage for the loss and the insurer had no notice of the other policies

_____ 11. This provision is made part of the policy to prevent an insured from receiving more money from disability insurance than he would earn by working

_____ 12. Allows deduction of premiums due but not paid from any claim benefits

A. Insurance with Other Insurers
B. Relation of Earnings to Insurance
C. Illegal Occupations
D. Change of Occupation
E. Unpaid Premium

> ☞ ***Answers to Review Questions are located at the back of the book.***

OTHER HEALTH INSURANCE PROVISIONS

The Policy Face

The face of the policy is a standard printed form containing the name of the insurance company and providing enough information to give the insured a capsule summary of what type of policy and what type of coverage is provided by the contract. The policy face identifies the insured and states the term of the policy (when it goes into effect and when coverage expires). The policy face also states how the policy can be renewed.

The policy face usually gives a brief statement of the type or types of benefits. However, it is essential to examine the benefit provisions within the body of the contract to obtain a complete understanding of the coverage provided.

Free Look

Many states now require that all health policies contain a clause allowing the policyholder a period of 10 days (or even 30 days) from date of receipt of the issued policy in which to inspect it and, if dissatisfied for any reason, return it for a refund of the full amount paid at the time of application or delivery. This is a full refund, not pro rata. In the event of cancellation by the policyholder, the company is not liable for any claims originating during the 10-day free look period.

Insuring Clause

The insuring clause represents the insurer's promise to pay benefits and the conditions under which these benefits will be paid. This clause further identifies the insurer and the insured, and states what kind of loss is covered. An example of an insuring clause would be:

The insurer, ABC Mutual, agrees to pay disability income benefits to the insured upon receipt of proof of loss and the timely payment of premiums by the insured. All benefits will be paid in accordance with the policy's provisions contained herein.

Consideration Clause

Consideration means giving something of value as part of a contractual agreement. The insurer agrees to provide something of value (policy benefits) in exchange for value received from the insured; this value being the premium and the statements on the health insurance application.

Renewability Clause

The renewal provision, which contains the terms and conditions for renewal of the policy, must appear on the first page of the policy. Renewal provisions vary, but they can be categorized into five types.

Cancellable. A health insurance policy which is cancellable may be canceled at any time with proper written notice from the insurer and a refund of any unearned premium. Cancellation of the policy does not relieve the insurer of any claim's responsibility. If the insured was in the midst of a claim at the time the policy was cancelled, the insurer must continue to honor the claim. (This type of renewability is not very common.)

Optionally Renewable. The insurer may elect not to renew the policy for any reason or no reason at all. If the election of nonrenewal is made, it can only be exercised on the policy's premium due date or the policy's anniversary. The policy's anniversary date is the "birthday" of the policy; that is, the anniversary of the policy's effective date. The insurer can also elect to renew the policy on the anniversary and it may also increase the policy's premium.

Conditionally Renewable. This provision is very similar to the optionally renewable provision. The primary difference is that a conditionally renewable policy may be nonrenewed for specific conditions contained in the policy. Optionally renewable policies basically do not require a policy condition or any reason for nonrenewal. Premiums may also be increased on the policy's anniversary date if the policy is to be renewed.

Guaranteed Renewable. This type of renewability guarantees that the insured has the right to continue the policy in force until a specified age by timely payment of the premiums. The insurer cannot refuse to renew the policy. What is not guaranteed is the premium. The insurer has the right to increase the premium on each policy anniversary. However, premiums may be increased but only for the entire class of insureds, not for an individual. This is a very common form of renewability, especially in hospitalization policies.

Noncancellable. A noncancellable policy is one which provides for the guarantee of both renewability and the premium. The insurer cannot cancel the policy or increase the premium. This type of renewability is most common with some forms of disability income policies.

Thus, there are two types of renewability which guarantee that the policy cannot be cancelled by the insurer — guaranteed renewable and noncancellable. However, it should be understood that under either type of renewability, the guarantee not to cancel typically only applies until age 65. At age 65, if the insured owns a medical expense policy, he or she becomes eligible for Medicare and normally, the medical expense policy will not be renewed past age 65. If the insured owns a disability income policy, the policy will only be renewed beyond age 65 if the insured provides evidence that he or she continues to work at a full time job. In this situation, usually the policy may be renewed for one year periods from age 65 to age 70 or 72.

Finally, it should be noted that the only type of renewability which guarantees that the premium cannot be increased is noncancellable. All other renewability provisions allow the insurer to increase premiums on the policy's anniversary.

Benefit Payment Clause

This clause describes the type of benefits provided by the policy and the circumstances under which they will be paid. Often information on the specific benefit amounts, duration of the benefit and elimination periods is contained in a benefit schedule, which is a detachable page appended to the policy.

Certain benefits, referred to as mandated benefits, are required by state law to be included in certain types of policies. Mandated benefit requirements usually apply to individual and group policies on an expense-incurred basis and to service plans such as Blue Cross and Blue Shield. Examples of mandated benefits include coverage of newborn children, and coverages for mental, emotional or nervous disorders. Some benefits must be provided as options, such as optional coverage for obstetrical services or for alcohol and drug dependence in certain types of policies.

Exclusions and Reductions

These provisions limit the insurer's obligation to pay. An **exclusion** or **exception** is a provision that entirely eliminates coverage for a specified risk. A **reduction** is a decrease in benefits as a result of specified conditions.

Most health insurance policies exclude war and act of war, self inflicted injuries, aviation, military service and overseas residence. Benefits will not be provided if the cause of a loss is due to military service, a war or civil disorder, a self inflicted injury such as an attempted suicide, or if the loss is due to aviation as a pilot.

Generally, coverage is temporarily suspended if an individual resides in a foreign country for a specified period of time or if the individual is serving in the military. Coverage is reinstated or reactivated when the insured returns to the United States or not longer is serving in the military.

Preexisting Conditions

Preexisting conditions can be excluded from coverage under a health insurance policy. This exclusion may be permanent or temporary. By definition, a preexisting condition is usually defined as any condition for which the insured sought treatment or advice prior to the effective date of the policy.

Further, a preexisting condition can also be defined as any symptom that would cause a reasonable and prudent person to seek diagnosis and medical treatment. This concept prevents an applicant who suspects that he or she may have a serious medical problem from buying health insurance and then going to a doctor for diagnosis and treatment.

Preexisting conditions may be covered by the insurer if they are indicated on the application. The insurer will then review the medical information and depending on the condition may elect to cover the problem or exclude it. Usually, only serious or chronic conditions will be excluded.

Probationary Period

A probationary period is a waiting period that frequently applies to group insurance coverage. It is the number of days or months that an individual joining a group has to wait before becoming eligible for coverage. For example, a new employee may have to work continuously for at least 30 days before becoming eligible for coverage under the employer's group disability insurance plan.

Nonoccupational Coverage

Often health insurance policies are issued which provide nonoccupational coverage only. This means that no benefits will be provided for losses due to an occupational cause. If a worker is injured on the job, his or her basic health insurance plan will not provide benefits if the policy is written as nonoccupational. In these situations, benefits are provided by workers compensation.

Occupational coverage is basically full coverage. If the health policy provides 24-hour coverage, then occupational losses will be covered as well as any other type of loss.

Case Management Provisions

In order to control the costs associated with medical care, many insurers are instituting methods to reduce costs while giving the insured options for health care. The **second surgical opinion** is a provision that can be included in policies that offer surgical expense benefits. This coverage allows the insured to consult a doctor, other than the attending physician, to determine alternative methods of treatment. While the use of this provision is sometimes optional, it is more often mandatory for certain procedures, such as tonsillectomy, cataract surgery, coronary bypass, mastectomy, and varicose veins. Some insurance companies have medical examiners review claims, and the examiner's decision to approve or deny a claim is considered the required second opinion.

One cost control mechanism being used by insurers and employers is **utilization review**. Utilization review consists of an evaluation of the appropriateness, necessity, and quality of health care, and may include preadmission certification and concurrent review.

Under the **precertification provision** (also known as precertification authorization or prospective review) the physician can submit claim information prior to providing treatment to know in advance if the procedure is covered under the insured's plan and at what rate it will be paid. This way both the physician and the insured know in advance what the benefit will be and can plan accordingly. This provision allows the insurance company to evaluate the appropriateness of the procedure and the length of the hospital stay.

Under the **concurrent review** process the insurer will monitor the insured's hospital stay to make sure that everything is proceeding according to schedule and that the insured will be released from the hospital as planned.

Recent evidence has shown that many treatments can be satisfactorily provided without the need for a hospital stay. **Ambulatory outpatient care** is the alternative to the costly inpatient diagnostic testing and treatment. Today, ambulatory care is best known to operate in hospital outpatient departments. However, this care can be provided by special ambulatory care health centers, group medical services, hospital emergency rooms, multi-specialty group medical practices, and health care corporations. These ambulatory facilities provide, in addition to diagnosis and treatment, preventive care, health education, family planning, and dental and vision care.

Waiver of Premium

Under this provision, the insurer waives premium payments after the insured has been totally disabled (as defined in the policy) for a specified period of time, usually three or six months. If the insured remains totally disabled, no further premium payments will be required from the insured. The insurer will pay the premiums until the insured attains age 65. If the insured recovers from the disability, then he or she will resume paying the premiums.

Policy Premiums and Cancellations

Insurance premiums are generally paid in advance and coverage does not take effect until a premium has been paid. For this reason, if a policy is cancelled in mid-term, a portion of the premium is usually returned to the policyowner. An **earned premium** is that portion of the premium that has been used up, or "earned" by the insurance company, as of the date of cancellation. An **unearned premium** is that portion of the premium that has not yet been used by the insurance company to provide coverage. For example, if a one-year policy is cancelled exactly six months into the policy term, approximately one-half of the annual premium would be earned and one-half would be unearned.

Whether a policyowner is entitled to a refund of the full unearned premium upon cancellation depends on the nature of the cancellation. There are generally three methods of returning unearned premium when a policy is cancelled.

A **pro rata cancellation** means that the premium is adjusted proportionally based upon the exact amount of time that the policy has been in force. This method is usually used when the insurer cancels a policy.

A **short rate cancellation** means that the premium returned to the insured is not in exact proportion to the number of days remaining in the policy period. In effect, the insured pays a slight penalty (to cover policy issuing costs and administrative expenses) for terminating a policy before the expiration date. This method is generally used when the insured requests cancellation.

A **flat cancellation** means that a policy is cancelled as of its effective date. Usually this means that no premium is charged. For example, when an insured returns a policy during a "free look" period, any premium payment will be fully refunded.

REVIEW QUESTIONS

13. The ________________ contains a general definition of the coverage provided in the policy.
14. The ________________ states the term of the policy.
15. A(n) ________________ renewable term policy can be renewed at the discretion of the insurer only for any reason or no reason at all.

Answers to Review Questions are located at the back of the book.

GROUP INSURANCE POLICY PROVISIONS

Conversion Privilege

The conversion privilege allows the insured to convert his or her group coverage to individual coverage without evidence of insurability. This privilege goes into effect only when the insured is no longer eligible for group coverage when:

- The insured's employment is terminated
- The insured becomes ineligible for coverage because the "class" he or she was insured under is no longer eligible for coverage. (For example, to save expenses, a company that formerly provided coverage for all employees working not less than 20 hours per week, may now only provide coverage to the "class" of employees who do not work less than 40 hours per week.)
- The insured's dependent child reaches the age specified in the policy as the age of terminating dependent coverage.

The insured has 31 days from the time of ineligibility to convert to the new plan of insurance. The new plan of insurance is an individual plan, normally a hospitalization policy, which will not provide the same benefits that the group plan did. Usually, the group medical expense benefits are more liberal than the converted policy's benefits. Often, those who elect to exercise this conversion privilege, do so because frequently they may have insurability problems. To limit adverse selection against the company, the insurer typically offers this conversion plan with reduced or limited benefits.

Certificates of Insurance

The certificate provision requires that insured persons be issued a certificate summarizing the coverage under the group policy. Information is usually provided on benefits, age limits, notice of loss and proof of loss requirements, the insurer's right of examination, and conversion. Certificates are sometimes issued in booklet form.

Dependent Coverage

Life or health insurance benefits may be extended to the primary insured's dependents. Dependents may be any of the following individuals:

- The insured's spouse
- The insured's children
- The insured's dependent parents
- The person on whom dependency can be proved

The insured's children can be stepchildren, foster children or adopted children. Dependent children must be under a specified age, usually to age 19, or to age 21 if attending school full time. The law further requires that any other person dependent on the insured is eligible for coverage. Such dependency is proved by the relationship to the insured, residency in the home, or the person being listed on the insured's income tax return as a dependent.

A child may be a dependent beyond the ages of 19 or 21 if that child is permanently mentally or physically disabled prior to the specified age.

Also a dependent child may be offered coverage beyond the limiting age of 19 if he or she is a full time college student in an accredited college. Usually, dependent coverage will be extended until age 21 or even to age 25.

Coordination of Benefits

A coordination of benefits (COB) provision is included in group health insurance policies to reduce overinsurance. Under this provision, when a person is covered under more than one plan, total benefits payable cannot exceed total medical expenses incurred. Without a COB provision, all plans could pay the full benefits of each plan. The insured would make money to the extent that the benefits exceeded medical expenses or loss of wages.

Under a COB provision, one plan is determined to be the primary plan and others secondary plans. If only one plan has a COB provision, the plan without the provision is the primary insurer and pays first.

If all plans have the COB provision, the order of payment is determined in one of the following ways:

John and his wife, Mary, work for different companies and both are covered by group medical expense insurance. John carries his wife as his dependent on his plan and Mary covers John as her dependent where she works. Thus, they both have double coverage. In this situation, each person's coverage as employee is considered the primary carrier.

For example, if John has a medical claim, his coverage where he works will pay first. If the entire claim is not paid in full, the unpaid portion will be paid by his wife's coverage as the secondary carrier. However, Mary's coverage will only pay what was not covered by the primary carrier. Thus, the husband cannot collect twice or double on the amount of the claim.

Let's assume that John and Mary have dependent children covered under their respective plans as well. If a medical expense claim involves a child under both parent's plans, one of two rules for determining the primary carrier will be used, depending on state laws.

The **gender rule** requires that the father's coverage will automatically be considered the primary carrier and thus pay first. The **birthday rule** requires that the coverage of the parent whose birthday falls earliest in the year will be identified as the primary carrier.

If parents are divorced or separated, the plan of the parent with custody of the children is considered the primary plan.

The primary carrier or plan pays benefits without regard to other plans. The secondary carrier pays unpaid portions of a claim and adjusts its benefit payments so that the total benefits paid do not exceed the total expenses incurred.

Records and Recordkeeping

This provision contains information as to whether the insurer or the policyholder will maintain records on the insureds. It provides for the policyholder to furnish the insurance company with necessary information to determine premiums and administer coverage.

Clerical Error. A clerical error provision provides that if there is an error or omission in the administration of a group policy, the person's insurance is considered to be what it would be if there had been no error or omission.

For example, an employer has the responsibility to send group enrollment forms for newly hired employees to the insurer. Sean is a new employee and through an administrative error, his enrollment form is never forwarded to the insurance company. A few months later he submits a medical expense claim to the insurer and is told that they have no record of his coverage.

This recordkeeping and clerical error provision protects the new employee in this type of situation. Usually, the insurer would accept an enrollment form and all of the past due premium and proceed to pay the medical claim.

REVIEW QUESTIONS

16. The conversion privilege allows the insured to convert group coverage to individual coverage without ______________________________

____
17. All of the following could be considered dependents **except**:
    a. the insured's adopted children.
    b. the insured's parents.
    c. the insured's 25-year-old child who became physically disabled at age 24.
    d. the insured's 21-year-old child who is attending college full-time.
18. The coordination of benefits provision provides that when a person is covered under more than one plan, total benefits cannot exceed ______________.

> ☞ ***Answers to Review Questions are located at the back of the book.***

FEDERAL & STATE REGULATIONS AFFECTING GROUP POLICIES

A number of federal regulations enacted over the past 20 years affect group life and health insurance policies. These are known by the acronyms COBRA, OBRA, TEFRA, and ERISA. Also, the health reform package passed in 1996 has major implications for group health insurance policies.

1996 HEALTH REFORMS

Legislation which takes effect July 1, 1997, ensures "portability" of group insurance coverage, and includes various mandates for small employers, the self-employed, pregnant women, and the mentally ill.

Portability

The new law makes it easier for individuals to change jobs and still maintain continuous health coverage. Employers now must make full health care coverage available immediately to newly hired employees who were previously covered at another job (the individual must have had coverage for at least 18 months). Prior to this change, coverage for preexisting conditions could be delayed for six months to one year, and new hires were subject to a waiting period before being eligible for health insurance. If the worker goes without health insurance for more than 63 days between jobs, the waiting period can be reinstated.

Also, an individual with group health insurance who leaves to become self-employed cannot be denied coverage (although the premium charged may be higher).

Group plans cannot impose more than a 12 month preexisting conditions exclusion for a person who sought medical advice, diagnosis, or treatment within the previous six months. However, this exclusion cannot be applied in the case of newborns, adopted children, or pregnancies existing on the effective date of coverage.

Mandated Benefits

The new law guarantees coverage for a 48-hour hospital stay for new mothers and their babies after a regular delivery (96 hours for a ceasarean section birth). Also, it expands coverage for mental illness by requiring similar coverage for treatment of mental and physical conditions. The law eliminates the special limitations included in many policies such as lifetime spending limits and annual limits applied only to mental health coverage.

Small employers (those with 2-50 employees) now cannot be denied group health insurance coverage because one or more employees are in poor health.

CONTINUATION OF BENEFITS (COBRA)

The Consolidated Omnibus Budget Reconciliation Act (COBRA) is a federal law that requires employers with 20 or more employees to provide for a continuation of benefits under the employer's group health insurance plan, for former employees and their families. Coverage may be continued for 18 to 36 months. Employees and other qualified family members, who would otherwise lose their coverage because of a qualifying event are allowed by COBRA to continue their coverage at their own expense at specified group rates. COBRA specifies the rates, coverage, qualifying events, qualifying beneficiaries, notification of eligibility procedures, and time of payment requirements for the continuation of insurance. Below are the terms and concepts most important to the understanding of COBRA and its limitations.

Qualifying Event. A qualifying event is an occurrence that triggers an insured's protection under COBRA. Qualifying events include: the death of a covered employee, termination or reduction of work hours of a covered employee, Medicare eligibility for the covered employee, divorce or legal separation of the covered employee from the covered employee's spouse, the termination of a child's dependent status under the terms of the group insurance plan, and the bankruptcy of the employer. Termination of employment is not a qualifying event if it is the result of gross misconduct by the covered employee. In short, a qualifying event occurs when the employee, spouse, or dependent child becomes ineligible for coverage under the group insurance contract.

Qualified Beneficiary. A qualified beneficiary is any individual covered under an employer-maintained group health plan on the day before a qualifying event. Usually this includes the covered employee, the spouse of the covered employee and/or dependent children of the employee. Changes made in 1996 amend the definition of "qualified beneficiary" to include children born or adopted during the 18 month coverage period.

Notification Statements. Employers are obligated to provide notification statements to individuals eligible for COBRA continuation. This notification must be provided under the following circumstances:

- When a plan becomes subject to COBRA

- When an employee is covered by a plan subject to COBRA
- When a qualifying event occurs

In addition to notifying current employees, the company must also notify new employees when they are informed of other employee benefits. Initial notification made to the spouse of an employee, or to his or her dependents must be made in writing and sent to the last known address of the spouse or dependent.

Following the notification of eligibility for continuation of benefits an individual has 60 days in which to elect such continuation. If continued coverage is not elected within 60 days the option to do so is forfeited.

Duration of Coverage. An employer is not required to make continuation coverage available indefinitely. The rationale behind COBRA is to provide transitional health care coverage until the employee or family member can obtain coverage or employment elsewhere. The maximum period of coverage continuation for termination of employment or a reduction in hours of employment is **18 months**. For all other qualifying events the maximum period of coverage continuation is **36 months**. There are also certain **disqualifying events** that can result in a termination of coverage before the time periods specified above. The dates of these events are as follows:

- The first day for which timely payment is not made
- The date the employer ceases to maintain any group health plan
- The first date on which the individual is covered by another group plan (even if coverage is less)
- The date the individual becomes eligible for Medicare

It should be remembered that COBRA deals with **continuation** of the exact same group coverage that the employee had as a covered employee. This distinction is important so as not to confuse this provision with the conversion of group coverage to a lesser amount of insurance as part of an individual plan.

Not only is the type of coverage the same that the insured had while employed, the premium is also the same except now the terminated employee will pay the entire premium to the employer for the privilege of continuing the group benefits. To cover any administrative expense that the employer may incur, the terminated individual may also pay an additional amount each month not to exceed 2% of the premium. It should also be noted that only the health benefits can be continued under COBRA. Any group life insurance under the plan may not be continued. It can of course be converted.

Recent amendments to COBRA require the continuation of coverage if a preexisting condition limitation is included in the new group health coverage. However, the new group health coverage is primary and the continuation coverage is secondary.

OBRA

The Omnibus Budget Reconciliation Act of 1989 (OBRA) extended the minimum COBRA continuation of coverage period from 18 to 29 months for qualified beneficiaries disabled at the time of termination or reduction in hours. The disability must meet the Social Security definition of disability, and the covered employee's termination must not have been for gross misconduct. Changes to COBRA in 1996 permit individuals who become disabled during the first 60 days of the 18-month coverage period to extend their coverge to 29 months, to extend coverage until the person would become eligible for Medicare (the five month waiting period plus 24 months of eligibility for Social Security disability benefits).

Under OBRA '89, an employer may terminate COBRA coverage because of coverage under another health plan provided the other plan does not limit or exclude benefits for a beneficiary's preexisting conditions.

OBRA '89 also clarifies that COBRA coverage may be terminated only because of Medicare entitlement, not merely eligibility. Before terminating COBRA coverage for beneficiaries at age 65, an employer must first be certain that the individual has actually enrolled under Medicare. Also, 36 months of COBRA coverage must be provided for the spouse and dependent children of a covered employee who becomes entitled to Medicare.

TEFRA

TEFRA (the Tax Equity and Fiscal Responsibility Act of 1982) is intended to prevent group term life insurance plans (usually always part of group health insurance programs) from discriminating in favor of "key employees." Key employees include officers, the top 10 interest-holders in the employer, individuals owning 5% or more of the employer, or owning more than 1% who are compensated annually at $150,000 or more.

TEFRA amends the Social Security Act to make Medicare secondary to group health plans. TEFRA applies to employers of 20 or more employees, and to active employees and their spouses between ages 65 and 69. TEFRA also amends the Age Discrimination in Employment Act (ADEA) to require employers to offer these employees and their dependents the same coverage available to younger employees.

ERISA

The Employee Retirement Income Security Act of 1974 (ERISA) was intended to accomplish pension equality, but it also protects group insurance plan participants. ERISA includes stringent reporting and disclosure requirements for establishing and maintaining group health insurance and other qualified plans. Summary plan descriptions must be filed with the Department of Labor and an annual financial report must be filed with the IRS. For other qualified plans, legal documentation of the trust agreement, plan instrument, plan description, plan amendments, claim and benefit denials, enrollment forms, certificates of participation, annual statements, plan funding, and administrative records must all be maintained.

STATE REGULATION

Many states have some form of mandated group health benefits. These commonly include required coverage for adopted or newborn children, continued coverage for handicapped dependents, coverage for treatment of alcoholism or drug abuse, and coverage for mammograms and pap smears.

Some state statutes mandate continuation of coverage for individuals whose group insurance has terminated. Most often, COBRA satisfies the state continuation of coverage requirements. In instances where the state requirements are more generous than COBRA, the employer must follow the more generous plan.

Extension of benefits is similar to continuation of coverage. In this case, benefits which began to be paid while a health insurance policy was in force continue, or are extended, after the insurance contract is terminated. Some states require group policies to provide for extension of benefits for a covered member who is totally disabled at the time of policy discontinuance.

States often regulate the marketing and advertising of accident and health insurance policies to assure truthful and full disclosure of pertinent information when selling these policies. As a rule, the insurer is held responsible for the content of advertisments of its policies. Advertisements cannot be misleading or obscure, or use deceptive illustrations, and must clearly outline all policy coverages as well as exclusions or limitations on coverage (such as preexisting condition limitations).

REVIEW QUESTIONS

19. ______________________ is a federal law that requires employers with 20 or more employees to include in their group insurance plan a continuation of benefits provision for all eligible employees.
20. ______________________ is a federal law intended to prevent group term life insurance plans from discriminating in favor of "key employees."
21. ______________________ is a federal law that extends the minimum continuation of coverage period from 18 to 29 months for qualified beneficiaries disabled at the time of termination or reduction in hours.
22. ______________________ is a federal law intended to accomplish pension equality, but it also protects group insurance plan participants.

☞ ***Answers to Review Questions are located at the back of the book.***

12

DISABILITY INCOME INSURANCE

Health insurance is concerned with two perils: accidental injury, and illness. Disability income insurance provides periodic payments when the insured is unable to work because of injury or illness. These policies pay a weekly or monthly income benefit to replace a portion of the salary or wages lost due to the insured's inability to work.

While it is not often recognized, the financial impact of total disability may be greater than the financial impact of death. A person may live for many years totally disabled and therefore unable to generate an income to pay for the higher medical and living expenses caused by the disability. Disability income insurance, sometimes referred to as **loss of time coverage**, is designed to protect an individual's most important asset — the ability to earn an income.

DEFINITIONS & BENEFITS

Disability income insurance can be defined as a contract which normally pays a monthly benefit, following the elimination period for total disability due to accident or sickness. Disability benefits may also be paid for partial or residual disability as well as total disability. An understanding of each of these terms is important because as agent, you must be able to explain to the insured how this policy will work if he or she becomes disabled. Benefits will be paid in accordance with the policy's terms and conditions.

Elimination Period

An elimination period is another kind of waiting period. It is a period of time during which an insured person must be disabled before any benefits begin. The elimination period may be thought of as a time "deductible" rather a dollar deductible, because benefits are not payable for the elimination period. Benefits begin only after this period of time is satisfied. For example, if an insured has an elimination period of 30 days and is totally disabled for 75 days, benefits would be payable only for the 45 days in excess of the elimination period.

The elimination period may be 30, 60, 90, 180 days or longer depending on the period elected by the insured. The longer the elimination period, the smaller the insurance premium, since the insured is willing to go without benefits for a longer period of time and the insurer will not have to pay for short term claims.

Benefit Period

After the elimination period has been satisfied and monthly disability benefits begin, they will be paid for a specific period of time provided the insured remains totally disabled. This period of time is known as the **benefit period**. Typical benefit periods are one year, two years, five years and to age 65.

Thus, if an insured has a disability income policy with a monthly benefit of $1,000 payable after a 30-day elimination period with a benefit period of five years, the insured would be entitled to five full years of benefits following the elimination period for each total disability (assuming that he or she continues to be totally disabled throughout the benefit period).

The longer the benefit period, the higher will be the policy's premium.

Total Disability

The definition of total disability will vary from policy to policy. This definition is important because it will determine whether the insured is totally disabled and thus eligible for benefits. One liberal definition of total disability is the inability to perform the duties of one's **own occupation**.

Let's assume that Dr. Jones is a neurosurgeon and develops an ailment which causes his hands to tremble and he can no longer perform surgery. His disability income policy defines total disability as the inability to perform the duties of his own regular occupation. Thus, Dr. Jones is eligible for benefits since he can no longer perform the duties of his occupation as a surgeon. Further, if Dr. Jones decided to become a teacher or real estate salesman, he would still be eligible to collect disability benefits even though earning an income in one of these other professions because of the liberal definition of total disability (the inability to perform the duties of the insured's "own occupation").

A more restrictive definition of total disability would be the inability to perform the duties of **any occupation**. Basically, this definition implies that the insured will only be considered totally disabled when he or she cannot work at any job whatsoever. Thus, if Dr. Jones' disability income policy contained this definition of total disability, as soon as he began to do the work of the teacher or real estate salesman, he would no longer be eligible to collect disability benefits.

Between these two definitions of total disability, there are several variations. In fact, some policies use a two-tier definition that refers to the insured's "own occupation" during an initial period of disability and then shifts to "any occupation." These policies usually define total disability as the inability to perform the duties of the insured's own occupation for a period of two to five years, and thereafter the inability to perform the duties of any occupation for which the insured is suited by reason of education, training, experience or prior economic status. This is known as the **loss of earnings** test for disability.

Some older policies also require that in addition to meeting the definition of total disability, the insured must also be confined to the house and under the treatment of a doctor. This is called **medically defined** disability.

Partial Disability

Contracts sometimes provide partial disability benefits. Partial disability is often defined as the "inability of the insured to perform one or more of the regular duties of his or her own occupation." The partial disability benefit usually pays up to 50% of the weekly or monthly indemnity payable for total disability for a period of **three to six months.**

Residual Disability

Some policies include residual disability benefits which are paid for loss of earnings after a return to work if the insured cannot earn as much as he or she did before becoming disabled. Frequently residual benefits are paid only following a period of total disability. Residual benefits are usually paid monthly, based on the percentage of income that the insured has lost due to the residual disability.

For example, Lucy has a policy that provides a monthly benefit of $1,000 for total disability and also pays residual disability benefits. She has a serious heart attack and is totally disabled for several months. During this time she suffers a total loss of her pre-disability income. After she satisfies the elimination period, she would be eligible to collect 100% of her disability benefit ($1,000 each month) while she remains totally disabled, since she has a 100% loss of pre-disability income.

After a few months, Lucy returns to work for a few hours, two or three days per week. She is compensated by her employer and receives 25% of her pre-disability compensation for this "part time" work. A typical "total disability only" policy would cease to pay her any further benefits at this point. However, since her policy includes residual disability benefits, it will continue to pay benefits.

Since Lucy is now receiving 25% of her pre-disability income, her loss of income is 75%. Lucy will therefore receive 75% of her total disability benefit or $750 ($1,000 x 75%). This benefit would be adjusted each month in proportion to the insured's loss of pre-disability income.

Recurrent Disability

A recurrent disability provision in a disability income policy is similar to a relapse provision. If the insured suffers a relapse (another disability which is related to a prior disability) and if this relapse occurs within six months of the insured's return to work, then the second disability will be considered a continuation of the initial disability. This works to the insured's advantage because the elimination period does not have to be satisfied a second time.

For example, Sam is paid disability income benefits for several months due to a heart attack. On June 1, he returns to work following his recovery. On September 1 (within six months of his return to work), he suffers a second heart attack (a relapse). Since the second heart attack is related to the initial disability, the September 1 claim will be considered a continuation of the initial disability claim. Accordingly, Sam will not have to satisfy a new elimination period and his monthly benefits will begin immediately.

However, if the second heart attack occurred nine months after the first attack, it would not satisfy the definition of a recurrent disability. In that case, the second heart attack would constitute a new claim and Sam would have to satisfy a new elimination period. Also, if Sam had suffered a second period of disability due to an unrelated cause, such as a broken leg, it would also constitute a new claim.

Presumptive Disability

Disability is presumed to be total and permanent in cases involving the loss of sight, hearing, speech, or the loss of any two limbs. Under these circumstances the insurance company does not require the insured to submit to periodic examinations to prove continuing disability.

Permanent Disability

Disability is usually defined as to whether it is permanent or temporary, in addition to whether it is total or partial. A permanent disability is one that reduces or eliminates the insured's ability to work for the rest of his or her life. Permanent disability results from injury to a limb or organ that is not expected to recover from the injury, such as loss of or loss of use of an eye, hand, or foot.

Temporary Disability

A temporary disability occurs when an insured is unable to work while recovering from an illness or injury, but is expected to fully recover from that illness or injury. Examples would be a broken leg or a sprained back.

INJURY VERSUS SICKNESS BENEFITS

Disability income benefits are paid for disabilities caused by accidental injury or sickness. While the benefit amount is usually the same for either cause of disability, the primary difference between coverage for accidents and sickness lies in the elimination period. Elimination periods for sickness may range from seven days to one year. Frequently, accident coverage has a reduced elimination period or no elimination period.

For example, an insured may have total disability coverage with a 30-day elimination period for sickness. The same policy may provide that benefits for a disability caused by accidental injury begin immediately (no elimination period), or begin after an elimination period of only three days or seven days (reduced elimination period).

Definition of Accidental Injury

Of the different terms used to define "accident" the two that will be discussed here are accidental bodily injury and accidental means.

Accidental bodily injury is defined as an injury (the **result** of an accident) which is unintentional and unforeseen. **Accidental means** is an injury of which the **cause** is unintentional and unforeseen. That is, the accident was not caused by any action taken by the injured person or by any activity performed by the injured person. Accidental means is a very restrictive definition of accidental injury, and is rarely, if ever, used today.

For example, Mary is carrying a heavy bag of groceries and strains her back. This accident would be defined as accidental bodily injury because Mary did not intentionally strain her back. However, while the injury was caused by accident it could not be defined as accidental means because the cause of the accident was foreseeable. That is, using reasonable judgment Mary could foresee that carrying too heavy a load could produce problems, such as the bag breaking and the contents spilling out and injuring her foot, or, as in this example, the heavy load creating a strain on her back. If the policy under which Mary was covered defined accident in terms of accidental means, she would not receive benefits.

On the other hand, if while carrying this same heavy bag of groceries, a dog runs in Mary's path causing her to fall and break her arm, she would be covered under the definition of accidental means. This is because the injury was caused by circumstances that could not reasonably be foreseen. Mary could not possibly foresee that a dog would run in her path; and that in running in front of her the dog would cause her to fall; and that in falling she would break her arm. There are too many contingencies to be planned for. Also, the cause of the fall was not based on any action taken by Mary, or by any activity in which Mary was engaged.

Definition of Sickness

Sickness or illness may not be defined in any manner that is more restrictive than, "sickness or disease which first manifests itself after the effective date of the policy." If a policy provides nonoccupational coverage only, the definition of sickness may exclude work-related disabilities.

For example, Susan applies for and is issued a disability income policy with an effective date of May 1, 1996. Approximately one month later she begins to have a digestive problem which is subsequently diagnosed on August 15, 1996, as a gall bladder problem requiring surgery. Medically, her symptoms first appeared after the effective date of the policy and thus, this sickness claim would be honored by the insurer.

On the other hand, let's assume that Susan begins to have the digestive problem on May 1, 1996. She contacts her doctor and he suggests that she take some antacid medication which she purchases from her local drug store. By June 1, the problem appears to be no better but Susan does nothing about it. Susan purchases some disability income insurance with an effective coverage date of July 1, 1996. One month later she consults with her doctor who after prescribing some tests, diagnoses her gall bladder problem. Even though the diagnosis occurred after the effective date of the disability income policy, the symptoms appeared prior to the effective date of the policy. Should a claim arise and all the facts become known, the insurer could determine that the gall bladder problem preexisted the effective date of the insurance and deny the claim.

The definition of sickness is very important because it could be used to permanently exclude benefits for conditions that existed prior to the effective date of coverage.

BENEFIT CALCULATIONS

Following are some sample benefit calculations which utilize the concepts discussed thus far.

Beth has a disability income policy with a 30-day elimination period, a $2,000 monthly income benefit for total disability, and a benefit period to age 65. Beth becomes totally disabled on January 1, 1997 and is unable to work for three months. She returns to work on a part-time basis, April 1, 1997 and is able to earn 40% of her pre-disability compensation during the month of April. In May she earns 60% of her pre-disability income. By June 1, she is working full time, earning 100% of her pre-disability income. Let's consider how Beth's benefits would differ under a policy that provides total and residual disability benefits and a policy that provides total disability benefits only.

It can be seen in the benefit calculation that a policy that pays residual disability benefits provides an incentive for the insured to return to work, because it pays proportional benefits. A more traditional "total disability only" policy implies that an insured cannot i return to work for any length of time without losing all benefits. While it appears that the insurance company in the example would pay less (by terminating benefits as soon as Beth returned to work on a part-time basis in April), it might actually end up paying as much or more than the policy providing residual benefits (because without partial benefits Beth might not return to work until she is fully recovered in June, and might claim total disability benefits for two additional months).

TYPES OF DISABILITY BENEFITS

Short-Term Disability

Most group short-term policies provide for short elimination periods (usually 30 days or less) and short benefit periods. The benefit period is normally for six months but not longer than one year. The benefit amount is limited to a percentage of compensation, such as 60 or 70%.

One of the rationales for short-term disability has been that the worker presumably is eligible for Social Security disability benefits after the five-month Social Security waiting period. In reality, this may or may not be true depending on whether the worker can qualify for Social Security disability benefits. In addition, if the person does qualify for benefits, the first benefit check will likely not be received before one year from the onset of disability. In any event, short-term disability benefits were designed to fill the gap until Social Security began paying benefits to the claimant.

Long-Term Disability (LTD)

LTD policies provide for longer elimination and benefit periods than short-term. Typically, the elimination period will be 90 days or six months with benefits provided for two or five years or to age 65. Most often LTD policies provide benefits to age 65.

BENEFIT CALCULATION

Month	Income Loss	Total and Residual Benefit Policy	Total Disability Only Policy
January	100%	None — satisfying the elimination period	None — satisfying the elimination period
February	100%	$2,000 — 100% of the total disability benefit	$2,000 — total disability benefit
March	100%	$2,000 — 100% of the total disability benefit	$2,000 — total disability benefit
April	60%	$1,200 — 60% of the total disability benefit	None — performing occupational duties
May	40%	$800 — 40% of the total disability benefit	None — performing occupational duties
June	0	None — no loss of income	None — performing occupational duties

CHART 12-1

The amount of the long-term benefit is limited to a percentage of the worker's compensation such as 60% or 70%. Like short-term policies, LTD coverage may be occupational or non-occupational.

Additionally, LTD policies usually provide for **integration** of plan benefits with other disability income benefits payable to the insured. The LTD benefit may be offset by any of the following:

- Any benefits provided by another formal employer plan
- Benefits payable under workers compensation or any similar statutory program
- Any benefits payable under Social Security

The purpose for having integration with these other sources of disability income is to prevent overinsurance on the part of the insured.

Lump Sum Benefits

Lump sum benefits under disability policies were once paid more frequently than today. With modern safety measures and enforcement, accidents in the workplace are less frequent. With the increase in medical technology total and permanent disability is a less frequent outcome. Therefore, installment disability income payments are still most frequently used to pay disability income benefits. Today lump sum benefits, if paid, will usually be paid under presumptive disability, or under special policies covering business buy-sell agreements.

Occupational versus Nonoccupational

Disability insurance policies can be written on an occupational or nonoccupational basis. Occupational coverage provides payment for disability arising out of accidents occurring on or off the job. Nonoccupational coverage provides payment only for disability that is not work related. Usually, group health insurance policies do not include occupational coverage because it is covered by workers compensation insurance. An occupational policy pays benefits whether or not the disability is covered under workers compensation; while a nonoccupational policy does not pay if workers compensation pays. Of course, nonoccupational coverage costs less than occupational coverage. The trend is to disallow coverage for occupational disability since workers compensation usually responds to such losses.

EXCLUSIONS

Common exclusions found in disability income policies are losses arising from war, military service, attempted suicide, overseas residence, aviation under certain circumstances (pilot or crew of aircraft), and losses that result when an insured is injured while committing a felony.

REVIEW QUESTIONS

Match the numbered definitions with the lettered terms below.

____ 1. Often defined as inability to perform duties of any occupation for which the individual is suited by education, training, or experience

____ 2. Type of health insurance providing periodic payments when an insured cannot work because of sickness or injury

____ 3. The period of time immediately following the onset of disability during which benefits are not payable

____ 4. The inability of an insured to perform one or more of the regular duties of his occupation

____ 5. When the insured is unable to work, but is expected to fully recover from illness or injury

____ 6. Injury which is unintentional and unforeseen

____ 7. The most time disability benefits will be paid

____ 8. Disability policies with a benefit period of two years or more

____ 9. War, military service, attempted suicide, aviation under certain circumstances

____ 10. Benefits are based on the insured's loss of earnings rather than inability to perform the duties of an occupation.

A. Elimination Period
B. Total Disability
C. Disability Income
D. Partial Disability
E. Temporary Disability
F. Residual Disability
G. Accidental Bodily Injury
H. Long-Term
I. Common Exclusions
J. Maximum Benefit Period

Answers to Review Questions are located at the back of the book.

OPTIONAL DISABILITY INCOME POLICY BENEFITS & RIDERS

Rehabilitation Benefit

As a result of a disability, the insured may not be able to return to his or her occupation, but may still be able to work in another field. Moving to a new job or career may necessitate some vocational training.

While totally disabled and receiving benefits, if the insured elects to participate in some form of vocational rehabilitation which is approved by the insurer, total disability benefits will be continued as long as the insured is actively participating in the training program and remains totally disabled.

Some insurers may provide a lump sum benefit for vocational training. Whether a lump sum or a monthly disability benefit, this benefit enables the insured to take positive steps toward returning to work, even though it may be in another occupation. Thus, this option benefits both the insured and the insurer.

Future Increase Option

This option may also be referred to as the **Guaranteed Insurability Option** or **Guaranteed Purchase Option**, since it enables the insured to purchase additional disability income protection, regardless of his or her insurability, at specified future dates. However, the rate for this additional coverage will be at the insured's attained age at the time of purchase, not the age when the policy was originally issued.

This benefit has some limitations. The insured will only be able to purchase a specified predetermined amount of disability income insurance at each option date. To guard against overinsurance, the insurer will usually limit the amount of additional coverage to possibly $500 or less on each option date. Also, the insured's earned income must warrant additional coverage. That is, it is presumed that every few years, the insured's earned income will increase substantially, thus "leaving room" for additional disability insurance.

Another limitation is the number of option dates on which the insured may purchase additional coverage. Usually, these option dates will be every two or three years from ages 25 to 40 or possibly, even to age 50. These dates may be arbitrarily selected by the insurer or they may coincide with the insured's birthdays, marriage, and the birth of children.

Cost of Living Benefit

The purchasing power of fixed disability benefits may be eroded due to inflation and increases in the cost of living. To protect against these trends, most insurers will offer an optional cost of living benefit.

Under the provisions of this option, the insured's monthly disability benefit (total or residual) will be automatically increased once the insured is on claim (receiving disability income benefits). Typically, this increase will occur after the insured is on claim for 12 months and each 12-month period thereafter as long as the insured remains on claim.

Lifetime Benefits

This option extends the benefit period from age 65 to lifetime. This extension may apply to accident only benefits or to accident and sickness benefits. Normally, if the total disability is due to an accident and it occurs prior to age 65, benefits will be paid for the lifetime of the insured provided he or she remains totally disabled.

Most companies will place some time limitations for the lifetime sickness benefit. That is, the disabling sickness must begin prior to a specified age such as 50, 55 or 60. A policy providing lifetime sickness benefits may stipulate that if the sickness begins at age 55 or earlier, then 100% of the total disability benefit will be provided for the lifetime of the insured. However, if the disability begins after age 55, but before age 65, a reduced benefit will be paid for life.

For example, a policy might state the following:

If total disability, due to sickness, begins at age 55 or earlier, total disability benefits will be paid for the lifetime of the insured. If total disability benefits begin at age:

- 56 — total benefits are paid to age 65; then 90% of the benefit for the lifetime of the insured
- 57 — total benefits are paid to age 65; then 80% of the benefit for the lifetime of the insured
- 58 — total benefits are paid to age 65; then 70% of the benefit for the lifetime of the insured
- 59 — total benefits are paid to age 65; then 60% of the benefit for the lifetime of the insured
- 60 — total benefits are paid to age 65; then 50% of the benefit for the lifetime of the insured.

This progression of benefits would continue in this manner until age 65. If the total disability began at age 65 (normally the policy is not renewed past age 65), then the payment of total disability benefits would be limited to one or two years.

Social Security Rider

The Social Security Administration defines total disability as the inability to perform any substantial gainful work which may exist in the national economy.

In addition, the disability must be expected to last at least 12 months or end in death. This is a very rigid and ultra-conservative definition of total disability.

Annually, the Social Security Administration denies about two-thirds of all disability claims. It is clear that few claimants will collect disability benefits under Social Security. If a Social Security rider is added to an individual's disability income policy, an additional benefit is paid for a short period of time.

There are two different methods by which a rider may provide benefits:

- **All or Nothing Rider**: Under this concept, the insured will be paid a benefit if Social Security pays nothing. Conversely, if Social Security provides any benefit, then the rider pays nothing.
- **Offset Rider**: The benefit provided by the Social Security rider will be reduced, or offset, by the amount of any benefit provided by Social Security.

Social Insurance Supplements

One of the problems private insurers have is providing disability income for middle and low income families without overinsuring. Amendments enacted by Social Security have reduced the overinsurance under its programs, but it is possible for a worker to receive more in benefits than his or her earned income. Because of this situation, most insurers writing disability income take into account the overinsurance when writing disability income for middle and low income groups. The problem with supplementing Social Security in this way alone is that an insured may not receive the benefits that the insurer has used in calculating disability payments. For example, an insured may not receive workers compensation benefits because the loss is not covered, or the insured may not meet the Social Security definitions of total or permanent disability. To solve this problem some insurers are using **social insurance supplements.** These supplements may be included as part of the disability income policy benefits, or they may be added to the policy by rider. Under this supplement total disability benefits will be paid until workers compensation or Social Security benefits begin. If, for any reason, government benefits stop, the insurer will begin the monthly payments again. The benefits are only paid during the benefit period and only if the insured is still disabled.

Additional Monthly Benefit (AMB) Riders

Most insurers offer short term riders to provide additional benefits during the first six months or 12 months of a claim. They may entitle them "Social Security Riders" or they may simply be identified as an "Additional Monthly Benefit Rider." Regardless of the name of the rider, the purpose is the same — to provide additional disability income benefits during the first year of a claim while the insured is waiting for Social Security benefits to begin.

These Additional Monthly Benefit riders are also used to complement other disability income sources such as short-term group disability benefits provided through the employer.

Hospital Confinement Rider

This optional benefit results in the elimination period being waived when the insured is hospitalized as an inpatient. The payment of any disability benefits must include satisfying the elimination period. The hospital confinement benefit pays the regular total disability benefit during the elimination period when the insured is hospitalized.

The factor which triggers the payment of the benefit is any period of hospitalization during the elimination period. Benefits will only be paid for as long as the insured is hospitalized.

For example, an insured has a disability income policy with a 30-day elimination period and a $1,000 per month benefit for total disability, payable to age 65. The insured also has the hospital confinement option and is hospitalized for minor surgery for a period of two days. Following the hospitalization, the insured returns to work within three days. Total disability benefits will be paid for the period of two days. The amount paid would be 2/30 (or 1/15th) of $1,000, or $67.

Non-Disabling Injury Rider

This benefit does not pay a disability benefit but rather provides for the payment of medical expenses incurred due to injury which does not result in total disability.

Waiver of Premium (with Disability Income)

This rider specifies that in the event of disability, premiums will be waived retroactively to the beginning of the disability. The definition is usually "permanent and total" disability. Again, however, a few companies have gone to a definition in terms of occupation, as previously discussed.

SAMPLE SCHEDULE

Loss of:	Sum Equal to Weekly Indemnity for:
Both hands, or feet, or sight of both eyes	200 weeks
One hand and one foot	200 weeks
Either hand or foot and sight of one eye	200 weeks
Either hand or foot	100 weeks
Sight of one eye	65 weeks
Thumb and index finger of either hand	50 weeks

Accidental Death & Dismemberment (AD&D)

Accidental death policies or riders include a death benefit which is payable in the event of death resulting from accidental bodily injury. A companion coverage is provided for loss of limbs or sight, often called dismemberment coverage.

A schedule is made a part of the policy which lists various dismemberments and losses of sight for which a specified sum will be paid to the insured. In policies with weekly disability income benefits, the sum payable is usually expressed as a multiple of the weekly indemnity. In policies without weekly disability income benefits, the sums payable are usually expressed as percentages of the death benefit limit or sometimes as percentages of a limit in the policy known as the **principal or capital sum**. The capital sum might be $20,000 and the death benefit is usually the same amount ($20,000).

The intent of the dismemberment feature is to provide insureds with a lump sum which will help them over the period when they go through rehabilitation and, probably, training for work other than that for which they previously were qualified. If the policy has a disability income feature, once a dismemberment sum is paid, the disability income payments stop. In some cases the insured might be disabled for a while, and during the disability suffer one of the losses listed above. In that event, the insured would be paid disability income up to the time of the loss of limb or sight only.

Most company policies provide that, even if the insured is not disabled after an accident, if a loss of limb or sight occurs within 90 days of the date of the accident, the sums in the schedule will be paid.

Accidental death and dismemberment coverage provides both a life insurance and a health insurance benefit. However, the life insurance benefit applies only to accidental death and is not paid for death by natural causes.

Other Provisions

While disability income policies do not typically accumulate cash value or have a life insurance component, it is possible to purchase riders to the policy that provide benefits similar to life insurance policies. Thus, an **annual renewable term** life insurance feature may be attached to a disability income policy, providing a death benefit as well as disability income coverage.

Similarly, a **return of premium rider** may be attached to a disability income policy. This rider provides for the return of a percentage of premiums paid (usually 80%) during a specific term period (usually every 10 years) minus the claims paid during the term period. The refund is made every 10 years and at age 65 or as of the date of death. Essentially, for an additional premium, the policyholder gets 80% of his or her money back either in claims, premium refunds, or a combination of both. Various settlement options are offered for receiving the premium refund. Amounts left on deposit with the insurance company earn interest and constitute cash value and/or may be applied toward future premium payments.

REVIEW QUESTIONS

11. The benefit which enables a disabled insured to learn to work in another occupation is known as the:
    a. cost of living benefit.
    b. rehabilitation benefit.
    c. guaranteed insurability option.
    d. lifetime benefit option.
12. The benefit which protects against the erosion of purchasing power for fixed disability benefits is known as the:
    a. cost of living benefit.
    b. rehabilitation benefit.
    c. offset rider.
    d. lifetime benefit.
13. The rider which provides more benefits during the first six months or year of a claim is known as the:
    a. cost of living rider.
    b. rehabilitation rider.
    c. additional monthly benefit rider.
    d. lifetime benefit rider.

14. The benefit which pays the regular total disability benefit during the elimination period when the insured is hospitalized is known as the:
    a. hospital confinement rider.
    b. rehabilitation benefit.
    c. non-disabling injury rider.
    d. offset rider.
15. The option which allows an insured to purchase additional amounts of disability income protection is known as the:
    a. lifetime benefit option.
    b. additional monthly benefit option.
    c. all or nothing option.
    d. future increase option.
16. If the Consumer Price Index goes up under the Cost of Living Benefit, the benefits will go (up/down) ____________________.
17. What is the advantage of having the Future Increase Option? ____________________

    ____

    ____
18. Social insurance supplements provide disability income:
    a. before workers compensation and social security begin payments
    b. after workers compensation and social security end payments
    c. both are correct

> ☞ ***Answers to Review Questions are located at the back of the book.***

BUSINESS USES OF DISABILITY INCOME INSURANCE

Disability income insurance is designed to protect an individual's most important asset — the ability to earn an income. By protecting against the loss of income during periods of disability, this type of coverage enables the disabled insured to continue to provide for the basic necessities of life. The application and use of disability income coverage is not confined to individuals but also is very relevant in business situations.

The life insurance section of this book identified business uses of life insurance, i.e., to fund buy-sell agreements, key person insurance, etc. Life insurance benefits are paid to the business upon the death of a key person or the businessowner so that the business may continue. A similar concept applies for the business with regard to the disability of a key person or the businessowner. The living death of disability can have a serious impact on the continued existence and profitability of a business.

Business Overhead Expense (BOE)

The BOE policy is designed for the small businessowner. Its purpose is to cover certain overhead expenses which continue when the businessowner is disabled. Most insurers will limit the BOE policy to those businesses which are relatively small.

For example, General Motors would not be eligible for a BOE policy but a small firm consisting of the owner and three to four employees could purchase a BOE policy.

The policy will indemnify the business (not the owner) for such business expenses as: rent, taxes, insurance premiums, utility bills, employees' compensation (not the owner's salary), etc. By covering these expenses when the owner is disabled, the business is able to keep its doors open and continue to operate.

Naturally, the overall concept is that the small businessowner is so important to the profitability of the business that when he or she becomes totally disabled, the business will suffer economically and may even be forced to close. An example of such a situation would be a dentist. Typically, if the dentist cannot practice his or her profession, business income will eventually be impaired and the few employees working in the dentist's office may lose their jobs. As the business income slows, the bills still have to be paid as do the employees. The BOE policy will solve this problem.

Generally, BOE policies will have elimination periods of usually 15 or 30 days and benefit periods of one or two years. The benefit amount will be determined by the average eligible overhead expenses of the business. If the businessowner becomes disabled, after the elimination period is satisfied, the business will receive benefits equal to the actual overhead expenses incurred during the owner's disability.

BOE premiums are tax deductible to the business. The disability benefits received are thus taxable to the business. However, these taxable benefits are then used to pay tax deductible business expenses.

Key Person Disability Insurance

Just as key person life insurance serves to indemnify the business for the lost services of a key person due to death, so too does a key person disability income policy. This type of coverage pays a monthly benefit to a business to cover expenses for additional help or outside services when an essential person is disabled. The key person could be a partner or working stockholder of the business. The key person could also be a management person who is personally responsible for some very important functions such as a sales manager.

The key person's economic value to the business is determined in terms of the potential loss of business income which could occur as well as the expense of hiring and training a possible replacement for the key person. The key person's value then becomes the disability benefit which will be paid to the business. The benefit amount may be paid in a lump sum or in periodic monthly installments. Generally, the policy's elimination period will be 30-90 days and usually the benefit period will be one or two years.

The business is the owner and premium payor of the policy. Benefits are received by the business tax free because the premium paid is not tax deductible.

Disability Buy-Sell Insurance

When there is a buy-sell agreement funded with life insurance to buyout the interest of a deceased owner or partner, there should also be a provision in the agreement for the buyout of the owner's business interest in the event of disability. Naturally, this disability provision should be funded with buy-sell disability income insurance.

One of the critical considerations with reference to the disability buy-sell policy is the elimination period. Once the elimination period is satisfied benefits will begin to be made to the business for the purpose of buying out the interest of the disabled owner or partner. Generally, once the buyout begins it cannot be stopped. Thus, for example, a disabled partner does not want to be bought "too soon" and then possibly recover from the disability and find that he or she has no job and no business interest.

For this reason, the elimination period for disability buy-sell insurance will normally be one or two years. The buy-sell agreement will specify the value or a method of determining the value of the owner's business interest. This value will be paid to the business following the elimination period. The benefits may may be paid in a lump sum or in monthly installments. If the policy provides a monthly benefit, usually the benefit period will not exceed five years. The business of course uses the policy proceeds to buy out the interest of the disabled person.

Usually, the business is the owner and premium payor for the policy or policies. The premiums are not deductible but the benefits are received by the business, tax free.

Disability Reducing Term Insurance

It may happen that a businessowner incurs a loan or other financial obligation that requires monthly payments. However, the monthly payment can only be made as long as the businessowner remains able to run the business (is not disabled).

To protect the financial obligation, and the assets that could be lost in case of default, the business can purchase a "disability reducing term policy" which provides a monthly benefit in the case of total disability sufficient to cover the monthly financial obligation until it is satisfied (the end of the loan repayment period).

The business purchases and owns the policy, the businessowner is the insured, and the business is the beneficiary of the monthly benefit. Premiums are not tax-deductible to the business, but benefits are received tax free. "Reducing term" refers to the fact that the full monthly benefit is payable only for the remaining term of indebtedness or obligation.

TAXATION OF DISABILITY INCOME INSURANCE

Premiums paid by the insured for individually owned disability income insurance are not tax deductible. However, benefits paid in this type of situation are tax free to the insured.

In situations where the business is providing disability income coverage for its employees, the **premium paid by the business** is tax deductible as a business expense. This is true whether the coverage is provided by a group policy or individual contracts. Naturally, the benefits received by the employees would then be taxable as income.

In situations where the business is providing disability income coverage to protect itself (key person, disability buy-sell insurance), premiums paid by the business are not tax deductible as a business expense. The basic premise is that either the premium or the benefit will be taxed. If the premium is not deductible to the business, then the benefits will be received tax free. If the premium is deductible then the benefits are taxable as is the case with the BOE policy.

REVIEW QUESTIONS

19. Businesses use health insurance to fund:
    a. business overhead expenses.
    b. employee benefits.
    c. buy-sell agreements.
    d. all of the above.

Match the numbered definitions below with the lettered terms below.

_____ 20. Indemnify the business for expenses such as rent, taxes, insurance premiums, utility bills, employees' compensation, etc. when the businessowner is disabled.

_____ 21. Pays a lump sum or monthly installment to cover the potential loss of business income when an important employee who makes a specific contribution to the success of the business becomes disabled.

_____ 22. Indemnifies a businessowner for his or her business interest in the event of disability.

A. Disability Buy-Sell Insurance
B. Business Overhead Expense
C. Key Person Disability Insurance

23. Premiums for disability income coverage paid by the employer (are/are not) __________ tax deductible for the business, and benefits received by the employees (are/are not) __________ taxable as income.
24. Premiums for individually owned disability income coverage (are/are not) __________ tax deductible to the insured, and benefits received by the insured (are/are not) __________ tax free.

☞ ***Answers to Review Questions are located at the back of the book.***

NOTES

13

MEDICAL EXPENSE INSURANCE

Medical expense insurance provides benefits for medical care. Contracts may provide for payment of medical expenses incurred on a reimbursement basis (by paying benefits to the policyowner), on a service basis (by paying those who provide the services directly), or a contract may provide for payment of an indemnity (by paying a set amount regardless of the amount charged for medical expenses). Medical expense or hospitalization insurance may be written on an individual basis or on a group basis. Benefits provided cover the individual and eligible dependents.

Although there are many types of benefits available, medical expense insurance can generally be categorized as basic medical expense insurance, major medical insurance, comprehensive medical insurance and special policies. It should be noted that these products have largely been replaced by managed care alternatives and are not sold as standalone coverages any longer. These types of plans have been modified and replaced in response to changes in the health care field relative to cost containment and market competition. However, an understanding of basic medical, hospital and surgical plans can serve as a foundation for understanding the hybrid plans currently being marketed.

BASIC MEDICAL EXPENSE

Basic coverages provided by an individual medical expense policy include **hospital expense, surgical expense** and **medical expense**. These three basic coverages may be sold together or separately. Frequently this is written as "first dollar" coverage, which means it does not have a deductible.

Hospital Expense

Hospital expense coverage provides benefits for daily hospital room and board and miscellaneous hospital expenses (not including telephone and television) while the insured person is confined to the hospital. The policy may provide for a certain dollar amount for the daily hospital room and board benefit, although the trend is toward coverage of not more than the semi-private room rate unless a private room is medically necessary.

Room and board (R&B) rates will vary by geographical location but it is not unusual to find R&B rates ranging from \$300—\$500 per day or more. The hospital expense part of a basic medical expense policy accordingly would provide a R&B daily rate of a specified amount which may or may not be equal to the actual R&B expenses incurred.

For example, if the insured's R&B benefit was \$400 per day and the hospital actually charged \$500 per day, the insured is liable for the \$100 per day not covered by the policy. Thus, it could be said that a basic hospital expense policy has limitations with regard to benefit amounts.

In addition, there are normally time limitations associated with a basic hospital expense policy. For example, benefits may be provided for only 30 days, 60 or 90 days, after which no further benefits would be provided unless the insured were subsequently hospitalized at a later date with a different ailment.

If the insured is confined to an intensive care unit of a hospital, then the R&B benefits will be increased. Normally, benefits for intensive care will be at least twice the regular R&B benefit.

The **miscellaneous hospital expense** part of the basic hospitalization policy includes benefits for such things as surgical dressings, in-hospital drugs, charges for operating rooms, anesthetics, lab work, in-hospital diagnostic tests, etc. Except for the R&B charges and surgery, most other hospital expenses could be identified as miscellaneous expenses or hospital extras.

Usually miscellaneous benefits are limited to specific dollar amount (\$2,000, \$3,000, \$5,000, etc.). Most often the benefit is limited to a multiple of the plan's daily R&B benefit. For example, if the basic medical expense policy provides for a daily R&B benefit of $500, the miscellaneous benefit might be expressed as an amount equal to 10 or 20 times the R&B benefit or $5,000 or $10,000. Again, it should be noted that this is a limitation of the basic hospitalization plan in that only a specified amount may be paid for miscellaneous hospital expenses.

Generally, in-hospital miscellaneous expenses are very high. Depending on the reason for admittance to the hospital, the insured could exhaust a modest miscellaneous benefit of $5,000 in a matter of a couple of days or less.

Surgical Expense

Surgical expense coverage provides benefits for the surgical services of a physician performed in or out of the hospital. Surgical expense benefits are usually limited to a dollar amount, although they may be expressed as multiples of the hospital benefit maximum. Usually a **schedule** of operations is attached to the policy and the maximum amount payable for each operation is listed. The more serious and complicated the surgery the higher the benefit. Operations that are not listed on the schedule are covered and the limit that applies to them is determined by the insurer on a basis consistent with comparably listed operations.

Some surgical schedules do not list dollar amounts but assign a **relative value unit** to each procedure. For example, a schedule may be identified as a $1,000 schedule which basically means that the maximum benefit for a surgical procedure will be $1,000. Naturally, this maximum amount of $1,000 would be paid for the most serious types of surgery such as open heart surgery. All other surgical procedures would have a relative value in relation to this $1,000 schedule. This relative value would be expressed by a number and then multiplied by a conversion factor to arrive at the benefit to be paid.

To illustrate this point, let's assume that Stephanie is about to have her gall bladder removed. Her basic surgical expense policy has a $1,000 surgical schedule and gall bladder surgery has a relative value of 40. The schedule's conversion factor (which remains constant) is 20. Multiplying 40 x 20, results in a benefit of $800 for the gall bladder surgery.

The following benefit calculation will illustrate the principal benefits of the basic medical expense policy.

This calculation demonstrates the benefits to be paid and the limitations of the basic medical expense plan. The insured would be liable for $3,850 of medical expenses due to benefit limits.

Other Medical Expense

Hospital R&B, miscellaneous and surgical expenses incurred as an in-patient represent the major benefits provided by a basic plan. Thus, if the insured were hospitalized due to a sickness or an accident, daily R&B charges, miscellaneous hospital expenses and surgical charges would be paid in accordance with the policy and its limitations.

Other medical expense benefits may be included as part of the policy or as options added to the policy. Following is a description of some of the more common policy benefits or options.

In-Hospital Physician Visits. Frequently, a basic medical expense policy will include a daily benefit for expenses incurred when the insured's physician visits him or her in the hospital. This benefit is limited to a

BENEFIT CALCULATION
BASIC MEDICAL EXPENSE POLICY

Policy Benefits	Expenses Incurred	Benefits Paid	Unpaid Amount
R&B: $350 per day for up to 90 days for each hospitalization	$400 per day for 10 days = $4,000	$3500 ($350 x 10)	$500 (50 x 10)
Miscellaneous: 20 times the R&B limit ($7,000)	$10,000 for the 10 days	$7000 Policy maximum	$3000
Surgery: $1,000 Schedule	Appendectomy $950 charge	$600 (i.e., per schedule)	$350
TOTALS:	$14,950	$11,100	$3,850

Chart 13-1

dollar amount such as $25 or $30 per day. This amount would be paid for any charges made by the doctor for visiting the patient.

Emergency Accident Benefits. A basic plan may include a specific benefit for expenses incurred due to an accident when the insured is taken to the emergency room of a hospital as an outpatient. Typically, this benefit is stated as $300 or possibly, $500. The benefit is to cover the cost of treatment in the emergency room including physician expenses, X-rays, stitches, etc.

Maternity Benefits. Most often, maternity benefits are optional benefits which may be elected by the insured. As a benefit, maternity coverage is very expensive and to keep the cost of this benefit reasonable, the benefit amount is frequently very limited. For example, for an additional premium, the insured may add a maternity benefit of $1,000. This amount is the total benefit paid for prenatal care, delivery of the baby and the hospital confinement for mother and child due to the delivery.

Mental and Nervous Disorders. This benefit is usually part of the policy and covers expenses for outpatient mental and nervous disorders. Normally, this would include out-of-the-hospital therapy provided by a psychiatrist or clinical psychologist. The benefit is usually limited to a specific dollar amount per visit, such as $50. There is normally a lifetime maximum of $10,000 or possibly as high as $25,000.

Hospice Care. Most states require that any hospitalization policy (individual or group) include benefits for hospice expenses. The hospice is a facility designed to control pain and suffering of terminally ill patients until their death. It does not treat diseases nor does it attempt to cure. In addition, the hospice also provides counseling for the patient and the family of the terminally ill. Expenses covered include R&B, medication as well as outpatient services and expenses.

Home Health Care. This is usually an optional benefit which provides for reimbursement of expenses incurred by the insured for the services of a visiting nurse, a therapist or some other support-type person who due to a medical necessity, visits the insured in his or her home and provides necessary medical services.

Outpatient Care. Outpatient care refers to expenses incurred by the insured for doctor's office visits, out-of-the-hospital diagnostic services such as lab work and X-rays. Often a basic medical expense policy only covers in-hospital expenses (inpatient) whereby treatment is provided to the patient who has been assigned a room and a bed and is staying in the hospital for some period of time. Basic plans may add coverage for certain medical services provided to the insured as an outpatient.

In summary, it is quite evident that basic medical expense plans definitely have time and/or benefit amount limitations. Thus, the insured may well expect to have to pay a considerable amount out of pocket for medical expenses. The solution to this problem is another type of hospitalization coverage referred to as major medical insurance.

MAJOR MEDICAL INSURANCE

Unlike basic medical expense policies with benefit amount limitations, major medical coverage is designed to provide a large sum of money from which to pay covered medical expenses. Sometimes, major medical insurance is referred to as catastrophe insurance because its focus is on large, catastrophic medical expenses. Major medical policies may be issued as individual coverage or as a group hospitalization plan. Major medical is characterized by deductibles, coinsurance and large benefit maximums.

Deductibles. Major medical benefits begin to be paid after the deductible is satisfied. The policy's deductible is usually between $100 and $500; although higher deductibles are not that uncommon. The deductible is considered satisfied as long as the insured can show evidence of having incurred the necessary expense.

For example, let's assume that a major medical policy contains a $500 deductible. The insured has no other medical expenses and is hospitalized for surgery. His total hospital bill is $7,500. Of this amount, $7,000 would be eligible for major medical benefits and $500 would be identified as the deductible amount. Thus, the insured has incurred an expense equal to the deductible. Notice that payment of the deductible is not necessary; only incurring the expense is required to satisfy the deductible.

The deductible may be identified as a **per cause** deductible or a **calendar year** deductible. Each of these applies to each covered person. The per cause deductible requires that a deductible be satisfied for each separate claim. The calendar year (all cause) deductible specifies that one deductible needs to be satisfied for a calendar year period regardless of the number of claims.

If George has three different medical claims in a given year and his policy contains a $250 per cause deductible, then he must satisfy three separate deductibles. If the policy contained a calendar year deductible, he would only have to satisfy one deductible which would take care of the entire year.

Most policies provide that if a family is insured, a maximum of two or three deductibles will satisfy the deductible requirement for the **entire family** for a year.

Mary Beth covers herself, her husband and three children with her group major medical policy where she works. The plan has a calendar year or all cause deductible of $100 with a family maximum of $300 per year. Thus, this family of five will satisfy their family deductible of $300 when a total of $300 of expenses has been incurred by the family members.

Also related to the family situation is the **common accident provision** which states that if members of a family are injured in a common accident, only one deductible applies.

Most major medical policies will contain a **carry over provision**. This provision usually stipulates that if the insured had no claims during the year but does incur medical expenses in the last three months of the year, these late year expenses may be carried over to a new calendar year and applied to the new year's deductible.

Coinsurance (Percentage Participation). Most policies have a coinsurance provision. Under its terms, all expenses in excess of the deductible are shared on some basis between the insurance company and the insured. In a great many policies expenses are shared on an 80%-20% basis. The insurer pays 80%, the insured 20%. Other coinsurance percentages encountered are 75%-25% and 85%-15%.

Out of Pocket Limit. The out of pocket limit is the maximum amount an individual will be required to pay during a policy year. After a predetermined amount has been paid by the insured, the insurer will pay 100% of covered expenses for the remainder of the year, up to the policy limit.

A major medical policy may reflect a $500 deductible followed by 80%-20% coinsurance on the first $5,000 of covered expenses. If expenses exceed, $5,000, the insurer pays 100% as the insured's out of pocket limit will have been reached. Basically, this means that the insured would be expected to incur the $500 deductible and 20% of $5,000 of medical expenses or an additional $1,000. Thus, the insured would be liable for a maximum expense of $1,500 — regardless of how large the claim might be.

If a major medical claim was exactly $5,500, the insured is liable for $1,500 or approximately 27% of the entire amount. On the other hand, if the claim totaled $105,500, the insured is still responsible for $1,500 which represents only a little more than 1% of the entire claim.

Frequently, this out of pocket limit is also referred to as the insured's **stop loss**, which is the point at which the insured's loss (coinsuring the claim) stops and the insurer assumes responsibility for 100% of the claim. Thus, in the previous example, the stop loss limit is $1,500.

Maximum Benefit. Major medical plans include a maximum benefit which applies on a "lifetime" basis, "per person." The maximum benefit is usually substantial, such as $500,000 or $1 million. Each member of an insured family is separately insured for the maximum benefit amount.

Restoration of Benefits. Most major medical policies have a restoration of benefits provision. If a claim is paid, the total amount of insurance is reduced by the amount of the claim. A policy with a $250,000 limit and a $10,000 claim, would only have $240,000 of coverage after that claim had been paid. The restoration of benefits feature restores a certain amount of coverage, such as $2,500 or $3,000 each year to replace, in effect, the coverage lost as a result of the claim.

Covered Medical Expenses. The coverage provisions of major medical policies are very broad. One way of looking at a major medical policy is to consider that the insurer has opened a bank account in your name and almost all of your medical expenses pass through this account. The term, "covered expenses", usually includes doctors' fees, nursing fees, hospital R&B charges, miscellaneous expenses, surgical expenses, out of the hospital expenses such as doctor's office calls, prescription medication, diagnostic services, etc. These expenses are covered in accordance with the policy's deductible and coinsurance provisions up to the policy's maximum benefit.

Limits of Coverage. The limits of coverage are also established by the concept of reasonable and customary charges (also referred to as usual, customary and reasonable — UCR). These charge or expense factors represent the average charge in a given geographical area for the medical service provided. These factors are adjusted periodically to reflect changes. A major medical policy might specify that it will pay the reasonable and customary charges for various covered medical expenses up to the policy's lifetime maximum of $1 million.

This does not imply that the policy will pay all of the insured's medical expenses. It states it will pay what is reasonable and customary, and there may be inside limits; limits which apply to particular types of expense such as hospital room and board and surgery. The inside limit may be expressed as a maximum dollar amount. Inside limit amounts are higher than the amounts allowed under basic medical expense policies.

For example, David has his tonsils removed. The surgeon's fee is $750. However, upon review by the insurer, it is determined that the reasonable and customary charge for a tonsillectomy is $550. Thus the covered expense is $550 subject to the policy's deductible and coinsurance provisions. If the policy also had an inside limit of $500 for a tonsillectomy, that would be the most it would pay.

Supplemental Major Medical

In the past, major medical policies were frequently sold as supplemental coverage. The insured had a basic medical expense plan which paid specific dollar amounts for various medical services. These amounts were often referred to as "first dollar" benefits because there were no deductibles or coinsurance features and the basic plan covered expenses up to these first dollar limits.

However, as medical expenses soared, the basic medical expense plan quickly exhausted its benefit limits and the insured was in need of additional coverage. These additional benefits were often provided by a major medical policy which was initially designed to supplement the basic plan so that when basic benefits were reduced or used up, the supplemental benefits would pick up where the basic plan left off.

Today, due to the high cost of health care and the high cost of hospitalization insurance, most employers and individuals will carry major medical plans as their main source of health care insurance. Because of the deductibles, coinsurance features and lack of first dollar benefits, major medical plans are typically less expensive. The higher the plan's deductible, the lower the premium. The higher the stop loss point with regard to coinsurance, the lower the premium.

For example, a major medical plan with a $500 all cause deductible and 70%-30% coinsurance on the first $10,000 of covered medical expenses will be less costly than a first dollar plan or a major medical plan with a $100 deductible and 80%-20% coinsurance on the first $2,500 of covered medical expenses.

Comparison of Basic Medical Expense and Major Medical

Let's review the basic medical expense calculation from one of the previous pages and use a major medical policy to provide benefits instead of the basic hospitalization plan.

This calculation assumes that all expenses are reasonable and customary. The calculation of the miscellaneous benefits is broken down into two parts ($1,250 and $8,750) because the stop loss or out of pocket limit has been reached ($1,250) and benefits provided by the insurer thereafter are 100% of the covered expense.

As previously illustrated, the same expenses covered by a basic medical expense plan provided $11,100 in benefits, leaving the insured with a bill of $3,850 compared to the out of pocket expense in this example of $1,250.

COMPREHENSIVE MEDICAL EXPENSE

Comprehensive medical expense insurance is a combination of basic medical expense coverage (first dollar coverage) plus a major medical plan. Both major plans are simply combined into one policy.

The basic part of the plan provides first dollar coverage, usually without any deductibles or coinsurance features. Once the basic benefits are exhausted, the major medical portion of the plan "kicks in" subject to a corridor deductible and coinsurance provisions.

MAJOR MEDICAL BENEFIT CALCULATION

Major Medical Policy Features

Deductible:	$250
Coinsurance:	80-20% up to $5,000 100% thereafter
Maximum Benefit:	$1 million

Expenses Incurred	Benefit Calculation	Out of Pocket Expense
$400 per day for 10 days = $4,000	$4,000 of covered expenses less the $250 deductible = $3,750 $3,750 x 80% = $3,000	$250 deductible $3,750 x 20% = $750
Miscellaneous Expense—$10,000	$1,250 x 80% = $1,000 $8,750 x 100% = $8,750	$1,250 x 20% = $250
Surgery—$950	$950 x 100% = $ 950	
Total Expenses: $14,950	Total Benefits: $13,700	Total: $1,250

Chart 13-2

COMPREHENSIVE MEDICAL EXPENSE

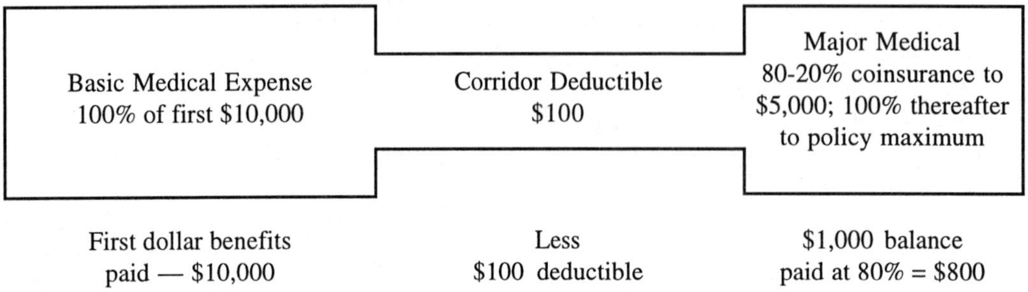

CHART 13-3

For example, let's assume that Keith has a comprehensive medical policy which provides 100% coverage of the first $10,000 of medical expenses followed by a deductible of $100 and a $1 million major medical plan with 80%-20% coinsurance on the next $5,000 of medical expenses with 100% paid thereafter. Keith incurs medical expenses totaling $11,100. His plan would pay as follows:

Keith's plan would cover $10,800 of the total expenses. It pays the first $10,000. Keith then pays the $100 deductible. The plan then pays 80% of the $1,000 balance and Keith pays 20%, or $200. Thus, Keith pays a total of $300.

Comprehensive plans will pay considerably more benefits in a typical situation than a basic hospitalization policy and slightly more benefits than a major medical plan. However, the inclusion of the block of first dollar benefits under the basic part of the comprehensive plan is an expensive item. This premium difference is often large enough to motivate many people to simply purchase a major medical plan with a reasonable deductible and a more reasonable premium.

MEDICAL EXPENSE LIMITATIONS

Reimbursement-type medical expense policies frequently provide limited coverage or benefits for certain medical conditions. Many plans will include limitations on the benefits to be provided for the following:

- Rehabilitation and skilled nursing/extended care facilities care
- Home health care
- Hospice care
- Ambulance services
- Outpatient treatment
- Medical equipment and supplies
- Reconstructive cosmetic surgery
- Treatment of AIDS
- Infertility and sterilization
- Maternity/complications of pregnancy/well baby care
- Psychiatric conditions
- Substance abuse
- Organ transplants
- Preexisting Conditions
- Reimbursement for non-physician services

Mental or Emotional Disorders. Lifetime benefit amounts are limited for outpatient treatment of these disorders. For example, a major medical policy may have a lifetime maximum of $1 million but the policy may limit coverage for outpatient treatment of mental or emotional disorders to a lifetime benefit of $25,000. In addition, frequently there may be a limitation with regard to the number of outpatient psychiatric visits per calendar year (such as a maximum of 26 visits per year) and/or the benefit amount paid per visit (such as a maximum benefit of $50 per visit or coverage for no more than 50% of the actual charges). These limits would not apply to inpatient treatment of mental or emotional disorders. (Note: New federal laws effective in 1997 remove these limitations for group coverage.)

Maternity. As previously discussed, maternity benefits are often optional. When elected, the amount of the maternity benefit is often limited. This limitation is frequently due to the high cost of a maternity claim and the corresponding high premium charged for the benefit.

For example, a maternity benefit may be limited to a total benefit of $1,000 regardless of the actual expenses incurred. Usually, the only time additional benefits are paid is if there are certain complications during the pregnancy or at the time of delivery. A very liberal maternity benefit (and a costly one) would be that maternity is treated as any other illness and thus a full range of benefits would be payable.

Substance Abuse. Outpatient treatment for drug or alcohol problems is usually limited in much the same way that nervous or emotional disorders are covered. Usually, if the insured is hospitalized as an inpatient for treatment of the substance abuse problem, then regular medical expense benefits would be payable.

Chiropractic Services. The treatment rendered by a chiropractor is normally a covered expense subject to a limitation with regard to total benefits (i.e. $10,000 lifetime) or a limitation with regard to the number of visits that will be covered in a given year and/or the amount that may be paid per visit.

Preexisting Conditions. Generally, a preexisting condition is any condition for which the insured sought treatment or advice prior to the effective date of coverage. Many policies contain a preexisting conditions limitation which excludes coverage for unspecified conditions for a period of time (usually six months). If an insurer wants to permanently exclude a preexisting condition, it usually has to specify the condition by name in the issued policy. Depending on the severity of the condition, it may be permanently excluded or temporarily excluded (i.e., the first 12 months following the effective date of coverage). Seldom is a preexisting condition covered by means of limited benefit amounts. Generally, it is either excluded or covered in full as any other condition.

Other Limitations

In past years, many health insurance contracts placed limitations on the kind of provider who could perform covered treatments and services. In many cases, coverage was limited to treatment rendered by a "physician." In effect, this eliminated coverage for treatments rendered by chiropractors, midwives, and other nontraditional healers.

In recent years, it has become recognized that many alternative providers who are subject to state licensing and/or standards of conduct imposed by professional organizations are qualified health care providers. Use of alternative providers can help to minimize health care costs and reduce the demand on hospitals and doctors. Under current laws in many states, policies must provide benefits for services given by various providers if benefits would be payable for the same services when given by a physician, as long as the providers are properly qualified and are acting within the scope of their profession. As a result, benefits for various services are often provided and may not be excluded when performed by the following types of health care professionals, if they are practicing within the scope of their license when rendering treatment:

- Chiropractors
- Optometrists
- Opticians
- Psychologists
- Podiatrists
- Clinical Social Workers
- Dentists
- Physical Therapists
- Professional Counselors

MEDICAL EXPENSE EXCLUSIONS

Medical expense policies contain many exclusions that are found in all health and disability policies: preexisting conditions, war, intentionally self-inflicted injuries, and active military duty. Exclusions which are common in medical expense policies include:

- Workers compensation
- Government plans (care in government facilities)
- Well-baby care
- Cosmetic surgery
- Dental care
- Eyeglasses
- Hearing aids
- Custodial care
- Routine physicals and medical care

Workers compensation and other government plans are included as exclusions to prevent overpayment of claims or overinsurance. If an injured employee will have his claim taken care of by workers compensation because the injury was work related, then individual or group medical expense plans will not pay the same claim. The same concept applies if for example an individual's medical care is to be provided by a veterans administration facility.

Some plans exclude well baby care since the purpose of medical expense coverage is to indemnify an individual who sustains a loss due to an accident or an illness. If a newborn baby is normal and healthy (a well baby) following delivery, then no benefits would be paid for any hospital claim while the child is in the hospital's nursery pending discharge of the mother. If the newborn has a medical problem following birth, then normal benefits would be paid.

Cosmetic surgery is usually excluded unless the reason for the surgery is due to a medical necessity such as an accident or a disease which disfigures a person. Cosmetic surgery is viewed as voluntary and thus not covered.

Routine dental care is usually excluded with individual medical expense policies but is frequently offered as an optional benefit under a group contract. Again, if a person is injured such as in an automobile accident and needs dental surgery for repair of damaged teeth, then this type of care would normally be covered.

Eyeglasses and hearing aids are normally excluded unless there is a medical reason for acquiring these devices such as injury which causes loss of hearing or vision. Reduced hearing or vision due to age and similar factors would not be covered.

Custodial care is care provided to assist the individual in the activities of daily living, which does not contribute to the improvement of a medical condition, and which can be performed by a person who does not have medical training. Coverage for these types of services may be excluded by a medical expense policy.

Routine physicals are normally also excluded from coverage. Routine physicals would include a person's "annual check up" when the reason for the physical is simply that it has been a year since the individual had a physical. Also excluded would be pre-employment physicals or a child's pre-school physical. There must be a medical reason for the physical before it would be considered a covered expense.

Also routine medical care such as routine immunizations are usually excluded. On the other hand if the insured is injured and requires a tetanus shot as a result of the accident, then this immunization would be covered. However, if a doctor simply told a patient that he or she should have a tetanus shot because it has been 10 years since the last shot, then this situation would not be covered.

It should be noted that many insurers now offer coverage for routine physicals and medical care because it is generally recognized that these preventive health care measures benefit the insured and the insurer. A routine physical exam could result in a potential major medical problem being diagnosed before it develops into a very large claim for the insurer.

OPTIONAL FEATURES & BENEFITS

Prescription Drugs

The prescription drug benefit is most often found in group health insurance policies. Some individual health insurance policies offer this benefit as a rider. Different policies offer different prescription card benefits. For example, some policies will cover birth control pills as part of the benefit, and in other policies they are specifically excluded. Usually prescription drug coverage requires a small deductible of typically, $2, $3 or $5.

A prescription drug benefit generally works one of two ways. Either insureds can be reimbursed for their prescription drug expenses using standard claim forms, or a prescription drug card can be issued. A prescription drug card allows prescriptions to be paid for by paying only the deductible with each prescription purchase. The pharmacy bills the insurer issuing the card directly for the prescription.

For example, Sally has a prescription drug card as part of her group medical plan which has a $5 deductible per prescription. Her doctor prescribes two medications for a serious cold. Each of these medications would cost Sally $5. The balance of the prescription cost will be billed to the insurer by the pharmacy.

Vision Care

Vision care includes eye examinations (refractions) and eyeglasses. Although not a very common benefit, it occasionally is offered as an optional benefit under group health insurance. Generally, this option will pay a specific amount or the entire cost of an annual eye examination. It normally also covers all or part of the cost of prescribed eyeglasses once in every two-year period.

Hospital Indemnity Rider

A hospital indemnity benefit provides for the payment of a daily benefit for each day that the insured is hospitalized as an inpatient. Available amounts are usually $50 to $100 per day or possibly slightly higher. In addition to any other medical benefits paid to the insured, the hospital indemnity benefit will pay the daily amount as long as the insured is hospitalized, usually for a benefit period of one or two years.

Nursing/Convalescent Home

Under this benefit, a daily maximum amount is paid for each day the insured is confined to a nursing or convalescent home after a hospital stay. Benefits are paid generally for as short as one month or up to one year.

Organ Transplants

More and more insurers are offering this coverage as it becomes less experimental and more commonplace. To provide coverage, many insurers require that a transplant must only be performed for life-threatening situations. Some of the more commonly covered transplants include bone marrow and kidney.

DENTAL EXPENSE

Dental insurance usually is offered only under group plans. It is most often excluded from medical expense insurance. Under group insurance it is usually offered as optional coverage.

Expenses Covered

Dental insurance may be covered under the benefits of a major medical plan on a scheduled or nonscheduled basis, in which case the dental coverage and medical coverage would be an integrated plan. The deductible amount can be met by either dental or medical expenses.

Dental expenses offered as an optional benefit (nonintegrated plan) may also be either scheduled or nonscheduled. A nonscheduled plan is paid on a usual, customary and reasonable basis (UCR). A scheduled plan has specific categories of dental treatment and dollar amounts are set for each category of dental care. The scheduled plan reimburses dental charges only up to the maximum amount specified on the schedule as to each covered service. A schedule would list the following categories:

- Preventive care
- Diagnostic care
- Restoration (which includes fillings, inlays, and crowns)
- Prosthodontics (which concerns bridgework)
- Oral surgery
- Periodontics (treatment of gum problems)
- Endodontics (treatment of problems with dental pulp, or root canals)
- Orthodontics
- Other

The scheduled maximum amounts differ from one part of the country to another. This difference in the amount of benefit payable on a particular procedure is based on the difference in dental costs throughout the nation. Dental costs in New York City, New York would be higher than dental costs in Des Moines, Iowa. There are many reasons for this, including, the higher office rents in New York than in Iowa.

Dental coverage may also be offered as a **combination plan** of scheduled and non-scheduled benefits. For example, routine dental care may be reimbursed on a UCR basis, with more advanced (and expensive) dental procedures being scheduled.

Limits

Limitations usually apply to prophylaxis (preventive care), no more than two, and only one fluoride treatment during any 12-month period. A bridge or denture will not be replaced within the first **five years,** except under special conditions. A kind of preexisting condition for dental coverage is the fact that teeth missing prior to the effective date of coverage will not be covered, or, if covered, the insured's copayment will increase.

Coinsurance and Deductible Provisions

Most dental plans have a deductible amount (e.g., $25, $50, $100) which must be met each calendar year. If the plan also covers the cost of preventive care, the deductible often does not apply to treatment for prevention (e.g., cleaning and routine examinations).

Most dental plans, as with most medical plans, have a coinsurance feature. That is, the insured pays some percentage of the dentist's charge, and the plan pays a percentage.

The plan will generally pay a maximum amount per calendar year (e.g., $500, $1,000, $5,000).

Exclusions

Dental services which are for cosmetic purposes, or are not considered to be standard procedure are usually not covered, except in rare instances, as when such benefits are offered to key employees or company executives.

Prepaid Dental Plans

Prepaid dental plan means a corporation, partnership, or other entity which, in return for a prepayment, provides or arranges for the provision of dental care services to enrollees or subscribers. The plan may be owned by a corporation, partnership, association trust, etc. and operated by a board of directors or trustees, executive committee, and/or principal officers.

Prepaid dental plans operate in much the same way as health maintenance organizations. They offer services based on **capitation,** or fixed per member per month payments where the provider assumes the full risk for the cost of contracted services without regard to the type, value, or frequency of the services provided.

Dentist Access to Membership. A prepaid dental plan shall provide that any licensed dentist may participate as a provider in the prepaid dental plan.

Benefits. Individual group contracts, evidence of coverage, and solicitation materials shall provide a statement of the services and benefits each member may receive. Reasonable exclusions, limitations, copayments, and deductibles may be included, provided they are clearly disclosed in contracts, evidence of coverage, and solicitation documents.

Member Choice of Provider. Subscribers must have the right to select any participating dentist as a provider. If a prepaid dental plan would restrict an enrollee's ability to receive services from a class of providers, the limitations must be described in the evidence of coverage, and in all solicitation documents.

Provider Contracts. The prepaid plan may contract with licensed dentists to provide dental care to subscribers in a specific service area or geographic location.

The dentists are paid (other than the copayment or deductible) by the prepaid dental plan. Provider contracts are subject to state laws designed to protect enrollees from becoming liable for services the prepaid dental plan fails to pay because of insolvency.

In an **open panel** system, dentists render services to both prepaid dental plan subscribers and to nonmembers. In a **closed panel** system, services are provided only to subscribers to the prepaid dental plan. The Plan must publish a list of participating providers, and enrollees are asked to choose a "primary" provider.

Under the **precertification** or **prior authorization** requirement, when the enrollee's dentist prescribes any course of treatment expected to exceed a specific amount (such as $200), the treatment must be outlined on a precertification form and submitted to the insurer for review and approval before it may be undertaken.

Evidence of Coverage. All enrollees must be issued an evidence of coverage describing the dental services covered, limitations on those services (including deductibles and copayments), how to obtain services and information, and methods for resolving complaints.

Complaint Procedure. The complaint system must establish reasonable procedures for resolving written complaints from both enrollees and providers. The organization must respond promptly to written complaints. Responses to written complaints regarding quality or appropriateness of care shall include a statement that the complainant may have the complaint reviewed by a consulting dentist and may submit the complaint to a professional peer review organization. Copies of complaints and responses must be maintained for three years.

Service Area — Geographic Location. Subscribers must have reliable access to qualified providers in the geographic area served by the prepaid dental plan. They also must have access to short-term emergency dental care services within the areas served, and the plan must pay for services when a dental emergency occurs outside the service area.

Quality Assurance Program. Each prepaid dental plan must provide appropriate, necessary, cost-effective, and professional services. Prepaid dental plans must have a quality assurance program to evaluate the quality of care given to enrollees, and provide for ways to correct deficiencies in provider or organizational performance. Provider contracts shall give disincentives (including termination) for providers rendering inappropriate, unnecessary or excessively costly care, or low quality care.

Underwriting

The underwriting procedures for group dental insurance are similar to those that apply to other types of group health insurance. Generally, when a group dental plan is initially effective, all employees or members must be covered or eligible for coverage. Under a contributory plan where the employee pays all or part of the premium, each eligible employee must elect to be covered. In order to minimize adverse selection, a probationary period usually applies to new employees who join the group after the effective date. Limitations on benefits may also be imposed on any employees who do not choose to be covered when first eligible, in order to avoid premium payments, but who elect coverage at a later date when they know they need dental treatment.

Since dental coverage is usually available only on a group basis, most plans do not include a conversion privilege. Members cannot convert to individual insurance when their membership in the group ends or the group plan is terminated.

REVIEW QUESTIONS

Match the numbered definitions with the lettered terms below.

____ 1. Type of health insurance providing high maximum coverage for medical care

____ 2. A combination of basic medical expense coverage and major medical expense coverage

____ 3. Type of policy covering doctor visits while the insured is in the hospital.

____ 4. Term meaning that all expenses in excess of the deductible are shared on some basis between the company and the insured

A. Basic Medical Expense Policy
B. Major Medical Insurance
C. Comprehensive Medical Insurance
D. Coinsurance

5. Maximum benefit amounts are the same from one part of the country to another under a single dental expense plan. (True/False)________________

6. Most dental plans have a coinsurance provision. (True/False)________________

7. If Harry's surgical expense coverage has a $1,000 surgical schedule, assigns a relative value of 30 to appendectomies, and the schedule's conversion factor is 20, what benefit will be paid for Harry's appendectomy? ________________

8. Expenses incurred to control pain and suffering of terminally ill patients until their death are known as ________________.
9. If members of the same family are injured in the same accident, only one deductible applies because of the ____________ provision.
10. Insured individuals may be required to pay coinsurance percentages of covered expenses up to a maximum amount, after which the insurer will pay 100% of covered expenses. This amount is known as the ____________.

> ☞ ***Answers to Review Questions are located at the back of the book.***

NOTES

14

SENIOR CITIZEN HEALTH PLANS

MEDICARE & MEDICARE SUPPLEMENT INSURANCE

MEDICARE

Medicare is a federal health insurance program for people 65 or older, people of any age with permanent kidney failure, and certain disabled people. It is administered by the Health Care Financing Administration.

Medicare has two parts — **Part A hospital insurance** and **Part B medical insurance.** Hospital insurance helps pay for inpatient hospital care and certain follow-up care. Medical insurance helps pay for doctors' services and many other medical services and items.

Hospital insurance is financed through part of the payroll (FICA) tax that also pays for Social Security. Medical insurance is financed from the monthly premiums paid by people who have enrolled for it and from general federal revenues.

Eligibility

An individual is eligible for Medicare hospital insurance at *no monthly premium* if:

- He or she is 65 or older and entitled to monthly Social Security or railroad retirement benefits
- He or she is 65 and is entitled to monthly Social Security benefits based on a spouse's work record, and the spouse is at least 62
- He or she is 65 or older and has worked long enough to be insured under Social Security or the railroad retirement system
- He or she is 65 or older and has worked long enough in federal, state, or local government employment to be insured for Medicare purposes
- He or she has been entitled to Social Security disability benefits for 24 months
- He or she has worked long enough in government employment and meets the requirements of the Social Security disability program

In addition to those who automatically qualify for Medicare, certain individuals who don't qualify for Medicare hospital insurance without premium charges (such as those who do not have the required work credits) may be covered if they *pay monthly premiums* for the coverage ($289 per month in 1996).

Hospital Insurance Benefits (Part A)

Medicare hospital insurance can help pay for inpatient hospital care, inpatient care in a skilled nursing facility, home health care, and hospice care.

Inpatient Hospital Care. Hospital insurance helps pay for up to 90 days in any participating hospital in each benefit period, for all covered services, subject to a deductible. The 1997 deductible is $760. The first 60 days are covered at 100% of approved hospital charges. The next 30 days are covered but are subject to a copayment of $190 per day. Every Part A recipient has a **lifetime reserve of 60 days** for hospital care. If more than 90 days of hospital care is needed in any benefit period, some or all of the 60 nonrenewable reserve days can be used, with a copayment of $380 per day.

Covered services include semi-private room, all meals, regular nursing services, operating and recovery room costs, hospital costs for anesthesia services, intensive care and coronary care, drugs, lab tests, X-rays, medical supplies and appliances, rehabilitation services, and preparatory services related to kidney transplant surgery.

Skilled Nursing Facility Care. Hospital insurance helps pay for up to 100 days in a participating skilled nursing facility in each benefit period, to provide for inpatient skilled nursing or rehabilitation, subject to a deductible. Medicare pays for all covered services during the first 20 days in a skilled nursing facility. From the 21st through the 100th day, there is a $95 daily copayment.

Covered services include semi-private room, all meals, regular nursing services, rehabilitation services, drugs, medical supplies, and appliances.

Home Health Care. For an individual confined to the home and meeting certain other conditions, hospital insurance can pay the full approved cost of home health visits from a participating home health agency. There is no limit to the number of covered visits.

Covered services include part-time skilled nursing care, physical therapy, and speech therapy. Hospital insurance also covers part-time services of home health aides, occupational therapy, medical social services, and medical supplies and equipment, if needed.

Hospice Care. Under certain conditions, hospital insurance can help pay for hospice care for terminally ill insureds, if the care is provided by a Medicare-certified hospice. Special benefit periods apply to hospice care. Hospital insurance pays for two 90-day periods and one 30-day period.

Covered services include doctors' services, nursing services, medical appliances and supplies including outpatient drugs for pain relief, home health aide and homemaker services, therapies, medical social services, short-term inpatient care including respite care, and counseling.

Hospital insurance pays part of the cost of outpatient drugs and inpatient respite care. For all other covered services, hospital insurance pays the full cost.

Medicare claims are paid on a reimbursement basis, in which case benefits are paid directly to the Medicare patient. Benefit payments may also be made directly to the participating provider. The calculation of benefit payments encompasses some important concepts.

Diagnostic-Related Groups. Under Part A of Medicare, when a patient is admitted to the hospital, it is due to the fact that the person is under the care of a physician who has made a diagnosis. The diagnosis identifies the patient's **Diagnosis-Related-Group (DRG).** Each of several hundred DRGs has a **Prospective Price** which represents the outside limit or maximum payment that Medicare will pay to the participating provider. When a provider is approved by Medicare as a **participating provider**, it agrees to accept the amount reimbursed by Medicare as payment in full.

For example, Art is admitted to the hospital for gall bladder surgery. A prospective price has been established for the DRG which represents the maximum amount that Medicare will pay to the hospital for the gall bladder diagnosis. Regardless of the length of the stay or the services provided to Art, the prospective price will be the maximum payment received by the hospital.

The DRG and prospective pricing concepts were implemented by Medicare in an effort to better control expenses and fees charged by medical providers. However, if a hospital is a non-participating provider, it may bill the patient for any excess expense which is not paid by Medicare.

What Part A Does Not Cover

Hospital insurance under Medicare does not cover:

- Private duty nursing
- Charges for a private room, unless medically necessary
- Conveniences, such as a telephone or television in an insured's room
- The first three pints of blood received during a calendar year (unless replaced by a blood plan)

Medical Insurance Benefits (Part B)

Medicare medical insurance helps pay for doctors' services and a variety of other medical services and supplies that are not covered by hospital insurance. Most of the services needed by people with permanent kidney failure are covered only by medical insurance.

Part B is optional and offered to everyone who enrolls in Part A. While Part A is financed through part of the Social Security tax, Part B is paid for by the individuals who enroll in it. There is a general enrollment period between January 1 and March 31 of each year. The 1997 monthly premium is $43.80.

After the annual medical insurance deductible ($100) is met, medical insurance generally will pay 80% of the approved charges for covered services received during the rest of the year.

Doctors' Services. Medical insurance covers doctors' services no matter where received in the United States. Covered doctors' services include surgical services, diagnostic tests and X-rays that are part of the treatment, medical supplies furnished in a doctor's office, and services of the office nurse.

Outpatient Hospital Services. Medical insurance covers outpatient hospital services received for diagnosis and treatment, such as care in an emergency room or outpatient clinic of a hospital.

Home Health Visits. Medical insurance can cover an unlimited number of home health visits if all required conditions are met, and the insured does not have Medicare hospital coverage.

Other Medical and Health Services. Under certain conditions or limitations, medical insurance covers other medical services and supplies. Some examples are: ambulance transportation; home dialysis equipment, supplies, and periodic support services; independent laboratory tests; oral surgery; outpatient physical therapy and speech pathology services; and X-rays and radiation treatments.

Drugs and Biologicals. Only medicines which are administered at the hospital or at a doctor's office are covered by Medicare. Drugs which can be self-administered (taken at home) are not covered, even if prescribed by a doctor.

Outpatient Treatment of Mental Illness. Medicare covers outpatient treatment by a doctor for mental illness, but with a 50% copayment, instead of the usual 20%.

The deductible and copayment provisions do not apply to the following:

- Second surgical opinions required by Medicare
- Most of the costs associated with home health care
- The costs of certain vaccines
- Diagnostic services provided by physicians who accept assignments or providers who are Medicare approved

Calculating Part B Benefits

The incredibly cumbersome method of calculating Part B benefits using allowable vs. customary charges was phased out in 1996.

The Health Care Financing Administration now publishes an annual fee schedule, based on national relative values for all doctor's fees. These fees are adjusted by geographical region to recognize the higher cost of medical care in metropolitan versus rural areas. Participating providers then accept the amount specified in the fee schedule as payment for the services rendered. **Nonparticipating providers** do not accept assignment. In these cases, benefit payments are made to the patient subject to deductible and coinsurance provisions, and it is the patient's responsibility to pay the provider.

Most often, the provider completes and files the actual Medicare claim regardless of participating or nonparticipating status, and just has the patient sign the claims form.

What Part B Does Not Cover

Medical insurance under Medicare does not cover:

- Private duty nursing
- Skilled nursing home care costs over 100 days per benefit period
- Intermediate nursing home care
- Physician charges above Medicare's approved amount
- Most outpatient prescription drugs
- Care received outside the United States (limited coverage for Canada and Mexico)
- Custodial care received in the home
- Dental care, routine physicals and immunizations, cosmetic surgery, eyeglasses, hearing aids, orthopedic shoes, acupuncture expenses
- Expenses incurred due to war or act of war

Claims and Appeals

If a doctor has not accepted a Medicare assignment, the doctor sends the bill directly to the patient. The patient fills out a Medicare claim form, and attaches itemized bills from the doctor including date of treatment, place of treatment, description of treatment, doctor's name, and charge for service. The form and accompanying documents are sent to the Medicare "carrier" (private insurance company) in the patient's area. Upon receiving the claim, the carrier will send a form called **Explanation of Medicare Benefits.** This form shows which services are covered and the amounts approved for each service.

If Medicare claims are denied, there is an appeal process a patient can go through. Within six months of the receipt of the Explanation of Medicare Benefits notice, the patient must file a written request for review. The carrier will check for miscalculations or other clerical errors. If the carrier, after review, declines to make a change, an appeal can be made (if the amount disputed is $100 or more) to the Social Security office. The patient must appear in person to attend a hearing and present evidence, such as a doctor's letter, to support his or her point. A written notice of the decision will be sent after the hearing.

Medicare and HMO Coverage

Health Maintenance Organizations are available to individuals on Medicare, just as they are through private insurance contracts. A growing number of HMOs have contracted with the Health Care Financing Administration (HCFA) to provide Part A and Part B services to Medicare beneficiaries. Medicare makes a monthly payment to the HMO on behalf of the recipient. About 65% of Medicare HMOs do not charge premiums beyond what is paid by Medicare. This payment may or may not cover Medicare deductibles and copayments, so additional payments from the recipient to the HMO may be required.

The advantages of an HMO for a Medicare recipient may be:

- No claim forms required
- Almost any medical problem is covered for a set fee so health care costs can be budgeted

- The HMO may pay for services not usually covered by Medicare or Medicare supplement policies, such as prescriptions, eye exams, hearing aids, and dental care (and thus, the individual probably does not need a Medicare supplement policy at all)

As with any HMO, all medical services must be received through the plan, except in emergencies. So if a recipient seeks care from a doctor outside of the HMO network, Medicare will not pay any part of the medical expenses. Also, HMOs may not be available in the insured's area.

Alternatives to Medicare

While an individual becomes eligible for Medicare upon turning age 65, federal laws extend primary coverage benefits under the employer's plan to active older employees regardless of age. In other words, the employers plan continues to be primary coverage and older employees defer eligibility for Medicare until retirement. Of course, employees have the right to reject the employer's plan and elect Medicare coverage.

OBRA requires the employer health plan to provide primary coverage for 18 months for individuals with end-stage renal (kidney) disease before Medicare becomes primary. Also, large group health plans (100 employees or more) must provide primary coverage for disabled individuals under age 65 who are not retired.

MEDICARE SUPPLEMENT POLICIES

Although Medicare pays a part of health care expenses, it does not pay them all. There are limits on some covered services and the Medicare program is subject to both deductibles and coinsurance provisions. To fill the gaps in protection left by Medicare, private insurers have developed special policies. Because of government support for HMOs, some supplementary medical care is provided by HMOs. As with most health insurance policies, Medicare supplement policies are sold on both an individual and group basis. These policies are also sometimes referred to as "Medigap" insurance policies since they are used to fill in the "gaps" not covered by Medicare (but in some states the terminology "MediGap" has been prohibited as misleading).

Medicare supplement policies pay some or all of Medicare's deductibles and copayments. Some policies may also pay for health services not covered by Medicare.

Medicare pays only for services determined to be medically necessary and only to the extent of what Medicare determines to be a reasonable charge. Most Medicare supplements follow the same guidelines and pay nothing for services Medicare finds unnecessary.

Not everyone needs private health insurance in addition to Medicare. Low income people who are eligible for Medicaid generally do not need this additional insurance. Medicaid pays almost all costs including long term nursing care.

Policies to supplement Medicare are neither sold nor serviced by the state or federal government. State Insurance Departments approve policies sold by insurance companies, but approval only means the company and policy meet the requirements of state law. No agent or company may make statements that they represent the Medicare program or any government agency.

Rating Considerations

Many insurance companies rate their Medicare supplement policies based on age. The insurer may base its determination on attained age, which means policy premiums are adjusted each year based on the policyholder's age. With issue age rating, premium is based on the age of the policyholder at the time of purchase and remains level. Many states have passed laws prohibiting or limiting the use of attained age rating, because studies have indicated that this practice is unfair to consumers because, after an average of six years, policyholders cumulatively have paid more premiums than they would under an issue age structure.

OBRA 1990

The Omnibus Budget Reconciliation Act of 1990 (OBRA 1990), which took effect on November 5, 1991, enhances the protections for Medicare supplement consumers. Under the law, Medicare supplement insurance may not be denied on the basis of an applicant's health status, claims experience, or medical condition during the first six months a Medicare beneficiary age 65 or older first enrolls in Part B of Medicare. This is known as the **open enrollment** requirement. (For people already covered by Medicare prior to age 65, the open enrollment period for Part B begins at age 65.)

Other features of this law include:

- Medicare supplement insurance may not be sold to a person who already has another health insurance policy that provides coverage for the same benefits. Likewise, a health insurance policy may not be sold if it duplicates coverage by a Medicare supplement policy. Insurers must ask applicants about their existing coverage in the application.
- Insurers must suspend insurance benefits upon request of a policyholder during the policyholder's entitlement to benefits under Medicaid

- Medicare supplement policies cannot exclude or limit benefits for losses incurred more than six months from the effective date of coverage for preexisting conditions
- If a Medicare supplement policy replaces another Medicare supplement policy which has been in effect for six months, the replacing policy must waive any time periods applicable to preexisting conditions, waiting periods, elimination periods, and probationary periods

Also, the law imposes new requirements that Medicare supplement policies be standardized. The National Association of Insurance Commissioners (NAIC) has developed 10 standard Medicare supplement policies, one of which is a **core benefit** policy with basic benefits that must be in all Medicare supplement policies.

For determining order of benefits, OBRA '90 requires that employer benefits are primary to Medicare benefits until October 1, 1995 (except for retirees and people with end-stage renal disease). Employers may not offer incentives to employees who are eligible for Medicare to terminate their group health coverage in order to avoid having the group health coverage be primary. Violators may be subject to a $5,000 penalty for each violation.

Core Benefits

The core package of basic benefits consists of the following:

- Coverage for Part A Medicare eligible expenses for hospitalization to the extent not covered by Medicare, from the 61st day through the 90th day in any Medicare benefit period
- Coverage of Part A Medicare eligible expenses incurred for hospitalization to the extent not covered by Medicare for each of the 60 lifetime reserve days
- Coverage of all Part A Medicare eligible expenses not covered by Medicare, after Medicare coverage has been used up, subject to a lifetime maximum benefit of an additional 365 days
- Coverage for the reasonable cost of the first three pints of blood, or equivalent quantities of packed red blood cells each calendar year
- Coverage for the 20% copayment under Medicare Part B

Additional Benefits

The following additional benefits may be included in the standardized Medicare supplement Plans "B" through "J":

- Medicare Part A deductible — Coverage for all of the Medicare Part A inpatient hospital deductible amount per benefit period
- Skilled nursing facility coinsurance — Coverage for the actual billed charges up to the coinsurance amount from the 21st day through the 100th day in a Medicare benefit period for the post-hospital skilled nursing facility care that is eligible under Medicare Part A
- Medicare Part B Deductible — Coverage for all of the Medicare Part B deductible amount per calendar year regardless of hospital confinement
- Part B excess charges at 80% or 100% — Coverage for the difference between the actual Medicare Part B charge as legally billed, not to exceed any charge limitation established by the Medicare program or state law, and the Medicare-approved Part B charge
- Basic prescription drug benefit — Coverage for 50% of outpatient prescription drug charges not covered by Medicare, after a calendar year deductible of $250, up to a maximum benefit of $1,250 per calendar year
- Extended Prescription drug benefit — Coverage for 50% of outpatient prescription drug charges not covered by Medicare, after a calendar year deductible of $250, up to a maximum benefit of $3,000 per calendar year
- Foreign travel benefit — Coverage for 80% of the actual billed charges not paid by Medicare for medically necessary, emergency hospital, physician and other medical care received in a foreign country, which would have been covered by Medicare if provided in the United States, so long as the care began during the first 60 consecutive days of each and any trip outside the United States, subject to a calendar year deductible of $250 and a lifetime maximum benefit of $50,000
- Preventive medical care — Coverage for the actual charges up to $120 per year, for a variety of preventive services not covered by Medicare (such as fecal occult blood tests, diabetes screening, mammograms, certain inoculations, and other tests or preventive measures determined appropriate by an attending physician)
- At-home recovery benefit — Coverage for the actual charges up to $40 per visit and an annual maximum of $1,600 per year for short term at-home assistance with "activities of daily living" (such as bathing, dressing, eating, and personal hygiene) for insureds recovering from an illness, injury, or surgery

In most jurisdictions, state-approved innovative benefits may be offered in addition to the standard plans.

Plans A-J

Every insurer must offer to each prospective insured Plan A, which contains only the core benefits. Insurers may offer any or all of the other plans described below as Plans B through J. The others provide various combinations of the additional available benefits. (Refer to the accompanying chart for a summary of the benefit combinations).

- **Plan A** is limited to coverage for the core benefits only (the basic benefits found in all plans)
- **Plan B** includes coverage for the core benefits and the Medicare Part A deductible
- **Plan C** includes coverage for the core benefits, the Medicare Part A deductible, skilled nursing facility coinsurance, the Medicare Part B deductible, and the foreign travel benefit
- **Plan D** includes coverage for the core benefits, the Medicare Part A deductible, skilled nursing facility coinsurance, foreign travel benefit, and the at-home recovery benefit
- **Plan E** includes coverage for the core benefits, the Medicare Part A deductible, skilled nursing facility coinsurance, foreign travel benefit, and preventive services
- **Plan F** includes coverage for the core benefits, the Medicare Part A deductible, skilled nursing facility coinsurance, the Medicare Part B deductible, 100% of the Medicare Part B excess charges, and the foreign travel benefit
- **Plan G** includes coverage for the core benefits, the Medicare Part A deductible, skilled nursing facility coinsurance, 80% of the Medicare Part B excess charges, the foreign travel benefit, and the at-home recovery benefit
- **Plan H** includes coverage for the core benefits, the Medicare Part A deductible, skilled nursing facility coinsurance, the foreign travel benefit, and the basic prescription drug benefit
- **Plan I** includes coverage for the core benefits, the Medicare Part A deductible, skilled nursing facility coinsurance, 100% of the Medicare Part B excess charges, the foreign travel benefit, the at-home recovery benefit, and the basic prescription drug benefit
- **Plan J** includes coverage for the core benefits, the Medicare Part A deductible, skilled nursing facility coinsurance, the Medicare Part B deductible, 100% of the Medicare Part B excess charges, the foreign travel benefit, the at-home recovery benefit, the extended prescription drug benefit, and preventive services

What Medicare Supplement Policies May Not Cover

It is important to look for certain policy provisions which may prohibit the insured from having the coverage he or she needs.

Preexisting Condition Exclusions. Many policies do not cover health problems an insured has at the time of policy issuance. However, most states require Medicare supplement policies to cover preexisting conditions after the policy has been in effect for six months.

Maximum Benefits. Some policies may restrict the number of days or the dollar amount that will be paid for treatment.

Right to Renew. Some companies do not guarantee the right to renew policies, although this is not very common any longer.

Regulation

Part A and Part B of Medicare plus one Medicare supplement will normally provide very complete coverage for the senior citizen. Medicare supplements may be purchased on an individual basis or they are frequently offered to the senior citizen through various associations such as the American Association of Retired Persons (AARP).

In addition to regulation by the federal government and the NAIC, Medicare supplements are heavily regulated by the state Insurance Departments. Often state requirements reflect federal regulations. For example, most states limit any period regarding payment for preexisting conditions to not later than six months following the effective date of coverage. States also frequently regulate disclosure provisions, renewability, the insured's right to return the policy, replacement, marketing standards, and the appropriateness of recommending the purchase of a Medicare supplement policy.

The state Insurance Departments also impose regulations on the agents who sell Medicare supplements. Because of the nature of the senior citizen market, it is important, even critical, that agents be professional and ethical when marketing these products. For example, there is no need for a senior citizen to have more than one Medicare supplement. Most states provide for severe agent penalties for those who duplicate existing Medicare supplement coverage. These agents may be substantially fined, lose their licenses and be subject to imprisonment.

MEDICARE SUPPLEMENT PLANS

MEDICARE SUPPLEMENT INSURANCE CAN BE SOLD IN ONLY TEN STANDARD PLANS. THIS CHART SHOWS THE BENEFITS INCLUDED IN EACH PLAN. EVERY COMPANY MUST MAKE AVAILABLE PLAN "A." SOME PLANS MAY NOT BE AVAILABLE IN ALL STATES.

BASIC BENEFITS: INCLUDED IN ALL PLANS

HOSPITALIZATION: PART A COINSURANCE PLUS COVERAGE FOR 365 ADDITIONAL DAYS AFTER MEDICARE BENEFITS END.
MEDICAL EXPENSES: PART B COINSURANCE (20% OF MEDICARE-APPROVED EXPENSES).
BLOOD: FIRST THREE PINTS OF BLOOD EACH YEAR.

A	B	C	D	E	F	G	H	I	J
BASIC BENEFITS	BASIC BENEFITS	BASIC BENEFITS	BASIC BENEFITS	BASIC BENEFITS	BASIC BENEFITS	BASIC BENEFITS	BASIC BENEFITS	BASIC BENEFITS	BASIC BENEFITS
		SKILLED NURSING CO-INSURANCE	SKILLED NURSING CO-INSURANCE	SKILLED NURSING CO-INSURANCE	SKILLED NURSING CO-INSURANCE	SKILLED NURSING CO-INSURANCE	SKILLED NURSING CO-INSURANCE	SKILLED NURSING CO-INSURANCE	SKILLED NURSING CO-INSURANCE
	PART A DEDUCTIBLE	PART A DEDUCTIBLE	PART A DEDUCTIBLE	PART A DEDUCTIBLE	PART A DEDUCTIBLE	PART A DEDUCTIBLE	PART A DEDUCTIBLE	PART A DEDUCTIBLE	PART A DEDUCTIBLE
		PART B DEDUCTIBLE			PART B DEDUCTIBLE				PART B DEDUCTIBLE
					PART B EXCESS (100%)	PART B EXCESS (80%)		PART B EXCESS (100%)	PART B EXCESS (100%)
		FOREIGN TRAVEL EMERGENCY	FOREIGN TRAVEL EMERGENCY	FOREIGN TRAVEL EMERGENCY	FOREIGN TRAVEL EMERGENCY	FOREIGN TRAVEL EMERGENCY	FOREIGN TRAVEL EMERGENCY	FOREIGN TRAVEL EMERGENCY	FOREIGN TRAVEL EMERGENCY
			AT HOME RECOVERY			AT HOME RECOVERY		AT HOME RECOVERY	AT HOME RECOVERY
							BASIC DRUGS ($1,250 LIMIT)	BASIC DRUGS ($1,250 LIMIT)	EXTENDED DRUGS ($3,000 LIMIT)
				PREVENTIVE CARE					PREVENTIVE CARE

SOURCE: NAIC

CHART 14-1

Buyers Guide and Outline of Coverage

The NAIC's **Guide to Health Insurance for People with Medicare** must be delivered to all applicants for health insurance policies (including Medicare supplement policies). Most states reiterate this requirement with a statute calling for delivery of a Medicare supplement **buyers guide.**

Most states also require delivery of an **outline of coverage** to ensure full and fair disclosure of policy features. Often, an acknowledgement of receipt is also required to be obtained from the applicant. The outline includes information on the various supplement plans available, the premium charges for each plan, comparative illustrations, a description of the principal benefits and features, and other required disclosures. The outline should state that it is a summary only, and advise the buyer to consult the policy for the governing provisions.

Medicare Select Policies

A new approach to providing affordable health coverage supplemental to Medicare is the Medicare Select policy. These policies are being offered on a trial basis in some states under special programs authorized by OBRA and state law.

A Medicare Select policy is a Medicare supplement policy with restricted network provisions. It can be thought of as a managed care, or HMO version of Medicare supplement insurance. Insureds must seek coverage through the approved network of health care providers in order to receive full benefits.

The health care provider network must meet approved standards for service, such as geographic location, hours of operation, and after-hour or emergency care. The Medicare Select provider must have the usual greivance procedure, quality assurance program, formal organizational structure, plan of operation, etc. required of health care insurers. As with HMOs, coverage provided by non-network providers may not be restricted for emergencies or when care is not available or it is not reasonable to obtain the care through a network provider.

Applicants must receive an outline of coverage describing the policy's benefits, provisions, restrictions, and limitations, as well as information about the network providers, coinsurance and deductible provisions, etc.

Individuals insured by a Medicare Select policy must have the right to request and purchase a Medicare supplement policy without restricted network provisions and having comparable or lesser benefits from the insurer. After the Medicare Select policy is in effect for six months, if the insured requests a Medicare supplement policy the insurer may not require evidence of insurability.

If Medicare Select policies are discontinued because the program is not reauthorized, the insurer must provide for continuation of coverage for Medicare Select policyowners.

LONG-TERM CARE

Better and better medical care means many individuals are living into their 80s, 90s, and beyond. Unfortunately, although life expectancy has increased, many older individuals have serious health problems that keep them from living on their own or completely caring for themselves. Long-term care pays for the kind of care needed for individuals who have a chronic illness or disability. It often covers the cost of custodial nursing care (nursing homes), but also provides coverage for home-based care — visiting nurses, chore services, and respite care for daily caregivers who need time away from these difficult duties.

Many people believe Medicare or Medicare supplement policies will pay for this care if they need it. None of them do. While Medicare and supplementary insurance pay for skilled nursing care, this is extremely limited. Medicaid does pay for nursing home care, but provides coverage only for needy families. Sadly, many people must pay for their own nursing home care, and eventually turn to Medicaid when their life savings are gone.

Spousal Impoverishment Act

Medicaid will pay for nursing home care only when an individual has little income and a very limited amount of non-exempt assets. This means that many middle class citizens who enter a nursing home while they have savings and assets are not initially eligible for Medicaid benefits. As a result, they exhaust their resources, by "spending down" to the point of poverty, at which point they may become eligible for Medicaid benefits.

For married couples, this presents a particular problem when one spouse is confined to a nursing home and the other spouse remains at home. Since the income and assets of both spouses is considered in determining eligibility for Medicaid, the process of income and asset depletion could, and often did, reduce the stay-at-home spouse to the point of poverty as well as the confined spouse. To remedy the situation, Congress passed the Spousal Impoverishment Act which protects a portion of the income and assets that a stay-at-home spouse may retain without terminating Medicaid eligibility for a confined spouse.

Under rules which took effect in 1989, an at-home spouse was allowed to keep some of the couple's joint monthly income (a minimum consisting of the first $815 of monthly income, up to a maximum of $1,565 of joint monthly income) and joint assets (a minimum of the first $12,000 of assets, not to exceed to maximum of $60,000 of assets). These amounts are indexed for inflation and increase annually.

The federal law provides a minor degree of protection for a stay-at-home spouse, but it is designed to be a safety net and is not a substitute for insurance. Without long term care insurance, most middle- and upper-class families would still be exposed to a considerable reduction in family resources if an extended stay in a nursing home became necessary.

Suitable Purchasers, Asset Protection, Medicaid Coverage

LTC insurance enables the senior citizen to maintain his or her independence. With adequate coverage, the individual does not have to rely on friends or family to provide custodial needs or necessary funds to help defray the costs of a nursing home stay.

Protection of personal assets may well be the most important reason for purchasing LTC insurance. Possibly, the question isn't "Can I afford to buy LTC insurance?," but rather, "Can I afford not to purchase LTC insurance?"

When an individual has substantial financial assets (and retirement income), the possibility that LTC expenses could mean a significant reduction in the person's assets and standard of living is a real threat. Thus, the purchase of LTC insurance to protect one's personal financial resources may well be a wise financial decision.

Paying periodic premiums is a more efficient and manageable way to provide for future LTC costs than having to rely on personal savings. LTC insurance provides that a person's financial resources need not be liquidated either to pay for nursing home expenses or to "spend down" to satisfy Medicaid eligibility.

For example, an individual with no dependents and few financial responsibilities may not have a very big need for life insurance. Likewise, a person without substantial assets at risk may have little need to purchase LTC insurance.

If a senior citizen's sole source of income is a relatively small pension and his or her financial assets are very minimal, then this person may already be "eligible" for Medicaid reimbursement of LTC expenses. Also, because of the individual's low income and limited financial resources, LTC insurance premiums may be unaffordable.

Example: Joe and Irene Brown are both 67 years old. Their only source of income is Social Security and a small pension ($200 monthly). They rent an apartment in a senior citizen complex, have a very small amount of life insurance (enough for burial) and usually maintain a savings account balance of no more than $1,000. They have no other assets other than personal possessions and an automobile. Are Mr. and Mrs. Brown prospects for LTC insurance? Probably not. First of all, it's doubtful that they could afford the premiums based on their relatively small retirement income. Secondly, they have no assets of any consequence to protect. They do not own a home, a large savings account or have other investments. In essence, they probably are already eligible for Medicaid benefits should they be forced into a nursing home.

Probability of Needing Care

In 1980, there were 25 million Americans 65 and older. It is estimated that by the turn of the century, the over 65 population will exceed 35 million, and by the year 2030 there will be more than 64 million Americans age 65 and over.

In addition, life expectancy is increasing in the United States. In 1980, life expectancy for males, 65 years old, was about 78, and for females, 81. It is estimated that by the year 2000, life expectancy for males will be age 81 and 86 for females. These retirees will face a greater potential need for long term medical care, simply due to longer life expectancy.

At age 65, the likelihood of a nursing home confinement is about 1 in 3. The odds increase as age increases. An individual 75 years of age, has a 2 to 1 chance of confinement in a nursing home. In 1990, there were approximately 7 million Americans, 65 or older, who needed long term care. This figure is expected to increase to more than 9 million by the year 2000 and will exceed 20 million by 2050.

Options Other Than Insurance

What are the available options for the senior citizen facing the reality of a stay in a nursing home? Following are some of the alternatives:

- Dependency on relatives
- Dependency on government programs
- Using personal assets

Dependency on friends and relatives for custodial type care may not be practical due to changing socioeconomic trends in today's society. Today's family is no longer a cohesive unit but rather a fragmented group whereby family members live great distances from each other.

The Medicare program is not designed to provide custodial care. It will cover a limited amount of rehabilitative care in a skilled nursing facility approved by Medicare. Since Medicare will only pay for rehabilitative services, it requires prior hospitalization before admission to the skilled nursing facility. Another avenue is Medicaid, which requires the individual to prove financial need. This normally requires that the individual "gets rid of" financial resources and "spends down" to a poverty level to obtain Medicaid eligibility. The Health Care Financing Administration reports that about one-half of all Medicaid spending goes to people who had financial resources when they entered a nursing home but reached the proverty level while in the nursing home.

Types of Long-Term Care Insurance Benefits

Nursing Facilities. LTC policies generally provide coverage for confinement in nursing facilities, which are licensed by the state and provide 24-hour a day nursing services under the supervision of a physician or registered nurse.

Home-Based Services and Community-Based Services. When the patient is in need of some health care but is able to generally function without being confined to a nursing home, occasional visits to the person's home by registered nurses, licensed practical nurses, licensed vocational nurses, or community-based organizations (such as hospice care) may be recommended or necessary. Home health care might include physical therapy and some custodial care such as meal preparations. Usually, the home health care benefit under the policy will be 50% of the regular daily nursing home benefit. Home health care must also be provided by state approved home health facilities and personnel.

Skilled nursing care is daily nursing and rehabilitative care that can only be provided by medical personnel, under a doctor's orders. It is almost always provided in an institutional setting.

Intermediate care is occasional nursing and rehabilitative care provided by medical personnel. It may be provided in an institutional setting or an alternative setting.

Custodial care is care for meeting personal needs such as assistance in eating, dressing, or bathing, provided under a doctor's orders, but by nonmedical personnel. This type of care is frequently provided in institutional settings, but may also be provided in the patient's home.

Triggers for Benefits

Activities of Daily Living (ADLs). ADLs are functions or activities which are performed by individuals without assistance, thus allowing personal independence in everyday living. These functions are used as measurement standards to determine the level of personal functioning capacity. Examples of ADLs would include:

- Mobility — the ability to walk
- Dressing — being able to adequately clothe one's self
- Personal Hygiene — being able to go to and from the toilet and bathe one's self
- Eating — being able to take in food

An individual who can not accommodate these needs will need some type of care.

Some of the newer LTC policies base eligibility for admission to a nursing home on the inability to perform some of the activities of daily living in lieu of sickness or injury. These contracts do not require prior hospitalization nor that the insured be admitted to a nursing facility as a result of sickness or injury.

Cognitive Impairment. A deficiency in the ability to think, perceive, reason or remember which results in the inability of individuals to take care of themselves without the assistance or supervision of another person. LTC policies may base eligibility for admission to a nursing home on cognitive impairment.

Medical Necessity. An LTC policy by definition provides coverage only for **medically necessary** diagnostic, therapeutic, rehabilitative, maintenance or personal care services.

Optional Coverages

Home Health Care is provided in the individual's home and must begin within a prescribed period of time following a nursing home stay. Usually, the home health care benefit under the policy will be 50% of the regular daily nursing home benefit. Home health care is an extension of intermediate or custodial care. The patient is in need of some health care, but is able to generally function without the need to be confined to a nursing home. Home health care might include physical therapy and some custodial care, such as meal preparations.

Adult Day Care is basically social and health care services for functionally impaired adults. This benefit provides reimbursement for expenses pertaining to an adult day care center such as a neighborhood recreational center, a community center, etc. Typically adult day care includes transportation to and from a day care center, and a variety of health, social, and related activities. This care usually also includes meals and certain medical services. Specialized care for Alzheimers victims is usually included in adult day care benefits.

Hospice Care is often offered as an optional benefit under LTC policies. The primary focus of hospice care is pain control, comfort and counseling for the terminally ill patient and the patient's family. A hospice is simply a facility whose purpose is to help terminally ill patients die with dignity and with as little suffering as possible. Typically, the expenses incurred in a hospice will be room and board and medication for pain.

Respite care is normally associated with hospice care. With this benefit, the patient is admitted to a nursing home for needed care for a short period of time, thus giving the family caregivers a respite or break from their responsibilities.

Types of LTC Policies

Most often LTC policies are purchased on an individual basis. LTC benefits are also appearing as part of group health insurance benefits. Occasionally, LTC benefits are provided by means of riders attached to other health or life insurance policies. Regardless of the form of the LTC policy (or rider), all usually provide coverages for the various levels of care discussed in the previous section.

Policy Provisions and Contract Limits

All long term care insurance policies contain the following common features.

Daily benefits/policy maximum limits. Initially, LTC policies were primarily indemnity contracts whereby the insured received a daily benefit ($25—$50 daily) for each day of nursing home confinement. Currently, many of these policies are still on an indemnity basis which feature benefits amounts of $50—$100 or more per day, and a maximum limit expressed as a period of time (the maximum benefit period). Expense incurred policies are also available in the market.

Elimination Periods. Similar to a disability income policy, no LTC benefits will be paid until the elimination period is satisfied. Most long term care policies provide for a period of time, usually expressed in days or months, at the beginning of a confinement in a long term care facility, during which no benefits are payable. The elimination period could be defined as a "time deductible." The elimination period could be 30 days or longer. Thus, after the insured is confined to a nursing home for a period of 30 days, LTC benefits would begin.

Benefit Periods. Following the elimination period, benefits will be paid for the benefit period selected as long as the insured remains confined in the nursing home. Most benefit periods are two to five years in duration.

Benefit Amounts. Most LTC policies provide a daily benefit during confinement. Benefit amounts range from $50 per day up to $150 or $200 per day. Some insurers may pay the actual charges incurred by the insured.

To illustrate these points, let's use the example of Kim who has a LTC policy with a 30-day elimination period, a daily benefit of $75 per day and a two-year benefit period. Kim is confined to a nursing home for a total of seven months. Her benefit calculation would be as follows:

- First 30 days: No benefit paid (elimination period)
- Next six months: $75 per day (assumes 30-day month)
- $75 x 180 = $13,500

If Kim's actual charges were more than $75 per day, the additional amount would have to be paid by her.

Scheduled Benefits. Most policies are defined in terms of the dollar amount per day that will be paid for skilled nursing care.

Length of Contract. The benefit period is usually one to five years or longer. Some policies may contain both a benefit period per stay plus a lifetime maximum benefit period.

Inside Limits. These are dollar limits applied to particular types of expense, such as skilled nursing care or home health care.

Deductibles. There may be a deductible amount that must be satisfied before the policy begins to pay.

Renewability. Most individual policies are **guaranteed renewable**. That is, the insurance company guarantees to renew the policy but does not guarantee at which premium the policy will be renewed. The insurer cannot cancel the policy but does reserve the right to increase premiums in accordance with the policy provisions. If the premiums are to be increased, they will be changed on the policy anniversary and the increased premium will be for an entire class of insureds, not just a single individual.

Some LTC policies are **noncancellable**, which means the insured has the right to continue the coverage by timely payment of premiums, and the insurer has no right to make any change in policy provisions, cannot decline to renew, and cannot change the premium rate at renewal for any reason.

Free Look. In most states, all buyers of LTC insurance are entitled to a 30-day trial examination period, or free look. If the insured returns the policy, for any reason, within the free look period, a total refund of all charges and premiums will be made.

Preexisting Conditions. All policies contain a preexisting condition provision which basically provides that no benefits will be paid for any preexisting condition during the first six months of policy.

Exclusions. LTC policies will contain some exclusions or limitations. Common exclusions include: war or act of war, intentionally self-inflicted injuries, losses covered by workers compensation or other government programs and losses due to personality disorders which are not subject to a physical or organic disease.

Premiums

Similar to life insurance, premiums are generally based on when an individual purchases this insurance. The younger the individual is at the time of purchase, the lower the premium. In addition, premiums will fluctuate according to the elimination and benefit periods selected — the longer the elimination period, the lower the premium; the longer the benefit period, the higher the premium. Finally, premium variations may result from underwriting considerations. Underwriters consider risk factors, including an applicant's current ability to perform activities of daily living (ADL). The premium will be higher if an applicant needs assistance with ADL at the time of application than it would be if the applicant did not need such assistance.

Waiver of Premium

Most LTC policies provide that after the insured is confined to a nursing home and receiving benefits for at least 90 consecutive days, the policy premium will be waived for the duration of the confinement as long as benefits continue to be paid.

Extension of Benefits Beyond Policy Termination

Termination of LTC insurance must be without prejudice to benefits payable for institutionalization which began while the insurance was in force and continues after termination. The extension of benefits may be limited by the policy's benefit periods, maximum benefits, waiting period, and other applicable policy provisions.

Eligibility

Subject to preexisting conditions, policies are generally available to individuals between the ages of 50 and 79. The younger an individual is when purchasing coverage, the lower the premium. Premiums are usually level and do not increase with age.

Emerging LTC Issues

Long term care insurance is still in an evolutionary state. There are literally hundreds of individual contracts, which have not been standardized like Medicare supplement policies. Some emerging issues in the LTC field include inflation protection and nonforfeiture provisions.

Inflation Protection. Many states require that insurers offer optional inflation protection at the time of policy purchase. The feature must either increase benefit levels annually or cover a specific percentage of actual or reasonable charges, or allow the insured to periodically increase benefit levels without needing to provide evidence of continued insurability.

Nonforfeiture Provisions. These protect the policyholder from forfeiting all policy values or benefits when the policyowner stops paying premiums and lapses the policy for any reason. Standard nonforfeiture options include cash surrender value (a lump sum payable upon policy surrender), reduced paid up (a reduced daily benefit payable for the policy's benefit period with no further premium payments required), or extended term (a limited extension of coverage for the full amount of policy benefits, without further premium payments required). Nonforfeiture provisions are not commonly included in LTC policies but are beginning to appear in some contracts.

Underwriting Considerations

Long term care underwriting is concerned with the same factors as health insurance underwriting but the major emphasis is on the likelihood of prolonged confinement in a nursing home. For example, a person who has a heart condition that could require surgery might not be a good candidate for health insurance, but might be accepted for LTC insurance because the condition would probably not result in a nursing home stay.

Once all the information (application, inspection reports, medical information) is gathered, the underwriter decides whether to decline the risk or accept the risk on a standard or substandard basis. Substandard risks may have to pay an extra premium or have the benefits reduced.

Regulation

Just as with Medicare supplement insurance, long term care policies are heavily regulated by the state Insurance Departments. States frequently regulate minimum standards, renewability, the insured's right to return the policy, replacement, marketing standards, and the appropriateness of recommending the purchase of LTC insurance. As with Medicare supplement insurance, frequently the delivery of a buyers guide and outline of coverage is mandatory.

Federal law allows the sale of long term care coverage that "substantially" duplicates that provided under Medicare or Medicaid (but not multiple policies) to Medicare beneficiaries, provided the company discloses the duplication and the policy pays without regard to other benefits.

TAXATION OF MEDICARE SUPPLEMENT AND LONG-TERM CARE INSURANCE

Individual Long-Term Care	Deductible*	Not taxable†
Group Long-Term Care	Deductible for employer	Not taxable
Individual Medicare Supplement	Deductible*	Not taxable
Group Medicare Supplement	Deductible for employer	Not taxable
*To the extent that combined premiums and unreimbursed medical expenses exceed 7.5% of adjusted gross income.	†In 1997, the first $175 of daily benefit is tax free.	#Benefits for permanent loss are not taxable

Chart 14-2

TAXATION OF MEDICARE SUPPLEMENT & LONG-TERM CARE INSURANCE

Individual Medicare suppplement insurance premiums are considered deductible medical expenses, to the extent that the combination of premiums paid plus other unreimbursed medical expenses exeeds 7.5% of adjusted gross income. Benefits are considered reimbursements for medical expenses already incurred, and are therefore received tax-free. Premiums paid by an employer for group Medicare supplement insurance is tax deductible to the employer, and benefits are received tax free.

Individually owned long-term care insurance also enjoys the same tax advantaged status as individually-owned medical insurance, thanks to the 1996 tax law changes. Also, the tax deduction is subject to age-related limits ranging from $200 per year for taxpayers under age 40 up to $2,500 per year for taxpayers age 71 and older (and these limits will be subject to annual indexing).

When group long-term care insurance premiums are paid by the employer, the premiums are tax deductible to the employer and benefits are tax free up to specified limits.

REVIEW QUESTIONS

1. The part of Medicare that helps pay for inpatient hospital care, inpatient care in a skilled nursing facility, home health care, and hospice care, is known as ____________.
2. The part of Medicare that helps pay for doctors services and medical services and supplies, and that is paid for by the individuals enrolled in it is known as ____________.
3. Which of the following would not be subject to the Medicare Part B deductible and copayment provisions?
   a. Radiation therapy
   b. Outpatient psychiatric care
   c. Second surgical opinions required by Medicare
   d. Anesthesiologist fees
4. Why is the HCFA annual fee schedule adjusted by geographical region?

   ____

   ____
5. The coinsurance percentage under Part B of Medicare is:
   a. 40%
   b. 25%
   c. 20%
   d. 15%
6. Most long-term care insurance policies are:
   a. conditionally renewable.
   b. guaranteed renewable.
   c. noncancellable.
   d. optionally renewable.
7. What types of policies are offered by private insurers to fill the gaps in Medicare protection?
   a. Major Medical
   b. Medicaid
   c. Social Security
   d. Medicare Supplement
8. Medicare supplement insurance cannot be denied based on an applicant's health status, claims experience, or medical condition during the first six months a Medicare beneficiary age 65 or older enrolls in Part B. (True/False) __________

9. Which of the following types of policies provides coverage for skilled, intermediate, and custodial nursing care?
   a. Medicare
   b. Long-term care
   c. Medicare supplement
   d. Limited health insurance

10. Medicare supplement policies generally do **not** cover:
    a. Medicare Part A insurance deductibles.
    b. the 20% copayment under Part B.
    c. preexisting conditions at policy inception.
    d. prescription drugs.

☞ ***Answers to Review Questions are located at the back of the book.***

SAMPLE POLICY SECTION

APPLICATION FOR INSURANCE — PART I

I hereby apply to *(Name of Insurance Company)* for insurance. I represent that the answers given below are full, true and complete, to the best of my knowledge and belief. I agree that they shall be used as the basis of any insurance issued hereon.

COMPLETE THIS SECTION FOR ALL POLICIES

1. Print full name and Residence Address of Proposed Insured. ☐ F ☐ M

First Middle Last

No. Street

City and State Zip Code

2. Date of Birth (Month Day Year) Age Nearest Birthday State of Birth Marital Status

3. Occupation
Other Occupations

4. Life Insurance and Annuities in force (if none, so state)

Company	Amount	Year Issued	Acc. Death Benefit	Disability Income

5. Is this insurance (or annuity) intended to replace or change insurance (or annuities) in this or any other company? (If "yes" explain under remarks) .... Yes ☐ No ☐

6. Has anyone proposed for coverage (a) participated in the past year in motor racing, scuba or sky diving or hang gliding? Yes ☐ No ☐ (b) within the last two years been convicted of two or more moving violations or had a drivers license suspended or revoked? .... ☐ ☐ (If "yes" explain under remarks)

7. GENERAL INFORMATION (Include all family members to be insured.) If answered "Yes" give details under "REMARKS", and name of person to which question applies. HAS ANY PERSON proposed for coverage:

	Yes	No
a. ever been deferred, rejected or discharged from military service because of a physical or mental condition?	☐	☐
b. within the past 5 years requested or received a pension, benefits, or payment because of an injury, sickness or disability?	☐	☐
c. contemplated flying or flown as pilot, student pilot or crew member during the last two years? (If "yes", complete Aviation Supplement.)	☐	☐
d. had any application or policy for life or health insurance declined, special rated, restricted, postponed, cancelled, reinstatement denied?	☐	☐
e. currently applied for or had a life or health application pending in any other company?	☐	☐

8. a. Have you smoked one or more cigarettes in the past 12 months? .... ☐ ☐
b. Do you use any other form of tobacco? .... ☐ ☐

REMARKS:

9. Beneficiary: Print full names and relationship to Proposed Insured.

Contingent Beneficiary, if any

Owner reserves right to change beneficiary unless otherwise stated.

10. Owner: Print name, address and relationship if other than Proposed Insured.

11. Automatic Premium Loan Provision will be included in policy unless otherwise indicated here .... ☐ No

COMPLETE THIS SECTION FOR POLICY OF LIFE INSURANCE

12. Life Insurance Applied For (Use Ratebook Description)
Amount $ ______ (Basic Plan Only) Plan ______ (No. of years)
☐ Non-Participating ☐ Participating

13. Additional Riders
- ☐ Five Year R&C Rider $ ______
- ☐ Increasing Term Rider $ ______
- ☐ Family Income Rider $ ______ for ______ Years
- ☐ Home Guardian Rider $ ______ for ______ Years
- ☐ Business Guardian Rider $ ______ for ______ Years
- ☐ Family Term Rider ☐ One Parent Family Rider ______ units
- ☐ Other ______ ☐ Childrens Term Rider ______ units
- ☐ Purchaser Benefit ☐ Death only ☐ Death and Disability

14. Additional Benefits Applied for
- ☐ Waiver of Premium Benefit
- ☐ Accidental Death Benefit $ ______
- ☐ Guaranteed Insurability Option $ ______

15. Premium Mode (Minimum premium is $15.00)
☐ Annual ☐ Semi-Annual ☐ Quarterly ☐ Special Monthly

16. Dividends (if participating)
☐ Cash ☐ Reduce Premium ☐ Paid-Up Additions ☐ Accumulate

17. Total amount of premium submitted herewith $ ______
Indicated premium allocation:
Life $______ Disability Income $______ Annuity $______

APPLICATION FOR INSURANCE — PART II

COMPLETE THIS SECTION IF FAMILY MEMBER(S) INCLUDED ON LIFE POLICY

Family Member(s)	Birth Date	Age	State of Birth	Relationship	Height	Weight	Ins. in Force
Purchaser Benefit	Birth Date	Age	State of Birth	Relationship	Height	Weight	Ins. in Force
Name of Purchaser ______							

Occupation ______ Duties ______

COMPLETE THIS SECTION FOR ANNUITY POLICY

ANNUITY APPLIED FOR

Immediate Single Premium
- ☐ Life Annuity — No Refund
- ☐ Life Annuity — Installment Refund
- ☐ Life Annuity ______ Years Certain
- ☐ Joint Life with ______ % to survivor
- ☐ Other (Specify):

Deferred to Policy Anniversary
- ☐ Single Premium (Accumulator) ______ Years Certain
- ☐ Flexible Premium
- ☐ Other (Specify):

Nearest Age ______
- ☐ Waiver of Premium Benefit

Annuity Payable		**Premium Payable**
☐	Annually	☐
☐	Semi-Annually	☐
☐	Quarterly	☐
☐ **Monthly**	Monthly	☐

Annual Premium $ ______

(or) Amount of Annuity Payment $ ______

COMPLETE THIS SECTION FOR POLICY OF ACCIDENT AND SICKNESS INSURANCE

Occupational Classification: ☐ **AAAA;** ☐ **AAA;** ☐ **AA;**

Premium Mode: ☐ **Annual** ☐ **Semi-Annual** ☐ **Quarterly** ☐ **Other** ______

Coverage Desired

☐ ACCIDENT & SICKNESS DIS. INCOME (Rate Book Plan ______) $ ______ Monthly indemnity (Total Dis.)	ELIMINATION PERIOD ______ Days	MAXIMUM BENEFIT PERIOD ______ Years

Optional Benefits
$ ______ Additional Mo. Ben. (Total Disability)
Maximum Benefit Period ______ Years

Social Program Benefit Replacement
______ Monthly Benefit

☐ BUSINESS OVERHEAD EXPENSE $ ______ Monthly Benefit	ELIMINATION PERIOD Sickness ______ days

Disability Income Insurance in force (if none, so state)

Company	Monthly Amount	Waiting Periods	Benefit Periods	Issue Date

What is your income?
Avg. mo. earned income
$ ______
Avg. mo. unearned income
$ ______
What is your net worth?
$ ______

HEALTH STATEMENT — PART III

INSTUCTION TO AGENT: Obtain information as to the Proposed Insured (unless he is to be medically examined) and for all the other family members on whom insurance is desired. Each question must be asked separately.

The following Questions and Answers relate to the following persons:

☐ Proposed Insured ☐ Family ☐ Purchaser

1. Proposed Insured's Height ______ft. ______in. Weight ______lbs.

2. To the best of your knowledge, within the past ten (10) years, has any person to be covered had or been told he had or been treated for: (Yes / No)
   a. Convulsions, paralysis, stroke, nervous or mental disorder? ☐ ☐
   b. Shortness of breath, asthma, emphysema or chronic respiratory disorder? ☐ ☐
   c. Chest pain, high blood pressure, rheumatic fever, heart murmur, heart attack or other disorder of the heart or blood vessels? ☐ ☐
   d. Jaundice, intestinal bleeding, ulcer, hernia, colitis or other disorder of the stomach, intestines gallbladder or liver including cirrhosis? ☐ ☐
   e. Disorder of the kidney, bladder, prostate or reproductive organs including venereal disease? ☐ ☐
   f. Diabetes, thyroid, neuritis, sciatica, arthritis, gout or other disorder of the muscles or bones, including the spine, back or joints? ☐ ☐
   g. Deformity, lameness or amputation? ☐ ☐
   h. Disorder of skin, lymph glands, tumor or cancer? ☐ ☐
   i. Allergies, anemia or other disorder of the blood? ☐ ☐

3. Has any person to be covered, within the past 5 years:
   a. had a checkup, consultation, illness, injury or operation? ☐ ☐
   b. been a patient in a hospital, clinic, sanitarium, or other medical facility? ☐ ☐
   c. had an electrocardiogram, or other diagnostic test or been advised to have such a test? ☐ ☐
   d. ever received treatment or counseling in connection with the use of alcohol or any drug? ☐ ☐

4. Is any person to be covered now under regular observation or taking treatment? ☐ ☐

5. In the past ten (10) years, has any applicant to be covered been advised of or taken treatment for any abnormality of menstruation, pregnancy or disorder of the reproductive organs or breasts? ☐ ☐

6.

	Age if Living?	Cause of Death?	Age at Death?
Father			
Mother			
Brothers and Sisters			

DETAILS of "Yes" answers. (IDENTIFY QUESTION NUMBER, CIRCLE APPLICABLE ITEMS: Include diagnosis, dates, duration and names and addresses of all attending physicians and medical facilities. Also, name of person to which question applies.)

Name and Address of Family Physician

Except as provided in the Receipt for First Premium which is attached hereto, no insurance applied for shall become effective unless a policy is issued and delivered to the applicant and the first premium paid while the insurability of any person proposed for coverage remains unchanged.

I acknowledge that I have received a copy of the "Medical Information Bureau Disclosure" and the "Underwriting Process".

I hereby authorize any licensed physician, medical practitioner, hospital, clinic or other medical or medically related facility, insurance company, the Medical Information Bureau or other organization, institution or person, that has any records or knowledge of me or my health, or of my family or their health, to give to the *(Name of Insurance Company)* or its reinsurors any such information.

A photographic copy of this authorization shall be as valid as the original.

Signed at ______________ (City, State) on ______________ (Month, Day, Year)

X ______________ Signature of Proposed Insured (Age 15 or older)

X ______________ Witness (Licensed Resident Agent if required)

Social Security No ______________

X ______________ Signature of Owner (Parent must sign for Proposed Juvenile)

AGENT'S REPORT — PART IV

1. Has Proposed Insured lived at present address 5 years?
   ☐ Yes ☐ No (If no, list previous address)
   Street and Number ______
   City and State ______
   How long have you known the Proposed Insured? ______
   (a) Are you related by blood or marriage? ☐ Yes ☐ No
   (b) If yes, please describe ______

2. What is Proposed Insured's Income?
   (a) Earned—$ ______
   (b) Unearned—$ ______
   (c) Source of Income ______
   (d) Amount of life insurance on applicant for benefit of spouse? ______

3. (a) Employer's name ______
   (b) Employer's address ______
   (c) Time in this Occupation ______
   (d) Describe duties ______

4. Is the insurance (or annuity) applied for intended to replace insurance (or annuities) in this or in any other Company? ☐ Yes ☐ No

5. Premium Notices will be sent to residence address unless otherwise indicated here: ______

6. Indicate which of the following requirements have been arranged.
   ☐ Medical examination by Dr. ______
   ☐ 2nd medical examination by Dr. ______
   ☐ Paramedical examination by ______
   ☐ EKG ☐ X-Ray ☐ SMA 12
   ☐ Other

7. Telephone number where we can reach proposed insured:
   ☐ Home ☐ Business (______) ______

8. If Proposed Insured Under Age 15
   Amount of insurance on head of household $ ______

9. If Proposed Insured is a Married Woman give maiden name if married within 2 years ______

10. If Owner is a Corporation
    (a) State in which Incorporated? ______
    (b) Does corporation own any other insurance on the life of the Proposed Insured? ☐ Yes ☐ No
    Amount $ ______
    Company ______

11. If Owner is a Partnership
    (a) Exact name of partnership ______
    (b) Current value of business $ ______
    (c) Full name of partners and percentage of business owned
    ______ % ______
    ______ % ______
    ______ % ______
    (d) Are all partners insured or applying for insurance?
    ☐ Yes ☐ No
    If no explain ______

12. If Owner or Beneficiary is a Trustee, give date of Trust ______

THIS SPACE FOR ADDITIONAL DETAILS

If this is a joint or split case, or if commission credits are to be other than in accordance with existing agency contracts, please give complete details.

13. I certify that I have truly and accurately recorded the information supplied by the insured.

______
Signature of Agent

______
General Agent

______
Agent's Name (Print)

RECEIPT FOR FIRST PREMIUM AND CERTIFICATE OF INTERIM INSURANCE

All premium checks must be made payable to the company: do not make check payable to the agent or leave the payee blank.

Received $ ______________________________ from ____
Name of Applicant

with an application for insurance on the ____________________ plan, bearing the same date and number as this receipt.

Countersigned at ____ on ____________________, 19 ________

____
(Signature of Agent)

If the amount paid with this application for insurance is equal to or greater than a monthly premium for the policy applied for, Interim Insurance Coverage may become effective. A description of such coverage is printed below. Please read it carefully.

Description of Interim Insurance Coverage

- **AMOUNT OF LIFE INSURANCE** : the **LESSER** of $250,000 and the amount applied for.
- **STARTING DATE** : the **LATER** of the date of this receipt and the date of any required physical examination.
- **TERMINATION** : the insurance provided by this receipt will terminate on the **EARLIEST** of:
  - a) the date we mail notice that we are unwilling to issue a policy as applied for;
  - b) 60 days from the date of this receipt;
  - c) the date we issue the policy.

LIMITATIONS AND EXCLUSIONS:
- a) no insurance is provided for any person age 61 or older;
- b) no insurance is provided if death results from self destruction;
- c) the amount of accidental death benefit insurance may not exceed $50,000.

MEDICAL INFORMATION BUREAU DISCLOSURE

*If owner is corporation or partnership, a corporate officer or partner must sign and state his title.

I hereby authorize any licensed physician, medical practitioner, hospital, clinic or other medical or medically related facility, insurance company, the Medical Information Bureau or other organization, institution or person that has any records or knowledge of me or my health, or of my family or their health, to give to the *(Name of Insurance Company)* or its reinsurors any such information.

____
(Signature of Proposed Insured) (Date)

I hereby authorize any licensed physician, medical practitioner, hospital, clinic or other medical or medically related facility, insurance company, the Medical Information Bureau or other organization, institution or person that has any records or knowledge of me or my health, or of my family or their health, to give to the *(Name of Insurance Company)* or its reinsurors any such information.

____
(Signature of Proposed Insured) (Date)

Information regarding your insurability will be treated as confidential. *(Name of Insurance Company)* or its reinsurors may, however, make a brief report thereon to the Medical Information Bureau, a non-profit membership organization of life insurance companies which operates an information exchange in behalf of its members. If you apply to another Bureau member company for life or health insurance coverage, or a claim for benefits is submitted to such a company, the Bureau, upon request, will supply such company the information it may have in its file.

Upon receipt of a request form you, the Bureau will arrange disclosure of any information it may have in your file. (Medical information will be disclosed only to your attending physician). If you question the accuracy of information in the Bureau's file, you may contact the Bureau and seek a correction in accordance with procedures set forth in the federal Fair Credit Reporting Act. The address of the Bureau's information office is Post Office Box A, Anytown, Anystate, 00000, telephone number (000)000-0000.

(Name of Insurance Company) or its reinsurors may also release information in its file to other life insurance companies to whom you may apply for life or health insurance, or to whom a claim for benefits may be submitted.

UNDERWRITING PROCESS

This is just to advise you that your recent applicant is being processed as quickly as possible. As part of our routine procedure.

(Name of Insurance Company) may require, at our expense, an investigative consumer report which would include information as to your character, general reputation, personal characteristics and mode of living. This information is obtained through personal interviews with your friends, neighbors and other associates.

Upon written request, additional information as to the nature and scope of the report, if one is made, will be provided. Thank you for considering us in this matter.

SAMPLE LIFE POLICY

The Company agrees to insure your life and pay the benefits listed, subject to the provisions of this policy.

The basic benefit of this policy is:

A DEATH BENEFIT. Upon receipt of due proof of your death while this policy is in force we will pay the Face Amount to the Beneficiary.

10 DAY RIGHT TO EXAMINE POLICY. This policy may be returned either to the Agent or to our Home Office for a full refund of any premium paid, for any reason, within 10 days after receipt and it will be deemed void from the beginning.

SECRETARY PRESIDENT

REGISTRAR

WHOLE LIFE INSURANCE POLICY	Proceeds payable at death. Premiums payable as stated in the policy schedule. A Participating Policy. (Dividends may be paid.)

. . . As a policyowner, you should contact your *(name of insurance company)* representative or the Home Office for information and assistance in the following:

Change of Address.

Collecting benefits under this policy. It is not necessary to employ any person or corporation for this purpose.

Suggestions to terminate or exchange this policy for any other policy or plan. Dropping existing policies to buy new policies is generally not advantageous and will usually result in loss to you through increased cost and less favorable benefits.

Please refer to your policy number when corresponding with the Home Office.

POLICY SCHEDULE

BENEFITS:	ANNUAL PREMIUM	PAYABLE TO AGE *
LIFE POLICY		100

*PREMIUMS PAYABLE AS STATED, OR UNTIL PRIOR DEATH OF INSURED.

QUARTERLY **SEMI-ANNUAL** **ANNUAL**

THIS POLICY IS IN A STANDARD PREMIUM CLASS.

POLICY NUMBER: 1800 **INSURED:** JOHN J. DOE

FACE AMOUNT: $10,000 **AGE:** 35

DATE OF ISSUE: JUNE 1, 1978 **POLICY DATE:** June 1,1978

TABLE OF GUARANTEED VALUES

ISSUE AGE 35 **FACE AMOUNT** $10,000

POLICY ANNIVERSARY IN	END OF POLICY YEAR	CASH OR LOAN VALUE	PAID UP INSURANCE	EXTENDED INSURANCE YEARS	EXTENDED INSURANCE DAYS
1980	1	.00	0	0	0
1981	2	.00	0	0	0
1982	3	160.00	410	3	320
1983	4	320.00	800	6	242
1984	5	490.00	1,190	8	321
1985	6	650.00	1,540	10	145
1986	7	820.00	1,900	11	241
1987	8	1,000.00	2,260	12	263
1988	9	1,170.00	2,580	13	163
1989	10	1,350.00	2,900	14	27
1990	11	1,530.00	3,210	14	196
1991	12	1,710.00	3,510	14	319
1992	13	1,890.00	3,790	15	39
1993	14	2,080.00	4,080	15	112
1994	15	2,270.00	4,350	15	156
1995	16	2,460.00	4,610	15	175
1996	17	2,650.00	4,860	15	173
1997	18	2,840.00	5,100	15	152
1998	19	3,030.00	5,320	15	114
1999	20	3,220.00	5,540	15	63
	AT AGE				
2004	60	4,190.00	6,540	14	72
2009	65	5,140.00	7,350	12	338
2014	70	6,030.00	7,990	11	173

NON-FORFEITURE FACTORS

POLICY YEARS	FACTORS
ALL	183.374

This contract is a legal contract between the contract owner and *(name of insurance company)*

READ YOUR CONTRACT CAREFULLY. It sets forth, in detail, the rights and obligations of both you and your insurance company. IT IS THEREFORE IMPORTANT THAT YOU READ YOUR CONTRACT CAREFULLY.

ALPHABETIC GUIDE TO YOUR CONTRACT

ADDITIONAL BENEFITS

The additional benefits, if any, listed on the Schedule of Coverage are described in the additional benefit rides that follow page 0.

DEFINITIONS

We, our, or us	the Company
You, your, or yours	the Insured.
Age	means age nearest birthday.
Policy Date	means the date shown on the Policy Schedule from which policy years, policy months, policy anniversaries and premium intervals will be determined.
Due Date	each premium after the first is due at the end of the period for which the preceding premium was paid.
Home Office	Our Company's principal place of business at ______________.
Proceeds	the net amount payable under this policy as a death benefit.
Payee	A person entitled to any payment under this policy.

Whole Life Insurance Policy Summary

This is a summary of your life insurance policy. A life insurance policy is a legal contract between you as the owner and the company as the insurer. Its purpose is to pay an amount of money upon your death, or the insured's death if you are not the insured, to the person you designate. In exchange for that benefit, you agree to pay premiums when due.

In this policy summary, some of the basic provisions of your life insurance policy are explained. Not everything can be explained here, however. If you have any questions about your policy that are not answered in this summary, the policy itself may contain the answers. If not, ask the agent or the company.

You have ten days after receipt of this policy to review it. If you decide you don't want to keep it, return it to the agent or the company within the ten day period and you will receive a refund of all premiums paid.

1. The amount of insurance. The face amount of insurance is shown on the Policy Schedule.

2. Premiums. The yearly premium on your policy is shown on the Policy Schedule. Any year by year variation in premiums is also shown. If you were charged an extra premium due to a health problem or any other reason, that too is shown. You may also pay the premium more often than once a year. There are extra charges for this right because the expenses are higher and because the company cannot earn as much interest as it would if it received the full premium at the beginning of the year.

- **a. Grace Period.** The law allows you to pay any premium without penalty during a grace period of 31 days after the due date. If you do not pay your premiums within the grace period, your policy will lapse unless any accumulated dividends are sufficient to pay the premium or you have elected the Automatic Premium Loan provision.
- **b. Reinstatement.** If the policy lapses, you have the right to reinstate the policy. That means put it back in force any time within five years after the due date of the premium you failed to pay. There are some conditions for this reinstatement and they are explained in the policy.

3. Policy Loans. After the policy has a cash value, you may borrow on your policy for any purpose. The loan will bear interest at 8%. Any amount of the loan outstanding plus interest will be deducted from the policy proceeds if you die or surrender the policy.

4. Dividends. This is a participating policy. This means that the company may pay dividends to the owner, depending upon mortality rates, interest rates and costs of doing business. Dividends can be paid in cash or they can be used in a number of ways such as the purchase of additional insurance. The choices you have are outlined in the Dividends and Dividend Options provisions of this policy.

5. Exclusions. There are certain situations in which the Company can refuse to pay the death benefit under this policy. Suicide within two years of the date of issue of the policy is one such situation. If you gave a material, false statement when you applied for this policy, and died within two years from its date of issue, the Company may refuse to pay the death benefit.

PREMIUMS AND REINSTATEMENT

(a) Payment. Each premium is payable on or before the due date. The first premium is due on the Policy Date. Upon request we will send a signed receipt.

(b) Frequency. Premiums may be paid once per pear, twice per year or once per quarter. The Owner may change the mode of payments if we approve.

(c) Grace Period. If a premium is not paid on or before the due date, it is in default. There is a grace period of 31 days from the due date. During this period, this policy will remain in force. After that, if your premium is unpaid this policy will expire except as provided in the Benefits on Lapse or Surrender Provisions. If you die during the grace period, a month's premium will be deducted from the policy proceeds.

(d) Premium Refund at Death. At your death we will refund as part of the policy proceeds the portion of any premium paid for a period beyond the policy month of your death.

Reinstatement. This policy may be reinstated at any time within 5 years after default in premium payment, if:
(a) The policy has not been surrendered for cash;
(b) You provide evidence of insurability accepted by us; and
(c) All past due premiums are paid and any indebtedness is paid or reinstated with compound interest on both at 6% per year.

LOAN AND REPAYMENT

Policy Loan. We will make loans on this policy. It must be in force other than as extended term insurance. The policy must be assigned to us as security for the loan. The loan value is the sum which with interest, shall not exceed the net surrender value: (a) on the date to which premiums have been paid; or, (b) if no further premiums are payable, on the next policy anniversary. Whenever indebtedness equals or exceeds the cash value, this policy will be void 31 days after notice has been mailed to the last known address of the Owner and any assignee shown on our records. We may defer making any loan, except to pay premiums, for not more than six months from receipt of written request for the loan.

Automatic Premium Loan. We will charge the amount of any premium not paid before the end of the grace period as a loan against the policy from the due date of that premium. To do this we require a written request received by us before the end of the grace period. If the loan value is not enough to pay the premium then due, no automatic premium loan shall be made and this policy will expire except as provided in the Benefits on Lapse or Surrender Provisions.
As long as the policy is in force under this provision, payment of premiums may be resumed without evidence of insurability.
The automatic premium loan may be stopped at any time by written request to us.

Interest and Repayment. Interest on loans will accrue at the yearly rate of 8% due on each policy anniversary. Any interest not paid when due will be added to the loan and will bear interest at the same rate. Indebtness may be repaid at any time while this policy is in force, other than as Extended Term or Reduced Paid-Up Insurance.

DIVIDENDS AND DIVIDEND OPTIONS

Dividend. This policy, while in force (except as extended term insurance), will share in any divisible surplus of our participating business as determined each year by us. Dividends, if any, are due on policy anniversaries. The dividend at the end of the first policy year will be payable only if the premium then due for the second policy year is paid.

Options. At the option of the Owner, each dividend may be:
(a) paid in cash; or
(b) used toward payment of any premium then due on this policy if the balance of such premium is duly paid; or
(c) held by us at interest at the rate we set, but not less than 2½% compounded annually; or
(d) used to buy participating paid-up additions to this policy; such additions would be paid upon receipt of due proof of your death; or
(e) used to buy a one-year term insurance addition (term additions); or
(f) used in any other manner to which we consent.

Term Additions. Option (e) may be chosen only if this policy is in a Standard Premium Class. It must be requested in the application for this policy or by written request received and approved by us. Option (e) shall apply only to dividends which become due after our receipt and approval of such request and before this option is cancelled by written request.
Each term addition shall be payble upon receipt by us of due proof that your death occurred within one year starting with the date such dividend became due. Each term addition shall expire without grace or notice at the end of said year so that only one term addition may be in force at any time. For policies in a Standard Premium Class, the charge for each term addition shall not exceed the net annual premium according to the Commissioners 1958 Extended Term Table and 3% interest with continuous functions.

General Provisions. Options (a), (b), (c), or (d) may be chosen for any part of any dividend not used under option (e) at any time within 31 days starting with the due date of such dividend.

Option (d) shall apply if no other option has been chosen for any part of any dividend within 31 days starting with the due date of such dividend. If they have not been used under the Benefits on Lapse or Surrender Provisions, dividends held by us and dividend additions (but not term additions) may be surrendered for their cash value less any indebtedness. If not otherwise used, dividend additions and dividends held by us will be paid at your death.

OWNERSHIP, BENEFICIARY AND ASSIGNMENT

Ownership. You are the Owner of this policy, unless someone else is named owner in the application or a written request approved by and filed with us. Unless otherwise provided: (a) the Owner may exercise policy rights during your life and (b) if the Owner dies during your life, all rights will vest in the Owner's estate.

Beneficiary. The beneficiary choice in the application will stay in effect unless changed by the Owner. If there is no beneficiary living or chosen, the proceeds will be paid to the Owner or his estate.

Change of Owner or Beneficiary. The Owner may transfer ownership or change the beneficiary by written request approved by us. When the request is filed at our Home Office, the transfer or change will be effective as of the date signed by the Owner, whether or not the Owner or Insured is living when the request is filed. We will not be liable for action taken by us before that filing.

Assignment. This policy may be assigned by the Owner. We are not bound by any assignment until it is received at our Home Office. We are not responsible for the validity of an assignment.

GENERAL PROVISIONS

Suicide. If you die by suicide, within 2 years from the Date of Issue your insurance shall be limited to the amount of premiums paid. This applies whether you are sane or insane at the time of suicide.

Incontestability. This policy may not be challenged after it has been in force during your life for 2 years from the Date of Issue except for failure to pay premiums. This provision does not apply to added benefits for disability or accidental death.

Contract. This insurance is granted in consideration of the application and payment of the scheduled premiums. This policy and the application attached at issue are the entire contract. All statements made in the application are deemed representations and not warranties. No statement shall void the policy or be used to defend a claim unless it is contained in the application.

Modification of this Policy. No person except the President, a Vice President, the Secretary or Assistant Secretary can modify this contract on our behalf. No agent may bind the Company by making a promise not contained in this contract.

Misstatement of Age or Sex. If your age or sex has been misstated, any amount payable shall be such as the premium paid would have purchased at the correct age or sex.

Payments by company. Payments by us are payable at our Home Office. Any indebtedness will be deducted from any payment under this policy.

Protection from Creditors. Unless contrary to law, (a) neither this policy, nor any policy payments are subject to the claims of creditors of the Owner or any payee and (b) the policy is not subject to attachment or judicial process.

BENEFITS ON LAPSE SURRENDER

Guaranteed Values. After premiums have been paid until this policy has a cash value, the owner may select, within 90 days after the due date of the premium in default, any one of the options listed below. If no written selection is made within the 90 days, then the automatic option will apply. The automatic option for a standard premium class policy is Option (c). The automatic option for a special premium class policy or a policy issued under a tax qualified retirement program is Option (b). Option (c) is not available if this is a special premium class policy.

The Net Surrender Value is the tabular cash value shown in the Table of Guaranteed Values, plus the present value of any dividend additions and the amount of any dividend accumulations, less any indebtedness. These values shall be calculated as of the due date of the premium in default, except that any indebtedness to be deducted shall include any indebtness charged against the policy after such due date.

(a) Surrender. This policy may be surrendered for the Net Surrender Value. We may defer payment up to 6 months. Interest at the yearly rate of 3% will be allowed on any payment of the Net Surrender Value which is deferred more than 30 days.

(b) Participating Paid-Up Insurance. This policy may be continued without any further premium payment as a paid-up participating contract payable upon receipt of due proof of your death. The Net Surrender Value of the policy shall be used as a net single premium at your then attained age to purchase the paid-up insurance. In no event shall the amount of paid-up insurance exceed a sum equal to the basic death benefit plus the amount of any dividend accumulations, less any indebtedness.

(c) Non-Participating Extended Term Insurance. This policy may be continued without further premium payment as non-participating Extended Term Insurance beginning with the due date of the premium in default. The amount of insurance shall equal the face amount of the policy, plus any paid-up additions and any dividend accumulations, less any indebtness. The amount of insurance shall not include any one year term insurance addition. The Net Surrender Value of the policy shall be used as a net single premium to determine the duration of insurance. This option is not available if the Net Surrender Value exceeds the present value of Extended Term Insurance for life.

Surrender of Paid-up or Extended Term Insurance. While it is in force as paid-up or extended term insurance, this policy may be surrendered to the Company at its Home Office for its cash value which shall equal the then present value of such paid-up or extended term insurance, including the then present value of any dividend additions and the then amount of any dividend accumulations to such paid-up insurance and less any indebtedness; except that within 31 days after any policy anniversary such cash value shall be calculated as of such anniversary.

Basis of Values. All net single premiums and present values referred to in this policy are based on the Commissioners 1958 Standard Ordinary Mortality Table except that net single premiums for extended term insurance are based on the Commissioners 1958 Extended Term Insurance Table. The calculations are based on continuous functions, age nearest birthday and with an interest rate of 3% per year.

On any policy anniversary the tabular cash value of this policy shall equal the excess, if any, of (a) the then present value of the future basic benefits as defined in the policy schedule, over (b) the then present value of a series of annual amounts beginning on such anniversary and continuing during the remaining premium paying period. Each such annual amount shall equal the Non-Forfeiture Factor shown in the table of Guaranteed Values for the appropriate policy year.

All guaranteed values in this policy are at least as great as the minimums required by the law of the state in which this policy is delivered.

Any supplemental agreement attached to this policy will not increase the cash values or paid-up insurance benefits unless otherwise provided in the agreement.

The Table of Guaranteed Values gives the values for the full face amount of this policy, provided this policy is free of indebtedness and has neither dividend additions nor accumulations. Allowance shall be made for lapse of time and payment of premiums beyond the beginning of each policy year. Any values not shown will be quoted on request. The entire loan value at the end of any policy year, less interest for the intervening period, will be available during the same year if the entire premium for that year has been paid.

OPTIONAL SETTLEMENT — METHODS OF RECEIVING POLICY PROCEEDS

While you are living, the Owner may elect settlement of the net policy proceeds under one or a combination of the following options and may revoke or change an election before any proceeds are so applied. If no such election is in force at your death, the beneficiary may elect settlement. Election of any option is subject to the conditions provided in this policy for changing a beneficiary and to the following:

(1) If the net proceeds for any one Payee under any option is less than $5,000, we will pay such amount as a single sum. We will lengthen payment intervals to make payments to any Payee at least $50.

(2) Election of any option by a corporation, partnership, association, assignee or fiduciary is permitted only with our consent.

(3) Options B or E may be elected only if the Payee is the Insured or Annuitant. Proof of the Payee's age is required if Option B or E is elected.

(4) Unless otherwise directed in the election of the option and approved by us, the Payee shall not have the right to commute, encumber or assign any installment or interest payment under any option, nor to withdraw any amount held by us under Option C or D. Under Option E no payment may be commuted, encumbered or assigned. We have the right to require 6 months written notice of any commutation or withdrawal.

The income under these options may be paid monthly, quarterly, semi-annually or annually.

Option A Fixed Period. Income to the Payee in equal installments for a specified number of years, the first installment being immediate. The amount will be as shown in the Option A Settlement Table, which is calculated at a 3% yearly rate of interest. Any share of surplus apportioned by us shall be paid on each anniversary of the first installment.

Option B Life Income. Income to the Payee, the first installment being immediate, for the lifetime of the Payee, or for a guaranteed period and as long thereafter as the original Payee shall live. The guaranteed period may be 5 years, 10 years, 20 years or a refund period such that the sum of the installments payable, including any fractional final payment, shall equal the proceeds applied. The amount of each installment shall be as declared by us and in effect at the time the first installment comes due, but shall not be less than the amount shown in the Option B Settlement Table, determined by the sex and adjusted age of the Payee on the due date of the first installment.

Option C Interest. Interest income to the Payee on the proceeds and applied at such rate as we declare each year, but never less than the equivalent of the yearly rate of 3%.

Option D Fixed Amount. Income to the Payee in equal installments, the first to be immediate, until the proceeds applied are exhausted. The amount payable in each year shall be not less than 5% of such proceeds. The final installment shall be the unpaid balance of such proceeds. On each anniversary of the first installment, interest will be added to the unpaid balance at such rate as we declare each year but never less than the yearly rate of 3%.

Option E Joint and Survivor Income. Income during the joint lifetime of the Payee and one Contingent Payee, on whose lives the option is based, and providing installments of the full amount if the Payee alone shall survive or installments of either the full amount or one-half the full amount, as elected, if the Contingent Payee alone shall survive. Payments shall be made jointly to the Payee and Contingent Payee while both are living. Thereafter the elected payment shall be made to the survivor while living. The amount of each installment shall be determined, in accordance with the Option E Settlement Table, by the sex and adjusted ages of the Payees on the due date of the first installment. The amount of income for any combination of adjusted ages not shown will be quoted upon request. This option shall not be available unless both Payees' adjusted ages at nearest birthday are at least 25 years.

Death of Payee. At the death of the Payee, any unpaid proceeds and accrued interest thereon under Option C or D, or the then commuted value of any installments certain then remaining unpaid under Option A or B, shall be payable in one sum to the executors or administrators of the Payee unless otherwise directed in the settlement election and approved by us.

Other Settlement Options. Provisions may be made for settlement of the net proceeds of this policy in any other manner approved by us.

Adjusted Ages. The adjusted age of the Payee is as follows:

Policy Year in which First Payment Falls Due	Adjusted Age of Payee is Age Nearest Birthday Plus
1 through 10	3
11 through 20	2
21 through 30	1
31 and over	0

SETTLEMENT TABLES

Monthly Installments Payable in Lieu of Each $1,000 Payable in One Sum

Option A — Fixed Period

Years	Amount	Years	Amount	Years	Amount	Years	Amount	Years	Amount
1	$84.47	6	$15.14	11	$8.86	16	$6.53	21	$5.32
2	42.86	7	13.16	12	8.24	17	6.23	22	5.15
3	28.99	8	11.68	13	7.71	18	5.96	23	4.99
4	22.06	9	10.53	14	7.26	19	5.73	24	4.84
5	17.91	10	9.61	15	6.87	20	5.51	25	4.71

Option B — Life Income

Adjusted Age		Period Certain		
Male	Female	10 Yrs.	20 Yrs.	Refund
	10 or under	$2.83	$2.82	$2.82
	11	2.84	2.84	2.83
	12	2.85	2.85	2.84
	13	2.87	2.86	2.85
	14	2.88	2.87	2.87
10 or under	15	2.89	2.89	2.88
11	16	2.91	2.90	2.89
12	17	2.92	2.92	2.91
13	18	2.94	2.93	2.92
14	19	2.95	2.95	2.94
15	20	2.97	2.96	2.95
16	21	2.99	2.98	2.97
17	22	3.00	3.00	2.99
18	23	3.02	3.01	3.01
19	24	3.04	3.03	3.02
20	25	3.06	3.05	3.04
21	26	3.08	3.07	3.06
22	27	3.10	3.10	3.08
23	28	3.12	3.12	3.11
24	29	3.15	3.14	3.13
25	30	3.18	3.16	3.15
26	31	3.20	3.19	3.18
27	32	3.23	3.21	3.20
28	33	3.26	3.24	3.23
29	34	3.29	3.27	3.25
30	35	3.32	3.30	3.28
31	36	3.35	3.33	3.31
32	37	3.38	3.36	3.34
33	38	3.42	3.39	3.37
34	39	3.45	3.43	3.41
35	40	3.49	3.46	3.44
36	41	3.53	3.50	3.48
37	42	3.57	3.54	3.52
38	43	3.62	3.58	3.56
39	44	3.66	3.62	3.60
40	45	3.71	3.66	3.64
41	46	3.76	3.71	3.68
42	47	3.82	3.75	3.73
43	48	3.87	3.80	3.78
44	49	3.93	3.85	3.83

Adjusted Age			Period Certain			
Male	Female	Life	5 Yrs.	10 Yrs.	20 Yrs.	Refund
45	50	$4.01	$4.00	$3.99	$3.90	$3.88
46	51	4.08	4.07	4.05	3.96	3.94
47	52	4.15	4.14	4.12	4.01	4.00
48	53	4.23	4.22	4.19	4.07	4.06
49	54	4.31	4.30	4.27	4.12	4.12
50	55	4.39	4.38	4.34	4.18	4.19
51	56	4.48	4.47	4.43	4.24	4.25
52	57	4.57	4.56	4.51	4.30	4.33
53	58	4.67	4.65	4.60	4.37	4.40
54	59	4.77	4.76	4.70	4.43	4.48
55	60	4.89	4.87	4.80	4.49	4.56
56	61	5.00	4.98	4.90	4.56	4.65
57	62	5.13	5.10	5.01	4.62	4.74
58	63	5.26	5.23	5.13	4.69	4.84
59	64	5.41	5.37	5.25	4.75	4.94
60	65	5.56	5.51	5.37	4.81	5.04
61	66	5.72	5.67	5.50	4.88	5.15
62	67	5.89	5.83	5.64	4.94	5.26
63	68	6.07	6.00	5.77	4.99	5.38
64	69	6.26	6.18	5.92	5.05	5.51
65	70	6.47	6.37	6.07	5.10	5.64
66	71	6.68	6.56	6.22	5.15	5.78
67	72	6.91	6.77	6.38	5.20	5.92
68	73	7.15	6.99	6.54	5.24	6.07
69	74	7.41	7.22	6.70	5.28	6.23
70	75	7.69	7.46	6.86	5.32	6.40
71	76	7.98	7.72	7.03	5.35	6.57
72	77	8.29	7.98	7.20	5.38	6.76
73	78	8.62	8.26	7.37	5.40	6.95
74	79	8.98	8.56	7.54	5.42	7.16
75	80	9.35	8.86	7.71	5.44	7.37
76	81	9.76	9.18	7.87	5.46	7.60
77	82	10.19	9.51	8.03	5.47	7.83
78	83	10.65	9.85	8.19	5.48	8.08
79	84	11.14	10.21	8.34	5.49	8.35
80 or over	85 or over	11.66	10.58	8.49	5.50	8.62

NOTE — To obtain the amount of each annual, semi-annual or quarterly installment under Option A, multiply the corresponding monthly Installment by ____________ respectively; under Option B multiply the corresponding monthly Installment by ____________ respectively.

SETTLEMENT TABLES

Monthly Installments Payable in Lieu of Each $1,000 Payable in One Sum

Option E — Joint and Full Survivor Income

Adjusted Age of other Specified Payee		The Income will be payable while both payees are living and all of such income will be continued to the survivor.															
		ADJUSTED AGE OF PAYEE															
Male		55	56	57	58	59	60	61	62	63	64	65	66	67	68	69	70
	Fem.	60	61	62	63	64	65	66	67	68	69	70	71	72	73	74	75
50	55	3.93	3.96	4.00	4.02	4.05	4.09	4.10	4.11	4.14	4.17	4.19	4.19	4.19	4.19	4.21	4.23
51	56	3.98	4.01	4.05	4.06	4.10	4.13	4.16	4.17	4.20	4.22	4.24	4.24	4.26	4.26	4.28	4.30
52	57	4.04	4.06	4.10	4.11	4.14	4.17	4.20	4.23	4.26	4.28	4.30	4.32	4.34	4.36	4.37	4.38
53	58	4.08	4.10	4.14	4.17	4.20	4.23	4.26	4.29	4.31	4.33	4.35	4.37	4.40	4.44	4.45	4.46
54	59	4.13	4.15	4.18	4.22	4.24	4.27	4.30	4.34	4.39	4.40	4.42	4.44	4.47	4.51	4.54	4.55
55	60	4.16	4.18	4.21	4.27	4.29	4.32	4.34	4.38	4.42	4.46	4.47	4.51	4.54	4.58	4.61	4.61
56	61	4.20	4.24	4.27	4.33	4.35	4.37	4.42	4.46	4.50	4.53	4.57	4.60	4.63	4.66	4.68	4.71
57	62	4.23	4.27	4.32	4.38	4.40	4.44	4.48	4.52	4.56	4.59	4.64	4.67	4.70	4.72	4.75	4.79
58	63	4.27	4.30	4.35	4.43	4.47	4.51	4.55	4.58	4.64	4.67	4.72	4.75	4.79	4.82	4.83	4.87
59	64	4.29	4.35	4.40	4.47	4.53	4.57	4.60	4.64	4.69	4.74	4.78	4.83	4.87	4.89	4.93	4.96
60	65	4.32	4.37	4.44	4.51	4.57	4.63	4.66	4.69	4.74	4.81	4.87	4.92	4.96	4.99	5.03	5.06
61	66	4.36	4.42	4.48	4.55	4.60	4.66	4.71	4.76	4.81	4.88	4.94	5.00	5.04	5.09	5.12	5.15
62	67	4.41	4.46	4.52	4.58	4.64	4.69	4.76	4.83	4.88	4.94	5.00	5.06	5.11	5.16	5.21	5.25
63	68	4.42	4.50	4.56	4.62	4.69	4.74	4.81	4.88	4.94	5.00	5.05	5.11	5.18	5.23	5.29	5.35
64	69	4.44	4.51	4.59	4.67	4.74	4.81	4.88	4.94	5.00	5.08	5.13	5.20	5.27	5.31	5.37	5.45
65	70	4.47	4.54	4.62	4.70	4.78	4.87	4.94	5.00	5.07	5.15	5.22	5.29	5.35	5.41	5.47	5.54
66	71	4.51	4.58	4.65	4.75	4.83	4.92	4.98	5.06	5.13	5.22	5.31	5.38	5.43	5.51	5.56	5.63
67	72	4.54	4.63	4.70	4.79	4.87	4.96	5.04	5.11	5.20	5.29	5.37	5.46	5.51	5.58	5.65	5.71
68	73	4.55	4.66	4.75	4.84	4.91	4.99	5.07	5.16	5.27	5.36	5.43	5.51	5.58	5.68	5.76	5.84
69	74	4.56	4.66	4.77	4.88	4.95	5.03	5.12	5.21	5.32	5.42	5.49	5.59	5.65	5.74	5.84	5.93
70	75	4.59	4.69	4.79	4.89	4.99	5.08	5.17	5.25	5.35	5.45	5.54	5.63	5.71	5.82	5.91	6.00
71	76	4.62	4.71	4.81	4.91	5.02	5.11	5.22	5.30	5.39	5.49	5.59	5.70	5.80	5.90	6.01	6.09
72	77	4.64	4.73	4.83	4.93	5.03	5.14	5.24	5.34	5.45	5.54	5.64	5.77	5.88	5.99	6.10	6.19
73	78	4.65	4.75	4.85	4.96	5.06	5.17	5.26	5.38	5.49	5.61	5.71	5.83	5.96	6.09	6.21	6.32
74	79	4.65	4.77	4.86	4.97	5.09	5.19	5.31	5.41	5.54	5.68	5.79	5.90	6.03	6.17	6.29	6.41
75	80	4.67	4.80	4.88	5.01	5.12	5.24	5.35	5.45	5.59	5.73	5.86	5.99	6.10	6.26	6.39	6.51

Option E — Joint and One-Half Contingent Survivor Income

Adjusted Age of Contingent Payee		The Income will be payable while the Payee is living and one-half of such income will be continued if the contingent payee alone survives.															
		ADJUSTED AGE OF PAYEE															
Male		55	56	57	58	59	60	61	62	63	64	65	66	67	68	69	70
	Fem.	60	61	62	63	64	65	66	67	68	69	70	71	72	73	74	75
50	55	4.36	4.42	4.50	4.56	4.63	4.71	4.78	4.84	4.92	5.00	5.08	5.15	5.22	5.29	5.37	5.46
51	56	4.39	4.45	4.53	4.59	4.66	4.74	4.82	4.88	4.96	5.04	5.12	5.19	5.27	5.34	5.43	5.51
52	57	4.42	4.48	4.56	4.62	4.69	4.77	4.85	4.92	5.00	5.08	5.16	5.25	5.33	5.41	5.50	5.58
53	58	4.45	4.51	4.58	4.66	4.73	4.81	4.88	4.96	5.04	5.12	5.20	5.28	5.38	5.48	5.56	5.65
54	59	4.48	4.53	4.61	4.68	4.76	4.83	4.91	5.00	5.09	5.17	5.25	5.33	5.43	5.53	5.63	5.71
55	60	4.50	4.55	4.62	4.71	4.79	4.86	4.94	5.03	5.12	5.21	5.29	5.39	5.48	5.58	5.68	5.76
56	61	4.52	4.59	4.66	4.75	4.82	4.90	4.99	5.08	5.17	5.26	5.35	5.45	5.54	5.64	5.74	5.84
57	62	4.54	4.61	4.69	4.78	4.85	4.94	5.03	5.12	5.21	5.30	5.40	5.50	5.59	5.69	5.79	5.90
58	63	4.56	4.63	4.71	4.81	4.89	4.98	5.07	5.16	5.26	5.35	5.46	5.55	5.66	5.76	5.85	5.97
59	64	4.57	4.65	4.73	4.83	4.93	5.01	5.10	5.19	5.29	5.40	5.50	5.61	5.72	5.81	5.92	6.03
60	65	4.59	4.67	4.76	4.86	4.95	5.05	5.14	5.22	5.32	5.44	5.56	5.67	5.77	5.88	5.99	6.10
61	66	4.61	4.69	4.78	4.88	4.97	5.07	5.17	5.27	5.37	5.48	5.60	5.72	5.83	5.95	6.06	6.17
62	67	4.64	4.71	4.81	4.90	4.99	5.09	5.20	5.31	5.41	5.52	5.64	5.76	5.88	6.00	6.12	6.24
63	68	4.65	4.74	4.83	4.92	5.02	5.12	5.23	5.34	5.45	5.56	5.67	5.79	5.92	6.04	6.18	6.31
64	69	4.65	4.74	4.85	4.95	5.05	5.16	5.27	5.37	5.48	5.61	5.72	5.85	5.98	6.10	6.23	6.38
65	70	4.67	4.76	4.86	4.96	5.08	5.19	5.30	5.41	5.53	5.65	5.78	5.90	6.03	6.16	6.29	6.44
66	71	4.69	4.78	4.88	4.99	5.10	5.22	5.32	5.44	5.56	5.70	5.83	5.96	6.08	6.23	6.36	6.50
67	72	4.71	4.81	4.90	5.02	5.13	5.24	5.36	5.47	5.60	5.74	5.87	6.01	6.13	6.27	6.41	6.56
68	73	4.72	4.82	4.93	5.04	5.15	5.26	5.38	5.50	5.64	5.77	5.91	6.04	6.18	6.33	6.48	6.64
69	74	4.72	4.83	4.94	5.06	5.17	5.28	5.40	5.53	5.67	5.81	5.94	6.08	6.22	6.37	6.53	6.70
70	75	4.73	4.84	4.95	5.07	5.19	5.31	5.43	5.55	5.69	5.83	5.97	6.11	6.26	6.41	6.58	6.74
71	76	4.75	4.85	4.96	5.08	5.21	5.33	5.46	5.58	5.71	5.85	6.00	6.15	6.31	6.46	6.64	6.80
72	77	4.76	4.86	4.97	5.09	5.21	5.34	5.47	5.60	5.75	5.88	6.03	6.19	6.35	6.52	6.69	6.86
73	78	4.77	4.87	4.98	5.11	5.23	5.36	5.48	5.62	5.76	5.92	6.07	6.22	6.40	6.58	6.75	6.94
74	79	4.77	4.88	4.99	5.11	5.25	5.37	5.50	5.64	5.79	5.96	6.11	6.27	6.44	6.63	6.80	6.99
75	80	4.78	4.90	5.00	5.13	5.26	5.39	5.53	5.66	5.82	5.98	6.15	6.31	6.48	6.68	6.86	7.05

NOTE: To obtain the amount of each annual, semi-annual, or quarterly installments, multiply the corresponding monthly installment by 11.72, 5.93, or 2.98 respectively.

SAMPLE HEALTH POLICY

BASIC HOSPITAL EXPENSE POLICY

POLICY RENEWAL

WE RESERVE THE RIGHT TO NON-RENEW ALL POLICIES OF THIS SAME FORM IN THE COUNTY WHERE YOU RESIDE. IF WE NON-RENEW, WE WILL NOTIFY YOU AT LEAST 31 DAYS PRIOR TO TAKING THIS ACTION.

EACH ADULT INSURED PERSON MAY BE INSURED TO AGE 65 OR UNTIL ELIGIBLE FOR MEDICARE, WHICHEVER FIRST HAPPENS. EACH DEPENDENT CHILD MAY BE INSURED TO AGE 25, TO THE DATE OF MARRIAGE, OR WHEN NO LONGER DEPENDENT ON YOU, WHICHEVER FIRST HAPPENS.

OTHER THAN AS STATED ABOVE, YOU HAVE THE RIGHT TO RENEW THIS POLICY BY PAYING THE CORRECT PREMIUM WHEN DUE. THE PREMIUM MUST BE PAID IN ADVANCE OF THE PREMIUM DUE DATE OR BEFORE THE END OF THE GRACE PERIOD.

PREMIUMS WILL INCREASE EACH YEAR. ALSO PREMIUMS MAY CHANGE IF YOU MOVE TO ANOTHER AREA. SEE PREMIUMS ON PAGE 7.

INSURING CLAUSE

WHEN WE RECEIVE PROOF OF A COVERED INJURY OR SICKNESS, AND SUBJECT TO THE PROVISIONS OF THIS POLICY, WE WILL PROVIDE BENEFITS FOR EXPENSE:

- WHICH IS INCURRED WHILE THE PERSON'S INSURANCE COVERAGE IS IN FORCE;
- LESS ANY DEDUCTIBLE AND COPAYMENT AMOUNT; AND
- UP TO ANY MAXIMUM PAYMENT THAT MAY BE SPECIFIED.

TEN DAY RIGHT TO EXAMINE THIS POLICY

THIS POLICY MAY BE RETURNED WITHIN TEN DAYS AFTER IT IS RECEIVED. RETURN IT TO OUR HOME OFFICE OR TO THE AGENT FROM WHOM IT WAS PURCHASED. WE WILL VOID THIS POLICY AND RETURN ANY PREMIUM YOU HAVE PAID.

THIS POLICY IS SIGNED FOR ______________ BY ______________

YOUR POLICY MAY NOT BE IN FORCE WHEN YOU HAVE A CLAIM! This policy was issued based on the information entered in the application, a copy of which is attached to this policy. If, to the best of your knowledge and belief, there is any misstatement in this application or if any information concerning your medical history has been omitted, advise us immediately regarding the incorrect or omitted information, otherwise your policy may not be a valid contract.

IMPORTANT MESSAGE TO OUR POLICYHOLDERS

Cancelling a health insurance policy which you already own and purchasing a new one, on account of encouragement by any agent, is called replacement. Some states have laws which forbid any misrepresentation or incomplete comparison by any agent that may occur at the time of replacement. Those laws require that a written and signed comparison of your existing policy and the recommended new policy be given to you.

Beware of anyone who encourages you to replace this policy without allowing you time to carefully investigate the replacement proposal, or discourages you from talking with a representative of the company whose policy is being recommended for replacement.

For your protection, if you are encouraged to replace this policy, we urge you to seek advice and to take the time to investigate any recommendation. Keep in mind that you can request changes in this policy long after its effective date.

______________________ ______________________

Secretary President

This policy is a legal contract between the company and the owner. Please read it carefully. We want you to understand the coverage which it provides. Omissions or misstatements in the application may cause a claim to be denied. Notify the company immediately of any misstated medical history.

Contents of Policy

Policy Index

When writing to ____________________ Company, please include the policy number, the insured person's full name, and the owner's name and current address.

POLICY SPECIFICATIONS

FORM ________ POLICY DATE JUNE 1, 1992 POLICY NUMBER SPECIMEN

SCHEDULE OF PREMIUMS	ANNUAL	SEMI-ANNUAL	QUARTERLY	MONTHLY	SPECIAL MONTHLY
*FIRST YEAR PREMIUMS	$	$	$	$	$

INSURED PERSONS

INSURED PERSON NUMBER	ISSUE AGE	NAME	INSURED PERSON NUMBER	ISSUE AGE	NAME
01	35	JOHN DOE			
02	30	MARY DOE			

INSURED PERSON NUMBER	DESCRIPTION OF COVERAGE	BENEFIT AMOUNT	FIRST YEAR PREMIUM
01	BASIC POLICY COVERAGE		
	HOSPITAL IN-PATIENT		
	ONE PERIOD OF CONFINEMENT — 365 DAYS		
	HOSPITAL ROOM — EACH DAY	$500.00	$
	MISCELLANEOUS HOSPITAL SERVICES MAXIMUM	10,000.00	
	DEDUCTIBLE AMOUNT — $100.00		
	OUT-PATIENT MEDICAL SERVICES AND SUPPLIES-MAXIMUM PER POLICY YEAR	500.00	
	OPTIONAL COVERAGE PURCHASED		
	EXTENDED CARE FACILITY — EACH DAY	100.00	
	EXTRA HOSPITAL MISCELLANEOUS — MAXIMUM	7,000.00	
	HOSPITAL INTENSIVE CARE UNIT — EACH DAY	500.00	
	PHYSICIAN'S VISITS — EACH	30.00	
	PRIVATE DUTY NURSE — EACH 8 HOUR SHIFT	50.00	
	SURGERY — MAXIMUM	2,000.00	
	PREMIUM		$
02	BASIC POLICY COVERAGE		
	HOSPITAL IN-PATIENT		
	ONE PERIOD OF CONFINEMENT — 365 DAYS		
	HOSPITAL ROOM — EACH DAY	$500.00	$
	MISCELLANEOUS HOSPITAL SERVICES MAXIMUM	10,000.00	
	DEDUCTIBLE AMOUNT — $100.00		
	OUT-PATIENT MEDICAL SERVICES AND SUPPLIES-MAXIMUM PER POLICY YEAR	500.00	
	*PREMIUM WILL INCREASE EACH YEAR. ALSO, PREMIUMS MAY CHANGE FOR OTHER REASONS. SEE PREMIUM PROVISION.		

POLICY SPECIFICATIONS

FORM ________ POLICY DATE JUNE 1, 1992 POLICY NUMBER SPECIMEN

SCHEDULE OF PREMIUMS	ANNUAL	SEMI-ANNUAL	QUARTERLY	MONTHLY

INSURED PERSONS

INSURED PERSON NUMBER	ISSUE AGE	NAME	INSURED PERSON NUMBER	ISSUE AGE	NAME
02					

INSURED PERSON NUMBER	DESCRIPTION OF COVERAGE	BENEFIT AMOUNT	FIRST YEAR PREMIUM
02	OPTIONAL COVERAGE PURCHASED		
	CHILDBIRTH COVERAGE	$2,000.00	$
	EXTENDED CARE FACILITY — EACH DAY	100.00	
	EXTRA HOSPITAL MISCELLANEOUS — MAXIMUM	7,000.00	
	HOSPITAL INTENSIVE CARE UNIT — EACH DAY	500.00	
	PHYSICIAN'S VISITS —EACH	30.00	
	PRIVATE DUTY NURSE — EACH 8 HOUR SHIFT	50.00	
	SURGERY — MAXIMUM	2,000.00	
	PREMIUM		$

DEFINITIONS

When we use the following words, this is what we mean:

complications of pregnancy

- Conditions requiring hospital confinement (when the pregnancy is not terminated) whose diagnoses are distinct from pregnancy, but are adversely affected by pregnancy, including but not limited to: acute nephritis, nephrosis, cardiac decompensation, missed abortion, and similar medical and surgical conditions of comparable severity, or
- Non-elective cesarean section, termination of ectopic pregnancy, and spontaneous termination of pregnancy occuring during a period of gestation in which a viable birth is not possible.

Complications of pregnancy do not include false labor, occasional spotting, physician prescribed rest during the period of pregnancy, morning sickness, hyperemesis gravidarum, preeclampsia, and similar conditions associated with the management of a difficult pregnancy not constituting a nosologically distinct complication.

dependent child
An insured person who is 25 years old or less, single and dependent on you.

effective date
This is the date the coverage for an insured person begins. For a person or coverage added to the policy after the policy date, it is the date shown on an amendment which is to be attached to this policy.

expense
The usual and customary charge for medical services and supplies for which this policy provides coverage.

extended care facility
An institution which:

- is recognized as a skilled nursing facility by the state in which such institution is located
- is regularly engaged in providing continuous skilled nursing care under the supervision of a graduate registered nurse for 16 hours and a graduate registered nurse or licensed practical nurse for the remaining eight hours
- maintains a daily medical record of each patient, and
- administers a planned program of observation and treatment by a physician (other than the proprietor or an employee of such facility) which is in accordance with existing standards of medical pratice for the injury or sickness causing confinement.

The definition of extended care facility, as herein defined, shall not include any home, facility or part thereof:

- used primarily for rest
- used for the aged or for the care of drug addicts or alcoholics, or
- used primarily for the care and treatment of mental or nervous disorders, or for custodial or educational care.

DEFINITIONS, Cont.

When we use the following words, this is what we mean:

hospital

an institution which:

- is operated according to law
- is primarily engaged in providing in-patient medical care and treatment to injured or sick persons for which a charge is made, and provides or operates (either on its premises or in facilities available to the hospital on a contractual, prearranged basis) medical, diagnostic and major surgical facilities under the supervision of a licensed physician, and
- provides 24 hour nursing service by or under the supervision of a graduate registered nurse.

A special unit of a hospital or any institution which provides primarily convalescent, rehabilitative, nursing, ambulatory or extended care is not considered a hospital as defined.

If treatment is for mental, emotional or nervous disorders, alcoholism or drug dependency, a hospital shall also include an institution which:

- is accredited by the Joint Commission on Accreditation of Hospitals; and
- offers medical, therapeutic and psychiatric care.

injury

Accidental bodily injury sustained, directly and independently of all other causes, from an accident occurring while the coverage is in force as to the person on whom the claim is made.

insured person

A person for whom insurance coverage is in force under this policy.

loss

An expense or an event for which this policy provides payment.

Medicare

The program of medical care coverage provided under Title XVIII of the Social Security Act of 1965, as amended.

mental or nervous disorder

a neurosis, psychoneurosis, psychopathy, psychosis, or mental or emotional disease or disorder of any kind, including physiological and psychological dependence on alcohol and drugs.

one period of confinement

- one continuous hospital confinement; or
- several hospital confinements for the same or related cause which are separated by less than 180 days.

Each hospital confinement must begin while the coverage is in force.

physician or surgeon

A person who is a practitioner of the healing arts who is licensed by the state to treat the injury or sickness causing the loss.

DEFINITIONS, Cont.

When we use the following words, this is what we mean:

policy date
The date shown on page 3. It will be used to determine anniversary dates and premium due dates.

pre-existing condition
The existence of symptoms which would cause an ordinarily prudent person to seek diagnosis, care or treatment within a six (6) month period preceding the effective date of the coverage of the insured person.

A condition for which medical advice or treatment was recommended by a physician or received from a physician within a six (6) month period preceding the effective date of the coverage of the insured person.

sickness
Disease or illness which manifests itself while this policy is in force. Sickness includes complications of pregnancy, as defined.

usual and customary charge
The prevailing charge which is made for the same type of or comparable care by most providers in the area in which the care is furnished.

we, our, us
The Insurer.

you, your
The owner of this policy. The owner may be someone other than an insured person.

GENERAL AGREEMENT

Why did we agree to issue this policy?

We agreed to issue this policy to you because you paid the first premium and we relied on the application you made. The application is attached and is a part of this policy. All dealings are between you and us.

Whom does this policy insure?

This policy insures any person shown on page 3 or any person added after the policy date.

How are changes in this policy shown?

Persons, coverage or benefits added or deleted after the policy date will be shown by amendment to be attached to this policy.

When does the policy term begin and end?

Each policy term begins and ends at 12 noon at the place where you reside. This policy will remain in force for any term for which we accept a premium.

PREMIUMS

How are premium due dates determined?	All premium due dates are determined from the policy date.
When and where do you pay your premiums?	The first premium is due before we deliver the policy. All other premiums are due in advance of the term for which they are to cover. Premiums after the first one are to be paid to our home office.
How may you pay your premiums?	You may pay premiums for a term of 12 months. A shorter term may be allowed by us if the method of premium payment and the payment amount meet our requirements.
When and how often will premiums increase?	On each annual anniversary date, we will increase premiums. The increase will reflect: ● the increased age of the insured persons ● the increasing costs of medical care, and ● the impact of any deductible. On the premium due date following a change of address, we will change your premiums to those that apply in your new area of residence.
Can the premiums of this policy be changed other than as stated above?	We reserve the right to change the premiums, but only if changed for all policies of this same form in your state of residence. Any change in premiums will be in accordance with and subject to the laws and regulations of the state.

TERMINATION FOR NON-PAYMENT OF PREMIUMS

What happens if a premium is not paid by the due date or within the grace period?	The coverage for an insured person will end if the right premium is not paid when due or within the grace period. This will not affect a claim for loss incurred before the coverage ended.

TERMINATION OF AN INSURED PERSON

Can the insurance for an adult insured person terminate other than if the policy is non-renewed or for non-payment of premium?	An adult insured person's insurance will terminate in the month after the first of these events happens: ● the person attains age 65, or ● the person becomes eligible for Medicare. The day of termination is that day of the month which coincides with the policy date.
Can the insurance terminate for a dependent child other than if the policy is non-renewed or for non-payment of premium?	A dependent child's insurance will terminate on the premium due date after the first of these events happens: ● the child attains age 25 ● the child marries, or ● the child is no longer dependent on you.
Will we terminate the insurance for a handicapped dependent child?	A dependent child's insurance will not terminate for the above reasons while the child: ● is incapable of self-support due to mental retardation or physical handicap ● is chiefly dependent on you for support and maintenance, and ● is not eligible for Medicare.

TERMINATION OF AN INSURED PERSON, Cont.

What must you do to continue the insurance for a handicapped dependent child?	To continue the handicapped dependent child's insurance, you must submit proof of the child's incapacity and dependency. The proof must be given to us within 31 days of the child's attainment of the limiting age.
Do we require proof of the handicapped child's condition more than once?	We reserve the right to require proof of the handicapped dependent child's continued incapacity and dependency. However, we will not require proof more than once a year after the dependent child attains age 27.
What rights and privileges does an insured person have when their insurance is terminated due to age?	When the insurance is terminated due to any of the reasons stated in this "Termination of an Insured Person" provision, we will: • continue that person's insurance for any term for which we accept the premium • consider any claim for which an expense was incurred before the insurance terminated • allow that person a conversion policy as set forth in the "Conversion Privilege" • extend the insurance for a limited time, as provided below, for a continuous loss that is due to an injury or sickness which began while the insurance was in force.

EXTENSION OF COVERAGE UPON TERMINATION OR NON-RENEWAL

What happens if an insured person is hospital confined or under continuous treatment when the insurance is terminated or non-renewed?	Other than for non-payment of premium, when coverage is terminated for reasons stated in the "Termination of an Insured Person" provision or if we should non-renew this policy, we will extend coverage for a continuous injury or sickness for which an insured person is being treated. The extension will be to the earliest of: • the date on which treatment is no longer required • the date on which the maximum payment is incurred • the date which is 90 days after the date on which the insurance should have ended, and • the date the coverage under a new policy with us (which has been issued subject to the "Conversion Privilege") becomes effective.

CONVERSION PRIVILEGE
(Other than when this policy is non-renewed)

Can this policy be converted if we non-renew it?	If we elect to non-renew this policy, there is no conversion privilege available.
Under what circumstances can this policy be converted?	Coverage can be converted on an adult insured • when their insurance terminates due to attainment of age 65 or when they become eligible for Medicare. The new policy will be that policy form, if any, which we are then offering in that person's resident state to those who are eligible for Medicare.

CONVERSION PRIVILEGE, Cont.
(Other than when this policy is non-renewed)

	continued Coverage can be converted on an insured dependent child • when such child's insurance terminates due to age, marriage or when no longer dependent. The new policy will be the policy form we are then offering in the person's resident state which is most similar to this policy. The benefits of the new policy will not exceed the benefits of this policy.
What must you do to convert this policy?	The new policy will be issued if we receive written application and the required premium at least 31 days prior to the date this insurance is to terminate.
When will the new policy be in force?	The new policy will be in force on the day after the date this insurance terminate.

PRE-EXISTING CONDITION LIMITATIONS

Are any conditions excluded from coverage?	You do not have any coverage for: • pre-existing conditions during the six months following the effective date of coverage as to an insured person; or • any disease or physical condition named or specifically described as excluded in any endorsement attached to this policy.

LIMITATIONS AND EXCLUSIONS

Are there any expenses for which we will not pay benefits?	We will not pay benefits for an expense which results from: • intentionally self-inflicted wounds • being intoxicated or under the influence of a narcotic, unless administered on the advice of and in such doses as are prescribed by a physician, except as otherwise provided in the Hospital In-patient Coverage • rest care, convalescent care, or rehabilitation, except as provided by any optional rider attached • the insured person committing or attempting to commit an assault, a felony or being engaged in an illegal occupation • injury or sickness covered by Workmen's Compensation or Employer's Liability Law • any act of war, declared or undeclared • dental treatment, except when due to injury • pregnancy, except complications of pregnancy as defined • normal childbirth, except as provided by any optional rider attached

LIMITATIONS AND EXCLUSIONS, Cont.

continued

- cosmetic surgery, except reconstructive surgery which is incidental to or follows surgery resulting from trauma, infection, or other diseases of the involved part, and reconstructive surgery due to congenital disease or anomaly of a covered newborn dependent child which results in a functional defect
- eye exams, glasses, contact lenses or hearing aids, except when due to injury
- elective sterilization
- hospital confinement or treatment for which you or the insured person are not legally required to pay, except Medicaid
- treatment of tonsils or adenoids within six months after the effective date, unless treatment is on an emergency basis
- injury sustained or sickness which manifests itself while on full-time duty in the military forces of any country. Upon notice, we will refund the proportion of unearned premium paid for the insured person while in such forces.

ADDITION OF PERSONS TO THE POLICY AFTER THE POLICY DATE

Is a newborn child automatically insured?

A child born to you while this policy is in force will be insured for 31 days from the date of birth.

For the child to continue to be insured, you must make written request and pay the premium for that child within 31 days after the child's birth. Premium for the child will be prorated from the date of birth to the next premium due date of this policy.

What does the coverage for a newborn child include?

The insurance on a newborn child will include coverage for congenital defects, birth abnormalities, as well as injury or sickness. Benefits are not payable for premature birth or routine well-baby care.

Can you add other persons to this policy?

Other dependents under age 64 may be added to this policy. To do so, you must

- make written application to us
- furnish proof that the person is insurable by our underwritting standards, and
- pay the additional premium due for that person. The first premium for the person to be added will be determined from the effective date of their coverage to the next premium due date.

GENERAL PROVISIONS

What constitutes the entire contract between you and us? Can the agent effect changes in this contract?

Entire Contract and Changes — This policy, including any attachments, is the entire contract. No one has the right to change this policy unless it is approved by one of our executive officers. The approval will be attached to the policy. No agent may change this policy in any way.

What is the time limit on certain defenses against misstatements and physical conditions which existed before the effective date?

Time Limit on Certain Defenses — (1) After two years from the effective date of an insured person's coverage, no misstatement, except fraudulent misstatement, made by you in the application will be used to void the policy or to deny a claim for loss incurred. (2) No claim for loss incurred after two years from the effective date of an insured person's coverage will be reduced or denied on the ground that a disease or physical condition had existed before the effective date unless, effective on the date of loss, the disease or physical condition has been excluded from coverage by name or specific description.

Does this policy have a grace period during which you may pay past due premium?

Grace Period — Unless within 31 days prior to a premium due date we deliver to you, or mail to you, at the last address as shown on the company's record, a written notice of our intention not to renew this policy beyond the period for which premium has been accepted, a grace period of 31 days will be granted for the payment of each premium falling due after the first premium. During the grace period, this policy will remain in force.

Can we deduct unpaid premiums from a claim payment?

Unpaid Premium — At the time of claim payment for insured expenses, the company reserves the right to deduct any unpaid premium due.

Can you reinstate this policy when it is terminated for non-payment of premiums?

Reinstatement — If premiums are not paid within the grace period and later we accept a premium without requiring an application, the policy shall be reinstated. However, if we require an application for reinstatement and issue a conditional receipt, the policy will be reinstated when we approve the application, or on the 45th day after the date the conditional receipt is signed, unless we have previously notified you, in writing, of its disapproval.

Upon reinstatement, the policy shall cover loss resulting from injury sustained after the date of reinstatement and loss due to sickness which begins more than 10 days after reinstatement. In all other respects, you and we shall have the same rights as we both had under the policy before the policy ended, subject to any conditions attached to this policy upon reinstatement. The premium we accept for a reinstatement shall be applied to a period for which premium has not been paid, but not to any period more than 60 days before the reinstatement date.

Our agents do not have authority to accept reinstatement premiums without requiring a reinstatement application and issuing a conditional receipt.

When and how should you notify us of a claim?

Notice of Claim — Written notice of claim must be given to us within 20 days after the occurrence of any covered loss, or as soon as reasonably possible. Notice given by or on behalf of the insured person to us at our Home Office, or to any of our authorized agents, with information sufficient to identify you or the insured person shall be considered as notice to us.

When will claim forms be furnished to you?

Claim Forms — Upon receipt of a notice of claim, we will furnish forms to the claimant for filing proof of the loss. If we do not furnish the forms within 15 days after we have been given the notice, we will consider the claimant to have complied with the requirements for filing proof of loss, provided we have received, within the time fixed in the policy for filing proof of loss, written proof of the occurrence, the character and the extent of the loss for which the claim is made.

GENERAL PROVISIONS, Cont.

When must you send proof of loss?	**Proof of Loss —** We must be furnished written proof of loss within 90 days after the date of loss. We will not reject or reduce any claim because we are not furnished proof in the time required if it is not possible for you to do so. However, proof must be furnished as soon as reasonably possible, and in no event, later than one year from the time proof is required, unless it is legally impossible to do so.
When can you expect payment of the claim?	**Time of Payment of Claim —** Any benefits payable under this policy will be paid immediately upon our receiving written proof of the loss.
To whom will payment of claims be made?	**Payment of Claims —** All benefits are payable to you. Any accrued benefits unpaid in the event of your death may, at our option, be paid to your estate. If any benefit is payable to your estate, or to an insured person who is a minor or otherwise not competent to give a valid release, we may pay such benefits (up to an amount not exceeding $1,000) to any relative by blood or connection by marriage of yours who we consider to be equitably entitled. Any payment made by us in good faith in accordance with this provision will fully discharge us to the extent of the payment.
When can you take legal action?	**Legal Actions —** No legal or equitable action can be taken against us under this policy prior to the expiration of 60 days after written proof of loss has been furnished in accordance with the requirements of this policy. No action will be brought against us after the expiration of 3 years after the time written proof of loss is required to be furnished.
Can we require any insured person to undergo a physical examination during the pendency of a claim?	**Physical Examination —** During the pendency of a claim, we will have the right and opportunity, at our own expense, to examine an insured person as often as we may reasonably require.
What happens when you misstate the age of any insured person?	**Misstatement of Age —** If the age of an insured person has been misstated, all amounts payable under this policy shall be such as the premium would have bought at the correct age.
What happens if this policy does not conform to state statutes?	**Conformity with State Statutes —** Any provision of this policy which, on its effective date, is in conflict with the statutes of the state in which you reside on such date is amended to conform to the minimum requirements of such statutes.

OUT-PATIENT MEDICAL SERVICES AND SUPPLIES COVERAGE

What benefits do we pay for expense for out-of-hospital medical services and supplies?

We will pay benefits for the out-patient medical services and supplies named below. We will pay:

- 80% of the expense incurred during a policy year;
- up to the maximum benefit amount shown on page 3.

Out-patient Medical Services and Supplies

- x-ray and fluroscopic examinations;
- radium, or other radioactive substance;
- electrocardiograms, microscopic, and laboratory tests;
- drugs and medicines which may be purchased only on the attending physician's written prescription and which are dispensed by a licensed pharmacist;
- casts, splints, braces, and crutches;
- artificial limbs;
- oxygen and equipment used for its administration;
- emergency room or operating room; and
- tetanus anti-toxin.

The above items are payable when furnished on an out-patient basis at a hospital, clinic, the doctor's office, or an ambulatory surgical center.

What is an ambulatory surgical center?

An Ambulatory Surgical Center is any public or private establishment that:

- is licensed by the state;
- has permanent facilities that are equipped and operated primarily for the purpose of performing surgical procedures;
- has continuous physician services and registered nursing service whenever a patient is in the facility; and
- does not provide services or accommodations for patients to stay overnight.

Is ambulance service covered?

We will pay benefits for emergency ambulance service which is required as the result of an injury.

We will pay up to $25.00 for such service from the accident to the hospital. Hospital confinement is not required. We will not pay more than the fee charged.

An ambulance must be a vehicle specifically equipped for, and used exclusively for, the transportation of persons who are sick, injured, or deceased.

Are all medical services and supplies covered?

No.

In order for benefits to be paid under this coverage, the service and supply must be rendered:

- as the result of an injury or sickness
- while this coverage is in force for the person who incurs the expense
- at the direction of and under the supervision of a physician or surgeon.

This coverage does not include benefits for professional services of a radiologist, pathologist, anesthesiologist, nurse, physician or surgeon.

HOSPITAL IN-PATIENT COVERAGE

What benefits do we pay for expense due to a confinement in a hospital? **What limits are imposed upon these expenses?**	**The benefits for confinement in a hospital are:** ● room (other than private room), board, and general nursing care, and ● miscellaneous hospital services. **HOSPITAL ROOM** — For each day of confinement in one period of confinement, we will pay up to the amount shown on page 3 for the insured person. See page 3 for the number of days we will pay during one period of confinement. **MISCELLANEOUS HOSPITAL SERVICES** — For any one period of confinement, we will pay up to the maximum amount shown on page 3 for the insured person. Hospital services do not include professional services of a radiologist, pathologist, anesthesiologist, nurse, physician or surgeon.
Are benefits payable for mental or nervous disorders, alcoholism, and drug dependency?	Benefits are payable in a hospital or in a mental hospital (which is licensed by the State) for the treatment of a mental, emotional or nervous disorder, alcoholism or drug dependency. We will pay the benefits which we would otherwise pay for the expense incurred in the treatment of a covered sickness. We will not pay for more than 30 days of active treatment in any one policy year.
What is meant by confinement in a hospital or a mental hospital?	Confinement in a hospital or a mental hospital, means: ● an insured person is confined to a hospital room for 24 hours or more, and ● a daily charge is made.
Are all hospital confinements covered?	No. In order for a hospital confinement to be covered: ● it must be for an injury or sickness ● it must begin while this coverage is in force for the person confined ● it must be at the direction of and under the supervision of a physician or surgeon.

CHILDBIRTH COVERAGE

(Check page 3 or any Amendment to the policy for names of insured persons for whom this coverage has been issued)

What benefit do we pay for normal childbirth or normal pregnancy?	The benefit we will pay due to nomal childbirth or normal pregnancy is shown on page 3.
What benefit do we pay for a Cesarean birth?	The benefit we will pay for a Cesarean birth will be 1½ times the benefit shown on page 3.
What do we mean by normal childbirth or normal pregnancy?	Normal childbirth or normal pregnancy means a pregnancy free of complications, as defined on page 4. Normal pregnancy includes false labor, occasional spotting, physician prescribed rest, morning sickness, hyperemesis gravidarum, pre-eclampsia or similar conditions associated with the management of a difficult pregnancy.
What conditions must be met for this benefit to be paid?	Benefits will be paid only if the childbirth occurs: ● 10 months or more from the effective date of this coverage for the insured person, and ● while this coverage is in force, except in event of the following. If we elect to non-renew this coverage, we shall provide for an extension of benefits for a pregnancy that began while this coverage was in force and for which we would have paid benefits had the coverage continued in force.

EXTENDED CARE FACILITY COVERAGE

(Check page 3 or any Amendment to the policy for names of insured persons for whom this coverage has been issued)

What benefit do we pay for expense while confined in an extended care facility?	The benefits for expense due to confinement in an extended care facility are: • up to the benefit amount per day which is shown on page 3 • for up to 30 days for any one accident of sickness
What requirements must be met for this expense to be paid?	In order for benefits to be paid under this coverage, the confinement: • must be for an injury or sickness • must begin while this coverage is in force for the person confined • must begin within 14 days after the person was confined in a hospital for 3 days or more • must be for treatment of the same injury or sickness which required the hospital confinement • must be authorized by and under the direction of a physician or surgeon.
What is an extended care facility?	See page 4 for the definition of an extended care facility.

EXTRA HOSPITAL MISCELLANEOUS EXPENSE COVERAGE

(Check page 3 or any Amendment to the policy for names of insured persons for whom this coverage has been issued)

What benefit do we pay under this coverage while confined in the hospital?	This coverage provides benefits when expense of $3,000 or more has been incurred for hospital services and supplies in one period of confinement. For any further expense incurred for such services and supplies in the same period of confinement for that person, we will pay: • 80 per cent of the expense incurred • up to the maximum benefit amount shown on page 3. The services do not include the expense for hospital room or for professional services of a radiologist, pathologist, anesthesiologist, nurse, physician, or surgeon.
What conditions must be met for this benefit to be paid?	In order for benefits to be paid under this coverage, the hospital confinement: • must be for an injury or sickness • must begin while this coverage is in force for the person confined • must be at the direction of and under the supervision of a physician or surgeon.

HOSPITAL INTENSIVE CARE UNIT COVERAGE

(Check page 3 or any Amendment to the policy for names of insured persons for whom this coverage has been issued)

What benefit do we pay for expense due to confinement in an intensive care unit of a hospital?	The benefit we will pay when confined in an intensive care unit of a hospital will be the expense, up to the daily amount shown on page 3 for the insured person.
What limits are imposed on this expense?	The benefit • will not be paid for more than 14 days during one period of hospital confinement • will not exceed the expense incurred, and • will be in lieu of the amount that would otherwise be paid for the hospital room.
What is an intensive care unit?	An intensive care unit means that part of a hospital which • is permanently equipped and staffed • provides more extensive care for the critically ill or injured patients than is available in other hospital rooms or wards • has trained and qualified personnel, including at least one graduate registered nurse in continuous attendance 24 hours a day, for the care and close observation of the confined patients and for which an additional hospital charge is made.
What conditions must be met for this benefit to be paid?	In order for benefits to be paid under this coverage, the hospital confinement: • must be for an injury or sickness • must begin while this coverage is in force for the person confined • must be at the direction of and under the supervision of a physician or surgeon.

COVERAGE FOR PHYSICIAN'S VISITS

(Check page 3 or any Amendment to the policy for names of insured persons for whom this coverage has been issued)

What benefit do we pay for expense due to a physician visit?	The maximum benefit amount we will pay for each visit by a physician is shown on page 3. We will not pay more than the amount charged for each visit. The visit must be for medical treatment.
Are there any limits imposed on physician's visits while hospital confined?	We will not pay for more than one visit per day. We will not pay for more than 31 visits during any one period of confinement.
Are benefits payable for a consulting physician while hospital confined?	If the attending physician requests a consulting physician's opinion, we will pay for up to 2 such consultations during one period of confinement for one accident or sickness The benefit amount shall be the same as we would otherwise pay for a physician visit.
Are there any limits imposed on physician's visits in the doctor's office, a clinic, or at home?	We will not pay for more than one visit per day. We will begin paying with the first visit for an injury and with the second visit for a sickness. We will not pay for more than 25 visits for any one accident or sickness.
What conditions must be met for these benefits to be paid?	In order for benefits to be paid under this coverage: • the treatment must be for an injury or sickness • the treatment must be begin while this coverage is in force for the person being treated, and • the medical treatment must be by a physician.
Are there any other limits imposed on this coverage?	Benefits will not be paid for a physician visit which relates to an injury or sickness for which surgery is performed.

COVERAGE FOR PHYSICIAN'S VISITS

(including Coverage for Clinical Social Worker)
(Check page 3 or any Amendment to the policy for names of insured persons for whom this coverage has been issued)

What benefit do we pay for expense due to a physician's or clinical social worker's visit?	The maximum benefit amount we will pay for each visit by a physician or clinical social worker is shown on page 3. We will not pay more than the amount charged for each visit. The visit must be for medical treatment.
Are there any limits imposed on physicians's visits or clinical social worker's visit while hospital confined?	We will not pay for more than one visit per day. We will not pay for more than 31 visits during any one period of confinement.
Are benefits payable for a consulting physician while hospital confined?	If the attending physician requests a consulting physician's opinion, we will pay for up to 2 such consultations during one period of confinement for one accident or sickness. The benefit amount shall be the same as we would otherwise pay for a physician visit.
Are there any limits imposed on physician's or clinical social worker's visits in their office, a clinic, or at home?	We will not pay for more than one visit per day. We will begin paying with the first visit for an injury and with the second visit for a sickness. We will not pay for more than 25 visits for any one accident or sickness.
What conditions must be met for these benefits to be paid?	In order for benefits to be paid under this coverage: • the treatment must be for an injury or sickness • the treatment must be begin while this coverage is in force for the person being treated, and • the medical treatment must be by a physician.
Are there any other limits imposed on this coverage?	Benefits will not be paid for a physician visit which relates to an injury or sickness for which surgery is performed.
What do we mean by a clinical social worker?	Clinical social worker shall mean an individual who is licensed as such by the state.

PRIVATE DUTY NURSE COVERAGE
(While Hospital Confined)

(Check page 3 or any Amendment to the policy for names of insured persons for whom this coverage has been issued)

What benefits do we pay for expense incurred for a private duty nurse while confined in the hospital?	The benefits for a private duty nurse when required during hospital confinement will be the expense incurred, subject to the following limits.
What limits are imposed on this expense?	For each day a private duty nurse is required, we will pay: • up to the amount shown on page 3 for the insured person for each 8 hour shift, and • up to 30 days of such service in one period of confinement.
What is a private duty nurse?	A Private Duty Nurse is a licensed Graduate Registered Nurse or a Licensed Vocational Nurse whose service is rendered solely for the insured person. A member of the insured person's immediate family shall not be considered a Private Duty Nurse.
What conditions must be met for this benefit to be paid?	In order for the service of a Private Duty Nurse to be covered: • the service must be rendered as the result of an injury or sickness • this coverage must be in force for the insured person when such service begins • the insured must be confined in the hospital • the service must be at the direction of and under the supervision of a physician or surgeon.

COVERAGE FOR SURGERY, DIAGNOSTIC PROCEDURES, AND FRACTURES

(Check page 3 or any Amendment to the policy for names of insured persons for whom this coverage has been issued)

What are the benefits for expense due to surgery?

The benefit for a surgical operation, diagnostic procedure or fracture is based upon the Schedule of Operations.

A certain percent is shown for each operation listed in the surgical schedule. We will pay up to this percent of the maximum surgical amount for that operation. The maximum surgical amount that will be paid for an insured person is stated on page 3. Our payment will not exceed the surgeon's fee.

When more than one surgical operation or diagnostic procedure is performed as the result of an accident or sickness, we will pay benefits a follows:

For Sickness

We will pay only the procedure which provides the larger benefit:

- when two or more surgical procedures are performed,
- when two or more diagnostic procedures are performed, and
- when both a surgical and diagnostic procedure are performed.

For Accident

If as the result of one accident multiple injuries are sustained which require more than one operation to be performed in separate operative fields and through separate incisions:

- we will pay up to the stated percent of the maximum for the most severe operation performed, and
- we will also pay 50% of the stated percent of the maximum for each additional operation or diagnostic procedure performed.

We will not pay for more than 3 operations (which includes diagnostic procedures).

If an operation or procedure is not listed in the Schedule of Operations, we will determine the amount to be paid based on other procedures of like severity.

Are benefits paid for anesthetic services?

Yes

We will pay 15% of the amount that is paid for an operation or diagnostic procedure performed. If more than one surgical operation is performed as the result of one accident or sickness, we will pay 15% of the greater benefit. We will not pay more than the amount charged or more than the expense.

Will benefits be paid if the insured person is not confined in the hospital?

The insured person need not be confined in the hospital for a benefit to be paid for this expense.

What conditions must be met for these benefits to be paid?

In order for benefits to be paid:

- the surgery must be for an injury or sickness
- this coverage must be in force for the person undergoing the surgery
- the surgery must be performed by a physician or surgeon.

SEE SURGICAL SCHEDULE

PART 1

SCHEDULE OF OPERATIONS

	% of Maximum Benefit
ABDOMEN	
Subtotal or hemi-gastrectomy, without vagotomy	76.0
Subtotal or hemi-gastrectomy, with vagotomy	84.0
Vagotomy and pyloroplasty, with or without gastrostomy	68.0
Enterectomy: resection of small intestine with anastomosis	68.0
Colectomy, partial, with anastomosis	72.0
Appendectomy	38.0
Exploratory laparotomy	40.0
Cholecystectomy	58.0
Pancreatectomy, subtotal	80.0
Pancreatectomy, whipple-type	100.0
Excision of lesion of pancreas (e.g., cyst, adenoma)	68.0
URINARY TRACT	
Nephrectomy (kidney removal) including partial ureterectomy, any approach	80.0
Nephrolithotomy, removal of kidney stone(s)	80.0
Cystotomy for excision of bladder tumor	64.0
Ureterolithotomy, middle one-third of ureter	72.0
Cystolithotomy: cystotomy with removal of calculus, without vesical neck resection	58.0
Cystourethroscopy with removal of ureteral calculus (stones)	28.0
CARDIOVASCULAR	
(Open heart surgery) mitral valve, valvotomy (commissurotomy), closed	100.0
Triple valve procedure, replacement and/or repair	100.0
Coronary angioplasty (endarterectomy, arterial implantation or anastomosis), with bypass	100.0
Aneurysm or occlusive disease, abdominal aorta	100.0
Ventricular septal defect, with bypass	100.0
Thromboendarterectomy combined aortailiac	100.0
Thromboendarterectomy, femoral and/or popliteal	100.0
Thromboendarterectomy, carotid or vertebral	100.0
Arterial embolectomy, direct aorta-iliac	80.0
Arterial embolectomy, direct, femoral-popliteal	64.0
Varicose veins ligation and division and complete stripping of long or short saphenous veins, unilateral	28.0
Ligation and division of long or short saphenous vein, bilateral	48.0

	% of Maximum Benefit
FRACTURES	
Clavicular fracture, closed manipulative reduction	12.0
Clavicular fracture, open (compound), with uncomplicated soft tissue closure, manipulative reduction	20.0
Humeral shaft fracture, closed manipulative reduction	20.0
Humeral shaft fracture, open (compound), open reduction, with or without internal or external skeletal fixation	44.0
Distal radial fracture (e.g. Colles' type) with or without fracture of ulnar styloid, closed (simple), manipulative reduction	16.0
Distal radial fracture (e.g. Colles' type), complex, requiring manipulative reduction, with or without internal or external skeletal fixation	24.0
Metacarpal fracture, single, closed manipulative reduction	9.6
Metacarpal fracture, single, open compound, open reduction, with or without internal or external skeletal fixation	28.0
Femur, fracture, proximal end, neck, closed (simple), closed manipulative reduction, including skeletal traction	38.0
Femur, fracture, proximal end, neck, open (compound), open reduction, internal fixation or prosthetic replacement	88.0
Femur, shaft fracture (including supracondylar), closed (simple), closed manipulative reduction	28.0
Femur, shaft fracture (including supracondylar), open (compound), with uncomplicated soft tissue closure, manipulative reduction	44.0
Tibia, shaft, fracture closed (simple), closed manipulative reduction	20.0
Tibia, shaft, fracture open (compound), open reduction with internal or external skeletal fixation	48.0
Tibia and fibula, fractures, shafts, closed (simple), closed manipulative reduction	26.0
Tibia and fibula, fractures, shafts, open (compound), with uncomplicated soft tissue closure, manipulative reduction	32.0
Tibia and fibula, bi-malleolar fracture ankle (including potts), closed (simple), closed manipulative reduction	20.0
Tibia and fibula, bi-malleolar fracture, ankle (including potts), open (compound), open reduction, with or without internal or external skeletal fixation	48.0

PART 1 **SCHEDULE OF OPERATIONS**

	% of Maximum Benefit
BRAIN	
Craniotomy — for removal of tumor, cyst or abcess	100.0
Burr Holes	
with exploration (no other surgery), unilateral	52.0
With removal of hematoma (blood tumor)	100.0
EYE	
Retina, reattachment (diathermy and/or cryotherapy), initial	80.0
with sclera buckling, resection or encircling tube, initial	100.0
Repair of retinal break(s) during same hospitalization	40.0
Cataract, extraction of lens, single	80.0
Muscle surgery, any number of muscles, one or both eyes	56.0
Pterygium, excision, simple	24.0
EAR	
Stapedectomy with prosthesis with fenestration of oval window	80.0
Tympanoplasty without mastoidectomy, post auricular or endaural approach	88.0
Fenestration of semicircular canal	88.0
Stapes mobilization, primary or secondary	48.0
Mastoidectomy, simple	48.0
Myringotomy, with or without eustachian tube inflation and/or aspiration	2.4
NOSE AND THROAT	
Tonsillectomy, with or without adenoidectomy	16.0
Sinus, antrotomy, radical, unilateral	48.0
Submucous resection, classic, for deviated septum	32.0
Laryngoscopy, operative, including foreign body removal	5.6
Bronchoscopy, with removal of foreign body	5.6
NECK	
Thyroidectomy, subtotal or partial	58.0
Thyroidectomy, total or subtotal, for malignancy with radical neck dissection	100.0
Excision of parotid-gland, total, with dissection of facial nerve	72.0
Thyroidectomy, total or complete	64.0
CHEST	
Lobectomy, total or partial	100.0
Thoracotomy, exploratory, including biopsy	48.0

	% of Maximum Benefit
CHEST (Cont.)	
Radical mastectomy, including muscles and lymph nodes, unilateral	72.0
Simple mastectomy, complete, unilateral	32.0
Simple mastectomy, complete, bilateral	40.0
Excision of cyst, or other benign tumor, unilateral	20.0
HERNIA	
Repair, diaphragmatic, transthoracic or transabdominal approach	68.0
Inguinal hernia, unilateral	36.0
Inguinal hernia, bilateral	48.0
Ventral hernia	44.0
Umbilical hernia	34.0
FEMALE GENITAL SYSTEM	
Total abdominal hysterectomy	64.0
Vaginal hysterectomy with anterior and/or posterior colporrhaphy	72.0
Combined anterior — posterior colporrhaphy for cystocele and rectocele	48.0
Dilation and currettage (nonpuerperal), and/or removal of polyps	16.0
Conization of cervix	19.2
Salpingo-oophorectomy (removal of tubes and ovaries)	48.0
MALE GENITAL SYSTEM	
Repair of hydrocele	24.0
Varicocele or ligation of spermatic veins for varicocele (independent procedure)	32.0
Prostatectomy, perineal, subtotal	80.0
Transurethral resection of prostate	80.0
RECTUM	
Hemorroidectomy, internal and external	28.0
Hemorroidectomy, external, complete	19.2
Fissurectomy, and hemorroidectomy	32.0
Fissurectomy, with or without sphincterotomy	19.2
Fistulectomy, subcutaneous	9.6
Complete proctectomy, combined abdominoperineal, one or two stages	100.0
SPINE	
Lumbar or thoracic disc excision, with bone graft (fusion, any approach)	100.0
Laminectomy, cervical or thoracic for intraspinal lesion	100.0
Vertebral body fracture and/or dislocation, open reduction	96.0
Excision of pilonidal cyst or sinus, simple	8.0
Excision of pilonidal cyst or sinus, extensive	28.0

PART 2 **SCHEDULE OF DIAGNOSTIC PROCEDURES**

	% of Maximum Benefit
Arteriogram	14.4
Angiogram,	
Unilateral	9.6
Bilateral	14.4
Biopsy	2.4
Bronchoscopy or Esophagoscopy	14.4

	% of Maximum Benefit
Cystoscopy	2.4
Gastroscopy	16.0
Gastroduodenscopy	19.2
Laparoscopy	5.6
Myelogram	2.4
Proctosigmoidoscopy	2.4

ANSWERS TO REVIEW QUESTIONS

— CHAPTER 1 — ANSWERS

1. risks
2. the insured
3. b. estimate future losses of a class or group of people.
4. b. a large group.
5. a. large number of homogeneous units
   b. loss must be ascertainable
   c. loss must be uncertain
   d. economic hardship
   e. exclusion of catastrophic perils
6. an annuity.
7. (1) facultative
   (2) treaty
8. (1) domestic
   (2) foreign
   (3) alien
9. Retaining risk
10. e. Insurer
11. b. Stock
12. The choices in this section are:
    (1) stock insurer
    (2) mutual insurer
    (3) reciprocal insurer
    (4) fraternal insurer
    (5) service insurer
    (6) government insurer
    (7) Lloyd's
    (8) assessment insurer
13. (1) agency
    (2) mass marketing
14. a. Independent agent
15. direct-response
16. a. Property/Casualty agent
17. (1) express
    (2) implied
    (3) apparent
18. do not have

If any of your answers were incorrect, please review the appropriate material.

— CHAPTER 2 — ANSWERS

1. *Paul v. Virginia* is the case that established the Supreme Court ruling that insurance conducted across state lines was not interstate commerce.
2. The South-Eastern Underwriters Decision is the case that reversed the *Paul v. Virginia* decision. With this decision it was decided that insurance conducted across state lines was, in fact, interstate commerce.
3. The purpose of the McCarran-Ferguson Act was to give the individual states authority to regulate insurance insofar as state laws did not conflict with existing federal law.
4. (1) Federal regulation
   (2) State regulation
   (3) Self-regulation
5. consumer
6. conducting pretext interviews
7. $5,000
8. To establish controls to protect the public from inaccurate or misused information.
9. disclosure authorization
10. $10,000, $50,000
11. annual statement
12. the Insurance Department
13. Rehabilitation
14. guaranty association
15. A.M. Best
16. capital and surplus
17. licensed
18. a, c, and d.
19. Countersignature is the signature of a resident agent on a policy sold by a nonresident agent.
20. b. resident agents

21. does not have
22. False. Notification must be immediate.
23. revocation, suspension, or refusal to renew
24. The insurer or the applicant
25. In the case of the applicant, the consideration consists of the statements made in the application and payment of the first premium. In the case of the insurer, it consists of the promises contained in the insurance contract.
26. The insured must be of legal age and mentally competent to enter into an insurance contract.
27. B. Insuring Clause
28. D. Exclusions
29. A. Policy Face
30. C. Conditions
31. C. Defamation
32. B. Twisting
33. A. Misrepresentation

If any of your answers were incorrect, please review the appropriate material.

— CHAPTER 3 —
ANSWERS

1. Transfer of the estate while the owner is alive
2. Transfer of the estate after the owner's death
3. Any four: Group retirement plans, savings, investments, annuities, Medicare, Medicaid, other income, Social Security
4. key person insurance
5. buy-sell agreement
6. False
7. (1) The primary insured's spouse
   (2) The primary insured's children
   (3) The primary insured's dependent parents
8. (1) whole life
   (2) term life
   (3) endowments
9. one year term insurance.
10. (1) Disability
    (2) Medicare
    (3) Retirement
    (4) Survivors
11. (1) average earnings under Social Security
    (2) age at retirement
    (3) additional earnings at retirement
12. False
13. C. Premiums
14. A. Dividends
15. D. Cash surrender value
16. B. Lump sum benefits

If any of your answers were incorrect, please review the appropriate material.

— CHAPTER 4 —
ANSWERS

1. adverse selection
2. True
3. is informed about the test and consents to it.
4. (1) mortality
   (2) interest
   (3) expenses
5. net
6. higher
7. premium mode
8. Reserves are accounting measurements of an insurer's liabilities to its policyholders.
9. a. and b.
10. c.
11. a, b, and c.
12. b, c, and d.
13. (1) list all replaced life insurance policies
    (2) give the applicant the Comparison Statement and Replacement Notice
    (3) give the insurer copies of the proposal and Comparison Statement
14. replacement actions are all in compliance with state regulations.

If any of your answers were incorrect, please review the appropriate material.

— CHAPTER 5 —
ANSWERS

1. Term
2. Convertible
3. Single premium
4. G. Whole Life insurance
5. B. Decreasing term
6. D. Limited payment whole life
7. H. Endowment insurance
8. A. Convertible
9. F. Single premium whole life
10. C. Level premiums
11. E. Term insurance
12. a. whole life and decreasing term
    b. whole life and level term
    c. whole life on head of household and term in smaller face amounts on other family members
13. B. Family Maintenance
14. J. Variable Life
15. C. Family Policy
16. G. Minimum Deposit
17. E. Joint Life Policies
18. A. Family Income

19. H. Modified Life
20. F. Juvenile Policies
21. D. Multiple Protection
22. I. Adjustable Life
23. K. Universal Life
24. small
25. weekly (or monthly)
26. False
27. False.
28. C. Return of Premium
29. A. Rider
30. D. Accidental Death
31. E. Waiver of Premium
32. B. Guaranteed Insurability
33. Under the generalized approach the benefits paid to the insured will not affect the life policy's face amount or cash value. The integrated approach links the LTC benefits paid to the life policy's face amount and/or cash value.
34. Payment of LTC benefits reduces the face amount of the life policy.

If any of your answers were incorrect, please review the appropriate material.

— CHAPTER 6 —

ANSWERS

1. H. Incontestability
2. D. Modifications
3. I. Entire Contract
4. A. Reinstatement
5. B. Assignment
6. F. Grace Period
7. C. Policy Loans
8. G. Free Look
9. E. Beneficiary
10. C. Class Designation
11. B. Contingent Beneficiary
12. D. Common Disaster
13. A. Revocable
14. Status clause and results clause
15. Two years

If any of your answers were incorrect, please review the appropriate material.

— CHAPTER 7 —

ANSWERS

1. Interest only, fixed-period income, fixed-amount income, and life income
2. The insurer holds the proceeds and pays the interest on them at periodic intervals. When the primary beneficiary dies, the interest may continue to be payable to a contingent beneficiary, or the principal may be paid to the estate of the insured or the beneficiary. Many companies hesitate to agree to pay the proceeds to the estate of the policyowner upon the death of a beneficiary because his or her estate may have been closed for years, and the delays and cost in reopening it to receive the proceeds may not be economical.
3. Generally speaking, fixed-period income should be used when it is desirable to have some income for a certain number of years (such as until children are grown up). Fixed-amount should be used when it is desirable to have as high an income as possible for at least some length of time (such as a period of time during which a family is readjusting from the loss of the earned income of a father, to earning its own way, and a higher income is needed until they find jobs, or until the mother completes a refresher course in business school to upgrade her job potential).
4. In the case of the former, the income ends when the recipient dies. In the second, it is guaranteed to someone for the period certain even if the recipient dies; if he or she survives the period certain, then it becomes life income to him or her only.
5. The income is paid jointly (either with or without a period certain) to more than one person, and some percentage of it is continued to the survivor after the death of the joint person(s).
6. Paid-up insurance, cash surrender value, extended term insurance
7. It ceases to be in force and he or she must surrender the policy.
8. Generally speaking, the insured should elect paid-up insurance when he or she wants to be sure to have some insurance for life (or to the maturity date of the original policy, if sooner). The insured should elect extended term when he or she wants to be sure the full amount of the original policy is in force for as long as the table of nonforfeiture values in the policy shows the extended term will run.
9. participating
10. paid-up additions
11. Cash

If any of your answers were incorrect, please review the appropriate material.

— CHAPTER 8 —
ANSWERS

1. An annuity is a periodic payment that commences at a stated or contingent date and continues for a fixed period or for the duration of a designated life or lives.
2. The life insurance policy provides that if the insured pays the insurer regular installments while he or she is alive or for a stated period, the insurer will pay his or her beneficiary a lump sum when he or she dies. The annuity contract provides that if the annuitant pays the insurer a lump sum or installments while he or she is alive, the insurer will pay him or her an income when he or she reaches a given age, or upon a certain date.
3. An annuity certain pays a stated periodic benefit for a stated number of years whether the annuitant lives or dies. (If he or she dies, it is paid to his or her beneficiary or estate.) A "life" annuity pays only so long as the annuitant lives, but it pays whether or not the total paid is in excess of the consideration paid.
4. A refund annuity pays a refund if the annuitant dies before the end of the guaranteed period or before the total amount of the premium has been paid back in annuity payments.
5. A variable annuity is an annuity that guarantees to pay an income for a specified duration with the amount of income varying according to the market value of funds invested in equities.
6. Three types of variable annuities are: single premium immediate variable annuity, single premium deferred variable annuity, and periodic payment variable annuity.
7. A. Keogh Plan
8. C. IRA
9. B. Pension Plan
10. D. Profit Sharing Plan

If any of your answers were incorrect, please review the appropriate material.

— CHAPTER 9 —
ANSWERS

1. The wage earner
2. Because the policy benefits are limited to payment only for loss due to cancer.
3. Accidental Death and Dismemberment
4. True
5. To cover groups such as campers, school athletic teams, and volunteer groups.
6. Medical expense insurance could be used to cover the individual's (and family's) health insurance needs, and disability income insurance could be used to cover ongoing family expenses (mortgage, living expenses).
7. True
8. True
9. It limits the employer's liability from potentially catastrophic claims in the case of a self-funded health care plan.
10. To provide insurance at reasonable rates to small groups who would not otherwise be able to obtain affordable insurance.
11. True
12. B. Medicaid
13. D. CHAMPUS
14. F. Preferred Provider Organization (PPO)
15. C. Health Maintenance Organization (HMO)
16. E. Third-Party Administrator (TPA)
17. A. Exclusive Provider Organization (EPO)
18. (1) Medical
    (2) Income
    (3) Death
    (4) Rehabilitation
19. True
20. 66 2/3%; minimum and maximum weekly limits.
21. covered individual; employer, union, trust, or other sponsoring organization.
22. credit health insurance.
23. The labor union must:
    (1) have a constitution and bylaws
    (2) be organized and maintained in good faith for purposes other than obtaining insurance
    (3) have insurance for the purpose of covering members, employees, or the employees of members for the benefit of persons other than the association or its officers or trustees
24. True
25. False
26. True
27. False
28. False

If any of your answers were incorrect, please review the appropriate material.

— CHAPTER 10 —
ANSWERS

1. approve, disapprove
2. True
3. a. The basic application requires the signature of the applicant.

4 agent
5. disciplinary action
6. application
7. True
8. (1) age
   (2) sex
   (3) occupation
   (4) physical condition
   (5) moral and morale hazards
9. rider.
10. c. cover all the insurer's policy payment obligations.
11. a. The agent is required to keep accurate records of all transactions involving the applicant's money.
12. c. no loss - no gain

If any of your answers were incorrect, please review the appropriate material.

— CHAPTER 11 —

ANSWERS

1. E. Time Limit on Certain Defenses
2. G. Proof of Loss
3. A. Grace Period
4. C. Uniform Mandatory Provisions
5. F. Payment of Claims
6. D. Reinstatement
7. B. Legal Actions
8. D. Change of Occupation
9. C. Illegal Occupations
10. A. Insurance with Other Insurers
11. B. Relation of Earnings to Insurance
12. E. Unpaid Premium
13. insuring clause
14. policy face
15. optionally
16. evidence of insurability
17. c. the insured's 25-year-old child who became physically disabled at age 24.
18. total medical expenses incurred
19. Consolidated Omnibus Budget Reconciliation Act (COBRA)
20. TEFRA
21. OBRA
22. ERISA

If any of your answers were incorrect, please review the appropriate material.

— CHAPTER 12 —

ANSWERS

1. B. Total Disability
2. C. Disability Income
3. A. Elimination Period
4. D. Partial Disability
5. E. Temporary Disability
6. G. Accidental Bodily Injury
7. J. Maximum Benefit Period
8. H. Long-Term
9. I. Common Exclusions
10. F. Residual Disability
11. b. rehabilitation benefit.
12. a. cost of living benefit.
13. c. additional monthly benefit rider.
14. a. hospital confinement rider.
15. d. future increase option.
16. up
17. The insured can purchase additional amounts of insurance without evidence of insurability.
18. c. Both are correct
19. d. all of the above
20. b. Business Overhead Expense
21. c. Key Person Disability Insurance
22. a. Disability Buy-Sell Insurance
23. are, are
24. are not, are

If any of your answers were incorrect, please review the appropriate material.

— CHAPTER 13 —

ANSWERS

1. B. Major Medical Insurance
2. C. Comprehensive Medical Insurance
3. A. Basic Medical Expense Policy
4. D. Coinsurance
5. False
6. True
7. $600 (30 x 20)
8. hospice expenses.
9. common accident
10. out of pocket limit.

If any of your answers were incorrect, please review the appropriate material.

— CHAPTER 14 —

ANSWERS

1. Part A, Hospital insurance benefits
2. Part B, Medical insurance benefits
3. c. Second surgical opinions required by Medicare
4. To recognize the higher health care costs of metropolitan vs. rural areas.
5. c. 20%

6. b. guaranteed renewable.
7. d. Medicare Supplement
8. True
9. b. Long-term care
10. c. preexisting conditions at policy inception.

If any of your answers were incorrect, please review the appropriate material.

SAMPLE EXAMINATION

Instructions

If you have completed your study of the material in this manual, you are ready to take the sample examination on the following pages. This sample examination will help you determine your preparedness for the licensing examination.

The test serves a dual purpose. First, it will help you determine whether or not your study of the material has been adequate. Second, it will help familiarize you with the kind of test you will take when you apply for your license. These sample questions are in the same style and format as the actual questions you will find on the licensing examination.

While taking the test, it may benefit you to circle any questions that you have difficulty with. Even if you choose the correct answer, it might be a good idea to review any material that you are unsure of. Use the blank Sample Examination Answer Sheet on the last page of this book to take the exam. After you complete the sample examination, check your answers against the Answer Sheet that follows the exam. Incorrect answers and circled questions will indicate the areas where you need to apply more study time. Whenever you return to sections of the manual for additional study, the review questions in each section may be used as a guide to determine whether you have mastered the material.

LIFE INSURANCE

1. In which company do stockholders share in the profits and losses of the insurer?
   (A) Stock
   (B) Mutual
   (C) Service
   (D) Assessment

2. In which company do policyholders receive policy dividends when there is a profit?
   (A) Stock
   (B) Mutual
   (C) Service
   (D) Assessment

3. All of the following persons would be considered as having INSURABLE INTEREST in the party they are insuring EXCEPT:
   (A) a citizen who wished to insure the life of the President of the United States.
   (B) a husband insuring the life of his wife.
   (C) a man insuring his own life.
   (D) a man insuring his business partner.

4. The LAW OF LARGE NUMBERS states that:
   (A) predictions become more accurate as the number of units being considered increases.
   (B) large losses are easier to predict.
   (C) small losses are predictable.
   (D) all losses are predictable.

5. Insurable risks must involve:
   (A) certain losses only.
   (B) the possibility of loss only.
   (C) certain and uncertain losses.
   (D) gambling.

6. An agent is a representative of:
   (A) the insured.
   (B) the policyowner.
   (C) the general agency system.
   (D) the insurance company.

7. BLUE CROSS and BLUE SHIELD PLANS are provided by what kind of insurer?
   (A) Stock
   (B) Mutual
   (C) Service
   (D) Assessment

8. An agent's responsibilities may include all of the following EXCEPT:
   (A) collection of premiums.
   (B) informing the principal of pertinent facts.
   (C) changing provisions in the policy
   (D) delivering the policy.

9. All of the following are powers of an insurance agent EXCEPT:
   (A) the express powers contained in the agency contract.
   (B) the apparent powers acquired through usage in the industry.
   (C) the implied powers the agent has exercised beyond his agency agreement which the company has failed to protest.
   (D) the power to reinstate a lapsed insurance policy by accepting past due premiums.

10. Which of the following terms means a voluntary abandonment or extinguishment by a party of a legal right or advantage?
    (A) Waiver
    (B) Estoppel
    (C) Parol evidence rule
    (D) Representation

11. Which of the following is NOT one of the traditional forms of life insurance?
    (A) Endowment
    (B) Whole life insurance
    (C) Group life insurance
    (D) Term insurance

12. All of the following statements regarding KEOGH PLANS are true EXCEPT:
    (A) they may be profit-sharing plans.
    (B) they apply to self-employed persons and their employees.
    (C) they may be funded by means of an annuity.
    (D) distributions prior to age 59½ are tax deductible.

13. A retirement plan set up as a fixed liability for corporate forms of business is called a(n):
    (A) Keogh plan.
    (B) Individual Retirement Account.
    (C) pension plan.
    (D) buy and sell agreement.

14. As a general rule, lump sum benefits payable to a beneficiary under a life insurance policy:
    (A) are totally subject to federal income tax.
    (B) are subject to federal income tax to the extent benefits exceed premiums.
    (C) are subject to federal income tax to the extent premiums exceed benefits.
    (D) are not subject to federal income tax at all.

15. GROUP LIFE INSURANCE is usually written as:
    (A) whole life insurance.
    (B) one-year term insurance.
    (C) an endowment.
    (D) five-year term insurance.

16. The Traditional Net Cost and Interest-Adjusted Cost methods of comparing the costs of life insurance policies are similar, EXCEPT the second method accounts for:
    (A) an interest rate.
    (B) the time value of money.
    (C) estate planning.
    (D) surrendering the policy before maturity.

17. In TERM INSURANCE, cash values are:
    (A) always provided.
    (B) usually not provided.
    (C) provided when the policy exceeds $10,000 face amount of insurance.
    (D) larger than for ordinary policies.

18. TERM INSURANCE is best used for those individuals with:
    (A) high incomes.
    (B) a need for accumulating loan values.
    (C) a need for temporary protection.
    (D) a need for lifelong coverage.

19. All of the following apply to a TERM POLICY EXCEPT:
    (A) it provides temporary insurance.
    (B) it usually builds no permanent values.
    (C) it may be converted to another type of policy.
    (D) it pays at the end of a stated period.

20. Which policy is not restricted to a stated period of time?
    (A) Increasing term
    (B) Decreasing term
    (C) Endowment
    (D) Whole life

21. Which policy may usually be converted into a different type?
    (A) Endowment
    (B) Whole life
    (C) Term
    (D) Industrial

22. DECREASING TERM INSURANCE:
    (A) increases the amount in force until the end of the term period.
    (B) decreases the amount in force to zero at the end of the term period.
    (C) provides permanent coverage.
    (D) none of the above statements are true.

23. If an insured purchased a 20-year FAMILY MAINTENANCE POLICY at age 25, and then died at age 35, how long would benefits be paid to his or her beneficiaries?
    (A) 5 years
    (B) 10 years
    (C) 20 years
    (D) 30 years

24. If an insured purchased a 20-year FAMILY INCOME POLICY at age 25, and then died at 35, how long would benefits be paid to his or her beneficiaries?
    (A) 5 years
    (B) 10 years
    (C) 20 years
    (D) 30 years

25. All of the following statements concerning ENDOWMENT policies are true EXCEPT:
    (A) they offer protection against death for a stated period of time.
    (B) if the insured dies during the endowment period, the beneficiary is paid nothing.
    (C) if the insured lives to the end of the endowment period, the policy pays the face amount to the insured.
    (D) an endowment policy may be used for retirement purposes.

26. Which of the following statements is true regarding INDUSTRIAL LIFE INSURANCE?
    (A) Premiums are payable yearly.
    (B) The face amount of insurance involved is at least $10,000.
    (C) It was designed for factory workers.
    (D) None of the above statements are true.

27. Which life insurance provision states that the company agrees not to use as a defense any error, concealment or misstatement on the part of the insured after the policy has been in effect a specified length of time?
    (A) Participating
    (B) Nonforfeiture
    (C) Incontestability
    (D) Insuring clause

28. The beneficiary of the proceeds of a life insurance policy can be:
    (A) a trust.
    (B) an estate.
    (C) a child.
    (D) all of the above.

29. Which life insurance provision recognizes the equity built up in the early years of a life insurance policy?
    (A) Nonforfeiture
    (B) Grace period
    (C) Payment of premiums
    (D) Incontestability

30. Which life insurance policy provision states that the insured has 30-31 days or one month from the premium due date to make a premium payment?
    (A) Nonforfeiture
    (B) Grace period
    (C) Payment of premiums
    (D) Incontestability

31. If the insured's age is misstated in a life insurance policy, what amount is payable under the policy?
    (A) Nothing
    (B) Half the stated amount
    (C) Twice the amount
    (D) The amount the premium would have purchased at the correct age of the insured

32. All of the following are EXCLUSIONS in life insurance policies EXCEPT:
    (A) suicide.
    (B) accidental death.
    (C) aviation.
    (D) war clause.

33. A "REVOCABLE" LIFE INSURANCE BENEFICIARY is one which:
    (A) cannot be changed.
    (B) can be changed without the knowledge or consent of the beneficiary.
    (C) can be changed with the knowledge of the beneficiary only.
    (D) can only be changed by the beneficiary.

34. Under the "UNIFORM SIMULTANEOUS DEATH LAW," who is considered to have died first if the insured and the primary beneficiary die simultaneously?
    (A) The insured
    (B) The beneficiary
    (C) Neither the insured nor the beneficiary
    (D) None of the above

35. Which of the following life insurance provisions means a transfer of all or a portion of the policyowner's rights under an insurance contract?
    (A) Assignment
    (B) Policy change
    (C) Policy year
    (D) Modifications

36. Which of the following statements is FALSE regarding loan values on life insurance policies?
    (A) After a policy that has a cash value element has been in force for some period of time (usually three years) it must contain some cash value which the policyowner may value.
    (B) The amount of any unpaid loan amount may be deducted from the death benefit.
    (C) The insurer is prohibited from charging the policyowner interest for borrowing his or her own money.
    (D) The insurer may defer a loan request for up to six months from the date of application.

37. A clause allowing the policyholder to inspect and, if dissatisfied, to return a policy for a full refund, is known as:
    (A) waiver of premium.
    (B) facility of payments.
    (C) probationary period.
    (D) free look.

38. If life insurance is used to protect against premature death, what is used to protect against the risk of living too long?
    (A) An annuity
    (B) A rider
    (C) A combination form
    (D) An endowment

39. All of the following statements regarding ANNUITIES are true EXCEPT:
    (A) annuities do not involve risk sharing.
    (B) annuities are sold by life insurance agents.
    (C) an annuity is a periodic payment.
    (D) the annuitant can pay the annuity premium in a lump sum.

40. What is the purpose of the VARIABLE ANNUITY?
    (A) To allow the annuitant an income relating to the variations in the cost of living
    (B) To allow the annuitant to pay off the annuity at different rates throughout the years
    (C) To allow the annuitant a discount on the cost of annuity
    (D) None of the above reasons

41. When does the insurer begin to pay the annuitant an annuity?
    (A) On the annuitant's 65th birthday
    (B) When the annuitant reaches a predetermined date
    (C) When the annuitant dies
    (D) Never

42. Which of the following is a NON-FORFEITURE OPTION?
    (A) Fixed-period installments
    (B) Extended term insurance
    (C) Accumulation at interest
    (D) Accelerated endowment

43. Which of the following is NOT a DIVIDEND OPTION?
    (A) Application to reduce premium
    (B) Extended term insurance
    (C) Cash
    (D) Paid-up insurance value

44. Which of the following descriptions accurately defines the ACCUMULATION AT INTEREST life insurance dividend option?
    (A) Dividends accumulate with interest paid on them at a rate specified in the policy.
    (B) Dividends are taken in the form of cash.
    (C) Dividends are used to pay part of the premium due when a dividend is declared.
    (D) Dividends are used to buy one-year term insurance.

45. All of the following statements are true regarding DIVIDEND OPTIONS in participating policies EXCEPT:
    (A) the dividend can be taken in the form of cash.
    (B) when the dividend is accumulated at interest, the interest is taxable.
    (C) the dividend may be applied toward the premium due.
    (D) additional paid-up participating insurance may not be surrendered for a cash surrender value.

46. A SETTLEMENT OPTION is an option for:
    (A) accumulating dividends.
    (B) donating proceeds to charity.
    (C) taking proceeds in other than a lump sum.
    (D) making a policy loan.

47. All of the following statements are true under the LIFE INCOME SETTLEMENT OPTION EXCEPT:
    (A) proceeds are retained by the insurer and paid to the beneficiary in equal installments.
    (B) the beneficiary receives installments for the rest of his or her life.
    (C) there is no refund of premium when the beneficiary dies.
    (D) only interest earned is paid to the beneficiary.

48. All of the following are true regarding optional modes of settlement EXCEPT:
    (A) with the fixed-amount option, the size of the payment determines the duration of the payments.
    (B) the fixed-period option is sometimes called the "amount option."
    (C) with the interest only option, only the interest on the policy proceeds is paid to the payee and at a guaranteed minimum rate.
    (D) with the fixed-period option, the duration of the payments determines the size of the payments.

49. Under what kind of life insurance settlement option is income paid throughout the lives of two or more beneficiaries?
    (A) Joint and survivor
    (B) Interest only
    (C) Life income
    (D) Fixed-period installments

50. If the insured chooses the PAID-UP INSURANCE NONFORFEITURE OPTION:
    (A) the paid-up insurance may be of any type the insured chooses.
    (B) he or she must pay a monthly premium until the paid-up insurance is an even dollar amount.
    (C) the amount purchased will be as much as the cash value will purchase at the insured's current age.
    (D) the face amount of the paid-up insurance will be the same as that of the original policy.

HEALTH INSURANCE

1. Which element of contract formation requires that an applicant for insurance have the legal capacity to make a contract?
   (A) Agreement
   (B) Consideration
   (C) Competent parties
   (D) Legal object

2. Which element of contract formation shows that each party is giving value or assuming responsibility?
   (A) Agreement
   (B) Consideration
   (C) Competent parties
   (D) Legal object

3. Which of the following terms means that an insurance contract is dependent upon chance or uncertain outcome?
   (A) Valued
   (B) Aleatory
   (C) Unilateral
   (D) Adhesion

4. All of the following statements regarding CONCEALMENT are false EXCEPT:
   (A) concealment is never grounds for rescission of a policy.
   (B) concealment is the failure to disclose any known fact.
   (C) if concealment is suspected, the burden of proof is on the insured.
   (D) concealment involves answering a question without an intent to defraud.

5. A WARRANTY in insurance is:
   (A) a failure to disclose a material fact.
   (B) a statement made by the applicant as an inducement to the formation of the contract.
   (C) a statement or condition that the applicant represents to be absolutely true.
   (D) a statement that the contract is not contrary to public policy.

6. All of the following statements are true about a REPRESENTATION EXCEPT:
   (A) a representation of a fact is the same as an expression of opinion.
   (B) it usually appears in an application.
   (C) a policy is usually voidable if a misrepresentation is of a material fact.
   (D) representations are sometimes given orally.

7. The FAIR CREDIT REPORTING ACT:
   (A) provides guidelines on premium financing.
   (B) is not applicable to the insurance industry.
   (C) sets up procedures for consumer reporting agencies.
   (D) prohibits the use of information on a consumer's character, general reputation and mode of living.

8. All of the following statements about consumer reporting agencies are true EXCEPT:
   (A) they have to reinvestigate disputed material.
   (B) the information they provide cannot be the sole reason for denial of insurance.
   (C) the consumer may file a brief statement with the agency concerning disputed material.
   (D) they must require identification of users of the information.

9. Which of the following contractual elements consists of the "offer" and "acceptance"?
   (A) Consideration
   (B) Agreement
   (C) Competent parties
   (D) Legal object

10. All of the following statements regarding health insurance are true EXCEPT:
    (A) policy coverages are regulated only by the federal government.
    (B) there is a wide assortment of policies available.
    (C) disability insurance may pay for loss of income due to accident.
    (D) disability insurance may pay for loss of income due to sickness.

11. All of the following are true statements about DISMEMBERMENT COVERAGE EXCEPT:
    (A) it is usually written with accidental death coverage.
    (B) loss of sight is usually covered.
    (C) loss must occur within 10 days of the date of the accident.
    (D) a schedule of payment is made a part of the policy.

12. Which of the following health insurance policies provides coverage for a business when the owner of the business is disabled?
    (A) Key employee disability insurance
    (B) Business overhead expense insurance
    (C) Social Security
    (D) Medicare

13. Insurance that would pay for hiring a replacement for an important employee who is disabled is known as:
    (A) key person disability insurance.
    (B) business overhead expense insurance.
    (C) blanket disability income.
    (D) group disability insurance.

14. Which of the following factors is not of primary importance in underwriting a HEALTH INSURANCE POLICY?
    (A) The physical condition of the applicant
    (B) The occupation of the applicant
    (C) The age of the applicant
    (D) The marital status of the applicant

15. If an insured malingers after an illness, collecting health insurance benefits, and not returning to work, what kind of hazard is this considered?
    (A) Physical
    (B) Morale
    (C) Certain
    (D) Uncertain

16. All of the following are true regarding the health insurance application EXCEPT:
    (A) The health insurance application is usually attached to and made part of the policy.
    (B) A physical exam is always required as part of the application process.
    (C) Insurers may use different application forms for different health insurance coverages.
    (D) The application must be signed by the insured, the policyowner, and the agent.

17. Under reimbursement plans benefits are paid to the:
    (A) hospital.
    (B) insured.
    (C) physician.
    (D) insurance company.

18. Which of the following groups could be covered under a group accident and health policy if qualified?
    (A) Employees of a corporation
    (B) An association of employers in the trucking industry
    (C) A labor union
    (D) All of the above

19. All of the following types of benefits are available under SOCIAL SECURITY EXCEPT:
    (A) retirement.
    (B) survivor.
    (C) workers compensation.
    (D) disability.

20. The two basic parts of the MEDICARE PROGRAM are:
    (A) hospital insurance and medical insurance.
    (B) inpatient hospital service and outpatient services.
    (C) hospital benefits and disability benefits.
    (D) hospital service and home health services.

21. All of the following statements are true about MEDICAID EXCEPT:
    (A) it provides medical assistance only.
    (B) it supplements Medicare for those aged 65 and over.
    (C) it is entirely funded by the state.
    (D) it provides medical assistance to the aged, the blind and the disabled.

22. Health coverage providers emphasizing preventive health care are called:
    (A) franchise health insurers.
    (B) service organizations.
    (C) health maintenance organizations.
    (D) group insurers.

23. Disability income is considered taxable income to the insured if:
    (A) the employer paid the premiums.
    (B) the insured paid the premiums.
    (C) it was the only income the insured received during the year.
    (D) he or she is not eligible for the disability income exclusion.

24. All of the following statements concerning MEDICARE are true EXCEPT:
    (A) both hospital insurance and medical insurance are mandatory.
    (B) it provides medical assistance to the aged.
    (C) home health service may be provided.
    (D) inpatient hospital services cover most hospital service.

25. Which of the UNIFORM MANDATORY PROVISIONS in a health insurance policy restricts agents from waiving any of the provisions in the policy?
    (A) Entire contract; changes
    (B) Time limit on certain defenses
    (C) Reinstatement
    (D) Legal actions

26. All of the following are UNIFORM MANDATORY PROVISIONS in individual health insurance policies EXCEPT:
    (A) change of occupation.
    (B) grace period.
    (C) entire contract; changes.
    (D) reinstatement.

27. Which of the following is the usual GRACE PERIOD for a semi-annual premium policy?
    (A) 7 days
    (B) 20 days
    (C) 31 days
    (D) 60 days

28. All of the following statements are true about REINSTATEMENT EXCEPT:
    (A) in some cases, it can be effected without an application.
    (B) the reinstatement premium cannot be applied retroactively prior to the date of reinstatement.
    (C) a reinstatement policy covers only injuries occurring after the date of reinstatement.
    (D) a reinstatement policy covers only sickness that begins ten days after the date of reinstatement.

29. All of the following are UNIFORM OPTIONAL PROVISIONS in individual health insurance policies EXCEPT:
    (A) notice of claim.
    (B) misstatement of age.
    (C) unpaid premiums.
    (D) intoxicants and narcotics.

30. All of the following are requirements for individual health insurance policies EXCEPT:
    (A) only an agent can alter a statement on the application.
    (B) effective and termination dates must be expressed in the policy.
    (C) false statements on the application bar recovery if material to the risk.
    (D) all money and other considerations must be expressed in the policy.

31. All of the following are true statements about the INSURING CLAUSE of a health policy EXCEPT:
    (A) it provides a general definition of coverage provided.
    (B) it identifies the insurer and the insured.
    (C) it includes a schedule of premium payments.
    (D) it states what kind of loss is covered.

32. All of the following are usually excluded in HEALTH INSURANCE POLICIES EXCEPT:
    (A) suicide.
    (B) accidents.
    (C) war.
    (D) overseas residence.

33. A clause allowing the policyholder to inspect, and if dissatisfied to return a policy for a full refund, is known as:
    (A) waiver of premium.
    (B) facility of payments.
    (C) probationary period.
    (D) 10-day free look.

34. Under the optional health insurance provision MISSTATEMENT OF AGE, what happens to benefits when the insured's age is misstated on the application?
    (A) They are not paid.
    (B) They are cancelled.
    (C) They are not paid for the first claim only.
    (D) They are paid according to what the premium actually paid would have purchased at the correct age.

35. Which of the following provisions states that claims for specific losses must be paid immediately upon receipt of proof of loss?
    (A) Grace period
    (B) Reinstatement
    (C) Notice of claim
    (D) Time of payments of claim

36. If the insured has no renewal right under the policy, his or her policy is:
    (A) conditionally renewable.
    (B) guaranteed renewable.
    (C) optionally renewable.
    (D) non-cancellable.

37. If a health insurance policy is NON-CANCELLABLE, the insurer may increase the premiums:
    (A) at renewal.
    (B) at any anniversary date.
    (C) at any premium due date.
    (D) the insurer may not increase the premiums.

38. According to the CONFORMITY WITH STATE STATUTES provision, if the policy is in conflict with state statutes:
    (A) it is amended to conform to the minimum requirements of state law.
    (B) it is null and void.
    (C) the insurer will be fined as a penalty.
    (D) the agent must change the conflicting provision of the policy.

39. Total disability typically means that an individual is unable to perform the duties of the occupation for which he is suited by:
    (A) education.
    (B) training.
    (C) experience.
    (D) any of the above.

40. DISABILITY INCOME POLICIES differ by:
    (A) whether or not coverage is provided in addition to workers compensation.
    (B) the elimination period required.
    (C) the definition of disability used.
    (D) all of the above.

41. An ELIMINATION PERIOD:
    (A) guards against preexisting conditions.
    (B) specifies a number of days which must expire after an accident before benefits will be paid.
    (C) guarantees that the contract will be renewable.
    (D) avoids adverse selection.

42. DENTAL EXPENSE coverage may include:
    (A) oral surgery.
    (B) periodontics.
    (C) preventive care.
    (D) all of the above.

43. BASIC MEDICAL EXPENSE POLICIES provide coverage in all of the following areas EXCEPT:
    (A) basic hospital expenses.
    (B) basic medical expenses.
    (C) basic surgical expenses.
    (D) yearly checkups.

44. All of the following statements are true concerning surgical expense benefits in BASIC MEDICAL EXPENSE POLICIES EXCEPT:
    (A) only operations listed on the schedule are covered.
    (B) benefits are usually limited to a dollar amount.
    (C) benefits may be expressed as multiples of the hospital benefit maximum.
    (D) a relative value may be used to determine the benefit amount available.

45. All of the following statements regarding miscellaneous expense benefits provided by BASIC MEDICAL EXPENSE POLICIES are true EXCEPT:
    (A) they may provide extended care benefits.
    (B) they are usually based on a multiple of the daily hospital room benefit.
    (C) they may be stated as a flat amount.
    (D) they are based on actual expenses incurred.

46. A MAJOR MEDICAL INSURANCE POLICY would cover expenses for all of the following EXCEPT:
    (A) doctor's fees for an operation.
    (B) charges covered under workers compensation insurance.
    (C) hospital room and board charges.
    (D) charges for cosmetic surgery necessitated by an accident.

47. All of the following statements regarding MAJOR MEDICAL INSURANCE POLICIES are true EXCEPT:
    (A) they provide first dollar coverage.
    (B) they pay for catastrophic medical expenses.
    (C) they often have a coinsurance provision.
    (D) maximum benefits apply per person in a family.

48. If the coinsurance feature in a MAJOR MEDICAL INSURANCE POLICY is 75%-25% with a $100 deductible, how much of a $2,100 bill would the insured pay?
    (A) $1,500
    (B) $100
    (C) $500
    (D) $600

49. Which of the following is true of MAJOR MEDICAL EXPENSE POLICIES?
    (A) they do not have deductible features.
    (B) they require a $100 per hospitalization deductible.
    (C) they have high maximum coverage.
    (D) they provide first dollar coverage.

50. MEDICARE SUPPLEMENT POLICIES:
    (A) are provided by the federal government.
    (B) only pay for the same health services covered by Medicare.
    (C) pay some or all of Medicare's deductibles and co-payments.
    (D) are usually necessary if an individual is covered by Medicaid.

SAMPLE EXAMINATION ANSWERS

LIFE INSURANCE

Q	A	Page Reference
1.	A	1-6
2.	B	1-6
3.	A	1-3
4.	A	1-3
5.	B	1-3
6.	D	1-10
7.	C	1-7
8.	C	1-14
9.	D	1-13
10.	A	1-13
11.	C	3-10
12.	D	8-9
13.	C	8-8
14.	D	3-17
15.	B	3-10
16.	A	3-3
17.	B	5-3
18.	C	5-3
19.	D	5-1
20.	D	5-3
21.	C	5-1
22.	B	5-2
23.	C	5-9
24.	B	5-9
25.	B	5-7
26.	C	5-19
27.	C	6-3
28.	D	6-7
29.	A	7-4
30.	B	6-2
31.	D	6-4
32.	B	6-10
33.	B	6-6
34.	B	6-9
35.	A	6-3
36.	C	6-2
37.	D	6-4
38.	A	8-1
39.	A	8-1
40.	A	8-6
41.	B	8-2
42.	B	7-4
43.	B	7-7
44.	A	7-7
45.	D	7-7
46.	C	7-1
47.	D	7-2
48.	B	7-1
49.	A	7-2
50.	C	7-4

HEALTH INSURANCE

Q	A	Page Reference
1.	C	2-15
2.	B	2-14
3.	B	2-15
4.	B	2-16
5.	C	2-16
6.	A	2-16
7.	C	2-2
8.	B	2-2
9.	B	2-14
10.	A	9-1
11.	C	9-1
12.	B	12-10
13.	A	12-10
14.	D	10-3
15.	B	10-3
16.	B	10-2
17.	B	9-4
18.	D	9-15
19.	C	9-10
20.	A	14-1
21.	C	9-11
22.	C	9-5
23.	A	12-11
24.	A	14-2
25.	A	11-1
26.	A	11-1
27.	C	11-1
28.	B	11-2
29.	A	11-4
30.	A	11-1
31.	C	11-7
32.	B	11-8
33.	D	11-7
34.	D	11-4
35.	D	11-2
36.	C	11-7
37.	D	11-7
38.	A	11-5
39.	D	12-2
40.	D	12-1,5
41.	B	12-1
42.	D	13-9
43.	D	13-1
44.	A	13-2
45.	D	13-1
46.	B	13-7
47.	A	13-3
48.	D	13-3
49.	C	13-3
50.	C	14-4

ABBREVIATED

GLOSSARY OF INSURANCE TERMS

NOTE: A completely separate bound edition of this glossary, with many more insurance terms, is available from Merritt. Please write or call for information concerning the "Glossary of Insurance Terms" to:

The Merritt Company
P.O. Box 955
1661 9th Street
Santa Monica, CA 90406
800-638-7597
310-396-4563 (Fax)

This glossary is a condensed edition of the *Glossary of Insurance Terms, 6th Ed.,* edited by Thomas E. Green, CPCU, CLU and The Merritt Company editorial staff.

To help you gain a quick reference point, definitions are immediately followed by one or more abbreviations for general categories of insurance, set in parentheses. The abbreviations for the reference categories used in this glossary are:

AN = *ANNUTIES*
AU = *AUTOMOBILE*
AV = *AVIATION*
C = *CRIME*
EP = *ESTATE PLANNING*
G = *GENERAL*
H = *HEALTH*
IM = *INLAND MARINE*
LE = *LEGAL*
LA = *LIABILITY*
LI = *LIFE*
OM = *OCEAN MARINE*
PE = *PENSION & PROFIT SHARING*
PR = *PROPERTY*
R = *REINSURANCE*
S = *SURETY*
WC = *WORKERS COMPENSATION*

In some areas, terms are cross-referenced with other terms appearing in the Glossary, in which case the referenced terms are also set in bold type. Cross-referencing is used for terms which have the same or similar meanings, terms which differ from related terms, and terms which are opposites.

This revised edition includes many new terms which have resulted from the introduction of new coverages and policy forms in recent years.

A

A&H, A&S — Accident and Health Insurance, Accident and Sickness Insurance. Once commonly used as generic designations for the entire field now called health insurance. See **Health Insurance. (H)**

Abandonment. A relinquishing of ownership of lost or damaged property by the insured to the insurer so that a total loss may be claimed. Abandonment is prohibited in most other types of property insurance. **(OM)**

Abandonment Clause. A clause in fire insurance policies and other property forms that prohibits the insured from abandoning partially damaged property to the insurer in order to claim a total loss. **(PR)**

Absolute Assignment. Assignment by a policyowner of all control of and rights in the policy to a third party. **(G)**

Accelerated Benefits. Riders on life insurance policies which allow the life insurance policy's death benefits to be used to offset expenses incurred in a convalescent or nursing home facility. **(H,LI)**

Accelerated Endowment. A dividend option allowing dividend accumulations to be applied to convert a life insurance policy into an endowment, or to shorten the endowment term. **(LI)**

Accident. An unplanned event, unexpected and undesigned, which occurs suddenly and at a definite place. See also **Occurrence. (G)**

Accident and Sickness Insurance (A&S). An older name for health insurance. See **Health Insurance. (H)**

Accident Insurance. A form of health insurance against loss by bodily injury. **(H)**

Accidental Bodily Injury. Traumatic damage to the body, of external origin, unexpected and undesigned by the injured person. Contrast with **Accidental Means. (G)**

Accidental Death and Dismemberment. A policy or a provision in a disability income policy which pays either a specified amount or a multiple of the weekly disability benefit if the insured dies, loses his or her sight, or loses two limbs as the result of an accident. A lesser amount is payable for the loss of one eye, arm, leg, hand, or foot. **(H)**

Accidental Means. Unexpected or undesigned cause of an accidental bodily injury. Under a definition of accidental means, the mishap itself must be accidental, not just the resulting injury. An example would be an individual chopping wood: If the axe slipped out of his hand and cut his foot, it would have been accidental means. However, if his finger got in the way of the axe, it would not have been. **(G)**

Accounts Receivable Insurance. Insurance against the loss that occurs when an insured is unable to collect outstanding accounts because of damage to or destruction of the accounts receivable records by a peril covered in the policy. **(PR)**

Accumulation Period. The period of time, prior to retirement, during which an annuitant is making payments or investments in an annuity. Such payments will accumulate on a tax deferred basis. **(AN)**

Accumulation Units. These are issued to owners of variable annuities during the accumulation period, as evidence of the annuitant's participation in the separate account. **(AN)**

Accumulations (or Accumulation Benefits). Percentage additions to policy benefits when the contract is continuously renewed. **(LI)**

Acquired Immunodeficiency Syndrome (AIDS). An infectious and incurable disease, commonly referred to as AIDS, which is caused by the human immunodeficiency virus, commonly referred to as HIV. **(H,LI)**

Acquisition Cost. The expenses incurred by an insurer or reinsurance company that are directly related to putting the business on the books of the company, including clerical work, medical examiners fees, inspection costs, etc. The largest portion of this cost is usually the agent's or sales representative's commission or bonus. **(G)**

Act of God. An event arising out of natural causes with no human intervention which could not have been prevented by reasonable care or foresight. Examples are floods, lightning, and earthquakes. **(G)**

Actual Cash Value. An amount equivalent to the replacement cost of lost or damaged property at the time of the loss, less depreciation. With regard to buildings, there is a tendency for the actual cash value to closely parallel the market value of the property. See also Market Value. **(G)**

Actuary. A specialist trained in mathematics, statistics, and accounting who is responsible for rate, reserve, and dividend calculations and other statistical studies. **(G)**

Additional Insured. A person other than the named insured who is protected under the terms of the contract. Usually, additional insureds are added by endorsement or referred to in the wording of the definition of "insured" in the policy itself. **(G)**

Additional Living Expense Insurance. A contract to reimburse the insured for increased living costs when loss of property forces the insured to maintain temporary residence elsewhere. Examples of these types of expenses are the cost for a hotel or motel, the extra cost for restaurant meals, and the cost of using a laundromat. The term Extra Expense Insurance is defined with regard to additional expenses incurred by businesses. See also **Loss of Use. (PR)**

Additional Monthly Benefit. Riders added to disability income policies to provide additional benefits during the first year of a claim while the insured is waiting for Social Security benefits to begin. **(H)**

Adjustable Life. A form of life insurance which allows changes on the policy face amount, the amount of premium, period of protection, and the length of the premium payment period. **(LI)**

Adjustable Premium. The right of an insurer to change the premium rate on classes of insureds, or blocks of business at the time of policy renewal. **(H,LI)**

Adjuster. A representative of the insurer who seeks to determine the extent of the firm's liability for loss when a claim is submitted. **(G)**

Adjustment. Determining the cause and amount of a loss, the indemnity recoverable by the insured and amount to be paid under the terms of the policy. **(G)**

Administrative Services Only. The services provided by an insurer, such as providing claim forms and processing claims, when the insurer is not the party funding the loss payments. **(H,LI)**

Admitted Company. An insurance company authorized and licensed to do business in a given state. **(G)**

Adverse Selection. The tendency of poorer than average risks to buy and maintain insurance. Adverse selection occurs when insureds select only those coverages that are most likely to have losses. **(G)**

Adverse Underwriting Decision. Any decision involving individually underwritten insurance coverages resulting in termination of existing insurance, declination of an application, or writing the coverage only at higher rates. For property and casualty insurance, it also includes placing the coverage with a residual market mechanism or an unauthorized insurer. **(G)**

Advertising Injury. Injury arising out of libel or slander, violation of the right to privacy, misappropriation of advertising ideas, or infringement of copyright, title or slogan committed in the course of advertising goods, products, or services. Contrast with **Personal Injury. (LA)**

Age Change. The date on which a person's age, for insurance purposes, changes. In most life insurance contracts this is the date midway between the insured's natural birth dates. Health insurers frequently use the age of the previous birth date for rate determinations. On the date of age change, a person's age may change to that of the last birth date, the nearer birth date, or the next birth date, depending upon the way in which the rating structure has been established by that particular insurer. **(H,LI)**

Age Limits. The ages below which or above which an insurer will not write certain forms of insurance or above which it will not continue a policy presently in force. **(G)**

Agency. When one person acts on behalf of another person, an agency is created with the first person being the agent and the second person being the principal. The principal generally can be held responsible for acts of its agents. **(LE)**

Agency. An insurance sales office which is directed by a general agent, manager, independent agent, or company manager. **(G)**

Agent. One who solicits, negotiates or effects contracts of insurance on behalf of an insurer. The agent's right to exercise various functions, authority, and obligations and the obligations of the insurer to the agent are subject to the terms of the agency contract with the insurer, to statutory law, and to common law. **(G)**

Agent's Appointment. Official authorization from an insurance company granting an agent the authority to act as its agent. In most states, agents must be appointed by at least one insurer in addition to being licensed by the state.

Agent's Appointment. Official authorization from an insurance company granting an agent the authority to act as its agent. In most states, agents must be appointed by at least one insurer in addition to being licensed by the state. **(G)**

Agent's Authority. The authority and power granted to an agent by the agency contract. The agent is also clothed with additional power under the legal concept of apparent agency. See also **Apparent Agency. (G)**

AIDS — See **Acquired Immunodeficiency Syndrome. (H,LI)**

AIDS Related Complex (ARC). The term given to a variety of symptoms and opportunistic infections and conditions which frequently manifest themselves in patients suffering from AIDS, or acquired immunodeficiency syndrome, which is caused by the human immunodeficiency virus. **(H,LI)**

All or Nothing Rider. A rider to a health insurance policy that provides additional benefits in the event no benefits are payable under Social Security. If Social Security benefits are payable, no additional benefit is paid under the rider. **(H)**

Allied Lines. Various insurance coverages for additional types of losses, and against loss by additional perils, which are closely associated with and usually sold with fire insurance. Examples include coverage against loss by perils other than fire, coverage for sprinkler leakage damage, and business interruption coverage. The fire insurance field consists of coverages for "fire and allied lines." **(PR)**

Allowable Charge. The lesser of the actual charge, the customary charge and the prevailing charge. It is the amount on which Medicare will base its Part B payment. **(H)**

All Risk Insurance. The term was once used to mean insurance against loss of or damage to property arising from any cause except those that are specifically excluded. Today, all risk type policies are know as special coverage forms. See **Open Peril.** Contrast with **Named Perils. (G,PR)**

Ancillary Benefits. Benefits for miscellaneous hospital charges. **(H)**

Annual (or Yearly) Renewable Term (ART). (1) Term Life Insurance that may be renewed annually without evidence of insurability until some stated age. (2) A form of life, and sometimes health, reinsurance in which the reinsurer assumes only the mortality risk, which is usually calculated as the face amount of reinsurance minus the terminal reserve. **(H,LI)**

Annual Statement. A report to the state insurance department of the year's financial results. The insurer's income and expenses are stated in detail as well as its assets and liabilities. **(G)**

Annuitant. The person who is covered by an annuity and who will normally receive the benefits of the annuity. **(AN)**

Annuity. (1) An amount of money payable yearly, or by extension, at other regular intervals; (2) An agreement by an insurer to make periodic payments that continue during the survival of the annuitant(s) or for a specified period. **(AN)**

Annuity Certain. An annuity that pays income for a fixed number of years regardless of whether the insured lives or dies. If it pays for life after the certain period, it is called an "annuity certain and for life thereafter." **(AN)**

Annuity Due. An annuity under which the benefits are paid at the beginning of the benefit period rather than at the end. **(AN)**

Annuity Option. A method if liquidating and distributing an annuity's principal and interest so that it lasts for the lifetime of the annuitant. **(AN)**

Annuity Period. The period of time, usually at retirement, during which the annuitant begins to receive annuity payments or benefits from the insurance company. **(AN)**

Annuity with Period Certain. An annuity that pays throughout the life of the insured, but also guarantees to pay income for a specific number of years regardless of whether the insured lives or dies. If the insured is living at the end of the time specified in the policy benefits continue beyond the guaranteed period until the death of the insured. **(AN)**

Apparent Agency. See **Presumption of Agency. (G)**

Apparent Authority. Authority of an agent that is created when the agent oversteps actual authority, and when inaction by the insurer does nothing to counter the public impression that such authority exists. **(G)**

Appeal. The right of a party who has received an adverse decision to take the case to a higher court for review. **(LE)**

Application. A form on which the prospective insured states facts requested by the insurer on the basis of which, together with information from other sources, the insurer decides whether to accept the risk, modify the coverage offered, or decline the risk. **(G)**

Apportionment. The method of dividing a loss among insurers in the same proportions as their participation when two of more companies cover the same loss. **(G)**

Appraisal. An evaluation of property made to ascertain either the appropriate amount of insurance to be written or the amount of loss to be paid. **(G)**

Approved Pension Plan. A pension plan qualifying for tax exemptions under provisions of the Internal Revenue Code. **(PE)**

Appurtenant Structures. Buildings on the same premises as the main building insured under a property insurance policy. Most dwelling property insurance policies cover appurtenant structures under most circumstances. **(PR)**

ARC — See **AIDS Related Complex. (H,LI)**

Arson. The willful and deliberate burning of property. **(LE)**

Assessment Company, Society or Insurer. An insurer who retains the right to assess policyholders additional amounts if premiums are insufficient for operations. In some cases, an assessment insurer may not charge a stipulated premium at all but will merely assess participants in the plan a pro rata share of each claim filed plus expenses. **(G)**

Assets. The items on the balance sheet of the insurer which show the book value of property owned. Under state regulations, not all property or other resources can be admitted in the statement of the insurer. This gives rise to the term "nonadmitted assets." See also **Nonadmitted Assets. (G)**

Assigned Risk. A risk which is not ordinarily acceptable to insurers and which is, therefore, assigned to insurers participating in an assigned risk pool or plan. Each participating company agrees to accept its share of these risks. **(G)**

Assignee. A person to whom policy rights are assigned in whole or in part by the original policyowner. **(LE)**

Assignment. An authorization to pay Medicare benefits directly to the provider. Medicare payments may be assigned to participating providers only. **(H)**

Assignment. Transfer by the policyowner of legal rights or interest in the policy contract to a third party. Most policies cannot be assigned without the permission of the insurer. **(LE)**

Assignment. The transfer of the ownership rights of a life insurance policy from one person to another. The term also refers to the document that effects the transfer. **(LI)**

Assumed Interest Rate (AIR). An assumed value which is assigned to the annuitant's account during the annuity period. It is an estimated return for the separate account. Monthly annuity payments are based on the AIR in relation to the actual rate of return experienced by the separate account of a variable annuity. **(AN)**

Assumed Liability. See **Contractual Liability. (LA)**

Assurance. Same as **Insurance. (G)**

Assured. Same as **Insured. (G)**

Assurer. Same as **Insurer. (G)**

Attained Age. The age an insured has reached on a given date. **(LI)**

Attending Physicians Statement (APS). A source of medical information used when underwriting a life or health insurance policy; usually obtained from the proposed insured's doctor. **(H, LI)**

Authorization. The amount of insurance an underwriter will agree to accept on a risk of a given class on specific property. It is given for the guidance and information of agents. **(G)**

Automatic Cover. Coverage given automatically by a policy, usually for a specified period and limited amount, to cover increasing values and newly acquired and changing interests. **(G)**

Automatic Premium Loan. A provision in a life policy authorizing the insurer to use the loan value to pay any premiums still due at the end of the grace period. **(LI)**

Automatic Reinstatement Clause. A stipulation in a property insurance policy which states that after a partial loss covered by the policy has been paid, the original limit of the policy will be automatically reinstated. **(PR)**

Automobile Fleet. Refers to a number of automobiles under the same ownership. For insurance purposes a fleet usually consists of five or more self-propelled units and generally qualifies for certain premium reductions and rating plans. **(AU)**

Average Rate. A rate for a policy established by multiplying the rate for each location by the value at that location and dividing the sum of the results by the total value. **(PR)**

Aviation Accident Insurance. A form of insurance which protects individuals as passengers or pilots, usually on scheduled aircraft, or which covers the flight travel of the employees of a company under a master policy. **(LI)**

Aviation Hazard. The extra hazard of death or injury resulting from participation in aeronautics, usually as other than a fare-paying passenger in licensed aircraft. This generally requires an extra premium rating or waiver of certain benefits or coverage. **(LI)**

Avoidance of Risk. Taking steps to remove a hazard, engage in an alternative activity, or otherwise end a specific exposure. One of the four major risk management techniques. See **Risk Management.** **(G)**

B

Bailee. A person or concern having possession of personal property entrusted to that person by the owner. An example would be a laundry which has custody of customers' clothing for washing or dry cleaning. Bailees are required to exercise the same care with the property of others as they would with their own property. **(LE)**

Bailees Customer Insurance. Insurance purchased by a bailee to protect the personal property of customers against loss caused by specific perils. An example would be a carpet cleaner who buys coverage to protect customers against loss or damage to their carpets while in the store's care. **(IM)**

Basic Coverage Form. Any of the commercial or personal lines property forms which provide basic coverages. These forms generally provide the most limited coverage, which is surpassed by broad forms and special forms. **(PR)**

Basic Extended Reporting Period. An automatic "tail" for reporting claims after expiration of a "claims-made" liability policy. It is provided without charge and consists of two parts: a **mini-tail** covers claims made within 60 days after the end of the policy; a **midi-tail** covers claims made within five years after the end of the policy period arising out of occurrences reported not later than 60 days after the end of the policy. **(LA)**

Basic Rate. The manual rate from which discounts are taken or to which charges are added to reflect the individual circumstances of a risk. **(G)**

Beneficiary. A person who may become eligible to receive or is receiving benefits under an insurance policy other than a participant. See also **Irrevocable Beneficiary, Secondary Beneficiary, Tertiary Beneficiary,** and **Contingent Beneficiary.** **(LI)**

Benefit. The amount to be paid to a participant of a retirement plan or to the participant's beneficiary at retirement, at death, or at termination of service. **(PE)**

Bid Bond. A bond filed with a bid for a construction or other project which guarantees that if the contractor has the low bid and is awarded the job, the required performance bond will be furnished. **(S)**

Binder. An agreement executed by an agent or insurer (usually the latter) putting insurance into force before the contract has been written or the premium paid. This term is not usually used in life insurance. **(G)**

Blanket A&H Policy. An Accident & Health Insurance policy that covers all of a class of persons not individually identified. **(H)**

Blanket Bond. A type of fidelity bond which covers losses caused by the dishonesty of all employees as opposed to bonds which specifically identify only certain employees to be covered. **(C)**

Blanket Crime Policy. A policy that once provided a package of coverages for employee dishonesty, loss of money and securities inside and outside the premises, depositor's forgery, loss of money orders, and loss due to counterfeit paper currency. This has been replaced by modern commercial crime coverage forms. **(C)**

Blanket Fidelity Bond. See **Blanket Bond.** **(C)**

Blanket Insurance. A contract of health insurance that covers all of a class of persons not individually identified in the contract. **(H)**

Blanket Insurance. A form of property insurance that covers, in a single contract, either multiple types of property at a single location or one or more types of property at multiple locations. **(PR)**

Blanket Position Bond. A Blanket Fidelity Bond in which the amount of coverage applies separately to each position covered. Contrast with **Commercial Blanket Bond,** which provides a single amount of coverage for any one loss, regardless of the number of employees involved in the loss. See also **Blanket Bond. (C)**

Blue Cross. Blue Cross plans are hospital expense prepayment plans designed primarily to provide benefits for hospitalization coverage, with certain restrictions on the type of accommodations to be used. **(H)**

Blue Shield. Blue Shield plans are prepayment plans offered by service organizations covering medical and surgical expenses. **(H)**

Bodily Injury Liability (BI). A legal liability that may arise as a result of the injury or death of another person. **(LA)**

Boiler and Machinery Insurance. Insurance against the sudden and accidental breakdown of boilers, machinery, and electrical equipment. Coverage is provided on (1) damage to the equipment, (2) expediting expenses, (3) property damage to the property of others, and (4) supplementary payments; and (5) automatic coverage is provided on additional objects. Coverage can be extended to cover consequential losses and loss from interruption of business. **(PR)**

Bond. A three-party contract guaranteeing that if one person, the principal, fails to perform as specified or proves to be dishonest, the person to whom the duty is owed, the obligee, will be financially protected by the issuer of the bond, the surety. **(S)**

Boycott. An unfair trade practice which occurs when someone in the insurance business refuses to have business dealings with another until he or she complies with certain conditions or concessions. **(G)**

Broad Form Personal Theft Policy. Theft coverage on personal property at private residences, usually on an open perils (all risk) basis. This type of coverage is most often part of a homeowners contract. A limited form of the Broad Form Personal Theft policy is known as the Personal Theft policy. **(C)**

Broad Form Storekeepers Insurance. A form of coverage for small storekeepers. It includes several specific crime perils on the same basis as a Storekeepers Burglary and Robbery policy, plus open perils (all risk) protection on money and securities, depositors' forgery, and a small limit on employee dishonesty. **(C)**

Broker. One who represents an insured in the solicitation, negotiation or procurement of contracts of insurance, and who may render services incidental to those functions. By law the broker may also be an agent of the insurer for certain purposes such as delivery of the policy or collection of the premium. **(G)**

Brokerage Department. A department of an insurer whose purpose is to deal with brokers in the placing of insurance. **(G)**

Builder's Risk Coverage Form. A commercial property coverage form specifically designed for buildings in the course of construction. **(PR)**

Builders Risk Insurance. Insurance against loss to buildings or structures in the course of construction. **(PR)**

Building and Personal Property Coverage Form. A commercial property coverage form designed to insure most types of commercial property (buildings, or contents, ot both). It is the most frequently used commercial property form, and has replaced the General Property Form, Special Building Form, Special Personal Property Form, and others. **(PR)**

Burglary. Breaking and entering into the premises of another with felonious intent, leaving visible signs of forcible entry or exit. **(C)**

Business. In property, liability, and health lines, it usually refers to the volume of premiums. **(G)**

Business. The face amount of life insurance written. **(LI)**

Business Auto Coverage Form. The latest commercial automobile insurance coverage form, which may be written as a monoline policy or as part of a commercial package. This form has largely replaced the Business Auto policy. **(AU)**

Business Income Coverage Form. A commercial property form providing coverage for "indirect losses" resulting from property damage, such as loss of business income and extra expenses incurred. It has replaced earlier Business Interruption and Extra Expense forms. **(PR)**

Business Insurance. Commercial insurance. The term is generally used to refer to insurance for businesses or commercial establishments as opposed to insurance for the personal protection of individuals. **(G)**

Business Insurance. Life and health policies written for business purposes, such as key employee, sole proprietorship, partnership, and corporation. **(H,LI)**

Business Interruption Insurance. A time element coverage that pays for loss of earnings when operations are curtailed or suspended because of property loss due to an insured peril. Now referred to as business income insurance. See **Business Income Coverage Form. (PR)**

Business Interruption Insurance, Contingent. Now referred to as coverage for business income from dependent properties. See **Business Income Coverage Form** and **Dependent Properties. (PR)**

Business Liability. The term used to describe the liability coverages provided by the Businessowners Liability Coverage form. It includes liability for bodily injury, property damage, personal injury, advertising injury, and fire damage. **(LA)**

Business Personal Property. Traditionally known as "contents," this term actually refers to furniture, fixtures, equipment, machinery, merchandise, materials, and all other personal property owned by the insured and used in the insured's business. **(PR)**

Buyers Guide. A consumer publication that describes the type of coverage being offered, and provides general information to help an applicant for life or health insurance compare different types of policies and reach a decision about whether the proposed coverage is appropriate. Also known as a Shoppers Guide. **(H)**

C

Cancellable. A contract of insurance that may be terminated by the insurer or insured at any time. Practically every form of insurance is cancellable, except life insurance and those health insurance policies designated as a "guaranteed renewable" or "noncancellable and guaranteed renewable." Some states also regulate when or if automobile policies can be cancelled. **(G)**

Cancellation. Termination of a contract of insurance in force by voluntary act of the insurer or insured in accordance with the provisions in the contract or by mutual agreement. **(G)**

Capital Stock Insurance Company. An insurance company having, in addition to surplus and reserve funds, a capital fund paid in by stockholders. **(G)**

Capital Sum. The maximum lump sum payable in the event of accidental death or dismemberment. **(G)**

Capitation (CAP). A rate paid, usually monthly, to a health care provider. In return, the provider agrees to deliver the health services agreed upon to any covered person. **(H)**

Carrier. Usually a commercial insurer contracted by the Department of Health and Human Services to process Medicare Part B claims payments. **(H)**

Carrier. Sometimes used to designate the insurer. The term "insurer" is preferred because of the possible confusion of "carrier" with transportation. See also **Insurer. (G)**

Carryover Provision. In major medical policies, allowing an insured who has submitted no claims during the year to apply any medical expenses incurred in the last three months of the year toward the new calendar year's deductible. **(H)**

Cash Surrender Value. The amount of cash due an insured who surrenders cash value life insurance. Such surrender, with consequent termination of all insurance benefits, is sometimes called "cashing out" or "cashing in" a policy. See also **Nonforfeiture Values. (LI)**

Casualty Insurance. That type of insurance that is primarily concerned with the legal liability for losses caused by injury to persons or damage to the property of others. It also includes such diverse forms as plate glass insurance, crime insurance, boiler and machinery insurance, and aviation insurance. Many casualty insurers also write surety bonds. Casualty insurers write forms of insurance not considered property forms. Contrast with **Property Insurance. (LA)**

Catastrophe Hazard. The hazard of large loss by reason of occurrence of a peril to which a very large number of insureds are subject. An example would be widespread loss due to a hurricane or tornado. **(G)**

Causes of Loss. Under the latest commercial property, inland marine and crime coverage forms, this term replaces the earlier term "perils" insured against. **(C,IM,PR)**

Causes of Loss Forms. Commercial property forms stating the perils insured against, additional coverages provided, and exclusions that apply. There are four Causes of Loss forms — **Basic, Broad, Special** and **Earthquake. (PR)**

Cease and Desist Order. An order of the state Insurance Commissioner or of a court requiring that a company or person stop engaging in a particular act or practice, usually involving insurance trade practices. **(LE)**

Certificate of Insurance. (1) A statement of the coverage and general provisions of a master contract in group insurance that is issued to individuals covered in the group. (2) A form which verifies that a policy has been written and states the coverage in general, often used as proof of insurance in loan transactions and for other legal requirements. **(G)**

Change of Occupation. A provision in a health insurance policy that allows the insurer to adjust policy benefits if the insured has changed to a more hazardous occupation. **(H)**

Churing. An illegal practice where insurance agents unnecessarily replace existing life insurance for the purpose of earning additional (higher) first year commission. **(LI)**

Claim. A demand made by the insured, or the insured's beneficiary, for payment of the benefits provided by the contract. **(G)**

Claims-Made Coverage. A policy providing liability coverage only if a written claim is made during the policy period or any applicable extended reporting period. For example, a claim made in the current year could be charged against the current policy even if the injury or loss occurred many years in the past. If the policy has a retroactive date, an occurrence prior to that date is not covered. Contrast with **Occurrence Coverage. (LA)**

Class Rate. A rate for risks of similar hazard. Class rates, for example, apply to dwellings. **(PR)**

Clause. A section of a policy contract or endorsement dealing with a particular subject. For instance, a subrogation clause deals with the rights of the insurer in the event of payment of a loss under the contract. **(G)**

Clerical Error. A provision in a group health insurance policy that provides if there is an error or omission in the administration of a group policy, the person's insurance is considered to be what it would be if there had been no error or omission. **(H)**

Closed Access. A situation where covered insureds must select one primary care physician. That physician is the only one allowed to refer the patient to other health care providers within the plan. Also called closed Panel or Gatekeeper model. **(H)**

Coinsurance Clause. A provision stating that the insured and the insurer will share all losses covered by the policy in a proportion agreed upon in advance, i.e., 80-20 would mean that the insurer would pay 80% and the insured would pay 20% of all losses. See also **Percentage Participation. (H)**

Coinsurance Clause. A clause under which the insured shares in losses to the extent that he or she is underinsured at the time of loss. The insurer grants a reduced rate to the insured providing the insured carries insurance 80, 90, or 100% to value. If, at the time of loss, the insured carries less coverage than required, the loss must be shared. For example, if an insured has a building worth $100,000 and carries an 80% coinsurance clause, it means that the insured agrees to carry at least $80,000 of insurance. If the insurance carried is just $60,000, then any loss under the policy would be paid for on the basis of the comparison of $60,000 (amount carried) divided by $80,000 (amount agreed upon in advance) times the amount of the loss. Thus, in the event of a $10,000 loss the insured would only receive 75% of a loss or $7,500. **(PR)**

Cold Lead Advertising. An illegal method of marketing insurance policies (often associated with Medicare supplement policies) which fails to disclose in a conspicuous manner that a purpose of the method of marketing is solicitation of insurance or other similar coverage, and that further contact will be made by an insurance agent, other producer or insurer. **(H)**

Collateral Assignment. Assignment of a life insurance policy or its value as security for a loan. In the event of default, the creditor would receive proceeds or values only to the extent of the creditor's interest. **(LI)**

Collision Insurance. A form of automobile insurance that covers loss to the insured's own vehicle caused by its collision with another vehicle or object or its upset but not covering bodily injury or property damage liability arising out of the collision. **(AU)**

Collusion. An agreement, usually secret, between two or more persons to defraud or deprive another or others of their property or rights. **(G)**

Combination Crime Coverage Plan. Under the latest commercial lines program, two combination crime coverage plans are available. When written with separate limits option, any combination of a variety of coverages may be included at different limits and the insurance is similar to the earlier Comprehensive Dishonesty, Disappearance and Destruction (3-D) policy. When written with a single limit, major coverages are mandatory, optional coverages may be included, but one limit applies to all coverages purchased and the insurance is similar to the earlier Blanket Crime Policy. **(C)**

Commercial Blanket Bond. This type of bond covers the insured against the dishonesty of all regular employees. A single amount of coverage applies to any one loss, regardless of the number of employees involved in the loss. See also **Blanket Bond**, and contrast with **Blanket Position Bond. (C)**

Commercial General Liability (CGL) Coverage Part. General liability coverage which may be written as a monoline policy or part of a commercial package. "CGL" now means "commercial" general liability forms which have replaced the earlier "comprehensive" general liability forms. The latest forms include all sublines, provide very broad coverage, and two variations are available — **"Occurrence"** or **"Claims-Made"** coverage. **(LA)**

Commercial Lines. This term is used to refer to insurance for businesses, professionals, and commercial establishments. See also **Business Insurance.** Contrast with **Personal Lines. (G)**

Commercial Package Policy (CPP). A commercial lines policy that contains more than one of the following coverage parts: Commercial Property, Commercial General Liability, Commercial Inland Marine, Commercial Crime, Boiler and Machinery Insurance, Commercial Automobile Insurance, and Farm Coverage. **(G)**

Commerical Property Coverage. Property coverage which may be written as a monoline policy or part of a commercial package. **(PR)**

Commission. That portion of the premium paid to the agent as compensation for services. **(G)**

Commission. An allowance made by the reinsurer to the original insurer for part of the original insurer's acquisition and other costs. It may also include a profit factor. **(R)**

Commissioner of Insurance. The title of the head of most state insurance departments. In some states, the title **Director** or **Superintendent** of Insurance is used instead. **(G)**

Common Carrier. An individual or organization that offers its services to the public for carrying persons or property from one place to another for payment. A common carrier cannot refuse to carry goods for one customer as opposed to another. **(IM)**

Common Law Liability. Responsibility based on common law for injury or damage to another's person or property which rests on an individual because of the individual's actions or negligence. This is opposed to liability based on statutory law. **(G)**

Common Policy Conditions. Under the latest commercial lines program, a form including six common conditions which apply to all coverage parts attached to a commercial policy. **(G)**

Common Policy Declarations. Under the latest commercial lines program, a common declaration page which is part of every commercial policy. It shows information applicable to the entire policy (policy number, insurer, insured, total premium, forms attached, etc.). Each individual coverage part may also have its own declarations page. **(G)**

Completed Operations Insurance. A form of insurance issued particularly to various types of contractors. It covers a contractor's liability for accidents arising out of jobs or operations that have been completed. **(LA)**

Comprehensive Coverage. Traditional name for physical damage coverage for losses by fire, theft, vandalism, falling objects, and various other perils. On personal auto policies, this is now called "other than collision" coverage. On commercial forms, it continues to be called "comprehensive" coverage. **(AU)**

Comprehensive General Liability. A policy covering a variety of general liability exposures, including premises and operations (OL&T or M&C), completed operations, products liability, and owners and contractors protective. Contractual liability and broad form coverages could be added. In most jurisdictions, the "Comprehensive" General Liability policy has been replaced by the newer "Commercial" General Liability (CGL) forms which include all the standard and optional coverages of the earlier forms. See also **Commercial General Liability. (LA)**

Comprehensive Glass Insurance Policy. A policy which covers the insured against loss by breakage of glass from almost any peril. Fire is usually excluded because it is covered under any basic property policy, and war is excluded. This policy has largely been replaced by a new commercial form. See **Glass Coverage Form. (PR)**

Comprehensive Major Medical. A plan of insurance which has a low deductible, high maximum benefits, and a coinsurance feature. It is a combination of basic coverage and major medical coverage which has virtually replaced separate hospital, surgical and medical policies with each having its own deductible requirements. Also see **Major Medical Insurance. (H)**

Comprehensive Personal Liability. This coverage protects individuals and families from liability for nearly all types of accidents caused by them in their personal lives as opposed to business lives. It is most commonly a part of the protection provided by a Homeowners policy. **(LA)**

Compulsory Insurance. Any form of insurance required by law. For example, some states have compulsory automobile insurance laws, some have compulsory disability benefits laws, etc. **(G)**

Computer Fraud. Fraudulent theft or transfer of money, securities or other property resulting from the use of any computerized equipment or systems. **(C)**

Computer Fraud Coverage Form. A commercial crime coverage form that protects against loss of money, securities, and property other than money and securities resulting from computer fraud. **(C)**

Concealment. The failure to disclose a material fact. **(LE)**

Concurrent Causation. A term referring to two or more perils acting concurrently (at the same time or in sequence) to cause a loss. This created problems for property insurers when one of the perils was covered and one was not, and it led to recent revisions in policy language. **(PR)**

Concurrent Insurance. Two or more policies with the same conditions and coverages that cover the same interest in the same property. If an insured has two or more property insurance policies, the policies should be concurrent (similar) or the property will not be insured properly if the policies are not concurrent (similar). **(PR)**

Concurrent Review. A case management technique which allows insurers to monitor an insured's hospital stay and to know in advance if there are any changes in the expected period of confinement and the planned release date. **(H)**

Conditional Binding Receipt. This is the more exact terminology for what is often called a binding receipt. It provides that if a premium accompanies an application, the coverage will be in force from the date of application or medical examination, if any, whichever is later, provided the insurer would have issued the coverage on the basis of the facts revealed on the application, medical examination and other usual sources of underwriting information. A life and health insurance policy without a conditional binding receipt is not effective until it is delivered to the insured and the premium is paid. **(H,LI)**

Conditionally Renewable. A contract that provides that the insured may renew it to a stated date or an advanced age, subject to the right of the insurer to decline renewal only under conditions stated in the contract. **(H)**

Condominium Association Coverage Form. A commercial property form designed to cover the joint insurance needs of members of a condominium association who collectively own commercial property. **(PR)**

Condominium Unit Owners Coverage Form. A commercial property form designed to cover the individual needs of commercial (not residential) condominium unit-owners. **(PR)**

Consent Order. A disciplinary action in which the party at fault (usually an insurance company or agent) agrees to discontinue a particular practice (usually an unfair trade or claims practice) through a written agreement with the Insurance Department. Consent orders (also known as consent decrees) may or may not involved a fine. **(G)**

Consequential Loss (or Damage). (1) An indirect loss arising out of the policyholder's inability to use the property over a period of time, as opposed to a direct loss that happens almost instantaneously. Business interruption, extra expense, rents insurance, and leasehold interest are the most common coverages included under the category of consequential loss coverages. (2) A loss not directly caused by a peril insured against, such as spoilage of frozen foods caused by fire damage to the refrigeration equipment. See also **Indirect Loss,** and contrast with **Direct Loss. (PR)**

Consideration. The exchange of values on which a contract is based. In insurance, the consideration offered by the insured is usually the premium and the statements contained in the application. The consideration offered by the insurer is the promise to pay in accordance with the terms of the contract. **(LE)**

Consolidated Omnibus Budget Reconciliation Act (COBRA) of 1986. Legislation providing for a continuation of group health care benefits under the group plan for a period of time when benefits would otherwise terminate. Continuation rights apply to enrolled persons and their dependents in companies with 20 or more employees. Coverage may be continued for up to 18 months if the insured person terminates employment or is no longer eligible. Coverage may be continued for up to 36 months in nearly all other cases, such as loss of dependent eligibility because of death of the enrolled person, divorce, or attainment of the limiting age. **(H)**

Consumer Report. A report ordered on an insured or applicant under which information about the person's credit, character, reputation, personal characteristics or lifestyle is obtained primarily through institutional sources. Contrast with **Investigative Consumer Report. (G)**

Contingent Beneficiary. A person(s) named to receive policy benefits if the primary beneficiary is deceased at the time the benefits become payable. **(LI)**

Contingent Business Interruption Insurance. Coverage for the loss of earnings of an insured because of a loss to another business which is one of the insured's major suppliers or customers. This insurance is now known as business income from dependent properties. See **Business Income Coverage Form** and **Dependent Properties. (PR)**

Continuous Premium Whole Life Policy. A whole life policy that stretches the premium payments over the insured's lifetime (to age 100). Also known as **Straight Life**. Compare with **Limited Payment Whole Life** and **Single Premium Whole Life. (LI)**

Contract Bond. A guarantee of the faithful performance of a construction contract and the payment of all material and labor bills incidental thereto. A bond covering faithful performance only is known as a Performance Bond, and one covering payment of labor and materials only is a Payment Bond. **(S)**

Contract Carrier. A transportation company that carries, for payment, the goods of certain customers only, as contrasted with a common carrier who carries goods for the public in general. **(IM)**

Contract of Insurance. The contract whereby an insurer agrees to indemnify an insured for losses, provide other benefits, or render services to or on behalf of the insured. The contract of insurance is often called an insurance policy, but the policy is merely the evidence of the agreement. **(LE)**

Contractual (or Assumed) Liability Insurance. This insurance protects the insured in the event a loss occurs for which the insured has assumed liability, express or implied, under a written contract. For example, under most construction agreements with a municipality, the contractor agrees to "hold the municipality harmless" for any accidents arising out of the job. Contractual liability insurance would thus protect the contractor from any loss for which the municipality would be liable in connection with the construction. **(LA)**

Contribution. (1) The share of a loss payable by an insurer when contracts with two or more insurers cover the same loss. See also **Apportionment.** (2) The insurer's share of a loss under a coinsurance or similar provision. (3) The amount of the premium for group insurance or a pension plan paid by the employee. **(G)**

Contribution Clause. See **Coinsurance Clause.** Both are similar in effect, but contribution clause is identified mostly with business interruption forms. **(G)**

Contributory. A general term used to describe a plan of employee coverage in which the employee pays at least part of the premium. **(H,LI)**

Conversion. (1) Wrongful use of property by one in lawful possession of it. (2) Change of one policy form to another, usually without evidence of insurability. This usually refers to life or health insurance contracts. **(G)**

Convertible. A policy that may be changed to another form by contractual provision and without evidence of insurability. Most term policies are convertible into permanent insurance. **(LI)**

Cost Basis. Money which has already been taxed; used in reference to taxation of investment dollars. **(PE)**

Cost Sharing. A situation where covered persons pay a portion of the health costs such as deductibles, coinsurance, or copayment amounts. **(H)**

Countersignature. The signature of a licensed agent or representative on a policy. **(G)**

Court Bond. Any bond required of a litigant to enable him or her to pursue a remedy in court. **(G)**

Cover. (1) A contract of insurance. (2) To effect insurance, that is, to "cover" an insured, for instance, for automobile insurance effective as of a given time. (3) To include within the coverage of a contract of insurance. For example, one could "cover" additional buildings under a property insurance contract. **(G)**

Coverage. The scope of the protection provided under a contract of insurance. **(G)**

Coverage Part. Any one of the individual commercial coverage parts that may be attached to a commercial policy. Under the latest commercial lines program, a coverage part may be issued as monoline policy or may be combined with others as part of a package policy. **(G)**

Coverage Trigger. A mechanism that determines whether a policy covers a particular claim for loss. For example, the difference between the coverage triggers of liability "occurrence" forms and "claims made" forms is that loss must occur during the policy period in the first case and the claim must be made during the policy period in the second case. **(LA)**

Credit Insurance. Insurance on a debtor in favor of a creditor to pay off the balance due on a loan in the event of the death or disability of the debtor. Liability insurance for abnormal loss from bad debts. **(H,LI)**

Custodial Care. Care that is primarily for meeting personal needs such as help in the activities of daily living (bathing, dressing, eating, taking medicine etc.). It can be provided by someone without professional medical skills or training but must be according to doctor's orders. **(H)**

Custodian. Under commercial crime insurance coverages, the named insured or any of the insured's partners or employees while having care and custody of insured property inside the insured's premises. **(C)**

Customary Charge. Used to determine Medicare benefit amounts, this usuallly means the average fee charged for a particular medical service in the geographical area in the preceding year. See also **Allowable Charge** and **Prevailing Charge. (H)**

D

Debit. (1) The amount of premium charged or debited to an agent to be collected. (2) The book of business represented by such premiums. (3) The territory where most of the insureds are located. (4) The total number of individual or home service insureds assigned to a given agent for collection of weekly or monthly premiums and for servicing, commonly referred to as "people in my debit." **(LI)**

Debris Removal Clause. A provision that may be included in a Property policy contract to provide the insured with indemnification for expenditures incurred in the removal of debris produced by the occurrence of an insured peril. Ordinarily a property policy covers only the direct damage caused by an insured peril. **(PR)**

Declaration. A formal written statement in which an individual avows under oath certain facts as personally known to him or her specifying of the facts constituting the plaintiff's cause of action against the defendant. **(LE)**

Declaration. A term used in insurance other than Life or Health to denote that portion of the contract in which is stated such information as the name and address of the insured, the property insured, its location and description, the policy period, the amount of insurance coverage, applicable premiums, and supplemental representations by the insured. **(LA,PR)**

Declination. Rejection of an application for insurance by the insurer. **(G)**

Decreasing Term. A form of life insurance that provides a death benefit which declines throughout the term of the contract, reaching zero at the end of the term. **(LI)**

Decreasing Term Insurance. A term life insurance policy where the death benefit decreases but the premium remains level for the policy term. See also **Increasing Term Insurance, Level Term Insurance** and **Term Insurance. (LI)**

Deductible. The portion of an insured loss to be borne by the insured before any recovery may be made from the insurer. **(G)**

Deductible, Calendar Year. A deductible that specifies that one deductible needs to be satisfied for a calendar year regardless of the number of claims. **(H)**

Deductible, Per Cause. A deductible that must be satisfied for each separate claim. **(H)**

Defamation. Under insurance law an unfair trade practice involving false, maliciously critical or derogatory statement intended to injure a person engaged in the insurance business. **(G)**

Deferred Annuity. An annuity contract that provides for the initiation of payments at some designated future date in contrast to one in which payment begins immediately on purchase. **(AN)**

Deferred Group Annuity. A group annuity contract providing for the purchase each year of a paid-up deferred annuity for each person covered in the group. The total amount of the annuity payments starts at a deferred date, usually retirement, and is the sum of the individual paid-up annuities. **(AN)**

Deflation. An economic period characterized by falling prices, high unemployment and a generally sluggish or slow economy. **(G)**

Demolition Clause. A provision that excludes liability for costs incurred in demolishing undamaged property, often necessitated by building ordinances requiring that structures must be demolished after a certain degree of damage has been sustained. **(PR)**

Dental Plan. A dental plan is any contractual arrangement for dental services provided or arranged for on a prepaid or postpaid individual or group service basis. **(H)**

Dental Plan Organization (DPO). A dental plan organization refers to a direct provider of dental services compensated on a prepaid or postpaid basis to individuals or groups. An arrangement for providing dental services indirectly through independent contractors or on a fee-for-service basis is not a DPO. A DPO may be an arrangement for dental services to be provided through an agreement with providers, or by employing dentists, where the dentists agree to treat enrollees of the plan in their private offices or a central facility. **(H)**

Dental Plan, Supplemental. A supplemental dental plan is an arrangement in which a dentist or group of dentists agree to relieve patients of paying any patient charges or copayments associated with dental insurance or other dental coverage for a predetermined fee. Supplemental dental plan may also refer to an arrangement which covers less than 50% of an enrollee's dental expenses, regardless of whether the enrollee has other coverage. **(H)**

Dependent Properties. Properties which an insured business does not own, operate or control, but upon which the insured's income depends. Examples include major suppliers or customers. Previously known as "contingent" properties. **(PR)**

Deposit Administration (DA). A group annuity providing for the accumulation of contributions in an undivided fund out of which annuities are purchased for each covered person in the group for retirement purposes. **(LI)**

Deposit (or Provisional) Premium. The premium paid at the inception of a contract which provides for future premium adjustments. It is based on an estimate of what the final premium will be. **(G)**

Depository Bond. A form of bond that guarantees to the government that its deposits with banks will not be subject to loss. **(S)**

Depreciation. A decrease in the value of any type of tangible property over a period of time resulting from use, wear and tear, or obsolescence. **(G)**

Direct Loss (or Damage). A loss which is a direct consequence of a particular peril. Fire damage to a refrigerator would be a direct loss. Spoiling of food in the refrigerator as a result of the fire damage would be an indirect loss. **(PR)**

Direct Selling System. A distribution system within which an insurer deals directly with its insureds through its own employees. This definition applies typically to property and liability insurance business. Included are mail-order insurance and the sale of insurance from vending machines at airport booths and elsewhere. **(G)**

Direct Writer. An insurer whose distribution mechanism is either the direct selling system or the exclusive agency system. **(LA,PR)**

Direct Writer. The insurer that negotiates with the insured as distinguished from the reinsurer. **(R)**

Disability Benefit. The benefit payable under a disability income policy or a provision of some other policy, such as a life insurance contract. **(H,LI)**

Disability Income Insurance. A form of health insurance that provides periodic payments to replace income, actually or presumptively lost, when the insured is unable to work as a result of sickness or injury. **(H)**

Discounted (Commuted) Value Table. A table showing the discounted or present value, for several interest rates, of dollars payable at various times in the future. **(G)**

Discovery Period. The period of time allowed an insured who has cancelled a bond to discover and report to the previous surety a loss that occurred during the term of that bond. Losses so reported are paid by the original surety even though another surety is on the risk at the time of the discovery. The usual discovery period is one year. **(S)**

Dismemberment. The loss of, or loss of use of, specified members of the body resulting from accidental bodily injury. **(H)**

Dividend. (1) The return of part of the premium paid for a policy issued on a participating basis by either a mutual or a stock insurer. (2) A portion of the surplus paid to the stockholders of a corporation. **(G)**

Dividend Additions. An option whereby the insured can leave dividends with the insurer, and each dividend is used to buy a single premium life insurance policy for whatever amount it will purchase. Also called **Paid-Up Additions.** **(LI)**

Dividend Option. Alternative ways in which insureds under participating life insurance policies may elect to receive their policyholder dividends. **(LI)**

Domestic Insurer (or Company). An insurer formed under the laws of the state in which the insurance is written. **(G)**

Double Indemnity. Payment of twice the basic benefit in the event of loss resulting from specified causes or under specified circumstances. For example, a life insurance contract may provide for twice the basic benefit if death is due to accident. Accident policies may provide double indemnity coverage for death due to an elevator accident. See also **Multiple Indemnity.** **(H,LI)**

Dread (or Specified) Disease Policy. Coverage, usually with a high maximum limit, for all types of medical expenses arising out of diseases named in the contract. Common diseases covered are poliomyelitis, diphtheria, multiple sclerosis, spinal meningitis, and tetanus. Cancer is sometimes covered or may be added with some companies by a rider. **(H)**

Dual Choice. The federal requirement that employers having 25 or more employees who are within the service area of a federally qualified HMO, who are paying at least minimum wage and offer a health plan to their employees, must offer HMO coverage as well as an indemnity plan. **(H)**

E

Earned Income. The money individuals earn as a result of working at some job or occupation for which they are paid a salary. **(G)**

Earned Premium. The amount of the premium that has been "used up" during the term of a policy. For example, if a one-year policy has been in effect six months, half of the total premium has been earned. **(G)**

Earth Movement. A peril including landslide, mudflow, earth sinking, rising or shifting, and earthquake. Usually excluded on homeowners' and commercial property policies. **(PR)**

Economic Risk. A risk experienced by those who invest in securities identified as the uncertainty of the economy. **(PE)**

Effective Date. The date on which the protection of an insurance policy or bond goes into effect. **(G)**

Electronic Data Processing (EDP) Coverage. Specialized type of insurance designed to cover computer equipment, data systems, information storage media and expenses or income loss related to EDP losses. **(PR)**

Elimination Period. A loosely used term, sometimes designating the probationary period, but most often designating the waiting period in a health insurance policy. See also **Probationary Period** and **Waiting Period. (H)**

Embezzlement. Fraudulent use of money or property which has been entrusted to one's care. **(S)**

Emergency. An injury or disease which happens suddenly and requires treatment within 24 hours. **(H)**

Employee Dishonesty Coverage Form. A commercial crime coverage form, which is actually a fidelity bond, providing coverage for losses resulting from employee dishonesty. This form covers losses of money, securities, and property other than money and securities. **(C)**

Employee Pension Benefit Plan or Pension Plan. Any program established and maintained by an employer or an employee organization providing retirement benefits to employees or deferred income until employment is terminated. **(PE)**

Employee Retirement Income Security Act (ERISA). This act prescribes federal standards for funding, participation, vesting, termination, disclosure, fiduciary responsibility, and tax treatment of private pension plans. **(LI)**

Employee Stock Ownership Plan (ESOP). A qualified employee plan which provides eligible employees with part ownership in the corporation for which they work. Stock is issued and held in trust for the benefit of the employees. **(PE)**

Employee Welfare Benefit Plan. Any program established or maintained by an employer or an employee organization to provide its participants or their beneficiaries with medical, surgical, or hospital care, or benefits in the event of sickness, accident, disability, death or unemployment. **(PE)**

Employers Liability Coverage. This is coverage B of the standard workers compensation policy. It provides coverage against the common law liability of an employer for injuries to employees as distinguished from the liability imposed by a workers compensation law. Employers liability applies in situations where a worker does not come under these laws. **(WC)**

Employers Non-Ownership Automobile Liability. (1) Liability arising out of the operation of an automobile not owned by the insured. This frequently results when an employee uses his own personal car in the business activities of the insured. (2) Insurance coverage for the liability exposure mentioned above. **(AU)**

Endorsement. A written or printed form attached to the policy which alters provisions of the contract. **(G)**

Endowment Insurance. A form of life insurance where the face amount is payable to the insured at the end of the contract period or to a beneficiary if the insured dies before that. An example would be an insured purchasing an endowment payable at age 65. Upon reaching that age, the proceeds would be payable to the insured. If the insured dies prior to that age, the proceeds would be payable to the designated beneficiary as a life insurance benefit. **(LI)**

Excess Interest. Interest credited to an insured's contract in excess of the amount guaranteed by the terms of the contract. **(LI)**

Exclusion Ratio. The relationship or ratio of cost basis to total expected return from an annuity; used to calculate the percentage of each annuity payment which is considered to be a return of cost basis. **(AN)**

Exclusions. Causes, conditions or property listed in the policy which are not covered and for which no benefits are payable. **(G)**

Exclusive Agency System. An insurance distribution system within which agents sell and service insurance contracts that limit representation to one insurer and which reserve to the insurer the ownership, use, and control of policy records and expiration date. See also **Direct Writer. (G)**

Exclusive Provider Organization (EPO). A type of preferred provider organization where individual members use particular preferred providers rather than having a choice of a variety of preferred providers. EPOs are characterized by a primary physician who monitors care and makes referrals to a network of providers. **(H)**

Expectation of Life. The average number of years of life remaining for persons of a given age according to a particular mortality table. Also called life expectancy. **(LI)**

Expected Mortality. The expected incidence of death within a given group during a given period of time as shown on a mortality table. **(LI)**

Expense Constant. A flat charge added to the premium of small accounts where the premium is so low that the cost of issuing and servicing the policy cannot be recovered. Most often used with workers compensation policies. **(G)**

Expense Guarantee. One of the guarantees of all annuities; that is, the guarantee that expenses, the cost of doing business, will not be increased or exceed a certain percentage of the annuity contributions. **(AN)**

Expense Ratio. The percentage of the premium dollar devoted to paying the expenses of an insurer, other than losses. **(G)**

Experience. (1) The loss record. It can be that of an insured, an agent, a territory, a type of insurance written, or any other category. (2) A statistical compilation relating losses to premiums. **(G)**

Experience Modification. The increase or decrease in premiums resulting from the application of an experience rating plan, usually expressed as a percentage. **(G)**

Experienced Mortality. The mortality that actually occurs to a group of inureds of a given insurance company in contrast to expected mortality. (See **Expected Mortality**.) **(LI)**

Expiration. The date indicated in an insurance contract as its termination date. **(G)**

Expiry. The termination of a term life insurance policy at the end of its period of coverage. **(LI)**

Explanation of Benefits (EOB). The statement sent to a participant in a health plan listing services, amounts paid by the plan, and total amount billed to the patient. **(H)**

Exposure. (1) The state of being subject to the possibility of loss. (2) The extent of risk as measured by payroll, gate receipts, area, or other standards. (3) The possibility of loss to a risk being caused by its surroundings. This is used in property insurance rating. (4) Surroundings producing a loss to the insured property. An example of definitions (3) and (4) would be an insured building suffering loss because a dynamite factory next to it exploded. **(G)**

Express Authority. Authority of an agent that is specifically granted by the insurer in the agency contract or agreement. **(G)**

Extended Care Facility. A facility such as a nursing home which is licensed to provide 24-hour nursing care service in accordance with state and local laws. Three levels of care may be provided—skilled, intermediate, custodial, or any combination. **(H)**

Extended Coverage (EC). A common extension of property insurance beyond coverage for fire and lightning. Extended coverage adds insurance against loss by the perils of windstorm, hail, explosion, riot and riot attending a strike, aircraft damage, vehicle damage, and smoke damage. At one time EC was added by endorsement. In recent years it has been included on many forms as either an optional coverage or as part of the minimum coverages provided. **(PR)**

Extended Reporting Period (ERP). A period allowing for making claims after expiration of a "claims-made" liability policy. Also known as a "tail." See also **Basic ERP, Supplemental ERP, Mini Tail, Maxi Tail. (LA)**

Extortion. The surrender of property away from an insured's premises as a result of a threat to do bodily harm to an insured or an employee, or to a relative or invitee of either, who is or allegedly is being held captive. **(C)**

Extra Expense Coverage Form. A commercial property form designed to cover extra expenses incurred by a business so it can remain in operation following a property loss. See **Extra Expense Insurance. (PR)**

Extra Expense Insurance. A form that provides reimbursement to the insured for the extra expenses reasonably incurred to continue the operation of a business when the described property has been damaged by a peril covered by the contract. This insurance is normally used by businesses where continuity of operation, regardless of cost, is a necessity as, for example, any business that would permanently lose customers if there were any suspension of operations. The term **Additional Living Expense Insurance** is defined with regard to extra expenses incurred by individuals, and such coverage is a common feature of homeowner policies. **(PR)**

F

Face. The first page of a life insurance policy. **(LI)**

Face Amount. The amount of insurance provided by the terms of an insurance contract, usually found on the face of the policy. In a life insurance policy, the death benefit. **(G)**

Facility-of-Payment Clause. A contract provision found in industrial life policies which permits the insurer to pay a portion of the proceeds of the policy to any relative or person who has possession of the policy and who appears equitably entitled to such payment. This provision is designed to facilitate payment when some doubt may exist as to who the beneficiary is and to save legal expenses in the settling of an estate. **(LI)**

Fair Credit Reporting Act. Public Law 91-508 requires that an applicant be advised if a consumer report may be requested and be told the scope of the possible investigation. Should the request for insurance be declined because of information contained in that report, the applicant must be given the name and address of the reporting agency. **(G)**

Family Expense Policy. A policy which insures the medical expenses of all members of a family. **(H)**

Family Income Policy. A policy that pays an income up to some future date designated in the policy to the beneficiary after the death of the insured. The period of payment is measured from the date of the inception of the contract, and at the end of the income period the face amount of the policy is paid to the beneficiary. If the insured lives beyond the income period, only the face amount is payable in the event of the insured's death. **(LI)**

Family Maintenance Policy. A policy that pays an income to the beneficiary starting after the death of the insured and continuing for a stated period of time. At the end of the income period, the face amount of the policy is paid to the beneficiary. **(LI)**

Federal Emergency Management Agency. A government agency that provides disaster relief during emergencies, such as floods, fire, earthquakes, etc. **(PR)**

Federal Estate Tax. The federal tax which is imposed on the deceased's estate which includes the total assets comprising a person's estate at death. **(G)**

Fidelity Bond. A bond which will reimburse an employer for loss up to the amount of the bond, sustained by an employer (the insured) by reason of any dishonest act of an employee (or employees) covered by the bond. **(C)**

Fiduciary. A person holding the funds or property of another in a position of trust, and who is obligated to act in a prudent and ethical manner. An example would be an attorney, bank trustee, the executor of an estate, etc.. **(G)**

Fiduciary Bond. A bond which guarantees the faithful performance of a fiduciary. **(S)**

Financial Responsibility Law. A state law which requires the insured to furnish evidence of ability to pay for losses. Some laws require this evidence before an accident, whereas others require evidence after the first accident. Evidence of ability to pay most often takes the form of an insurance policy with certain minimum limits of coverage. **(AU)**

Fire. Combustion which is rapid enough to produce a flame or glow. Property insurance only covers "hostile" fires, which means those that have escaped their intended limits or were not started intentionally. Fires in their proper contained area are called "friendly fires" and are not covered under most basic property insurance policies. **(PR)**

Fire Insurance. (1) Insurance contracts that indemnify an insured for loss caused by the destruction of the insured's property resulting from fire. (2) The field of insurance that provides insurance policies on the insured's property for a variety of perils, including fire. **(PR)**

"First" Named Insured. The first named insured appearing on a commercial policy. The latest forms permit the insurer to satisfy contractual duties by giving notice to the "first" named insured rather than requiring notice to all named insureds. **(G)**

Fixed-Amount Installments. A settlement option under which fixed, periodic benefits payments are made until the principal and interest are exhausted. **(LI)**

Fixed Dollar Annuity. Guarantees a fixed, minimum dollar payout, during each payout period. **(AN)**

Fixed-Period Installments. A settlement option under which the proceeds are guaranteed to be paid in equal installments for a specified period of time. **(LI)**

Flat Cancellation. A policy which is cancelled upon its effective date. Usually under a flat cancellation no premium charge is made. **(G)**

Flexible Premium Annuity. An annuity that allows the contract holder to vary the amount of the premium payment, or stop payments and resume payments at will. A flexible premium annuity is used to fund IRA and Keogh retirement plans because it allows the amount of premium to change as wages change. **(AN)**

Flexible Premium Policy. A life insurance policy under which the policyholder may vary the amount or timing of premium payments. **(LI)**

Floater. A form of insurance that applies to movable property, whatever its location, if it is within the territorial limits imposed by the contract. The coverage "floats" with the property. **(IM)**

Foreign Insurer. An insurer domiciled in a state of the United States other than the one in which the insured's insurance is written. **(G)**

Forgery. The false and fraudulent making or altering of a written instrument. **(C)**

Forgery Bond. See **Depositor's Forgery Insurance.** **(C)**

Forgery or Alteration Coverage Form. A commercial crime coverage form that protects the insured against losses resulting from forgery or alteration of outgoing checks, drafts, promissory notes and similar instruments drawn against the insured's accounts. **(C)**

Form. (1) An insurance document which, when attached to a policy, makes it complete. For example, a Standard Fire policy would have to have a Business Interruption form attached to it to make up a Business Interruption policy. (2) Any rider or endorsement, such as a Deductible Endorsement "form." **(G)**

401(k) Plan. A qualified elective deferral plan where employee contributions are made by means of a salary reduction agreement, with or without matching employer contributions. Authorized by section 401(k) of the Internal Revenue Code. **(PE)**

403(b). A section of the Internal Revenue Code authorizing tax sheltered annuities as qualified pension plans for employees of nonprofit organizations. **(PE)**

Franchise Insurance. A plan for covering groups of persons with individual policies having uniform provisions, although they may differ in benefits. Individual contracts are issued to each person with individual underwriting. It is usually applied to groups too small to qualify for true group coverage, and the solicitation of cases usually takes place among an employer's workforce with employer consent. In life insurance, it is sometimes called wholesale insurance. **(H)**

Fraternal Insurance. Insurance offered a special group of people, namely, members of a lodge or a fraternal order. Such insurance may be written on an assessment basis or on a legal reserve basis. **(H,LI)**

Free Look. A period of time (usually 10, 20 or 30 days) during which a policyholder may examine a newly issued individual policy of life or health insurance, and surrender it in exchange for a full refund of premium if not satisfied for any reason. **(H,LI)**

G

Garage Keepers Legal Liability Insurance. An insurance contract that protects a garage keeper against liability for damage to vehicles in the keeper's care, custody, or control caused by specific perils. **(LA)**

Garage Liability Insurance. Insurance to protect garage owners or automobile dealers for liabilities arising out of their business operations. **(LA)**

Gatekeeper Model. Under this model of HMO and PPO organizations, the primary care physician (the gatekeeper) is the initial contact for the patient for medical care and for referrals. This is also called a closed access or closed panel. **(H)**

General Account. An investment portfolio used by the insurer for investment of premium income. This portfolio generally consists of safe, conservative, guaranteed investments, such as real estate and mortgages. **(AN)**

General Agent (GA). An individual appointed by a life or health insurer to administer its business in a given territory. General agents are responsible for building their own agency and service force and are compensated on a commission basis, with possibly some additional expense allowances. **(H,LI)**

General Aggregate Limit. A Commercial General liability limit that applies to all damages paid for bodily injury, property damage, personal injury, advertising injury, and medical expenses, except damages included in the products-completed operations hazard. **(LA)**

Glass Coverage Form. A commercial property form used to insure plate glass, lettering, frames and ornamentation. It has replaced earlier commercial glass insurance forms. **(PR)**

Good Driver Discount. A system which entitles good drivers (as defined by driving safety record, number of miles driven annually, number of years driving experience, and other factors related to the risk of loss) to discounts on automobile insurance rates and premiums. See also **Safe Driver Plan.** **(AU)**

Grace Period. A prescribed period, usually 30 to 31 days from the premium due date, during which an insurance contract is in force and the premium may be paid. **(H,LI)**

Graded Premium. A modified life insurance policy for which the initial premium is low, and then increases in steps over a period of time (usually five years), after which it becomes a level premium. **(LI)**

Gross Earnings Business Interruption. An insurance form providing for a business to recover its gross earnings less expenses which discontinue in the event of a loss, such as a fire. **(G)**

Gross Line. The total limit accepted by an insurer on an individual risk, including the amount to be reinsured. **(G)**

Group Contract. A contract of insurance made with an employer or other entity that covers a group of persons identified by reference to their relationship to the entity buying the contract. The group contractual arrangement is generally used to cover employees of a common employer, members of a trade association or trusteeship, members of a welfare or employee benefit association, members of a labor union, or members of a professional or other association not formed only for the purpose of obtaining insurance. **(H,LI)**

Guaranteed Cash Value. In whole life insurance, the policy's cash value increases over the life of the policy until at the insured's age 100 the cash value is equal to the policy's face amount. **(LI)**

Guaranteed Insurability. An option in life and health insurance contracts that permits the insured to buy additional prescribed amounts of insurance at prescribed future time intervals without evidence of insurability. **(H,LI)**

Guaranteed Renewable. A contract that the insured has the right to continue in force by the timely payment of premiums for a substantial period of time as set forth in the contract. During that period of time, the insurer has no right to make any change in any provision of the contract other than a change in the premium rate for all insureds in the same class. Contrast with **Noncancellable,** from which Guaranteed Renewable should be distinguished. **(H,LI)**

Guest Property Coverage. Two commercial crime coverage forms are available for hotels, motels, inns and other lodging facilities to protect the property of guests against loss or damage. One form covers guests' property while it is in a safe deposit box on the insured's premises. The other form covers an insured's legal liability for loss or damage to guests' property while in the insured's premises or in the insured's possession. **(C)**

H

Hazard. A specific situation that increases the probability of the occurrence of loss arising from a peril, or that may influence the extent of the loss. For example, accident, sickness, fire, flood, liability, burglary, and explosion are perils. Slippery floors, unsanitary conditions, shingled roofs, congested traffic, unguarded premises, and uninspected boilers are also hazards. **(G)**

Health Insurance. Insurance against loss by sickness or bodily injury. The generic form for those forms of insurance that provide lump sum or periodic payments in the event of loss occasioned by bodily injury, sickness or disease, and medical expense. The term health insurance is now used to replace such terms as accident insurance, sickness insurance, medical expense insurance, accidental death insurance, and dismemberment insurance. The form is sometimes called accident and health, accident and sickness, accident, or disability income insurance. **(H)**

Health Maintenance Organization (HMO). An HMO is a prepaid medical service plan which provides services to plan members. Medical providers contract with the HMO to provide medical services to plan members. Members must use contracted providers. The emphasis is on preventive medicine, and it is an alternative to employee benefit plans. Employers of more than 25 persons are required to offer the alternative of HMO to employees, but not if the cost exceeds that of present employee benefit plans. **(H)**

High Pressure Tactics. An illegal method of marketing insurance policies (often associated with Medicare supplement policies) employing tactics having the tendency to induce the purchase or to recommend the purchase of coverage through force, fright, explicit or implied threat, or undue pressure. **(H)**

Hired Automobile. Autos the insured leases, hires, rents, or borrows, but not autos owned by employees or members of their households. **(AU)**

HIV. See **Human Immunodeficiency Virus. (LI,H).**

Hold Harmless Agreement. A contractual arrangement whereby one party assumes the liability inherent in a situation, thereby relieving the other party of responsibility. Such agreements are typically found in contracts like leases, sidetrack agreements, and easements. For example, a typical lease may provide that the lessee must "hold harmless" the lessor for any liability from accidents arising out of the premises. The effect of such an agreement is that the lessee must provide a defense for the lessor, and if any judgment is rendered against the lessor, the lessee would have to pay. **(LA)**

Home Service Insurance. A variation in the industrial life concept, home service life insurance policies are usually modest in size, ranging from $10,000 to $15,000 in face value, and are typically sold on a monthly debit plan (automatic bank draft) or payments by mail. **(LI)**

Homeowners Policy. A property and liability insurance contract that provides insurance against any of the property and liability perils to which a homeowner or renter is exposed. **(LA,PR)**

Hospital Benefits. Benefits payable for hospital room and board, plus miscellaneous charges resulting from hospitalization. **(H)**

Hospital Confinement Rider. An optional disability income rider that results in the elimination period being waived when the insured is hospitalized as an inpatient. **(H)**

Hospital Indemnity. Coverage that pays based on daily, weekly, or monthly limits regardless of the amount of actual hospital expenses. **(H)**

Hospitalization Expense Policy. A policy which covers daily hospital room and board charges and also covers miscellaneous hospital expenses (such as X-ray, etc.). It also often covers emergency treatment charges and many times will also include a surgical benefit. **(H)**

Hospitalization Insurance. A form of insurance that provides reimbursement within contractual limits for hospital and specific related expenses arising from hospitalization caused by injury or sickness. **(H)**

Hospital/Surgical Expense Policy. A policy combining benefits of hospital and surgical coverages. (See also Hospital Expense and Surgical Expense policies.)

HR-10. A qualified retirement plan for the self employed. Also known as a Keogh Plan. **(PE)**

Human Immunodeficiency Virus. The virus, commonly referred to as HIV, which causes acquired immunodeficiency syndrome, an infectious and incurable disease commonly referred to as AIDS. **(G)**

I

Illegal Occupation Provision. A health insurance policy provision that voids liability if the loss results from the insured's committing or attempting to commit a felony or from the insured's engaging in an illegal occupation. **(H)**

Impaired Insurer. An insurer which is in financial difficulty to the point where its ability to meet financial obligations or regulatory requirements is in question. **(G)**

Impaired Property. Tangible property which cannot be used or has become less useful because it incorporates the insured's product or work which is defective or inadequate, or because the insured has failed to fulfill a contractual obligation. **(LA)**

Implied Authority. Authority of an agent that the public may reasonably believe the agent to have. If the authority to collect and remit premiums is not expressly granted in the agency contract, but the agent does so on a regular basis and the insurer accepts, the agent has implied authority to do so. **(G)**

Improvements and Betterments. Additions or changes made by a lessee at his own cost to a building which he is occupying which enhance its value. These become part of the realty and require special insurance consideration. **(PR)**

Incidents of Ownership. Various rights that may be exercised under the policy contract by the policyowner. Some of the incidents of ownership would be: (1) the right to cash in the policy, (2) to receive a loan on the cash value of the policy, and (3) to change the beneficiary. **(LI)**

Incontestable Clause. A clause in a policy providing that after a policy has been in effect for a given length of time (two or three years), the insurer shall not be able to contest the statements contained in the application. A health insurance provision also states that after that time no claim shall be denied or reduced on the grounds that a condition not excluded by name at the time of issue existed prior to the effective date. In life policies, if an insured lied as to the condition of his or her health at the time the policy was taken out, that lie could not be used to contest payment under the policy if death occurred after the time limit stated in the incontestable clause. **(H,LI)**

Increasing Term Insurance. A term life insurance policy where the death benefit increases but the premium remains level for the policy term. See also **Decreasing Term Insurance, Level Term Insurance** and **Term Insurance. (LI)**

Incurred Losses. The losses occurring within a fixed period, whether or not adjusted or paid during the same period. As an example, in workers compensation claims losses occur during a given policy period, but benefits may continue to be paid for many years. The estimated value of the total claim would be an "incurred loss" for the policy period during which the loss occurred. **(G)**

Indemnify. To restore the victim of a loss to the same position as before the loss occurred. **(G)**

Indemnity Bond. A bond that indemnifies an obligee against loss which may arise as the result of failure to perform on the part of the principal. **(S)**

Independent Contractor. One who agrees to perform according to a contract and who is not an employee. **(G)**

Indirect Loss (or Damage). Loss resulting from a peril but not caused directly and immediately by that peril. For example: Loss of property due to fire is a direct loss, while the loss of rental income as the result of the fire would be an indirect loss. See also **Consequential Loss. (PR)**

Individual Contract. A contract made with an individual that covers that individual and perhaps also specified members of his or her family for benefits as described in the policy. **(H)**

Individual Retirement Account (IRA). A qualified retirement plan established by ERISA for anyone under age 70½ with earned income, allowing them to set aside up to $2,000 per year on a tax favorable basis for retirement purposes. **(PE)**

Industrial Life Insurance. One of the major classes of insurance. It is generally sold in amounts of less than $1,000 by agents who service insureds on debits. The premiums are collected weekly or monthly at the address of the insured. See also **Debit. (LI)**

Inflation. An economic period characterized by rising prices, low unemployment, an expanding economy and erosion of consumer's purchasing power due to the higher cost of living. **(G)**

In-Force Business. Life or health insurance for which premiums are being paid or for which premiums have been fully paid. The term refers to the total face amount of a life insurer's portfolio of business. In health insurance it refers to the total premium volume of an insurer's portfolio of business. **(H,LI)**

Inherent Explosion. An explosion caused by some condition existing in and natural to an insured's premises. An example would be a dust explosion in a grain elevator. **(PR)**

Inherent Vice. A fault in property that leads to its self-destruction. Insurance contracts usually exclude such damage. **(IM,PR)**

Inland Marine Insurance. A branch of the insurance business which developed from the insuring of shipments which did not involve ocean voyages. The inland marine forms borrowed their language from fire, ocean marine, theft and other contracts. Exposures eligible for this form of protection are described in the nationwide definition of marine insurance. Such diverse properties as bridges, tunnels, jewelry and furs can now be written under Inland Marine forms. **(IM)**

Inspection. Independent checking on facts about an applicant, policyholder, or claimant, usually by a commercial inspection agency. **(G)**

Installment Refund Annuity. An annuity which promises to continue the periodic payments after the death of the annuitant, until the combined benefits paid to the annuitant and to the beneficiary have equaled the purchase price of the annuity. **(AN)**

Installment Settlement. Payment of the proceeds of a life insurance policy or its cash value in installments rather than in a lump sum. The term refers to any one of the options in a life insurance policy that has this result. **(LI)**

Insurability. Acceptability to the insurer of an applicant for insurance. **(G)**

Insurable Interest. Any interest a person has in a possible subject of insurance, such as a car or home, of such a nature that a certain happening might cause that person financial loss. **(G)**

Insurable Risk. A risk which meets most of the following requisites: (1) The loss insured against must be capable of being defined. (2) It must be accidental. (3) It must be large enough to cause a hardship to the insured. (4) It must belong to a homogeneous group of risks large enough to make losses predictable. (5) It must not be subject to the same loss at the same time as a large number of other risks. (6) The insurance company must be able to determine a reasonable cost for the insurance. (7) The insurance company must be able to calculate the chance of loss. **(G)**

Insurance. A formal social device for reducing risk by transferring the risks of several individual entities to an insurer. The insurer agrees, for a consideration, to assume, to a specified extent, the losses suffered by the insured. **(G)**

Insurance Commissioner. The head of a state's insurance regulatory agency in most jurisdictions. In some states the title of Director or Superintendent is used. **(G)**

Insurance Company. See **Insurer. (G)**

Insurance Department. A governmental bureau in each state and the federal government in Canada charged with the administration of insurance laws, including the licensing of agents and insurers and their regulation and examination. In some jurisdictions the department is a division of another state department or bureau. **(G)**

Insurance Examiner. The representative of a state insurance department assigned to participate in the official audit and examination of an insurer. **(G)**

Insurance Policy. The printed form which serves as the contract between an insurer and an insured. **(G)**

Insured. The party to an insurance arrangement whom the insurer agrees to indemnify for losses, provide benefits for, or render services to. This term is preferred to such terms as policyholder, policyowner, and assured. See also **Named Insured. (G)**

Insured Contract. A definition which shapes the extent of contractual liability coverage by describing the types of contracts which are insured. On modern liability forms, "insured contract" includes leases of premises, sidetrack agreements, elevator maintenance agreements, easement agreements, and other agreements related to the insured's business. **(LA)**

Insurer. The party to an insurance arrangement who undertakes to indemnify for losses, provide pecuniary benefits, or render services. It is desirable to use the word "insurer" in preference to "carrier" or "company" since it is a functional word applicable without ambiguity to all types of individuals or organizations performing the insurance function. The word insurer is generally used in statutory law. **(G)**

Insuring Agreement (or Clause). That portion of an insurance contract which states the perils insured against, the persons and/or property covered, their locations, and the period of the contract. **(G)**

Intentional Injury. An injury resulting from an act intended to inflict injury. In an accident insurance contract, an intentionally self-inflicted injury is not covered (because it is not an accident). In general, intentional injuries inflicted on the insured are covered (assuming no collusion). **(H)**

Interline Endorsement. An endorsement that may apply to more than one coverage in a commercial package policy. Interline endorsements were developed to reduce redundancy. **(G)**

Interest, Post-Judgment. Money the plaintiff would have earned if the favorable judgment had been paid at the time of the first judgment, instead of at a later date due to an appeal. **(LA)**

Interest, Pre-Judgment. Money the plaintiff would have earned if the favorable judgment had been paid at the time of injury or damage, instead of at a later date when a judgment is made. **(LA)**

Interest Rate Risk. A risk faced by investors who invest in bonds characterized by an individual being locked into a lower interest rate when interest rates are generally increasing in the economy. **(G)**

Interest Sensitive Provision. Provisions in variable and flexible premium policies which guarantee certain interest earnings plus an additional interest percentage should the current interest rate rise above a specified percentage. **(LI)**

Interline Endorsement. Commercial endorsements that apply, or could apply, to more than one coverage part of a package policy. **(G)**

Intoxicants and Narcotics Provision. A health insurance policy provision that voids liability if the loss results from the insured's being intoxicated or under the influence of any narcotic unless administered on the advice of a physician. **(H)**

Involuntary Unemployment Insurance. Insurance providing coverage for consumer credit repayment obligations when an insured is involuntarily unemployed due to individual or mass layoff, general strike, termination by employer, unionized labor dispute, and lockout. Usually sold to borrowers under a master group policy issued to a creditor (bank, association, or other financial institution). Also called **Job Loss Insurance**. Can be classified as either property/casualty or life/health insurance. **(G)**

Investment Company Act of 1940. A federal law which regulates the organization and activities of investment companies and requires the registration of investment companies with the federal government. **(G)**

Irrevocable Beneficiary. A beneficiary that cannot be changed without his or her permission. **(LI)**

Investigative Consumer Report. A report ordered on an insured or applicant under which information about the person's character, reputation, or lifestyle is obtained through personal interviews with the person's neighbors, friends, associates or acquaintances. Contrast with **Consumer Report**. **(G)**

J

Joint Life Insurance. See **Joint Insurance. (LI)**

Joint Life and Survivorship Annuity. A contract which provides income to two or more people and continues in force as long as any one of them survives. **(LI)**

Joint-Survivor Option. An annuity option which provides for a guaranteed income to the annuitant and upon death of the annuitant, a continued income to the annuitant's survivor. **(AN)**

Judgment Rates. See **"A" Rates. (G)**

Judicial Bond. A bond required in civil and criminal court actions. **(C)**

Juvenile Policies. In life insurance, policies modified to meet the needs of young children (usually under age 15). **(LI)**

K

Key Person (Key Employee) Insurance Policy. — An insurance policy on the life of a key employee whose death would cause the employer financial loss, owned by and payable to the employer. In health insurance, the term is also used to designate salary continuation insurance payable to a key employee or to a medical benefits plan, payable to that employee paying all or part of the premium. **(LI)**

Kidnapping Coverage. Insurance against the hazard of a person being seized outside the insured premises and forced to return and open the premises of a safe therein or to give information which will enable the criminal to do so. This has frequently been one of the perils covered under a package crime policy. See also **Extortion Coverage Form. (C)**

L

Lapse. Termination of a policy because of failure to pay the premium. In life insurance, the term refers to nonpayment before the policy has developed any nonforfeiture values. If it has, and the premium is not paid, it is said to have lapsed "except as to any nonforfeiture benefits that may apply." **(G)**

Laser Beam Endorsement. An endorsement to a "claims made" liability form used to exclude specific accidents, products, work or locations. It earned its nickname because it allows an insurer to zero in with a sharp focus to exclude specific exposures. **(LA)**

Lease. Contract whereby the owner or user of property (the lessor) agrees to let another party (the lessee) use the property for a consideration (money or rent). **(LE)**

Leasehold Insurance. Insurance for the tenant of property leased against the loss of value of the lease or of profit from a sub-lease through termination of the lease by fire or other peril insured against. **(PR)**

Leasehold Interest Coverage Form. Commercial property coverage form used to insure an insured tenant's interest in a favorable lease under which the rent paid is less than the rental value of alternative premises. Pays the difference between rent paid and the rental value if lease is cancelled because of property damage. **(PR)**

Legal Reserve. The minimum reserves required to be established for a life insurance contract under the laws of the jurisdiction within which an insurer operates. **(LI)**

Legal Reserve Life Insurance Company. A life insurer that maintains the reserves required by the jurisdiction within which it operates. **(LI)**

Legislative Risk. A risk faced by investors whereby changes in tax laws can result in adverse effects on the individual's investment results. **(G)**

Lessee. The person to whom a lease is granted. Commonly called the "tenant." **(LE)**

Lessee's Safe Deposit Box Coverage Form. A commercial crime coverage form that protects against loss of property other than money while it is in the insured's safe deposit box inside a depository premises. **(C)**

Lessor. The person granting a lease. Also known as the "landlord." **(LE)**

Level Premium Insurance. That form of insurance for which the premium remains the same throughout the life of the contract. Most whole life insurance is paid for in this way. The amount of a level premium is higher than needed for the protection afforded in the early years of the contract but less than needed for protection in the later years. It is a method of leveling off the cost of insurance so as not to have it increase each year until it becomes inaffordable. **(LI)**

Level Term Insurance. A term life insurance policy where the death benefit and premium remain level for the policy term. See also **Decreasing Term Insurance, Increasing Term Insurance** and **Term Insurance. (LI)**

Liability. See **Legal liability. (LE)**

Liability Insurance. That insurance which pays and renders service on behalf of an insured for loss arising out of his or her responsibility to others imposed by law or assumed by contract. **(LA)**

Liability Limits. The maximum amount for which a liability insurance company provides protection in a particular policy. **(LA)**

License and Permit Bonds. Bonds often required by jurisdictions to be posted by persons performing certain services, such as security dealers and plumbers. It provides indemnification in the event that the licensee fails to conform to pertinent regulations of the jurisdiction. **(S)**

Life Annuity. A contract that provides a stated income for life, payable annually or more frequently. **(AN)**

Life Expectancy. The average number of years remaining for a person of a given age to live as shown on the mortality or annuity table used as a reference. **(LI)**

Life Insurance (Generic). A contractual system of risk sharing under which contributions are accumulated and redistributed to meet the economic consequences of the uncertain duration of life. **(LI)**

Life Insurance (Narrow). An agreement that guarantees the payment of a stated amount of monetary benefits upon the death of the insured, or under other circumstances specified in the contract, such as total disability. **(LI)**

Life Insurance Cost Surrender Index. The guaranteed cash surrender value of a life insurance policy is often required to be calculated into an index for presentation to prospective life insurance buyers. Such an index determines the guaranteed cash surrender value, if any, available at the end of the 10th and 20th policy years according to the accumulation of the annual cash dividends at 5% interest compounded annually to the end of a selected period, if the policy is a participating policy. **(LI)**

Life With Period Certain. An annuity option which provides a lifetime income to the annuitant plus an extra guarantee of income for a specified period of time such as 5 or 10 years. The period certain provides income to the annuitant or the annuitant's survivor. **(AN)**

Lifetime Policy. (1) A policy guaranteed renewable or noncancellable to age 65 or some later date. (2) A policy paying disability benefits for life. **(LI)**

Limit of Liability. The maximum amount for which an insurer is liable as set forth in the contract. **(LA)**

Limitations. Exceptions to coverage and limitations of coverage as contained in an insurance contract. For instance, a limit of liability would be one limitation on an automobile policy. Another example would be policies written to cover only certain described automobiles, or, in the case of general liability insurance, certain described premises. **(G)**

Limited Agent. An agent authorized to transact only a limited form of insurance, such as travel-accident or credit insurance. In many states, limited agents are exempt from licensing examination and education requirements. **(G)**

Limited Health Insurance. Special health insurance policies that provide limited coverage for specific injuries or illnesses, such as travel accident, hospital income, and specified disease coverage. **(H)**

Limited Payment Life. A life insurance contract providing protection for the whole of life with premiums paid for an indicated number of years. See also **Life Paid Up At Age. (LI)**

Limited Payment Whole Life. A whole life policy that allows the policyholder to pay the entire premium in a shorter period of time (such as a 20 year period or to age 65). Compare with **Continuous Premium Whole Life** and **Single Premium Whole Life. (LI)**

Limited Policies. (1) Health insurance contracts, such as those offered by newspapers to their customers, with low limits and somewhat restricted forms. (2) Policies paid only upon the occurrence of certain contingencies, such as cancer, in contrast to policies covering all contingencies other than those excluded. **(H,LI)**

Limited Pollution Liability Coverage Form. Commercial form providing pollution liability coverage on a "claims made" basis, but not providing any coverage for clean-up costs. **(LA)**

Limits. (1) Ages below or above which the insurer will not issue a policy or above which it will not continue a policy presently in force. (2) The maximum amount of benefits payable for a given situation or occurrence, e.g., a limit of $50,000 on the contents of a home, or a $40,000 per accident limit for property damage liability. See also **Limit of Liability. (G)**

Livestock Insurance. A named perils contract that provides a prescribed lump sum payment to an insured upon the death of any animal covered by the policy. **(PR)**

Livestock Mortality Insurance. The equivalent of life insurance for livestock. **(PR)**

Living Need Benefits. A combination of life insurance and long-term care insurance which allows life insurance benefits to generate long-term care benefits. Up to a certain percentage of the life insurance policy's death benefit may be used in advance to offset nursing home or medical expenses, reducing the face amount of the life policy. **(H)**

Lloyd's Broker. A person who has the authority to negotiate insurance contracts with the underwriters on the floor at Lloyd's. See also **Lloyd's. (G)**

Loading. The amount added to the pure insurance cost to cover the cost of the operations of an insurer, the possibility that losses will be greater than statistically expected, and fluctuating interest rates on the insurer's investments. The "pure" insurance cost is that portion of the premium estimated to be necessary for losses. **(G)**

Long-Term Disability Insurance. A group or individual policy which provides coverage for longer than a short term, often until the insured reaches age 65 in the case of illness and for life in the case of accident. See also **Short-Term Disability Insurance. (H)**

Loss. Generally refers to (1) the amount of reduction in the value of an insured's property caused by an insured peril, (2) the amount sought through an insured's claim, or (3) the amount paid on behalf of an insured under an insurance contract. **(G)**

Loss Constant. A flat amount included in the premium for small workers compensation policies, for dwellings in some jurisdictions, and for some prescribed inland marine insurance lines. The purpose of the loss constant is to offset the greater-than-average loss experience which most small risks have when compared to all other risks in a given classification. **(G)**

Loss-Of-Income Benefits. Benefits paid for inability to work for remuneration because of disability resulting from accidental bodily injury or sickness. The loss of income may be real or presumptive. **(H)**

Loss of Income Insurance. Insurance paying loss of income benefits. **(H)**

Loss Prevention Service. Engineering and inspection work done by an insurance company or independent organization with the aim of removing or reducing dangerous conditions in order to prevent losses. **(G)**

Loss Ratio. The losses divided by the premiums paid. The numerator (losses) can be losses incurred or losses paid, and the denominator (premium) can be earned premiums or written premiums, depending on what use is going to be made of the loss ratio. **(G)**

M

Major Medical Insurance. A type of health insurance that provides benefits up to a high limit for most types of medical expenses incurred, subject to a large deductible. Such contracts may contain limits on specific types of charges, like room and board, and a percentage participation clause sometimes called a coinsurance clause. These policies usually pay covered expenses whether an individual is in or out of the hospital. **(H)**

Malpractice. Professional misconduct or lack of ordinary skill in the performance of a professional act which renders the practitioner liable to suit for damages. **(LA)**

Managed Care. A system of health care where the goal is a system that delivers quality, cost effective health care through monitoring and recommending utilization of services, and cost of services. **(H)**

Manual. A book giving rates, classifications, and underwriting rules for some line of insurance. An example would be the Automobile Manual which gives such information for automobile insurance. **(G)**

Manual Rates. Rates based on average claims data for a large number of groups. These rates are then adjusted for specific groups based on that group's characteristics, such as the type of industry, changes in benefits from the standard, etc. **(H)**

Manual Rates. Usually the published rate for some unit of insurance. An example is in the Workers Compensation Manual where the rates shown apply to each $100 of the payroll of the insured, $100 being the "unit." **(G)**

Manufacturers and Contractors Liability Insurance (M&C). A form of premises and operations liability insurance designed to cover manufacturing or contracting risks. The basis of premiums for this coverage is the payroll. **(LA)**

Market Conduct. Used to measure how insurance companies and insurance agents comply with state laws regulating the sales and marketing, underwriting, and issuance of insurance products. Proper market conduct means conducting insurance business fairly and responsibly. **(G)**

Market Conduct Examination. When state insurance department investigators examine the business practices and operations of an insurer and its agents in order to determine their authority to conduct insurance business in the state. **(G)**

Market Risk. A risk experienced by those who invest in securities which is the risk of possible loss of investment since there are no guarantees associated with such investments. **(G)**

Market Value Clause. A provision that may be used in certain property insurance forms which obligates an insurer to pay the established market price of destroyed or damaged stock rather than its cost to the insured, as is usually provided in the Standard Fire policy. This coverage is only available to manufacturers with finished products, not to wholesalers or retailers. **(PR)**

Master Policy. (1) The policy contract issued to an employer or other entity authorized by state law for a group insurance plan. See also the first definition of **Certificate of Insurance.** (2) A property insurance policy issued to an insured who can issue certificates of coverage to cover the property of others. **(G)**

Maturity Date. The date at which the face amount of a life insurance policy becomes payable by reason of either death or endowment. **(LI)**

Maxi Tail, or Full Tail. Unlimited extended reporting period allowing for making claims after expiration of a "claims-made" liability policy. See also **Supplemental Extended Reporting Period. (LA)**

Medicaid. A medical benefits program administered by states and subsidized by the federal government. Under this plan, various medical expenses will be paid to those who qualify. It is technically referred to as Title XIX Benefits. **(H)**

Medical Examination. The examination of an applicant for insurance or a claimant by a physician who acts in the capacity of the insurer's agent. **(H,LI)**

Medical Expense Insurance. A form of health insurance that provides benefits for medical, surgical, and hospital expenses. This term is used to include coverage under the names hospital-surgical expense insurance and medical care insurance. **(H)**

Medical Savings Account (MSA). An employer-funded account linked to a high deductible medical indemnity plan. Usually, the employer raises the plan deductible (usually by 300% to 400%) and in turn returns a portion of the premium savings to employees as contributions to the medical savings account. Employees can use the contributions to pay for health care expenses throughout the year, and at the end of the year may withdraw whatever remains in the account as cash. **(H)**

Medicare Benefits. Benefits provided by a Federal program as part of the Social Security program. It applies to persons over 65 years of age and certain disabled beneficiaries under the Social Security program. Benefits provide hospital insurance and supplementary medical insurance. **(H)**

Medicare Select Policy. A Medicare supplement policy or certificate that contains restricted network provisions conditioning the payment of benefits on the use of network providers. **(H)**

Medicare Supplement Insurance. Insurance coverage sold on an individual or group basis which helps to fill the gaps in the protection provided by the Medicare program. Medicare supplements cannot duplicate any benefits provided by Medicare, but may pay part or all of Medicare's deductibles and copayments, and may cover some services and expenses not covered by Medicare. **(H)**

Mercantile Robbery and Safe Burglary Policy. A once popular crime insurance form used by retail establishments to insure money and securities. This has been replaced by modern commercial crime coverage forms. **(C)**

Messenger. Under commercial crime insurance coverages, the named insured or any of the insured's partners or employees while having care and custody of property outside the insured's premises. **(C)**

MIB — Medical Information Bureau. An organization serving as a clearing house of medical information on impaired risks reported to it by insurance companies which are members of the service and reported to them as a source of underwriting information on applicants. **(H)**

Mini Tail. Automatic 60-day extended reporting period allowing for the making of claims after expiration of a "claims-made" liability policy. See also **Extended Reporting Period. (LA)**

Minimum Premium. A cost plus arrangement whereby the employer pays the insurer only a portion of the premium which is to be used for administration costs. The remainder is placed in a "bank account" which is then used by the insurer to pay claims. **(H)**

Minimum Premium. The smallest amount of premium for which an insurer will issue coverage under a given policy. **(G)**

Miscellaneous Expenses. Ancillary expenses, usually hospital charges other than daily room and board. Examples would be X-rays, drugs, and lab fees. The total amount of such charges that will be reimbursed is limited in most basic hospitalization policies. **(H)**

Misrepresentation. The use of oral or written statements that do not truly reflect the facts either by an insured on an application for insurance or by an insurer concerning the terms or benefits of an insurance policy. **(LE)**

Mode of Premium Payment. The method of premium payment (mode) elected by the policyowner. Modes generally available are monthly, quarterly, semiannually, and annually. **(G)**

Modified Endowment Contract. An endowment contract where the amount payable upon survival of the endowment period is greater than the face amount and the amount payable at death is the greater of the face amount or cash value. Modified endowment contracts are subject to taxation and subsequent penalties. **(LI)**

Monoline Policy. Any insurance coverage written as a single line policy. Contrast with **Package policy. (G)**

Moral Hazard. A condition of morals or habits that increases the probability of loss from a peril. An extreme example would be an individual who previously burned his or her own property to collect the insurance. **(G)**

Morale Hazard. Hazard arising out of an insured's indifference to loss because of the existence of insurance. The attitude, "It's insured, so why worry," is an example of a morale hazard. **(G)**

Morbidity. The relative incidence of disease. **(H)**

Mortality. Death. A mortality table shows the incidence of occurrence of death as a morbidity table shows the incidence or occurrence of sickness (or disability). **(G)**

Mortality Guarantee. The provision that an annuitant is guaranteed an income for life regardless of changes in the mortality of the population. **(AN)**

Mortgage. Interest in real property conveyed to mortgagee as security for the loan of money by the mortgagee to the mortgagor, often the money being used by the mortgagor for the purchase of the real property from its seller (this is known as a purchase money mortgage). **(LE)**

Mortgage (or Mortgagee) Clause. A provision attached to a Fire or other direct damage policy that covers mortgaged property, specifying that the loss reimbursement shall be paid to the mortgagee as the mortgagee's interest may appear, that the mortgagee's rights of recovery shall not be defeated by any act or neglect of the insured, and giving the mortgagee other rights, privileges, and duties. For instance, one duty is that the mortgagee must report to the insurer any change in hazards that he becomes aware of. **(PR)**

Mortgage Insurance. In life and health insurance, a policy covering a mortgagor from which the benefits are intended (1) to pay off the balance due on a mortgage upon the death of the insured, or (2) to meet the payments on a mortgage as they fall due in the case of the insured's death or disability. Also called **Mortgage Redemption Insurance. (H,LI)**

Motor Truck Cargo Policy — Carrier's Form. This form indemnifies the policyholder, a trucker, for loss or damage resulting from legal liability as a carrier while transporting the property of others. It does not insure against any loss for which he is not legally liable. Statutory law requires a truckman to carry a minimum amount of coverage. **(IM)**

Motor Truck Cargo Policy — Owner's Form. This form insures the owner of a truck against loss to his or her own property while being transported. It pays for the loss or damage of cargo for the perils insured against, regardless of the legal liability. **(IM)**

Multiple Indemnity. A provision that some or all of the benefits under a policy will be increased by a stated multiple, such as 100% or 200%, in the event that a peril occurs in a specified way, e.g., double indemnity on life insurance for accidental death. **(LI)**

Mutual Insurer. An incorporated insurer without incorporated capital owned by its policyholders. Although mutual insurers do distribute their earnings to their policyholders in the form of dividends, the term should not be used in a sense that makes it synonymous with participating. In most jurisdictions, a mutual insurer is free to issue nonparticipating insurance if it chooses and a stock insurer is free to issue participating insurance. Contrast with **Stock Insurer. (G)**

N

NAIC. See **National Association of Insurance Commissioners. (G)**

Name Schedule Bond. A type of fidelity bond which covers losses caused by the dishonesty of only those employees specifically named in the bond. Contrast with **Blanket Bond. (C)**

Named Insured. Any person, firm, or corporation, or any member thereof, specifically designated by name as the insured(s) in a policy. Others may be protected as insureds even though their names do not appear on the policy. A common application of this latter principle is in automobile policies where, under the definition of insured, protection is extended to cover other drivers using the car with the permission of the named insured. **(G)**

Named Non-Owner Policy. An automobile insurance policy issued to someone who does not own an automobile, but who drives borrowed or rented autos. **(AU)**

Named Peril Policies. Named peril policies specify what perils are insured against, contrary to so-called all risk policies. **(G,PR)**

National Association of Insurance Commissioners (NAIC). Originally National Convention of Insurance Commissioners. An association of state insurance commissioners formed for the purpose of exchanging information and of developing uniformity in the regulatory practices of the several states through drafting model legislation and regulations. The NAIC has no official power to enforce compliance with its recommendations. **(G)**

National Flood Insurance Program (NFIP). Federal program providing flood insurance for fixed property. Under a "dual" program coverage may be written directly by the NFIP or by private carriers whose losses may be reimbursed by the NFIP. **(PR)**

Natural Death. Death by means other than accident or homicide. **(G)**

Negligence. Failure to use that degree of care which an ordinary person of reasonable prudence would use under the given or similar circumstances. A person may be negligent by acts of omission or commission or both. **(G,LE)**

Net Cost. Premiums paid minus cash value and any policy dividends paid as of the date the calculation is being made. In the life business, it is common to draw up net cost comparisons at the end of 10 and 20 years. **(G)**

Net Premium. (1) The amount of premium minus the agent's commission. (2) The premium necessary to cover only anticipated losses, before loading to cover other expenses. (3) The original premium minus dividends paid or anticipated in participating life insurance when the insured elects to use dividends toward payment of the premiums. Contrast with **Gross Premium. (G)**

Newly Acquired Autos. Any automobile purchased after the effective date but before the end of the term of an automobile policy. Newly acquired autos receive some automatic coverage but the insured must notify the insurance company of the acquisition within 30 days. **(AU)**

Nonadmitted Assets. Assets that do not qualify under state law for insurance statement purposes. Examples would be furniture, fixtures, agents' debit balances, and accounts receivable which are over 90 days old. **(G)**

Nonadmitted Insurer. An insurer not licensed to do business in the jurisdiction in question. Same as **Unauthorized Insurer** and **Unlicensed Insurer. (G)**

Nonassignable. A policy that the owner cannot assign to a third party. Most policies are nonassignable unless approval is given by the insurer. **(G)**

Noncancellable ("Non-Can"). A contract of health insurance that the insured has a right to continue in force by payment of premiums, as set forth in the contract, for a substantial period of time, also as set forth in the contract. During that period of time, the insurer has no right to make any change in any provision of the contract. The NAIC recommends that the term "noncancellable" not be permitted to be used to designate any form that is not renewable to at least age 50 or for at least five years if issued after age 44. Note that this is in contrast to guaranteed renewable, on which the premium may be increased by classes. The premium for noncancellable policies must remain as stated in the policy at the time of issue. Contrast with **Guaranteed Renewable. (H)**

Nonconcurrency. The situation that exists when a number of insurance policies intended to cover the same property against the same hazards are not identical as to the extent of coverage. Nonconcurrency usually results in an insured not being fully covered for a loss. Modern forms have minimized the problem of nonconcurrency. **(PR)**

Nonconfining Sickness. Sickness that does not confine the insured indoors. **(H)**

Noncontributory. A plan or program of insurance, usually group, for which the employer pays the entire premium and the employee contributes no part of the premium. **(H,LI)**

Non-Disabling Injury. An injury that does not qualify the insured for total or partial disability benefits. A Disability Income policy may contain a provision for a small benefit in the case of such an injury, including medical costs of up to 25% or 50% of one month's disability benefit payment. **(H)**

Nonforfeiture Values. Those values in a life insurance policy that by law the policyowner cannot forfeit even if he ceases to pay the premiums. These benefits are the cash surrender value, the loan value, the paid-up insurance value, and the extended term insurance value. The policyowner may choose one of these nonforfeiture options, but even if he fails to do so, the one specified in the contract for such a case automatically goes into effect. **(LI)**

Nonmedical (Non-Med). A contract of life or health insurance underwritten on the basis of an insured's statement of health with no medical examination required. **(H,LI)**

Non-Occupational Policy. A policy or provision of a policy which excludes accidents occurring on the job, when such employment is covered by workers compensation. **(H)**

Non-Ownership Automobile Liability Insurance. Protection of the policyholder against claims for bodily injury and property damage liability caused by his employees or others using autos not owned or hired by the insured in conducting his business. **(AU)**

Nonparticipating (Non-Par). Insurance contracts on which no policy dividends are paid because there is no contractual provision for the policyowner to participate in the surplus. Contrast with **Participating. (G)**

Nonprofit Insurers. Insurers organized under special state laws, usually exempting them from some taxes imposed on regular insurers, to supply medical expense reimbursement insurance, usually on a service basis. "Blue" plans (Blue Cross and Blue Shield) in most states are an example. **(H)**

Nonqualified Plan. A benefit type of plan, such as a retirement plan, which may be discriminatory, need not be filed with the IRS and does not provide a current tax deduction for contributions. **(PE)**

Nonresident Agent. An agent licensed in a state in which he does not live. **(G)**

O

Obligee. Broadly, anyone in whose favor an obligation runs. This term is used most frequently in surety bonds where it refers to the person, firm, or corporation protected by the bond. The obligee under a bond is similar to the insured under an insurance policy. In the case of a construction bond, the person for whom the building is being built is the obligee. **(S)**

Obligor. Commonly called the principal. One bound by an obligation. In the case of a construction bond, the contractor is the principal. **(S)**

Occupancy. This refers to the type or character of use of the property in question. The type of occupancy has a bearing on its desirability and also effects the rate for the policy. **(PR)**

Occupational Accident. An accident arising out of or occurring in the course of one's employment and caused by hazards inherent in or related to it. **(G)**

Occupational Disease. Impairment of health caused by continued exposure to conditions inherent in a person's occupation or a disease caused by an employment or resulting from the nature of an employment. **(H)**

Occupational Disease. Sickness or disease arising out of or in the course of employment. State compensation laws provide coverage for this type of loss. **(WC)**

Occupational Hazard. A condition in an occupation that increases the peril of accident, sickness, or death. **(H,LI,WC)**

Occurrence Coverage. A policy form providing liability coverage only for injury or damage that occurs during the policy period, regardless of when the claim is actually made. For example, a claim made in the current policy year could be charged against a prior policy period, or may not be covered, if it arises from an occurrence prior to the effective date. Contrast with **Claims-Made Coverage. (LA)**

Office Burglary and Robbery Policy. A special policy designed for offices. It usually consists of several crime coverages on office equipment and supplies which are purchased as a package. There is relatively low limit for each coverage and very little flexibility in that the policyholder must buy the complete package. **(C)**

Old Age, Survivors, Disability, and Health Insurance. The system of social insurance benefits for the aged, surviving dependents, and disabled workers set up by the Social Security Act of 1935, plus amendments and additions. **(G)**

Omnibus Budget Reconciliation Act. A federal law which extends the minimum COBRA continuation of group health care coverage from 18 to 29 months for qualified beneficiaries who are disabled at the time of qualification. **(H)**

Open Access. Allows a participant to see another participating provider of services without a referral. Also called **Open Panel. (H)**

Open End Investment Company. An investment company managed by professional investment advisors who invest in stocks and bonds on behalf of shareholders. Also known as a mutual fund. **(PE)**

Open Perils. Insurance against loss of or damage to property arising from any cause except those that are specifically excluded. See **All-Risk Insurance.** Contrast with **Named Perils. (G,PR)**

Optionally Renewable. A contract of health insurance in which an insurer reserves the unrestricted right to terminate coverage at any anniversary or, in some cases, at any premium due date. It may not do so in between. **(H)**

Ordinary Life Policy. A whole life policy for which premiums are paid continuously as long as the insured lives. Same as **Straight Life Policy.** See also **Whole Life Insurance. (LI)**

Other Insurance. The existence of other contracts covering the same interest and perils. See also **Concurrent Insurance. (G)**

Other Insurance Clause. A provision found in almost every insurance policy except life and sometimes health stating what is to be done in case any other contract of insurance embraces the same property and/or hazards. See also **Apportionment. (G)**

Outline of Coverage. A document presented to applicants for life or health insurance that provides a brief description of proposed coverages, premiums, benefits, limitations and exclusions. It generally warns an applicant that it is a summary only and encourages the applicant to read the actual policy or certificate carefully. An Outline of Coverage may include various disclosures, and inform the applicant of certain rights, such as the right to a "free look" — the right to return the policy and receive a full refund of premium within a stipulated time period if not satisfied for any reason. **(H,LI)**

Outpatient. A patient who is not a bed patient in the hospital in which he or she is receiving treatment. **(H)**

Overinsured. A term used to describe the condition that exists when an insured has purchased coverage for more than the actual cash value or replacement cost of a subject of insurance. It is also used to describe a situation where so much insurance is in force as to constitute a moral or morale hazard, such as having so much disability income insurance in force that it becomes profitable to be disabled. **(G)**

P

Package Policy. Any insurance policy including two or more lines or types of coverages in the same contract. Personal and commercial package policies are very common today. In fact, most policies sold are package policies. **(G)**

Paid-For. Insurance on which the premium has been paid. **(G)**

Paid-Up Insurance. Insurance on which all premiums are paid but which has not yet matured by either death or endowment. An example would be a limited payment life policy for which the premium-paying period is over. **(LI)**

Paid-Up Adds. Abbreviation for Paid-Up Additions. Additional single premium life insurance paid for by policy dividends and added to the face amount. **(LI)**

Partial Disability — A condition in which, as a result of injury or sickness, the insured cannot perform all of the duties of his or her occupation but can perform some. Exact definitions vary from policy to policy. **(H)**

Partial Loss. A loss covered by an insurance policy which does not completely destroy or render worthless the insured property. **(G)**

Participating (Par). (1) Insurance that pays policy dividends. In other words, it entitles a policyowner to participate in allocations of the insurer's surplus. In life insurance there are several options available for the use of such dividends. (2) Insurance that contributes proportionately with other insurance on the same risk. **(G)**

Payor Benefit. A rider or provision often found in juvenile policies under which premiums are waived if the person paying the premium, usually one of the parents, becomes disabled or dies while the child is still a minor. **(LI)**

Payor Clause. Provides that the premiums on a child's insurance will be waived in the event the premium payor (usually a parent of the insured child) dies or becomes totally disabled prior to the child's attainment of a specified age. **(LI)**

Pension Plan. A risk experienced by those who invest in securities identified as the uncertainty of the economy. **(PE)**

Percentage Participation. A provision in a health insurance contract which states that the insurer will share losses in an agreed proportion with the insured. An example would be an 80-20 participation where the insurer pays 80% and the insured pays the 20% of losses covered under the contract. Often erroneously referred to as coinsurance. **(H)**

Peril. The cause of a possible loss. Compare to with **Hazard** and **Risk. (G)**

Permanent and Total Disability. Total disability from which the insured does not recover. When used as a definition in a policy (usually a life insurance policy rider), "permanent" is presumed after a stated period of time, commonly six months. **(H)**

Permanent Life Insurance. A term loosely applied to life insurance policy forms other than group and term, usually cash value life insurance, such as endowments and whole or ordinary life policies. **(LI)**

Persistency. The tendency or likelihood of insurance business not lapsing or being replaced by another insurer's product; an important underwriting factor. **(G)**

Persistency. The staying quality of insurance policies, i.e., the renewal quality. High persistency means that a high percentage of policies stay in force to the end of the period coverage, while low persistency means that a high percentage of policies lapse for nonpayment of premiums. **(LI)**

Personal Articles Floater. (PAF) Originally an inland marine policy. It can be sold as a separate policy or attached to an existing property insurance policy, such as a homeowners form. The PAF is used for listing items to be covered, such as furs and jewelry, with an amount shown for each item. This is usually an open perils (all risk) form. See also **Floater. (IM,PR)**

Personal Effects Floater. A policy covering personal effects usually carried by tourists. It can be written on either an open perils (all risk) or specified-peril form. It covers worldwide but excludes coverage at the insured's residence, as it provides travel coverage only. **(IM)**

Personal Injury. Injury other than bodily injury arising out of false arrest or detention, malicious prosecution, wrongful entry or eviction, libel or slander, or violation of a person's right to privacy committed other than in the course of advertising, publishing, broadcasting or telecasting. Contrast with **Advertising Injury. (LA)**

Personal Injury Coverage. Liability insurance coverage for third party claims for damages which are other than physical such as, libel, slander, false arrest, wrongful eviction, invasion of privacy, etc.

Personal Injury Protection (PIP). The formal name usually given to no-fault benefits in states that have enacted mandatory or optional no-fault automobile insurance coverages. PIP usually includes benefits for medical expenses, loss of work income, essential services, accidental death and funeral expenses. **(AU)**

Personal Lines. This term is used to refer to insurance for individuals and families, such as private passenger automobile insurance and homeowner policies. Contrast with **Business Insurance** and **Commercial Lines. (G)**

Personal Property. Any property of an insured other than real property. Homeowner policies protect the personal property of family members, and commercial forms are used to protect many types of business personal property of an insured. **(PR)**

Personal Property Floater. A Broad Form policy covering all personal property worldwide, including at the insured's home. Similar coverage is available by endorsement as part of the "Special" homeowners policy form. **(PR)**

Personal Property of Others. Property, other than real property, which is not owned by an insured. Liability forms have traditionally excluded coverage for property of others in an insured's care, custody or control. Modern homeowner forms and commercial property forms provide some coverage for property of others. **(G)**

Personal Theft Policy. See **Broad Form Personal Theft Policy. (C)**

Physical Exam and Autopsy. A standard health insurance policy provision that allows the insurer at its own expense to examine the insured when a claim is pending, and in the event of death perform an autopsy where not prohibited by law. **(H)**

Physical Hazard. Any hazard arising from the material, structural, or operational features of the risk itself apart from the persons owning or managing it. **(G)**

Physicians and Surgeons Equipment Form. A form used to cover equipment, materials, supplies and office furniture of individuals in the medical and dental professions. **(IM)**

Physicians and Surgeons Professional Liability Insurance. Malpractice insurance for physicians and surgeons. See **Malpractice. (LA)**

Pilferage. Petty theft, particularly theft of articles in less than package lots. This term is associated with the insuring of cargo under an inland marine insurance form. **(G)**

Policy. The written statement of a contract effecting insurance, or certificates thereof, by whatever name called, and including all clauses, riders, endorsements, and papers attached thereto and made a part thereof. **(G)**

Policy Dividend. The return of a portion of the premium paid on a participating policy. It represents the difference between the gross premium charged and the actual cost assessed against the policy by actuarial formula. **(G)**

Policy Fee. (1) A one-time charge added to the first premium to help defray acquisition costs, now illegal in many states. (2) A flat, per policy charge that does not change with the size of the policy and thus serves as a form of quantity discount. Various insurers call it by other names, such as quantity discount factor and quantity adjustment fee. **(LI)**

Policyholder. Literally, the person who has possession of the policy. Thus the term is non-functional as commonly used. See comment under **Insured. (G)**

Policy Loan. A loan made by the insurance company to the policyowner with the cash value of the policy as security or collateral. One of the usual Nonforfeiture options. **(G)**

Policyowner. The person who has the right to exercise the rights and privileges in the policy contract. Such person may or may not be the insured, depending on policy ownership and assignment, if any. **(G)**

Policy Proceeds. The amount actually paid on a life insurance policy at death or when the insured receives payment at surrender or maturity. It includes any dividends left on deposit and the value of any additional insurance purchased with dividends; and it excludes any loans not repaid, plus unpaid interest on those loans. **(LI)**

Policy Reserve. See **Unearned Premium Reserve. (H)**

Policy Reserve. A reserve which exists because of the concept that each policy has a pro rata share of the total reserve established for all policies. **(LI)**

Policy Summary. A document that summarizes the coverages, benefits, limitations, exclusions, cost and terms of a proposed life insurance policy. Cost and benefit information usually includes annual premiums, guaranteed amounts payable at death, guaranteed cash surrender values at the end of various years, life insurance cost indexes, and (if applicable) dividend information. In many jurisdictions Policy Summaries are required to be delivered to applicants in connection with any solicitation or replacement transaction. **(LI)**

Policy Year. The period between policy anniversary dates.. **(G)**

Policy Year Experience. The measure of premiums and losses for each 12-month period a policy is in force. Losses occurring during this 12-month period are assigned to the period regardless of when they are actually paid. **(G)**

Policyholder. (1) The person in actual possession of an insurance policy. (2) Often used loosely to refer to the policyowner and/or insured. See also **Insured. (G)**

Pollution Liability Coverage Form. Commercial form providing pollution insurance on a "claims made" basis, and also including coverage for clean-up costs. Contrast with **Limited Pollution Liability Coverage Form. (LA)**

Pollution Liability Extension Endorsement. An endorsement to general liability insurance which removes part of the pollution exclusion, creating liability coverage for pollution injury or damage. **(LA)**

Position Schedule Bond. See **Name Position Bond** and **Name Schedule Bond. (C)**

Power of Agency. See **Agent's Authority. (G)**

Power of Attorney. (1) The authority given to one person or corporation to act for and obligate another to the extent set forth in the agreement creating the power. (2) The authority given to the chief administrator of a reciprocal insurance exchange, who is called an attorney in fact, by each subscriber. See also **Reciprocal Insurance Exchange. (G)**

Preauthorization Check Plan. A premium-paying arrangement by which the policyowner authorizes the insurer to draft money from his or her bank account for the payments. This is usually done on a monthly basis. **(LI)**

Precertification Authorization. A cost containment technique which requires physicians to submit a treatment plan and an estimated bill prior to providing treatment. This allows the insurer to evaluate the appropriateness of the procedures, and lets the insured and physican know in advance which procedures are covered and at what rate benefits will be paid. **(G)**

Preexisting Condition. A physical condition that existed prior to the effective date of a policy. In many health policies these are not covered until after a stated period of time has elapsed. **(H)**

Preferred Provider Organization (PPO). An organization of hospitals and physicans who provide, for a set fee, services to insurance company clients. These providers are listed as preferred and the insured may select from any number of hospitals and physicians without being limited as with an HMO. Coverage is 100%, with a minimal copayment for each office visit or hospital stay. Contrast with **Health Maintenance Organization. (H,LI)**

Preferred Risk. Any risk considered to be better than the standard risk on which the premium rate was calculated. **(G)**

Premises Burglary. A burglary which occurs on an insured premises. Various commercial insurance forms distinguish between coverage provided on and off an insured premises. Premises burglary coverage may be written separately or as part of a broader package of crime coverages. **(C)**

Premises Theft — Outside Robbery Coverage Form. A commercial crime coverage form that protects against loss of property other than money and security by theft on the premises or robbery outside the premises. **(C)**

Premium. The price of insurance protection for a specified risk for a specified period of time. **(G)**

Premium Loan. A loan made by the insurance company to the insured, with the cash value of the policy as security, to pay a premium due. **(G)**

Premium Notice. A form notice from an insurer or agency to a policyowner that a premium will be due on a given date. **(G)**

Pre-Paid Hospital Service Plan. The common name for Health Maintenance Organization plan (HMO). It provides comprehensive health care, usually by salaried personnel, for members who pay a flat fee for the services, whether out-patient or hospital treatment is needed. **(H)**

Presumption of Agency. A legally binding agency relationship when, in fact, no formal agency agreement is in effect. If an insurer acts to give the appearance of agency, perhaps by furnishing letterhead and applications before a person has been licensed and appointed, an agency relationship exists under the law and the insurer may be legally bound by the acts of a person acting as agent. **(G)**

Prevailing Charge. Used to determine Medicare benefit amounts, this usually means the typical charge in the area where the patient lives. See also **Allowable Charge** and **Customary Charge. (H)**

Principal. The individual or corporation whose performance is guaranteed in suretyship. **(S)**

Principal Sum. The amount payable in one sum in the event of accidental death or certain accidental dismemberments. When a contract provides benefits for both accidental death and accidental dismemberment, each dismemberment benefit is an amount equal to the principal sum or some fraction thereof. Examples would be half the principal sum for loss of one arm, half the principal sum for the loss of one leg, etc. **(H,LI)**

Pro Rata. (1) Distribution of the amount of insurance under one policy among several objects or places covered in proportion to their value or the amounts shown. (2) Distribution of liability among several insurers having policies on a risk, usually in the proportion that the amount of coverage in each policy bears to the total amount of coverage in all policies. **(G)**

Pro Rata Cancellation. The termination of an insurance contract or bond, premium charge being adjusted in proportion to the exact time the protection has been in force. **(G)**

Pro Rata Distribution. A provision, also known as the **Pro Rata Distribution clause**, used in the writing of certain blanket policies. Its purpose is to divide the amount of insurance carried under a single item in the policy form among the several subjects of insurance, in that proportion which the value of each subject of insurance bears to the total value of all property covered under that single item in the policy form. **(G)**

Pro Rata Liability Clause. Provides that losses will be paid in the proportion that the amount of the policy bears to the entire amount of insurance on all policies covering the loss. This provides for insurance companies to appropriately share in the loss when more than one policy exists yet prevents the insured from collecting in total from several insurance companies and making a profit. **(G)**

Probationary Period. A period of time between the effective date of a health insurance policy, and the date coverage begins for all or certain physical conditions. **(H)**

Proceeds. The amount payable by a policy, usually in reference to the face amount of a life insurance policy, payable at the death of the insured. **(LI)**

Producer. A term applied to an agent, solicitor or other person who sells insurance. **(G)**

Products Liability Insurance. Provides protection against claims arising out of the use, handling or consumption of a product. (See also **Completed Operations insurance.**) **(PR)**

Professional Liability Insurance. (1) See **Malpractice Insurance** for the definition applicable to the healing arts. (2) See **Errors and Omissions Insurance** for the definition applicable to those in professions such as law and accounting. Errors and omissions exposure exists for many other kinds of businesses, like travel agencies and telephone exchanges. **(LA)**

Profit-Sharing Plan. A plan under which some of the profits of a company are set aside for distribution to qualified employees. The plan may provide for immediate distribution, or distribution upon death, disability, termination, or attainment of a specific retirement age. Such plans are subject to special tax exemption if they meet the requirements of the Internal Revenue Code. **(PE)**

Proof of Loss. A formal statement made by a policyowner to an insurer regarding a loss. It is intended to give information to the insurer to enable it to detemine the extent of its liability. **(G)**

Property Damage Liability Insurance. Protection against liability for damage to the property of another, including loss of the use of the property, as distinguished from liability for bodily injury to another. In the majority of cases it is written along with Bodily Injury liability protection. **(LA)**

Property Insurance. Insurance that indemnifies a person with an interest in physical property for its loss or the loss of its income producing abilities. This definition encompasses all lines of insurance written by property and inland marine insurers and can also include certain kinds of insurance written by casualty insurers, e.g., Burglary and Plate Glass coverages. **(PR)**

Property Other than Money and Securities. Under commercial crime insurance coverages, any tangible property other than money and securities that has intrinsic value, such as merchandise, supplies, raw materials and office equipment. **(C)**

Proration of Benefits. The adjustment of health insurance policy benefits by reason of the existence of other insurance covering the same contingency. **(H)**

Protected Risk. A property risk which is within the geographical area protected by a fire department. **(PR)**

Protection. (1) A term used interchangeably with "coverage" to denote insurance provided under the terms of a policy. (2) The fire-fighting facilities in the area in which a risk is located. **(G)**

Proximate Cause. The effective cause of loss or damage. It is an unbroken chain of cause and effect between the occurrence of an insured peril or a negligent act and resulting injury or damage. **(LE)**

Public Employee Bond. A fidelity bond to insure the faithful performance of a public employee, usually one entrusted with finances. **(C)**

Public Employees Dishonesty Coverage. Commercial crime coverage written for public entities to cover losses of money, securities, or other property caused by employee dishonesty. Coverage may be written on a "per loss" or "per employee" basis. **(C)**

Public Official Bond. A surety bond under which the company (surety) guarantees that the principal (public official) will faithfully perform his or her official duties and will account for all funds entrusted to his or her care. **(S)**

Punitive Damages. Damages awarded over and above compensatory damages to punish a negligent party because of wanton, reckless, or malicious acts or omissions. General liability policies cover punitive damages when included with compensatory damages in a lump sum, but it is up to the courts to decide whether or not they are to be awarded. Also known as **Exemplary Damages. (LE)**

Pure Premium. A term used in insurance rate making. It refers to that portion of the total premium which is needed to pay expected losses. It does not take into account money needed for other company expenses. **(G)**

Pure Risk. Uncertainty as to whether a loss will occur. Under a pure risk situation, there is no possibility for gain. Contrast with **Speculative Risk. (G)**

Q,R

Qualified Plan. A retirement plan which has been filed and approved by the IRS, which does not discriminate as to participation, and where the contributor (usually the employer) receives a tax deduction for plan contributions, and investment income is tax deferred until paid out. **(PE)**

Rate. The cost of a given unit of insurance. For example, in ordinary life insurance, it is the price of $1,000 of the face amount. In disability income insurance, it is usually the price per $10 or per $100 of monthly benefits. In property insurance, it is the rate per $100 of value to be insured. The premium, then, is the rate multiplied by the number of units of insurance purchased. **(G)**

Rate. The percent or factor applied to the ceding company's subject premium to produce the reinsurance premium or the percent applied to the reinsurer's premium to produce the commission. See also **Premium. (R)**

Rated. Coverages issued at a higher rate than standard because of impairment of the insured. Usually used as an adjective in such expressions as "rated risk," "rated policy," and "rated up." **(LI)**

Rating Bureau. A private organization that classifies and promulgates manual rates and in some cases compiles data and measures the hazards of individual risks in terms of rates in geographic areas, the latter being true especially in connection with property insurance. **(G)**

Rebate. A portion of the agent's commission returned to an insured or anything else of value given an insured as an inducement to buy. The payment of policy dividends, retroactive rate adjustments, and reduced premiums that reflect the savings of direct payment to an agent or home office are not usually considered to be rebates. In most cases rebates are illegal, both for the agent or insurer to give a rebate and for an insured to receive one. **(G)**

Reciprocal Insurance Exchange. An unincorporated group of individuals, called subscribers, who mutually insure one another, each separately assuming his or her share of each risk. Its chief administrator is an attorney in fact. **(G)**

Recurring Clause. A health insurance policy provision defining the duration of a period of time during which the recurrence of a condition will be considered a continuation of a prior period of disability or confinement. **(H)**

Reduced Paid-Up Insurance. A form of insurance available as a nonforfeiture option. It provides that the cash value of the policy be used as a single premium to purchase paid-up insurance in whatever amount the cash value will provide, which will be less than the original face amount in most cases. See also **Nonforfeiture values. (LI)**

Reduction. A decrease in the benefits in an insurance policy because of a specified condition. For example, benefits may be reduced because a disability is caused by a specific condition. **(G)**

Reduction of Risk. Taking steps to reduce the probability or severity of a possible loss. For example, installing alarms and sprinkler systems to reduce the risk of fire loss to a building. One of the four major risk management techniques. See **Risk Management. (G)**

Refund Life Annuity. An annuity paying installments as long as the insured lives and installments after death to the beneficiary until the amount paid equals the principle sum of insurance. **(AN)**

Register. A record of all policies charged to a debit account. **(LI)**

Regulatory Information Retrieval Service (RIRS). A database product developed by the National Association of Insurance Commissioners in conjunction with state insurance departments which lists regulatory actions such as suspensions, revocations, fines, penalties, cease and desist orders, consent orders. etc. against insurance firms and individuals. **(G)**

Reimbursement. Payment of an amount of money upon the occurrence of a loss covered by the policy. **(G)**

Reinstatement. (1) Restoration of a lapsed policy. (2) Restoration of the original amount of a type of policy that reduces the principal amount by the amount of claims. **(G)**

Reinstatement. Putting back into effect a catastrophe reinsurance coverage that has been reduced by the payment of a reinsurance loss as the result of one catastrophe. This is usually effected by the payment of a reinstatement premium. **(R)**

Reinsurance. A type of insurance that involves acceptance by an insurer, called the reinsurer, of all or a part of the risk of loss covered by another insurer, called the ceding company. It is a way for an insurer to avoid having to pay for large or catastrophic losses. **(R)**

Relation of Earnings to Insurance. A health insurance provision used in noncancellable and guaranteed renewable contracts that states if when a disability begins the insured's total disability income exceeds his or her earned income, the benefits will be reduced proportionally and premiums for any excess coverage will be refunded. **(H)**

Relative Value Schedule. A surgical schedule which basically compares the value of one surgical procedure to another and establishes the surgical fee to be paid. **(H)**

Release. (1) To give up, abandon, and discharge a claim or an enforceable right of one person against another. (2) The name of the instrument evidencing such an act. For example, if a claim representative obtains a release from a claimant, this means that the claimant has given up all further rights against the insurance company. **(G)**

Renewable Term. Term insurance that may be renewed for another term without evidence of insurability. **(LI)**

Rent Insurance. See **Rental Value Insurance. (PR)**

Rental Value Insurance. A form of property insurance that provides indemnity (1) for the loss of the rental value of property when the owner or tenant is deprived of the use of the property because it has been damaged by an insured peril, or (2) for the loss by the owner-landlord of the rent that would have been payable by a tenant of the property, under the terms of the lease or by statute, when he is relieved of liability for the payment of rent during a period of untenantability due to an insured peril. **(PR)**

Replacement Cost. The cost of replacing property without a reduction for depreciation. By this method of determining value, damages for a claim would be the amount needed to replace the property using new materials. Contrast with **Actual Cash Value. (PR)**

Reporting Form. The form for a periodic report to an insurer by an insured that covers the fluctuating values of stocks of merchandise, furniture and fixtures, and improvements and betterments. Premiums are adjusted annually, based on the average values insured during the policy period. An insured with fluctuating inventories might use this form. **(PR)**

Representation. A statement made on an application for insurance that the applicant represents as correct to the best of his or her knowledge and belief. See also **Warranty. (LE)**

Rescission. (1) Repudiation of a contract. A party whose consent to a contract was induced by fraud, misrepresentation or duress may repudiate it. A contract may also be repudiated for failure to perform a duty. (2) The termination of an insurance contract by the insurer when material misrepresentation has occurred. **(G,LE)**

Reserve. (1) An amount representing actual or potential liabilities kept by an insurer to cover debts to policyholders. (2) An amount allocated for a special purpose. Note that a reserve is usually a liability and not an extra fund. On occasion a reserve may be an asset, such as a reserve for taxes not yet due. **(G)**

Residence Premises. In homeowners insurance, the dwelling, other structures and grounds, or that part of any other building where the named insured lives. **(LA,PR)**

Residual Disability. That form of disability which becomes defined as partial disability when an insured has returned to work immediately following a period of total disability. **(H)**

Residual Markets. Various insurance markets outside of the normal agency-company marketing system. Residual markets include government insurance programs, specialty pools (aviation risks and nuclear risks), and shared market mechanisms (assigned risk plans). **(G)**

Retention. The portion of the premium which is used by the insurance company for administrative costs. **(H)**

Retention. The amount of liability retained by the ceding company and not reinsured. **(R)**

Retention of Risk. Assuming all or part of a risk instead of purchasing insurance or otherwise transferring the risk. One of the four major risk management techniques. See **Risk Management.** **(G)**

Retroactive Date. Date on a "claims made" liability policy which triggers the beginning period of insurance coverage. A retroactive date is not required. If one is shown on the policy, any claim made during the policy period will not be covered if the loss occurred before the retroactive date. **(LA)**

Return of Premium. A rider or provision in a health insurance policy agreeing to pay a benefit equal to the sum of all the premiums paid, minus claims paid, if claims over a stated period of time do not exceed a fixed percentage of the premiums paid. **(H)**

Return of Premium. A rider on a life insurance policy providing that, in the event of the death of the insured within a specified period of time, the policy will pay, in addition to the face amount, an amount equal to the sum of all premiums paid to date. This is a form of increasing term insurance and is used as a sales tool. **(LI)**

Return Premium. A portion of the premium returned to a policyowner as a result of cancellation, rate adjustment, or a calculation that an advance premium was in excess of the actual premium. See also **Pro Rate** and **Short Rate.** **(G)**

Revocable Trust. A type of trust instrument in which the grantor maintains control over the trust assets and can revoke the trust. **(EP,LE)**

Rider. An attachment to a policy that modifies its conditions by expanding or restricting benefits or excluding certain conditions from coverage. See **Waiver** and **Endorsement.** **(G)**

Risk. (1) Uncertainty as to the outcome of an event when two or more possibilities exist. See also **Pure Risk** and **Speculative Risk.** (2) A person or thing insured. Contrast with **Hazard** and **Peril.** **(G)**

Risk. The physical units of property insured or the physical units of property at risk. Contrast with **Peril** and **Hazard.** **(PR)**

Risk Management. Management of the pure risks to which a company might be subject. It involves analyzing all exposures to the possibility of loss and determining how to handle these exposures through such practices as avoiding the risk, reducing the risk, retaining the risk, or transferring the risk, usually by insurance. **(G)**

Risk Retention Groups. Liability insurance companies owned by their policyholders. Membership is limited to people in the same business or activity which exposes them to similar liability risks. The purpose is to assume and spread liability exposure to group members and to provide an alternative risk financing mechanism for liability. **(G)**

Robbery. The felonious taking, either by force or fear of force, of the personal property of another. **(C)**

S

Safe Depository Coverage. Two commercial crime coverage forms are available for firms other than financial institutions that rent safe deposit boxes to others. One covers an insured's legal liability for loss or damage, while the other covers direct losses regardless of liability. Both cover customers' property on the insured's premises while in a safe deposit box or vault, or while being deposited or removed from such containers. **(C)**

Salvage. Property taken over by an insurer to reduce its loss. **(G)**

Salvage. Property recoverable by salvagers under maritime law. **(OM)**

Schedule. A list of the items covered by an insurance policy with their descriptions and valuations. **(IM)**

Schedule. A list of individual items covered under one policy, such as various buildings and contents. **(PR)**

Second Injury Fund. Special funds set up by each state to pay all or part of the compensation required when a partially disabled employee suffers a subsequent injury. Because the compound effect of two injuries can be greater than the effect of the same two injuries in isolation, employers might be reluctant to hire the handicapped if they had to bear the full burden for a second injury. Second injury funds relieve employers of some of this burden. **(WC)**

Secondary Beneficiary. The second person named to receive benefits upon the death of an insured if the first-named beneficiary is not alive or does not collect all the benefits before his or her own death. See also **Contingent Beneficiary.** **(LI)**

Securities Act of 1933. A federal law which requries full and fair disclosure and the use of a prospectus in the sale of securities. **(G)**

Securities Deposited With Others Coverage Form. A commercial crime coverage form that protects against loss by theft, disappearance or destruction of securities which have been deposited with others, such as a bank, trust company, or stock broker. **(C)**

Securities Exchange Act of 1934. A federal law which requires the registration of companies and agents with the federal government if they are selling securities. **(G)**

Self-Inflicted Injury. An injury to the body of the insured inflicted by himself or herself. **(H)**

Self-Insurance. Making financial preparations to meet pure risks by appropriating sufficient funds in advance to meet estimated losses, including enough to cover possible losses in excess of those estimated. Few organizations are large or dispersed enough to make this a sound alternative to insurance. **(G)**

Service Insurer. Relating to an agreement by the insurance company (insurer) to pay certain vendors of health care services, under arrangements with them for rendering such services to covered persons. These arrangements may preclude or limit any additional charges for the defined services. (Blue plans are the best known, but not the only form of service insurers.) **(H)**

Service Plans. Plans of insurance where benefits are the actual services rendered rather than a monetary benefit, such as the benefits provided by Blue Cross and Blue Shield. **(H)**

Settlement Options. The various methods for the payment of the proceeds or values of a life insurance policy that may be selected in lieu of a lump sum. **(LI)**

Shoppers Guide. A consumer publication that describes the type of coverage being offered, and provides general information to help an applicant for life or health insurance compare different types of policies and reach a decision about whether the proposed coverage is appropriate. Also known as Buyers Guide. **(H,LI)**

SGLI — Servicemens Group Life Insurance. — Group Life insurance issued to members of the armed forces while in the service. Convertible after separation to individual coverage in participating or eligible private insurance companies. **(LI)**

Shoppers Guide. A consumer publication that describes the type of coverage being offered, and provides general information to help an applicant for life or health insurance compare different types of policies and reach a decision about whether the proposed covreage is appropriate. Also known as Buyers Guide. **(LI,H)**

Short Rate. The term "short rate" in insurance and bonding is used to describe the charge required for insurance or bonds taken for less than one year, and in some cases, the earned premium, including a penalty, for insurance or bonds cancelled by the insured before the end of the policy period or term of bond. **(G)**

Short-Term Disability Income Policy A disability income policy with benefits payable for "Short-Term," usually less than two years, as opposed to a long-term disability income policy. **(H)**

Sickness Insurance. A form of health insurance against loss by illness or disease. It does not include accidental bodily injury. **(H)**

Simplified Employee Pension Plan (SEP). A plan where the employer contributes a specific amount into an eligible employee's IRA on behalf of the employee. **(PE)**

Single Interest Policy. Insurance protecting the interest of only one of the parties having an insurable interest in property, such as insurance protecting a mortgagee but not a mortgagor or protecting a seller but not a buyer. **(PR)**

Single Premium Whole Life. A whole life policy which is paid with a single premium payment at the time of purchase. Compare with **Continuous Premium Whole Life** and **Limited Payment Whole Life. (LI)**

Sinkhole Collapse. The peril of a sudden sinking or collapse of land into underground empty spaces created by the action of water on limestone or similar rock formations. This peril is now covered by the latest commercial property forms. Other forms of earth movement continue to be excluded in most cases. **(PR)**

Social Security Rider. An optional disability income rider that provides an additional benefit depending on the amount of disability benefits payable by Social Security. **(H)**

Solicitor. An individual appointed and authorized by an agent to solicit and receive applications for insurance as the agent's representative. Solicitors are not usually given the power to bind coverage but are required to be licensed. **(G)**

Special Coverage Form. Any of the commercial or personal lines property forms which provide coverage on an open perils (all risk) type basis. These forms provide the broadest coverage and do not list covered perils, but do include a lengthy list of exclusions. See also **Open Peril.** Compare with **Named Peril. (PR)**

Special Multi-Peril (SMP). A business policy which combined into one contract the coverages normally purchased under several. Property and liability coverages were mandatory, Crime and boiler and machinery were optional. Many other options and endorsements allowed the SMP to be tailor made for each policyholder. Largely replaced by new commercial forms. See **Commercial Package Policy. (LA)**

Specific Rate. A rate applying to an individual piece of property. **(PR)**

Specified Disease Policy. See **Dread Disease Policy. (H)**

Speculative Risk. Uncertainty as to whether a gain or loss will occur. An example would be a business enterprise where there is a chance that the business will make money or lose it. Speculative risks are not normally insurable. Contrast with **Pure Risk. (G)**

Sprinkler Leakage Insurance. Insurance against damage done by the accidental discharge of water from an automatic sprinkler system, as contrasted with discharge because of heat from a fire. **(PR)**

Standard Risk. A risk that is on a par with those on which the rate has been based in the areas of health, physical condition, and morals. An average risk, not subject to rate loadings or restrictions because of poor health. **(LI)**

Standard Provisions. (1) Provisions prescribed by state law that must appear in all policies issued in that jurisdiction. (2) Provisions adopted by the NAIC to apply to group life insurance as minimum protection. They are required by law in most states. (3) Formerly, a set of prescribed provisions regulating the operating conditions of a health insurance policy required by law in most jurisdictions between about 1912 and 1950. They are now superseded by uniform provisions for individual accident and health insurance policies which contain an NAIC model bill. These have been enacted in virtually all jurisdictions. **(H,LI)**

Stated Amount. An agreed amount of insurance which is shown on the policy, and which will be paid in the event of total loss regardless of the actual value of the property. **(PR)**

Stock Insurer. An incorporated insurer with capital contributed by stockholders, to whom the earnings are distributed as dividends on their shares. Contrast with **Mutual Insurer. (G)**

Stop Loss. Any provision in a policy designed to cut off an insurer's losses at a given point. In effect, a stop loss agreement guarantees the loss ratio of the insurer. **(G)**

Storekeepers Liability Policy. A single limit package policy covering bodily injury and property damage liability claims in the operation of the storekeeper's business. It includes limited coverage on contractual and products liability. **(LA)**

Straight Life Policy. See **Ordinary Life Policy. (LI)**

Straight Life Policy. A whole life policy that stretches the premium payments over the insured's lifetime (to age 100). Also known as Continuous Premium Whole Life. **(LI)**

Sublimit. Any limit of insurance which exists within another limit. For example, special classes of property may be subject to a specified dollar limit per occurrence, even though the policy has a higher overall limit; a health insurance policy may limit certain benefits to fixed dollar amounts or maximum amounts per day, even though the overall coverage limit is higher. **(G)**

Subordination. Putting below in importance. Sometimes the creditors of a contractor will subordinate their interests in the obligations owed them until a construction project is completed. This has the effect of increasing the contractor's working capital. **(S)**

Subrogation. The right of one who has taken over another's loss to also take over the other person's right to pursue remedies against a third party. It is never used in life insurance and seldom in health. **(LE)**

Subrogation. The right of a surety, in its name or in the name of the obligee under a bond, to pursue a course of action against the principal or any other party liable for a loss paid by the surety. **(S)**

Subrogation Waiver. A waiver by the named insured giving up any right of recovery against another party. Normally an insurance policy requires that subrogation (recovery) rights be preserved. In commercial property insurance, a written waiver of subrogation rights is permitted if it is executed before the loss occurs. **(PR)**

Subscriber. This term has two meanings — first, it refers to a person or organization who pays the premiums, and second, the person whose employment makes him or her eligible for membership in the plan. **(H)**

Substandard Risk. A risk not measuring up to underwriting standards. It may still be written but usually at a surcharged premium. **(G)**

Superintendent of Insurance. The title of the head of a state or provincial insurance department used in some jurisdictions. In most states the title "commissioner" is used. **(G)**

Supplemental Contract. A rider usually relating to the method of settlement of the proceeds of a life insurance policy. **(LI)**

Supplemental Dental Plan. See **Dental Plan, Supplemental. (H)**

Supplemental Extended Reporting Period. An optional "maxi tail" or "full tail" which extends for an unlimited period of time after expiration of a "claims-made" liability policy, and covers claims made after the policy period. **(LA)**

Supplementary Payments. A provision in most liability policies under which the insurer agrees to pay defense costs, premiums on various bonds, interest accruing after a judgment, and other reasonable expenses in addition to the limit of liability. **(LA)**

Surety. One who guarantees the performance or faithfulness of another. A surety can be either a corporation or an individual, but it is usually an insurance company. **(S)**

Surety Bond. A bond guaranteeing that a principal will carry out the obligation for which he is bonded. A surety bond is most often issued to a contractor, a person seeking a license or permit, or someone involved in a court case. **(S)**

Suretyship. The means by which one person or entity, the surety, guarantees another entity, the obligee, that a third entity, the principal, will or will not do something. It differs from insurance by being a three-party contract, but most sureties today are insurers. **(S)**

Surgical Insurance Benefits. A form of health insurance against loss due to surgical expenses. **(H)**

Surgical Schedule. Usually part of a basic medical expense plan which itemizes various surgical procedures and the monetary benefit allocated to each procedure. **(H)**

Surgical Schedule. See **Schedule. (H)**

Surplus Lines. A risk or a part of a risk for which there is no market available through the original broker or agent in its jurisdiction. Therefore, it is placed with nonadmitted insurers on an unregulated basis, in accordance with the surplus or excess lines provisions of the state law. **(G)**

Surrender. To give up a whole life policy. The insurer pays the insured the cash value which the policy has built up if it is surrendered. **(LI)**

Survivor. The beneficiary of an annuity contract, i.e., the annuitant's survivor. **(AN)**

T

Tail. This term has been used to describe both the exposure that exists after expiration of a policy and the coverage that may be purchased to cover that exposure. On "occurrence" forms a claims tail may extend for years after policy expiration, and the losses may be covered. On "claims made" forms tail coverage may be purchased to extend the period for reporting covered claims beyond the policy period. See **Mini, Midi, Maxi Tail. (LA)**

Tax Basis. Money which has yet to be taxed, usually part of a qualified plan benefit or distribution. **(PE)**

Tax Equity and Fiscal Responsibility Act. A federal law intended to prevent group term life insurance plans from discriminating in favor of "key" employees, and which amends the Social Security Act to make Medicare secondary to group health plans. **(H,LI)**

Tax Sheltered Annuity. (TSA) An annuity program under which contributions reduce the taxable income of participating employees, and the benefits are not taxable until distributed. **(LI)**

Temporary Agent. A person who is licensed to act as an agent for a brief period of time (usually 90 days) without taking a written examination. Temporary licenses are commonly granted to allow someone to continue the business of an agent who has died, become disabled, or entered active military service. **(G)**

Tenants in Common. Where two or more persons have undivided ownership and possession of real property, but (unlike joint tenancy) each owner may transfer or dispose of their share of ownership. **(LE)**

1035 Exchange. A nontaxable exchange of life insurance policies and annuities as provided under section 1035(a) of the Internal Revenue Code. **(LI)**

Term. The period of time for which a policy or bond is issued. **(G)**

Term Insurance. The type of life insurance policy that provides protection only for a specified period of time. A common policy period would be one year, five years, 10 years, or until the insured reaches age 65 or 70. It does not build up any of the nonforfeiture values associated with whole life policies. See also **Decreasing Term Insurance, Increasing Term Insurance** and **Term Insurance**. Contrast with **Whole Life Insurance. (LI)**

Tertiary Beneficiary. A beneficiary designated as third in line to receive proceeds or benefits if the primary and secondary beneficiaries do not survive. **(LI)**

Theft. The act of stealing. It includes such acts as larceny, burglary, and robbery. **(C)**

Third Party Insurance. A term for liability insurance. Liability always involves a third party, the one who has suffered a loss, in addition to the insurer and the insured. See also **Liability Insurance. (LA)**

Time Element Insurance. Insurance which covers expenses consequent to damage or destruction by an insured peril that continue over a period of time. The amount paid depends on the length of time during which the expenses accumulate. An example would be Business Interruption insurance, which pays for the loss of earnings during the time it takes to repair the property. **(PR)**

Time Limit on Certain Defenses. One of the uniform individual accident and sickness provisions required by state law to be included in every individual health policy. It sets a limit on the number of years after a policy has been in force that an insurer can use as a defense against a claim the fact that a physical condition of the insured existed before the policy was issued, but was not declared at that time. **(H)**

Time Limits. The limits of time within which notice of a claim and proof of a loss must be submitted. **(G)**

Time of Payment of Claims Provision. A health insurance provision that requires that claims be paid immediately upon receipt of proofs of loss. Some states specify a number of days in place of the word "immediately". **(H)**

Total Disability. A degree of disability from injury or sickness that prevents the insured from performing the duties of any occupation from remuneration or profit. The definition in any given case depends on the wording in a covering policy. **(H)**

Transacting Insurance. The solicitation, inducement, and preliminary negotiations effecting a contract of insurance and the subsequent carrying on of business pertaining to it. The exact definition will vary somewhat according to the state laws regulating insurance. **(G)**

Transfer of Risk. Shifting all or part of a risk to another party. Insurance is the most common method of risk transfer, but other devices, such as hold harmless agreements, also transfer risk. One of the four major risk management techniques. See **Risk Management. (G)**

Traumatic Injury. An injury to a person's physical body caused by an outside source, as distinct from physical disability caused by sickness or disease. **(G)**

Travel Accident Insurance. A form of health insurance limiting coverage to accidents occurring while the insured is traveling. **(H)**

Travel Ticket Insurance. Accident insurance issued for the duration of a specified trip by common carrier. Name is derived from the fact that it was originally issued in the form of an extra stub on a travel ticket. **(H,LI)**

Trip Transit Insurance. A type of policy which provides coverage for goods in transit for a specified trip and by a specified mode of transportation. **(IM)**

Trust Agreement. (1) A supplemental agreement attached to and made a part of a life insurance policy setting forth the manner in which the proceeds are to be paid, in lieu of having them paid in a lump sum or under one of the other installment settlement options in the policy itself. (2) An agreement or instrument under which a corpus (fund/property) is given over to the management of the trustee named in a trust instrument for the benefit of the beneficiaries of the trust. (3) A written agreement between two parties — the employer and the trustee — setting forth the provisions of a pension plan. **(EP,LI,PE)**

24-Hour Care Coverage. A health insurance concept that blends occupational and nonoccupational benefits in order to provide round-the-clock coverage for injuries or diseases whether or not they are work-related. **(H, WC)**

Twisting. Misrepresenting a policy or making incomplete comparisons of policies to induce a policyowner to change or replace an existing policy. **(G)**

UV

Umbrella Liability Policy. A coverage basically affording high limit coverage in excess of the limits of the primary policies as well as additional liability coverages. These additional coverages are usually subject to a substantial self-insured retention. The term "umbrella" is derived from the fact that it is a separate policy over and above any other basic liability policies the insured may have. **(LA)**

Unallocated Benefit. A benefit providing reimbursement of expenses up to a maximum but without any schedule of benefits as such. **(H)**

Unauthorized Insurer. See **Nonadmitted Insurer.** **(G)**

Underinsurance. A condition in which not enough insurance is carried to cover the insurable value. **(G)**

Underwriter. A technician trained in evaluating risks and determining rates and coverages for them. The term derives from the practice at Lloyd's of each person willing to accept a portion of the risk writing his or her name under the description of the risk. **(G)**

Underwriters Laboratories, Inc. (UL). A testing laboratory for manufactured items to determine their safety propensities. **(G)**

Underwriting. The process of selecting risks and classifying them according to their degrees of insurability so that the appropriate rates may be assigned. The process also includes rejection of those risks that do not qualify. **(G)**

Unearned Premium. That portion of the written premium applicable to the unexpired or unused part of the period for which the premium has been paid. Thus, in the case of an annual premium, at the end of the first month of the premium period eleven-twelfths of the premium is unearned. **(G)**

Unfair Claim Settlement Practices Law. State laws designed to protect the consumer against unfair practices in the reporting, investigation, payment, and final resolution of insurance claims. **(G)**

Unfair Trade Practices Law. State laws designed to protect the consumer against misleading, deceptive, monopolistic, or otherwise unfair practices in the business of insurance. **(G)**

Uniform Provisions. A set of provisions regarding the operating conditions of individual health policies developed in a model law recommended by the National Association of Insurance Commissioners and required, with minor variations by almost all jurisdictions, and permitted in all jurisdictions. **(H)**

Uniform Provisions. A set of provisions required by state law in life insurance policies. The actual wording of the provisions can vary, but the intent must be the same as the wording of the uniform provisions. **(LI)**

Uniform Simultaneous Death Act. State law which states that if the insured and beneficiary die in the same accident and it cannot be determined which died first, it will be assumed that the beneficiary died first, and all proceeds will then pass to the insured's contingent beneficiary. **(CIC)**

Unit Investment Trust (UIT). An investment company which invests on behalf of investors in a portfolio of securities such as stocks and bonds. The trust does not have a management function. It merely holds the assets. **(PE)**

Universal Life. A combination flexible premium, adjustable life insurance policy. The premium payer may select the amount of premium he or she can pay and the policy benefits are those which the premium will purchase. Or, the premium payer may change the amount of insurance and pay premium accordingly. Many believe this is the only true solution to the "buy term invest the difference" problem. **(LI)**

Unpaid Premium Provision. A provision in a health insurance policy that allows deduction of unpaid premiums from claims payments. **(H)**

Utilization Review. A cost control mechanism by which the appropriateness, necessity, and quality of health care is monitored by both insurers and employers. **(H)**

Utmost Good Faith. Acting in fairness and equity with a sincere belief that the act is not unlawful or harmful to others. The insurance contract requires that each party is entitled to rely upon the representations of the other without attempts to conceal or deceive. **(G,LE)**

Valuable Papers and Records Coverage. An open perils (all risk) coverage for physical loss or damage to valuable papers and records of the insured. It includes practically all types of printed documents or records except money. **(PR)**

Value Reporting Form. Commercial form designed for businesses that have fluctuating merchandise values during the year. As values are reported (monthly, quarterly or annually) the amount of insurance is adjusted. Reporting forms help eliminate problems of overinsurance and underinsurance, as well as the need to continually endorse a policy. **(PR)**

Variable Annuity. An annuity contract in which the amount of the periodic benefit varies, usually in relation to security market values, a cost-of-living index, or some other variable factor in contrast to a fixed or guaranteed return annuity. As a hedge against inflation, the variable annuity presents investment risks to the annuitant. **(AN)**

Variable Life Insurance. A form whose face value varies depending upon the value of the dollar or securities or other equity products at the time payment is due. **(LI)**

Variable Universal Life. — A combination of the features of variable life insurance and universal life insurance under the same contract. Benefits are variable based on the value of equity investments, and premiums and benefits are adjustable at the option of the policyholder. **(LI)**

VGLI — Veteran's Group Life Insurance. Group insurance available to veterans who were covered under SGLI (Servicemen's Group Life Insurance) if converted within 120 days of separation from the service. **(LI)**

Viatical Settlement. A written contractual agreement under which the policyholder of a life insurance contract covering the life of a terminally ill person assigns, transfers ownership, or otherwise irrevocably designates all control and rights in the contract to another person or entity in exchange for the advance payment of a portion of the death benefits. Under these arrangements, a portion of the proceeds is paid to the insured or policyholder prior to the actual death of the insured person. **(LI)**

Viatical Settlement Company. A company or firm that specializes in negotiating viatical settlements with policyholders of life insurance contracts covering the lives of terminally ill persons. **(LI)**

W

Waiting Period. The period of time between the beginning of a disability and the start of disability insurance benefits. Also called **Elimination period.** **(H)**

Waiver. (1) A rider waiving (excluding) liability for a stated cause of injury or sickness. (2) A provision or rider agreeing to waive premium payments during a period of disability of the insured. (3) The act of giving up or surrendering a right or privilege that is known to exist. In property and liability fields, it may be effected by an agent, adjuster, company, employee, or company official, and it can be done either orally or in writing. **(G,LE)**

War Clause. A provision excluding liability of an insurer if a loss is caused by war. **(H,LI)**

Warranty. A statement made on an application for most kinds of insurance that is warranted as true in all respects. If untrue in any respect, even though the untruth was not known to the applicant, the contract may be voided without regard to the materiality of the statement. By contrast, statements in life and health applications are not warranties except in cases of fraud, and the trend in more recent court decisions in other lines has tended to modify the doctrine of warranty to an application only when the statement is material to a risk or the circumstances of a loss. See also **Representation.** **(LE)**

Watchperson. Under commercial crime insurance coverages, any person retained to have care and custody of the insured's property inside the premises, and who has no other duties. **(C)**

Whole Life Insurance. Insurance which may be kept in force for a person's whole life and which pays a benefit upon the person's death, whenever that may be. All whole life policies build up nonforfeiture values, but they are paid for in three different ways. Under a straight or ordinary life policy, premiums are paid for as long as the insured lives. A single premium policy is paid for at one time in one premium. Between these two types there are many limited-payment plans, under which the insured pays premiums for a certain period or until reaching a certain age. Contrast with **Term Insurance.** **(LI)**

Wholesale Group Insurance. See **Franchise Insurance.** **(H,LI)**

Workers Compensation (WC). (1) A schedule of benefits payable to an employee by the employer without regard to liability, required by state law in the case of injury, disability, or death as the result of occupational hazards. (2) Insurance agreeing to pay workers compensation law benefits on behalf of the insured employer. **(WC)**

Write. To insure, to underwrite, or to accept an application. **(G)**

Written Business. Insurance on which an application has been taken out but which is not yet delivered and/or the first premium settled. **(LI)**

LIFE/HEALTH SOURCEBOOK 1997 INDEX

MERRITT

AGENT'S LICENSING SOURCEBOOK

SAMPLE EXAMINATION ANSWER SHEET

LIFE

1	Ⓐ Ⓑ Ⓒ Ⓓ	26	Ⓐ Ⓑ Ⓒ Ⓓ
2	Ⓐ Ⓑ Ⓒ Ⓓ	27	Ⓐ Ⓑ Ⓒ Ⓓ
3	Ⓐ Ⓑ Ⓒ Ⓓ	28	Ⓐ Ⓑ Ⓒ Ⓓ
4	Ⓐ Ⓑ Ⓒ Ⓓ	29	Ⓐ Ⓑ Ⓒ Ⓓ
5	Ⓐ Ⓑ Ⓒ Ⓓ	30	Ⓐ Ⓑ Ⓒ Ⓓ
6	Ⓐ Ⓑ Ⓒ Ⓓ	31	Ⓐ Ⓑ Ⓒ Ⓓ
7	Ⓐ Ⓑ Ⓒ Ⓓ	32	Ⓐ Ⓑ Ⓒ Ⓓ
8	Ⓐ Ⓑ Ⓒ Ⓓ	33	Ⓐ Ⓑ Ⓒ Ⓓ
9	Ⓐ Ⓑ Ⓒ Ⓓ	34	Ⓐ Ⓑ Ⓒ Ⓓ
10	Ⓐ Ⓑ Ⓒ Ⓓ	35	Ⓐ Ⓑ Ⓒ Ⓓ
11	Ⓐ Ⓑ Ⓒ Ⓓ	36	Ⓐ Ⓑ Ⓒ Ⓓ
12	Ⓐ Ⓑ Ⓒ Ⓓ	37	Ⓐ Ⓑ Ⓒ Ⓓ
13	Ⓐ Ⓑ Ⓒ Ⓓ	38	Ⓐ Ⓑ Ⓒ Ⓓ
14	Ⓐ Ⓑ Ⓒ Ⓓ	39	Ⓐ Ⓑ Ⓒ Ⓓ
15	Ⓐ Ⓑ Ⓒ Ⓓ	40	Ⓐ Ⓑ Ⓒ Ⓓ
16	Ⓐ Ⓑ Ⓒ Ⓓ	41	Ⓐ Ⓑ Ⓒ Ⓓ
17	Ⓐ Ⓑ Ⓒ Ⓓ	42	Ⓐ Ⓑ Ⓒ Ⓓ
18	Ⓐ Ⓑ Ⓒ Ⓓ	43	Ⓐ Ⓑ Ⓒ Ⓓ
19	Ⓐ Ⓑ Ⓒ Ⓓ	44	Ⓐ Ⓑ Ⓒ Ⓓ
20	Ⓐ Ⓑ Ⓒ Ⓓ	45	Ⓐ Ⓑ Ⓒ Ⓓ
21	Ⓐ Ⓑ Ⓒ Ⓓ	46	Ⓐ Ⓑ Ⓒ Ⓓ
22	Ⓐ Ⓑ Ⓒ Ⓓ	47	Ⓐ Ⓑ Ⓒ Ⓓ
23	Ⓐ Ⓑ Ⓒ Ⓓ	48	Ⓐ Ⓑ Ⓒ Ⓓ
24	Ⓐ Ⓑ Ⓒ Ⓓ	49	Ⓐ Ⓑ Ⓒ Ⓓ
25	Ⓐ Ⓑ Ⓒ Ⓓ	50	Ⓐ Ⓑ Ⓒ Ⓓ

HEALTH

1	Ⓐ Ⓑ Ⓒ Ⓓ	26	Ⓐ Ⓑ Ⓒ Ⓓ
2	Ⓐ Ⓑ Ⓒ Ⓓ	27	Ⓐ Ⓑ Ⓒ Ⓓ
3	Ⓐ Ⓑ Ⓒ Ⓓ	28	Ⓐ Ⓑ Ⓒ Ⓓ
4	Ⓐ Ⓑ Ⓒ Ⓓ	29	Ⓐ Ⓑ Ⓒ Ⓓ
5	Ⓐ Ⓑ Ⓒ Ⓓ	30	Ⓐ Ⓑ Ⓒ Ⓓ
6	Ⓐ Ⓑ Ⓒ Ⓓ	31	Ⓐ Ⓑ Ⓒ Ⓓ
7	Ⓐ Ⓑ Ⓒ Ⓓ	32	Ⓐ Ⓑ Ⓒ Ⓓ
8	Ⓐ Ⓑ Ⓒ Ⓓ	33	Ⓐ Ⓑ Ⓒ Ⓓ
9	Ⓐ Ⓑ Ⓒ Ⓓ	34	Ⓐ Ⓑ Ⓒ Ⓓ
10	Ⓐ Ⓑ Ⓒ Ⓓ	35	Ⓐ Ⓑ Ⓒ Ⓓ
11	Ⓐ Ⓑ Ⓒ Ⓓ	36	Ⓐ Ⓑ Ⓒ Ⓓ
12	Ⓐ Ⓑ Ⓒ Ⓓ	37	Ⓐ Ⓑ Ⓒ Ⓓ
13	Ⓐ Ⓑ Ⓒ Ⓓ	38	Ⓐ Ⓑ Ⓒ Ⓓ
14	Ⓐ Ⓑ Ⓒ Ⓓ	39	Ⓐ Ⓑ Ⓒ Ⓓ
15	Ⓐ Ⓑ Ⓒ Ⓓ	40	Ⓐ Ⓑ Ⓒ Ⓓ
16	Ⓐ Ⓑ Ⓒ Ⓓ	41	Ⓐ Ⓑ Ⓒ Ⓓ
17	Ⓐ Ⓑ Ⓒ Ⓓ	42	Ⓐ Ⓑ Ⓒ Ⓓ
18	Ⓐ Ⓑ Ⓒ Ⓓ	43	Ⓐ Ⓑ Ⓒ Ⓓ
19	Ⓐ Ⓑ Ⓒ Ⓓ	44	Ⓐ Ⓑ Ⓒ Ⓓ
20	Ⓐ Ⓑ Ⓒ Ⓓ	45	Ⓐ Ⓑ Ⓒ Ⓓ
21	Ⓐ Ⓑ Ⓒ Ⓓ	46	Ⓐ Ⓑ Ⓒ Ⓓ
22	Ⓐ Ⓑ Ⓒ Ⓓ	47	Ⓐ Ⓑ Ⓒ Ⓓ
23	Ⓐ Ⓑ Ⓒ Ⓓ	48	Ⓐ Ⓑ Ⓒ Ⓓ
24	Ⓐ Ⓑ Ⓒ Ⓓ	49	Ⓐ Ⓑ Ⓒ Ⓓ
25	Ⓐ Ⓑ Ⓒ Ⓓ	50	Ⓐ Ⓑ Ⓒ Ⓓ

- - - - - - - - - - - - - - - - CUT HERE - - - - - - - - - - - - - - - -